The Drawings of Vincent van Gogh

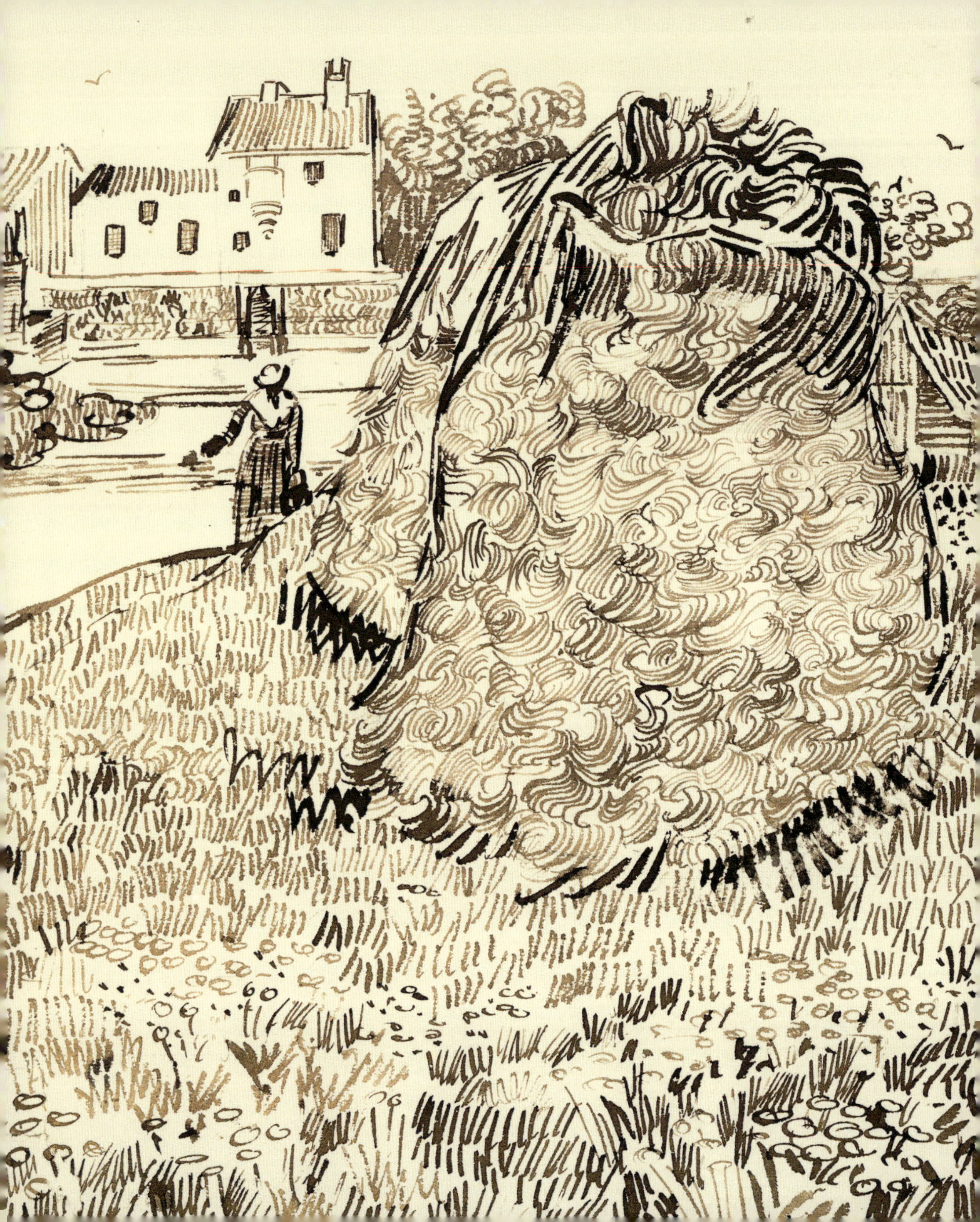

Christopher Lloyd

The Drawings of Vincent van Gogh

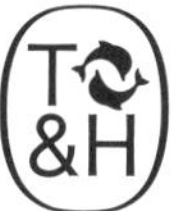

Drawing is becoming more and more of a passion, and it's just like a sailor's passion for the sea.

Vincent van Gogh to Theo van Gogh, Letter 200, on or about 14 January 1882

Drawing is the most important thing, no matter what they say, and far and away the most difficult.

Vincent van Gogh to Theo van Gogh, Letter 205, 18 February 1882

Whoever had witnessed this wrestling, struggling and sorrowful existence could not but feel sympathy for the man who demanded so much of himself that it ruined body and mind. He belonged to the breed that produces the great artists. . . . Whenever in the future I shall remember that time, and it is always a delight for me to recall the past, the characteristic figure of Vincent will appear to me in such a melancholy but clear light, the struggling and wrestling, fanatic, gloomy Vincent, who used to flare up so often and was so irritable, but who still deserved friendship and admiration for his mind and highly artistic qualities.

*Anthon van Rappard to Vincent van Gogh's mother, Anna van Gogh-Carbentus, written on hearing of the death of the artist (*The Complete Letters of Vincent van Gogh*, London, 1958, p. XXXI)*

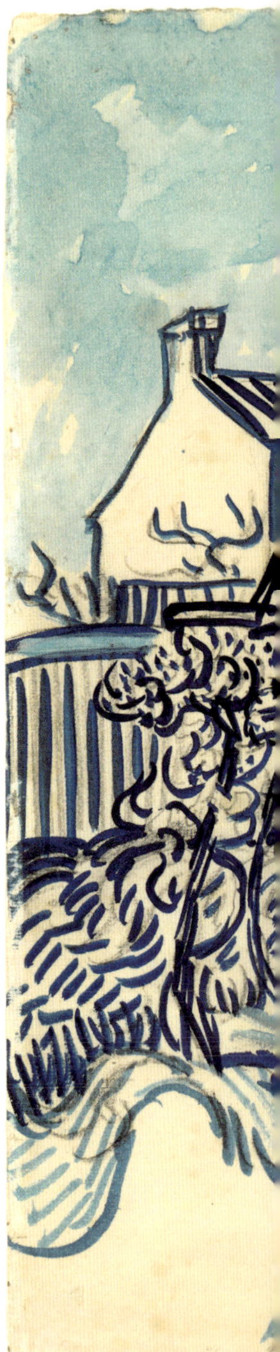

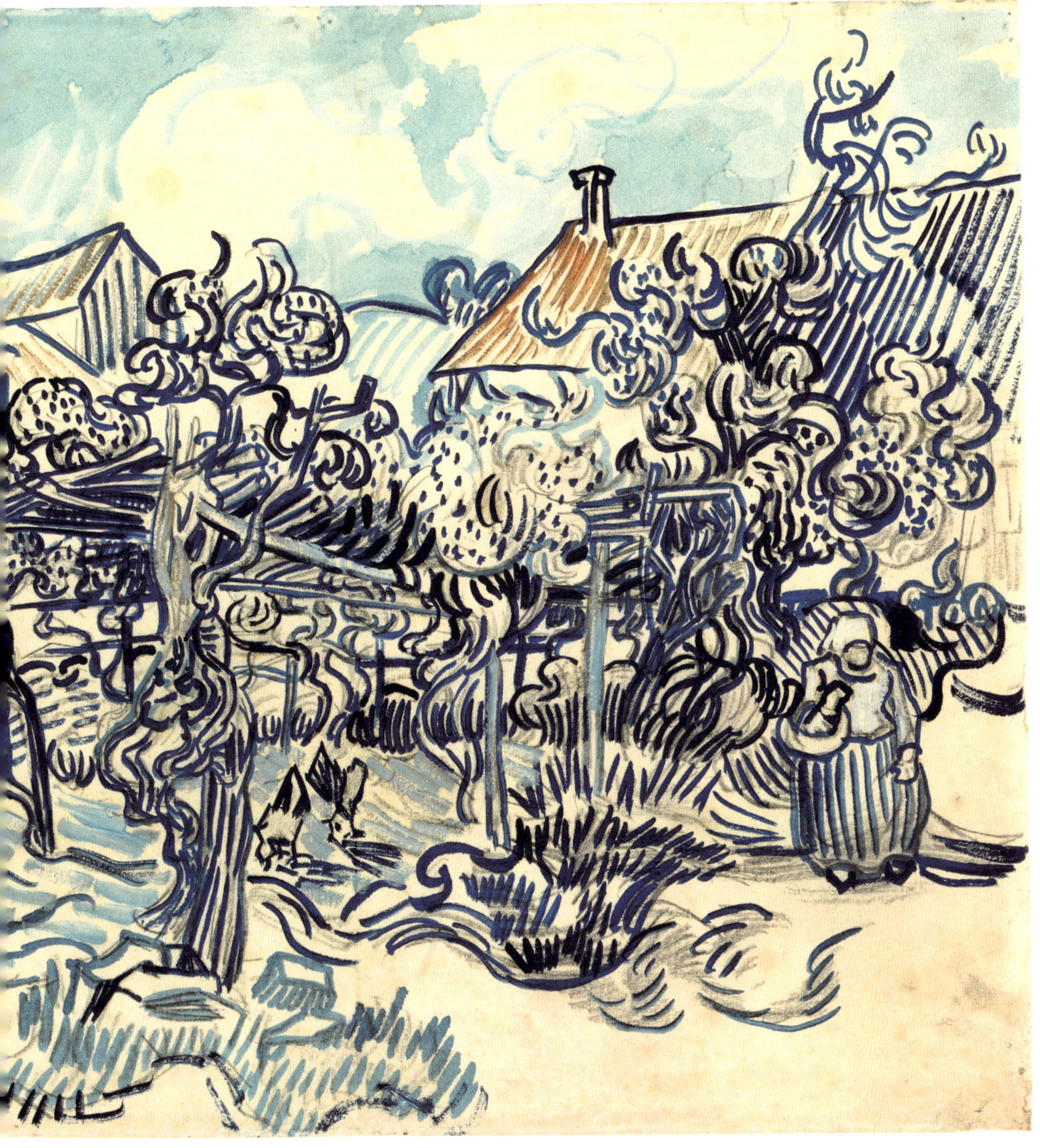

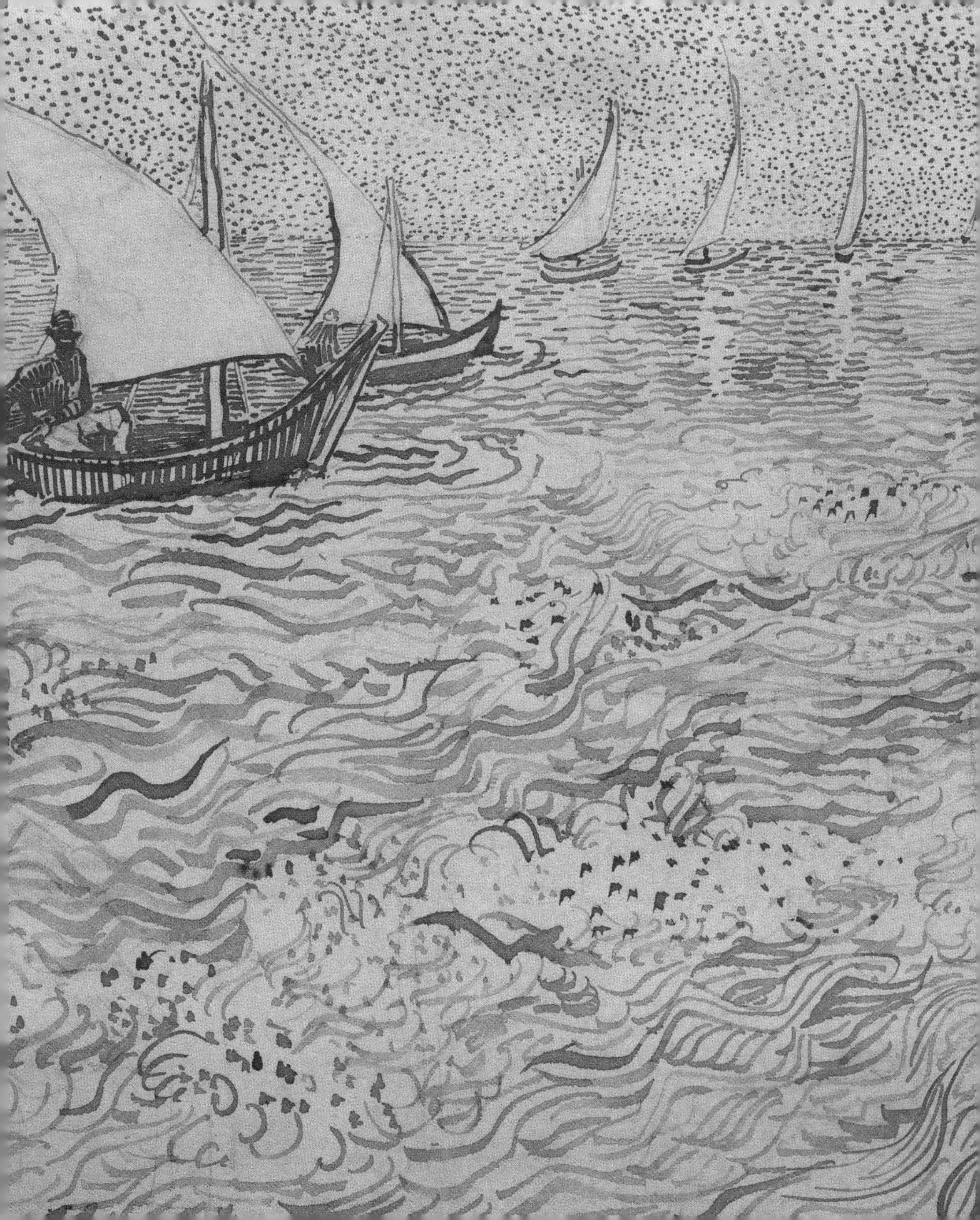

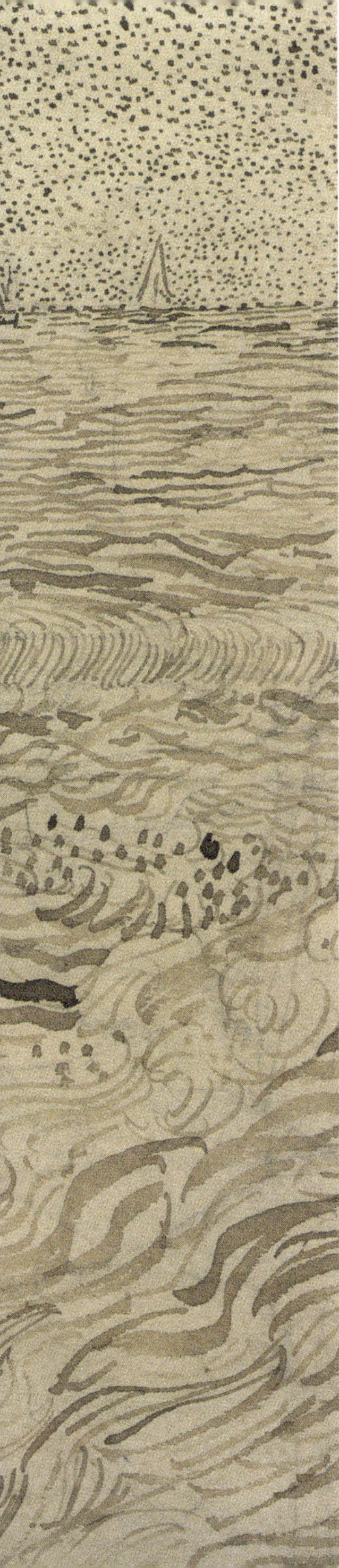

Contents

Preface

Portrait of Patience Escalier, early August 1888. Reed pen and ink over pencil, on paper, 49.4 × 38 cm (19½ × 15 in.). FOGG MUSEUM, HARVARD ART MUSEUMS, CAMBRIDGE, MASS.

Anyone writing on the drawings of Vincent van Gogh today finds themselves in a privileged and enviable position. Both of the recognized catalogues raisonnés published to date – the first compiled by J.-B. de la Faille in 1928 and revised in 1970; the second, by Jan Hulsker in 1980 – included the works on paper. As is well known, Van Gogh illustrated many of his numerous letters with sketches, as well as often enclosing drawings. The texts of the nine hundred or so letters with accompanying illustrations were definitively published in six volumes in 2009 and are now available online. The two largest collections of Van Gogh's drawings are to be found in the Van Gogh Museum in Amsterdam and the Kröller-Müller Museum in Otterlo, both of which have been fully catalogued in an informative and exemplary manner. Pioneering work on Van Gogh's sketchbooks was undertaken by Johannes van der Wolk which he published as *The Seven Sketchbooks of Vincent van Gogh* in 1987.

Several exhibitions have proved to be crucial for the study of Van Gogh's drawings, beginning with the two displays organized by the Metropolitan Museum of Art in New York in 1984 ('Van Gogh in Arles') and in 1986–87 ('Van Gogh in Saint-Rémy and Auvers') and culminating in the centenary exhibition of drawings held in 1990 at the Kröller-Müller Museum. In more recent years, the most significant contribution to the subject has been the exhibition devoted exclusively to the drawings organized jointly by the Van Gogh Museum, Amsterdam, and the Metropolitan Museum of Art in 2005. The range and quality of the selection, combined with the results of the scientific work undertaken to coincide with the exhibition, made the catalogue indispensable. 'The Real Van Gogh: The Artist and his Letters', held at the Royal Academy of Arts in London in 2010, set the artist's drawings in a wider context.

Accompanying the important exhibition that took place in Amsterdam and New York in 2005 was the book *Van Gogh: The Master Draughtsman* by Sjraar van Heugten, then Head of Collections at the Van Gogh Museum. The text of that publication is arranged chronologically and provides a clear and coherent account of Van Gogh's development as a draughtsman. The chapters in the present book, however, treat Van Gogh's drawings thematically and is intended to be a fresh, if not innovative, approach to the subject. The inspiration for this approach lies in *The Drawings of Rembrandt: A New Study* by Seymour Slive, published in 2009; I hope it will be as rewarding to read.

Note

Quotations from letters written by or to Van Gogh are taken from www.vangoghletters.org, the official website of the Van Gogh Museum in Amsterdam, and are referenced in parentheses with the letter number; for example, the reference '(726)' refers to a letter from Vincent to Theo, dated Monday, 17 or Tuesday, 18 December 1888.

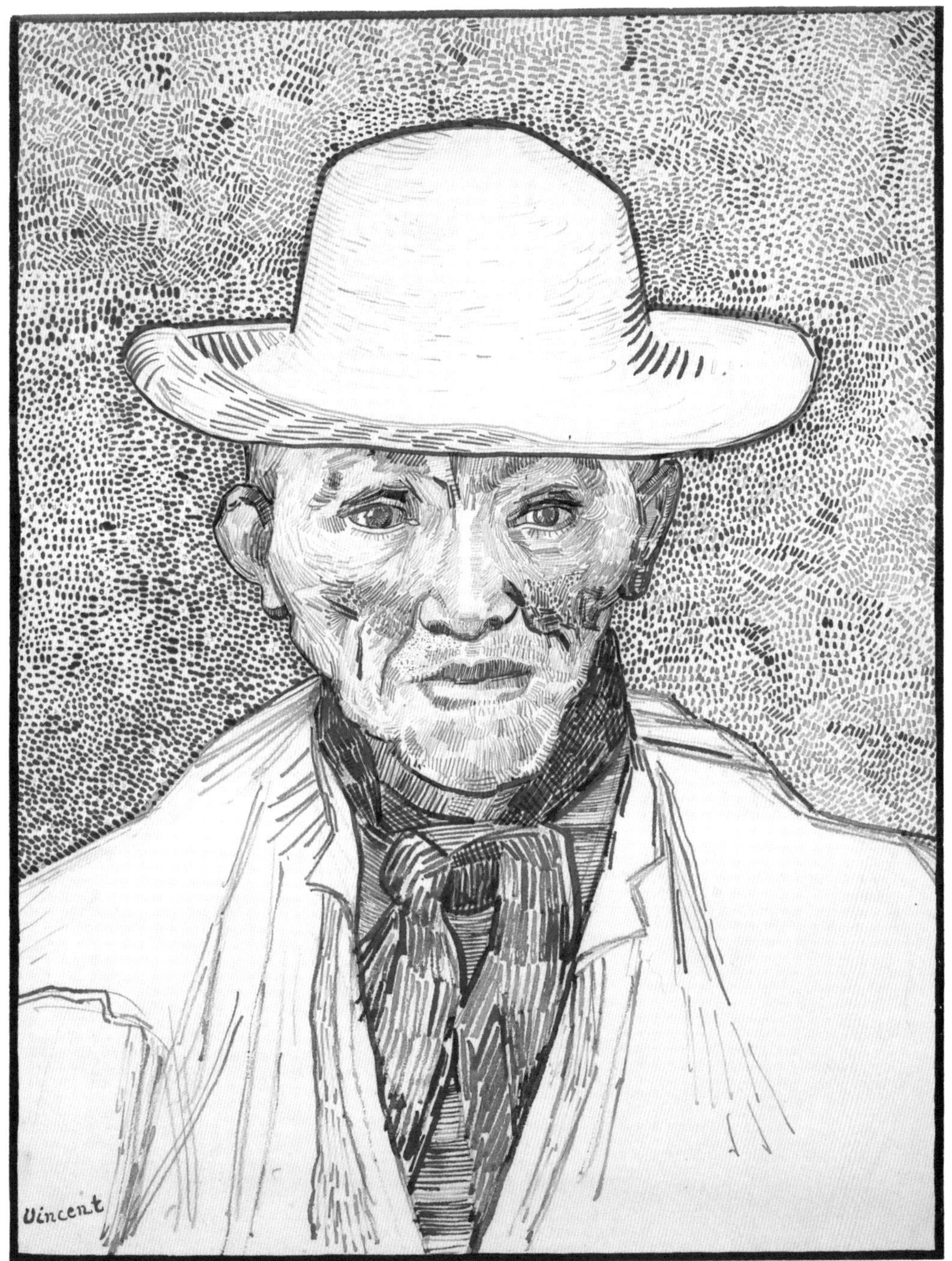
Vincent

Brief Chronology of the Life of Vincent van Gogh

1853
Born 30 March in Groot Zundert in North Brabant. The eldest child of the Revd Theodorus van Gogh and Anna Cornelia van Gogh-Carbentus, he will have five siblings: Anna Cornelia (1855–1930), Theodorus (Theo) (1857–1891), Elisabeth (Lies) (1859–1936), Willemina (Wil or Willemien) Jacoba (1862–1941) and Cornelis (Cor) Vincent (1867–1900).

1869
Appointed junior apprentice at the branch in The Hague of the art dealer Goupil & Cie and subsequently transferred to the branch in London (1873–75) and the headquarters in Paris (1875–76), before being dismissed (1 April 1876).

1876
Returns to England, where he works as a teacher in Ramsgate (Kent) and Isleworth (Middlesex).

1877
Takes up a position in a bookshop in Dordrecht, followed by a short period of theological studies in Amsterdam.

1878–79
Secures temporary appointments as a lay preacher in the Borinage, a mining district in southern Belgium.

1880
Decides to become an artist in August and, two months later, moves to Brussels to broaden his experience. Here he briefly attends the Royal Academy of Fine Arts.

1881
Theo van Gogh assumes financial responsibility for his brother, offering guidance and support for the rest of the artist's life. In April, Vincent bases himself in the family home at Etten and works with the artist Anthon van Rappard, mainly on drawings. Moves to The Hague, where he meets up with his cousin by marriage, the artist Anton Mauve, from whom he takes drawing and painting lessons.

1882
Establishes a relationship with a former prostitute, Sien Hoornik, and her family. She works as his model until September 1883.

1883
Travels to Drenthe in the north-east of the Netherlands before living for almost two years with his parents in the vicarage at Nuenen in North Brabant.

1885
His father dies on 26 March 1885. Moves to Antwerp in November.

1886
Studies at the Royal Academy of Fine Arts in Antwerp for one month, also visiting churches and museums. Moves to and settles in Paris in February, living with Theo, and studies briefly (March–April) at the studio of Fernand Cormon, where he meets several artists associated with the avant-garde.

1888
In February, leaves Paris for the south of France, settling in Arles in Provence for fourteen months. In May, rents four rooms in the Yellow House (2 place Lamartine) to use as a studio and, in September, moves in, using it as a base for his 'Studio of the South', in which he hopes to encourage other artists to participate. Paul Gauguin arrives in Arles on 23 October but returns to Paris on 25 December.

1888–89
Following a marked deterioration in his mental health and his increasingly erratic behaviour towards the end of December, he is admitted to the hospital (Hôtel Dieu) in Arles until 7 January 1889.

1889
Returns to hospital on 7 February where he remains until his departure for Saint-Rémy three months later. On 18 April, Theo van Gogh marries Johanna (Jo) Bonger. Vincent agrees on 8 May to be admitted to the asylum of Saint-Paul-de-Mausole in Saint-Rémy, to the north-east of Arles, where he suffers intermittent breakdowns interspersed with periods of lucidity that allow him to work.

1890
Leaves the asylum on 16 May and returns north to stay briefly with his brother, now the father of a son, Vincent Willem, in Paris, before settling in Auvers-sur-Oise to the north-west of Paris. Shoots himself in the chest on 27 July and two days later dies of his wounds, with Theo at his side. Is buried in the cemetery at Auvers-sur-Oise.

1891
Theo dies on 25 January in Utrecht, and his remains are transferred in 1914 to the cemetery at Auvers-sur-Oise, where the brothers lie side by side.

Chapter 1

Setting Out

Of Vincent van Gogh (Fig. 1) it might legitimately be said that he became an artist only as a last resort. His final, much delayed decision to pursue art as a single ambition seems to have been taken in the summer of 1880, when he was aged twenty-seven. This was done with the encouragement of his brother Theo (1857–1891) and ultimately with the approval, even relief, of his whole family. Such a development occurred, however, after a series of false starts, to the extent that it is perhaps more accurate to describe Van Gogh at the outset to have been more a student of life than a student of art.

Born in 1853, the eldest son of Theodorus van Gogh (1822–1885), a pastor, and Anna Cornelia van Gogh-Carbentus (1819–1907), Van Gogh had five siblings: two brothers and three sisters. As a result of his father's affiliation with the Groningen School branch of the Dutch Reformed Church, he was brought up and lived in rural parsonages in North Brabant – Zundert, Helvoirt, Etten and Nuenen – places in the south of the Netherlands, close to the Belgian border, that he depicted and remembered with considerable affection. Although living for so many years in poorer areas of the country, in accordance with Theodorus's religious principles, the Van Gogh family was itself avowedly middle class, with social and commercial ambitions to match, particularly with regard to their children. Theodorus himself had followed his own father's calling and gone into the ministry, but his brothers had struck out in new directions. One, Johannes, was a high-ranking naval officer, and no fewer than three others were involved with the art or book trades: Hendrik ('Uncle Hein') and Vincent ('Uncle Cent') both held positions with the French dealer Goupil & Cie (renamed Boussod, Valadon & Cie in 1884), while Cornelis ('Uncle Cor') became an independent bookseller and art dealer.

It was naturally assumed that their nephew, Vincent, might be suited to a similar career, and so in 1869 Van Gogh became apprenticed to Goupil & Cie, working in their branches in The Hague and also intermittently in London and at their headquarters

Lange Vijverberg, The Hague, autumn 1872–spring 1873 (detail of Fig. 9).

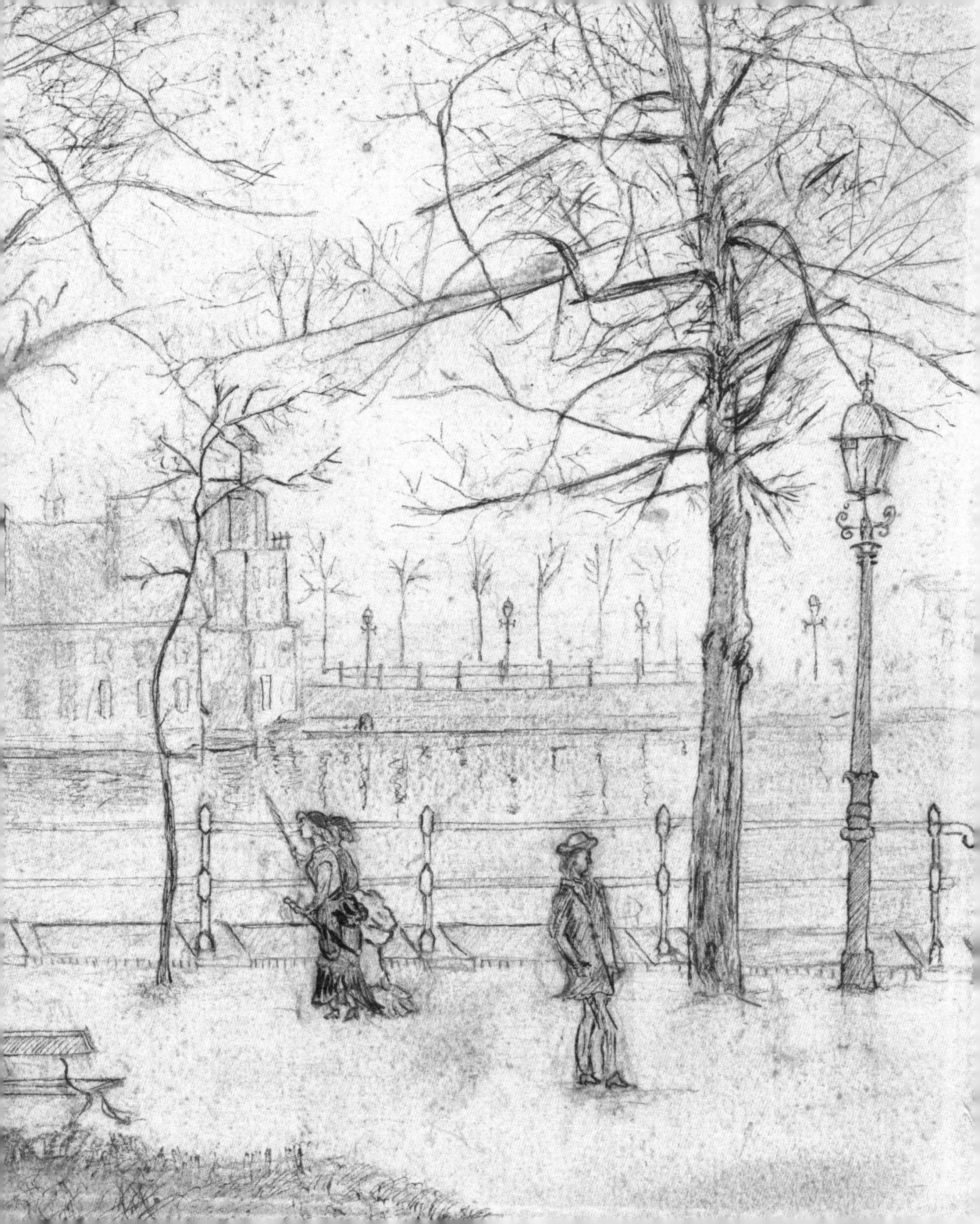

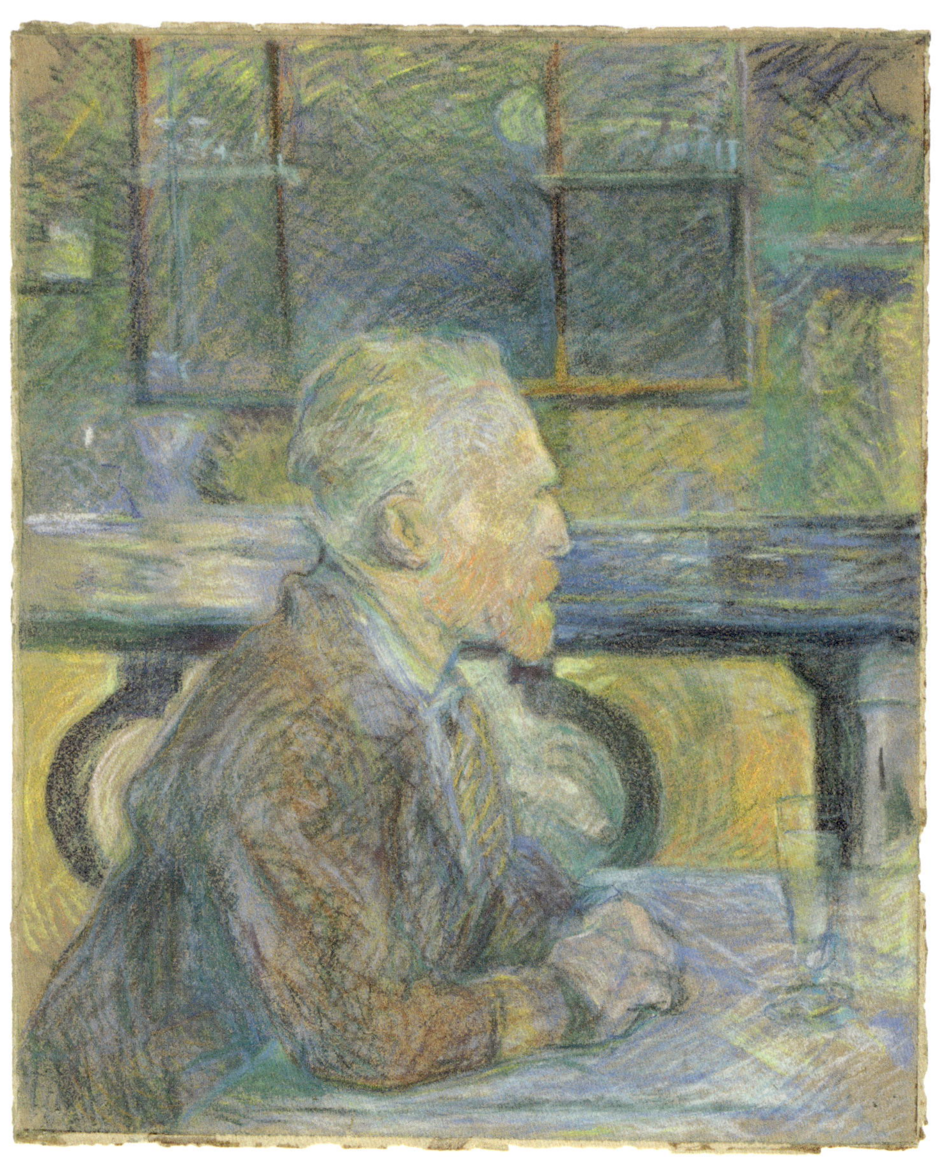

1 Henri de Toulouse-Lautrec
Portrait of Vincent van Gogh, 1887.
Chalk on paper,
57 × 46.5 cm (22½ × 18⅜ in.).
VAN GOGH MUSEUM, AMSTERDAM

in Paris. Although he was given notice on 4 January 1876, on the grounds that he lacked the necessary skills for a salesman, and left the firm on 1 April, in the long run Van Gogh benefited enormously from the opportunities that were presented by working in the capital cities of Europe, where there were active artistic communities and institutions. By contrast, Theo, who followed his elder brother to Goupil & Cie in 1873, was appointed to a permanent position six years later, succeeded as an art dealer and remained with the company until his death. This gave Theo the means to support Vincent financially, professionally and emotionally, although at times not without difficulty or exasperation and often in a state of personal anguish. Theo, in fact, died only six months after Vincent, and both are now buried side by side in the cemetery at Auvers-sur-Oise.

Following his setback at Goupil & Cie, Vincent van Gogh sought to establish himself as a teacher in England, first of all at a school in Ramsgate in Kent and then at two different schools in Isleworth in Middlesex. Here he became interested in religion, attending Methodist and Congregational churches, and, in October 1876, he preached his first sermon in a Weslyan Methodist church in Richmond. Interestingly, this sermon included a slightly confused reminiscence of a painting, *God Speed! Pilgrims setting out to Canterbury*, by George Boughton, which was shown in 1874 at the Royal Academy, where it was seen by Van Gogh. Returning to the Netherlands early in 1877, he worked as an assistant in a bookshop in Dordrecht before pursuing theological studies in Amsterdam and training to be an evangelist in Brussels. In this last endeavour he was unsuccessful and was not formally accepted for any official posting. Nonetheless, at the beginning of 1879 Van Gogh fulfilled his ambition by working as an evangelist independently for six months in the Borinage, a mining region in southern Belgium near the French border. Here, while living in abject poverty, he gave Bible readings, visited the sick and tried to alleviate the hardships of his neighbours. It was during this period that his interest in practising art intensified, and he became preoccupied by drawing.

This last development was by no means sudden, but more a slow process of realization. Even so, the decision made by Van Gogh to commit himself to becoming an artist first on paper, as opposed to canvas, is significant. It is, for instance, reflected not only in the large number of drawings in his oeuvre, but also in the variety of uses to which he put those drawings and the moments in his career when he chose to give them priority. The full range of works on paper by Van Gogh is astonishing: preparatory studies for paintings, drawings made for sale, presentation drawings given to friends, records of completed paintings or work in progress (referred to affectionately as 'scratches' or 'scribbles') – frequently enclosed with or liberally illustrating his unusually extensive correspondence (Figs 2–6) – and even sketches of the various materials and instruments that

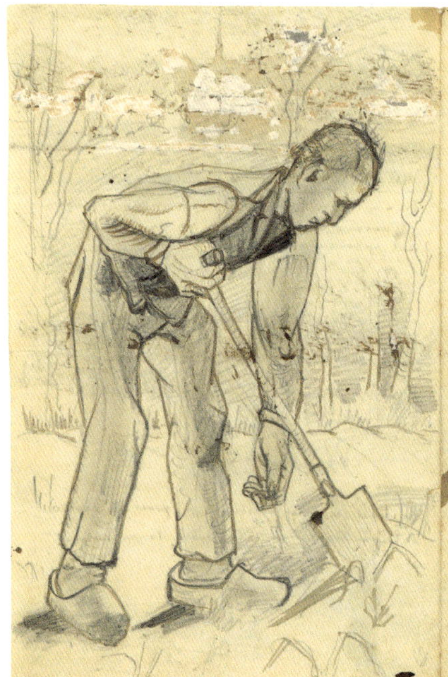

2 Letter from Vincent van Gogh to Theo van Gogh, mid-September 1881 (Letter 172). Sheet 1 (recto), with sketch of *Digger*. Pencil, pen and ink, watercolour, on paper, 20.7 × 26.3 cm (8¼ × 10⅜ in.).
VAN GOGH MUSEUM, AMSTERDAM

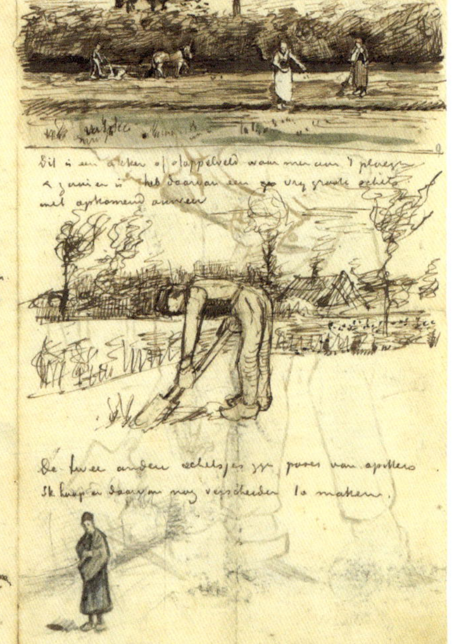

3 Letter from Vincent van Gogh to Theo van Gogh, mid-September 1881 (Letter 172). Sheet 1 (verso), with sketches of *Storm Clouds Over a Field*, *Digger* and *Figure of a Woman*. Pencil, pen and ink, watercolour, on paper, 20.7 × 26.3 cm (8¼ × 10⅜ in.).
VAN GOGH MUSEUM, AMSTERDAM

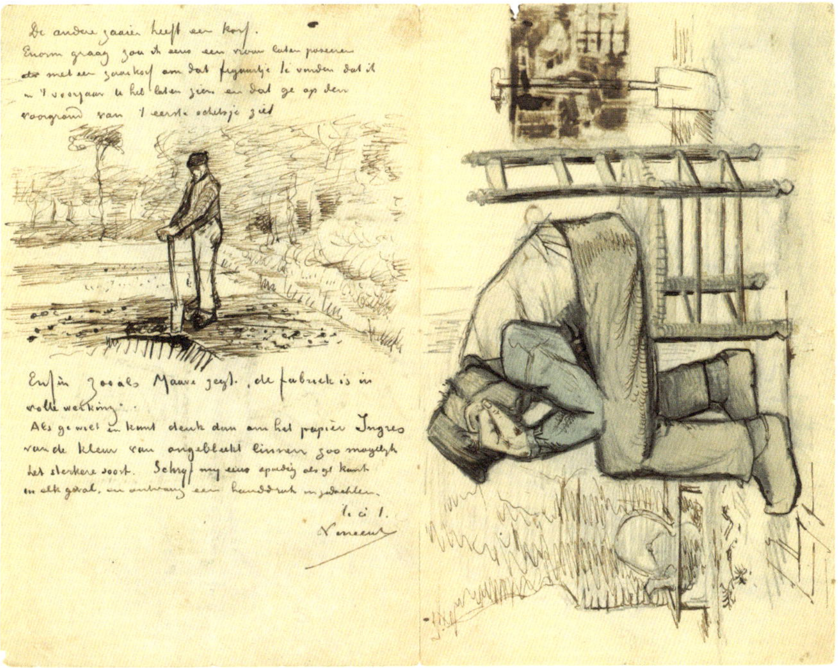

De andere zaaier heeft een korf.
Enorm graag zou ik eens een vrouw laten poseeren
ook met een zaaikorf om dat figuurtje te vinden dat ik
in 't voorjaar u heb laten zien en dat ge op den
voorgrond van 't eerste schetsje ziet

Enfin zooals Mauve zegt, „de fabriek is in
volle werking".
Als ge weet en kunt denk dan aan het papier Ingres
van de kleur van ongebleekt linnen zoo mogelijk
het sterkere soort. Schrijf my eens spoedig als ge kunt
in elk geval, en ontvang een handdruk in gedachten.

t. à t.
Vincent

4 Letter from Vincent van Gogh to Theo van Gogh, mid-September 1881 (Letter 172). Sheet 2 (recto), with sketches of *Man Leaning on his Spade* and *Man Sitting by the Fireplace ('Worn Out')*. Pencil, pen and ink, watercolour, on paper, 20.7 × 26.3 cm (8¼ × 10⅜ in.). VAN GOGH MUSEUM, AMSTERDAM

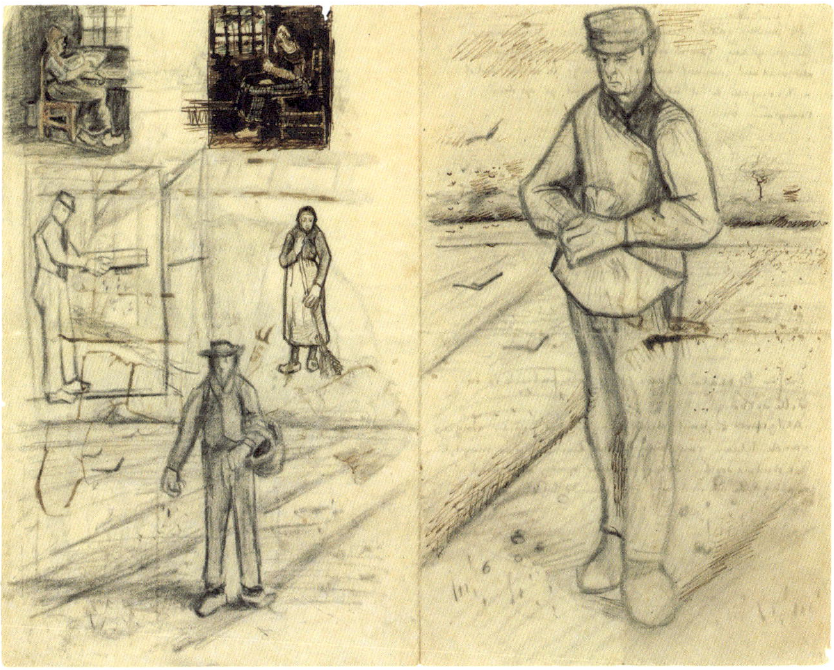

5 Letter from Vincent van Gogh to Theo van Gogh, mid-September 1881 (Letter 172). Sheet 2 (verso), with sketches of *Woman near a Window*, *Woman near a Window*, *Man with a Winnow*, *Woman with a Broom*, *Sower* and *Sower with a Sack*. Pencil, pen and ink, watercolour, on paper, 20.7 × 26.3 cm (8¼ × 10⅜ in.). VAN GOGH MUSEUM, AMSTERDAM

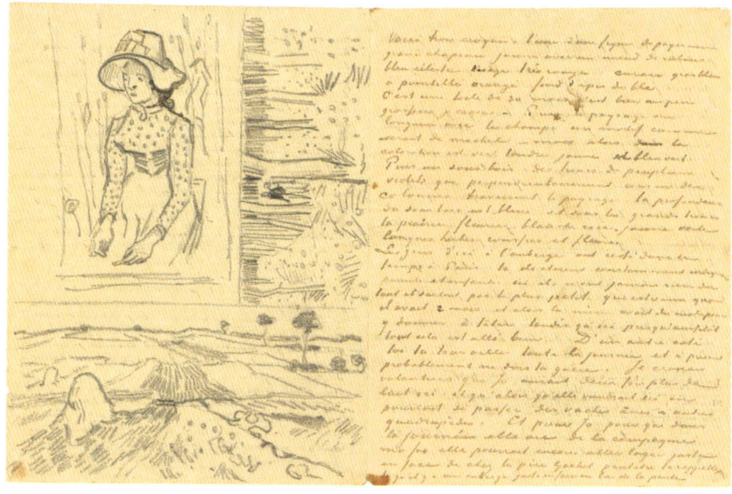

6 Letter from Vincent van Gogh to Theo van Gogh and Jo van Gogh-Bonger, 2 July 1890 (Letter 896), with sketches of *Girl against a Background of Wheat*, *Couple Walking between Rows of Poplars*, *Wheatfields*. Pencil, pen and ink, on paper, 27 × 41.8 cm (10¾ × 16½ in.)
VAN GOGH MUSEUM, AMSTERDAM

he needed or used for making drawings (Fig. 7). Most significantly, at times drawing often took precedence over painting. Few other artists resorted to drawing on so many different occasions or came to rely so heavily on it as a means of communication – in the process, revealing so much of themselves. Perhaps only Leonardo da Vinci (1452–1519), Albrecht Dürer (1471–1528), Michelangelo (1475–1564), Rembrandt (1606–1669) and Peter Paul Rubens (1577–1640) among his distant predecessors fall into this category.

Any assessment of Van Gogh's significance as an artist, therefore, has to take into account the importance that drawing held for him. It was not simply a preparatory exercise or an act of mediation, but an impassioned expression of his temperament and his response to the world in which he lived. A telling feature is the regularity with which, even from the outset, he signed his drawings and, furthermore, in so doing used his first name, as Rembrandt did. Another unusual aspect is the close dating that is possible for so many of the sheets, a result of the detailed knowledge of the artist's movements and his almost daily correspondence with his brother. It is difficult to nominate another artist whose career can be so closely monitored.

Throughout his working life, bursts of activity devoted solely to painting alternated with similar bursts of activity devoted to drawing. It is all the more remarkable that such a high level of intensity was restricted to a limited period of a single decade, in which the volume of output seems inversely proportional to the time actually spent as a fully fledged artist. Added to this is the extraordinary fact that Van Gogh was virtually self-taught and only very occasionally subjected himself to any kind of formal instruction or training.

The principal source for the study of Van Gogh's art beyond the works themselves is the extensive correspondence with

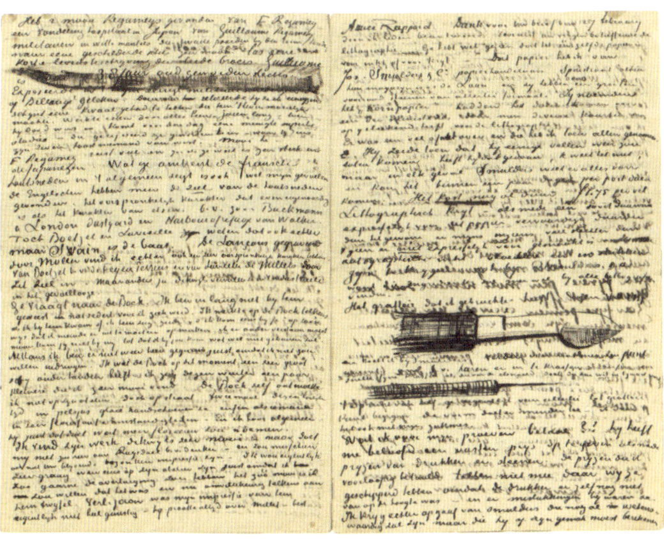

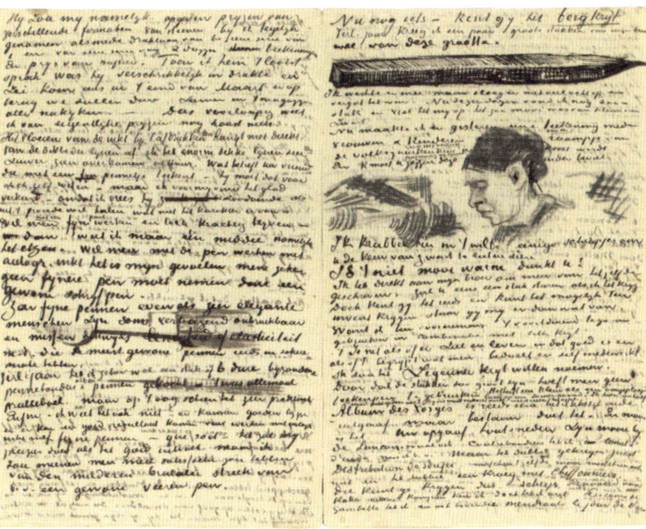

7 Letter from Vincent van Gogh to Anthon van Rappard, 5 March 1883 (Letter 325). Sheet 1 (recto), with sketches of *Scraper* and *Point*; sheet 1 (verso), with *Natural Chalk* and *Head of a Woman in Profile, and Two Drafts*. Pen and ink, natural chalk, on paper, 20.5 × 26.8 cm (8⅛ × 10⅝ in.).
PRIVATE COLLECTION

members of his family, principally Theo, and fellow artists such as Anthon van Rappard (1858–1892), Paul Gauguin (1848–1903) and Émile Bernard (1868–1941). The insights these letters provide into his emotions and thoughts, his interests and perceptions during the course of his short life reveal not only a great deal about the personal crises but also the surprisingly solid foundations on which his art lay and on which his natural artistic instincts were based. What the letters demonstrate also is how evocatively Van Gogh could write, both when describing his surroundings and when assessing the qualities or imperfections of works of art. Again, a comparison with the correspondence of Rubens, John Constable (1776–1837) or Eugène Delacroix (1798–1863) seems justified.

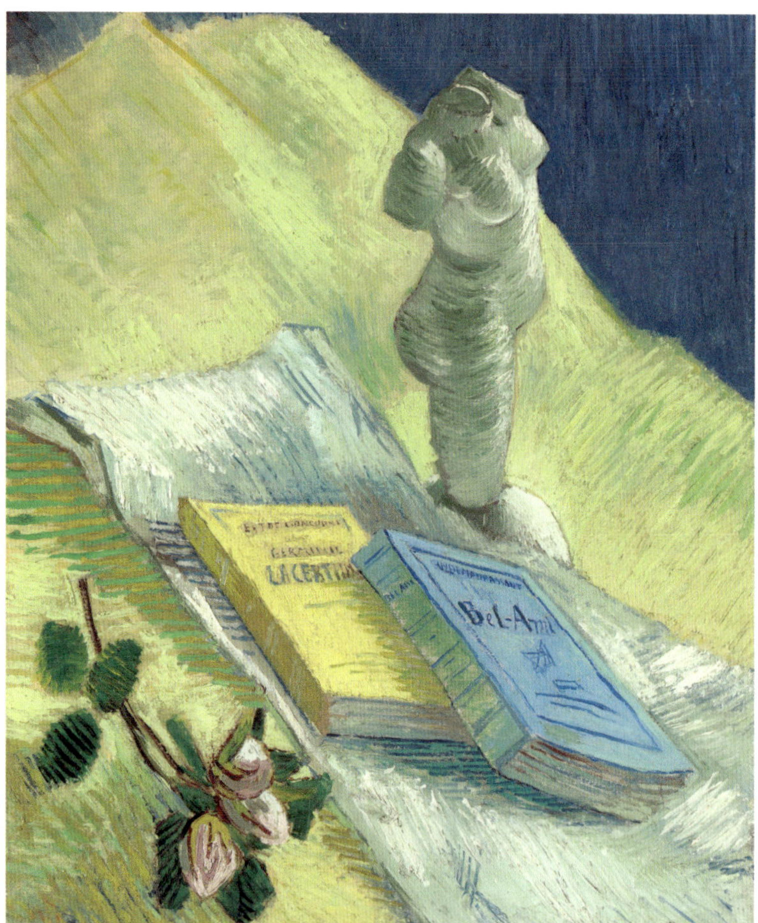

8 *Still Life with Plaster Statuette*, late 1887. Oil on canvas, 55 × 46 cm (21¾ × 18⅛ in.). KRÖLLER-MÜLLER MUSEUM, OTTERLO

Like many great artists, Van Gogh had innate intelligence, which in his case was combined with extensive reading in all categories of European and American literature, often in the original language. As might be expected, he could quote long passages from the Bible, and early on he read many religious works, such as those by Thomas à Kempis, Jacques Bossuet and John Bunyan. He particularly enjoyed exploring the plays of William Shakespeare and relished the novels and writings of such near contemporaries as Charles Dickens, George Eliot and Thomas Carlyle. Among American authors, he referred often to works by Harriet Beecher Stowe and Henry Longfellow. Of French authors, Honoré de Balzac, Gustave Flaubert, Alphonse Daudet, Émile Zola, Jules and Edmond de Goncourt, Jules Michelet, Victor Hugo and Guy de Maupassant held sway (Fig. 8). Titles by many of these writers were often read more than once, and he was adept at remembering plots and characters, as well as commenting on matters of style. This love of literature resulted in Van Gogh's frequent habit of copying out extended passages of religious texts and poetry for the benefit of his correspondents. In many respects, he lived his life through the art and literature with which he identified so closely.

There is a similar eclecticism about the artists Van Gogh admired or whose work he wanted to emulate. The range and diversity of his interests is demonstrated by the scrapbooks of prints, illustrations and reproductions (including photographs) that he compiled over the years, amounting to thousands of examples, some of which he hung on the walls of his various studios and most of which are preserved in the Van Gogh Museum in Amsterdam. These images reflected his experiences while working for Goupil & Cie – established in 1827 as a seller of prints after paintings – as well as his many later visits to museums, galleries, exhibitions and private collections. His eye was all-inclusive, in so far as he looked at works by other artists not so much in a judgmental way but more constructively, in accordance with his own concerns over the treatment of subject matter or technical procedures. Thus, he could become absorbed in equal measure by works by artists as diverse as Rembrandt, Jacob van Ruisdael (1628/29–1682), Delacroix, John Everett Millais (1829–1896), Pierre Puvis de Chavannes (1824–1898), Ernest Meissonier (1815–1891), Jean-François Millet (1814–1875), Ary Scheffer (1795–1858), Adolphe Monticelli (1824–1886) and Constantin Meunier (1831–1905), to name only a few, as well as the legions of British, French and American illustrators commissioned by such journals as *L'Illustration*, *The Graphic* and the *Illustrated London News*, of which he was particularly fond. In addition, Van Gogh was an ardent searcher for anecdotes about other artists in his reading of biographies and memoirs, such as Charles Blanc's *Les Artistes de mon temps* (The Artists of my Time; 1876), Théophile Silvestre's *Les Artistes français: Études d'après nature* (French Artists: Studies from Life; 1878 edn), Jean Gigoux's *Causeries sur les artistes de mon temps* (Conversations about the Artists of my Time; 1885) and anything by Jules and Edmond de Goncourt.

Exemplifying what is essentially an ingrained eclectic approach to visual sources is the visit that Van Gogh made with Gauguin in mid-December 1888 from Arles to the Musée Fabre in Montpellier. The purpose was to see the collection formed by the important patron and collector Alfred Bruyas, who had donated his collection to the museum in 1868. Van Gogh reported to his brother that of greatest interest for Gauguin and himself were the works (many of them portraits) acquired or commissioned by Bruyas from Delacroix, Gustave Courbet (1819–1877) and Octave Tassaert (1800–1874), but that they had also examined paintings by early Italian painters, Paulus Potter (1625–1654) and Puvis de Chavannes, in addition to bronzes by Antoine-Louis Barye (1795–1875) (726). The conversation that took place in the Bruyas Gallery in the museum at Montpellier was undoubtedly stimulating, but, at the same time, it served to demonstrate the differences of approach between these two artists. Van Gogh had been impressed by Bruyas's attempt to introduce contemporary art to the south of France and must have seen it as a forerunner to his own desire to establish a 'Studio of the South' in Arles. Gauguin was geographically much more adventurous in this respect.

It is abundantly clear that, when Van Gogh finally decided to become a full-time artist in 1880, he was not exactly a neophyte. Indeed, he had in place a secure base on which to establish his own priorities, which, in effect, were in due course to alter the development of European art. What he lacked initially, however, was the practical experience and technical knowledge to fulfil his ambitions. The way in which he acquired these necessary skills was unusual if not totally surprising.

Van Gogh's earliest surviving drawings were undertaken in 1872–73 in The Hague (Fig. 9), while he was working at Goupil & Cie, and also subsequently in England between 1873 and 1875. These are made in a mixed media of pencil and pen and ink, which was to become a favourite combination. The choice of motifs in many of these drawings would become familiar in Van Gogh's later works on paper. There is a certain aptitude in dealing with recession and spatial intervals in these first attempts, just as there is variety in the line and an eye for detail. But the overall effect is spoiled by uncertainties and missteps, which give the early drawings an untutored appearance with a tentative finish. Later, Van Gogh

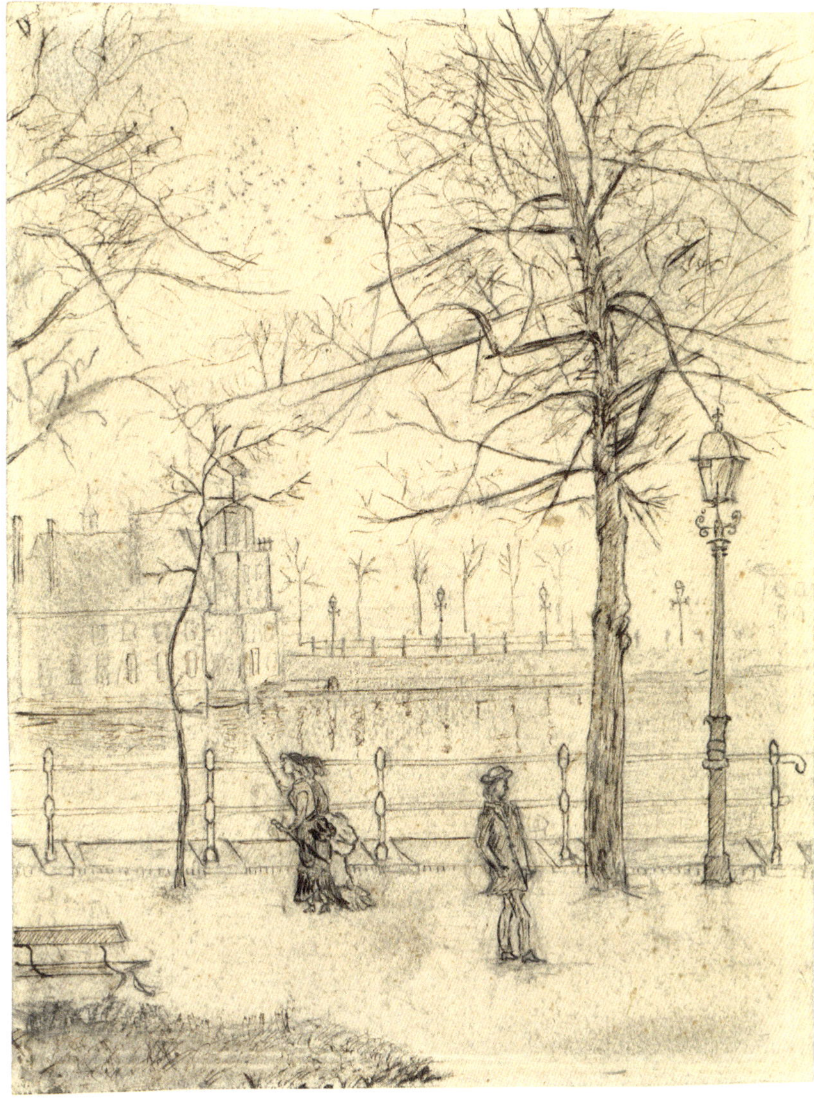

9 *Lange Vijverberg, The Hague*, autumn 1872–spring 1873. Pencil, pen and ink, on paper, 22.2 × 16.9 cm (8¾ × 6¾ in.). VAN GOGH MUSEUM, AMSTERDAM

reflected on his missed opportunities during this period: 'When I was in London, how often I would stand on the Thames Embankment and draw as I made my way home from Southampton Street in the evening, and it looked terrible. If only there had been someone then who had told me what perspective was, how much misery I would have been spared, how much further along I would be now' (394).

Faced, therefore, as a late starter, with the quandary of literally learning how to draw, Van Gogh had three courses of action. The first was to teach himself from the illustrated manuals, which could explain the fundamental principles, instruct him in such practical problems as the properties of the materials from which he could choose, and influence him by encouraging the copying of appropriate examples from the history of art in order to set him on the right path. There was a buoyant market for such manuals, which were frequently reprinted with revisions and very quickly went into several editions. Van Gogh duly equipped himself with many of them and was either given some or borrowed others. A leader in this field was Charles Blanc's *Grammaire des arts du dessin: Architecture, sculpture, peinture* (Grammar of the Arts of Drawing, Architecture, Sculpture, Painting; 1870). Mostly, however, the available titles covered very specific topics. Particularly important for Van Gogh as regards the study of the figure were two manuals by Charles Bargue, originally published by Goupil & Cie: *Cours de dessin exécuté avec le concours de J.-L. Gérôme* (Drawing Course, created with the Assistance of J.-L. Gérôme; 1868–71) and *Exercices au fusain pour préparer à l'étude de l'académie d'après nature* (Exercises in Charcoal in Preparation for Making Figure Studies from Life; 1871). Part 1 of the *Cours de dessin* (*Modèles d'après la Bosse* [Examples after Plaster Casts]) comprised seventy lithographs after plaster casts, and Part 2 (*Modèles d'après les maîtres de toutes les époques et toutes les écoles* [Examples after Masters of All Periods and Schools]), sixty-seven lithographs after works by famous artists, in this case particularly Hans Holbein the Younger (Fig. 10). So eager was Van Gogh to learn from the illustrations of charcoal figure studies in *Exercices au fusain* that, in 1880–81, he copied all sixty plates three times in quick succession.

Manuals by Armand-Théophile Cassagne covered specific areas of expertise, such as perspective (*Traité pratique de perspective appliquée au dessin artistique et industriel* [Practical Treatise on Perspective applied to Artistic and Industrial Drawing; 1866; revised and

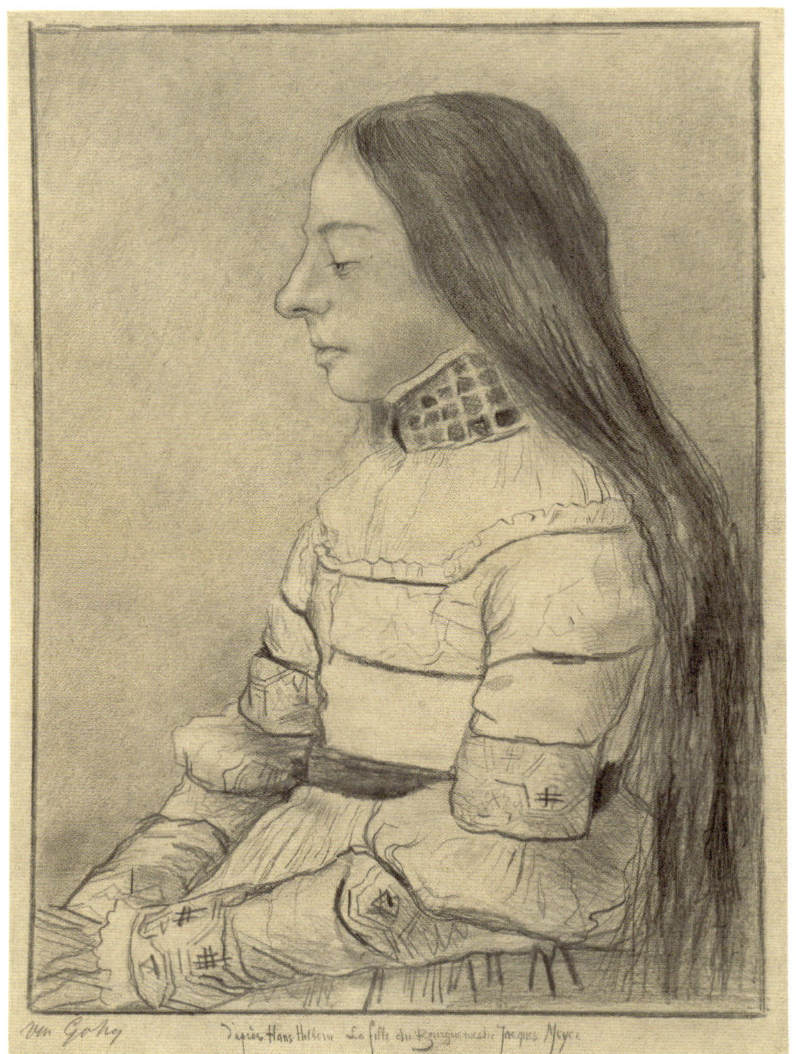

10 *The Daughter of Jacob Meyer (after Bargue after Holbein)*, October 1880–April 1881. Pencil on paper, 42.6 × 30.5 cm (16⅞ × 12⅛ in.).
VAN GOGH MUSEUM, AMSTERDAM

enlarged edn, 1879]) and the technique of watercolour (*Traité d'aquarelle* [Treatise on Watercolour; 1874]), as well as general introductions (*Guide de l'alphabet du dessin, ou l'art d'apprendre et d'enseigner les principes rationnels du dessin d'après nature* [Guide to the Alphabet of Drawing, or the Art of Learning and Teaching the Rational Principles of Drawing from Life; 1880]). For the use of charcoal, reference was made to Karl Robert (the pseudonym

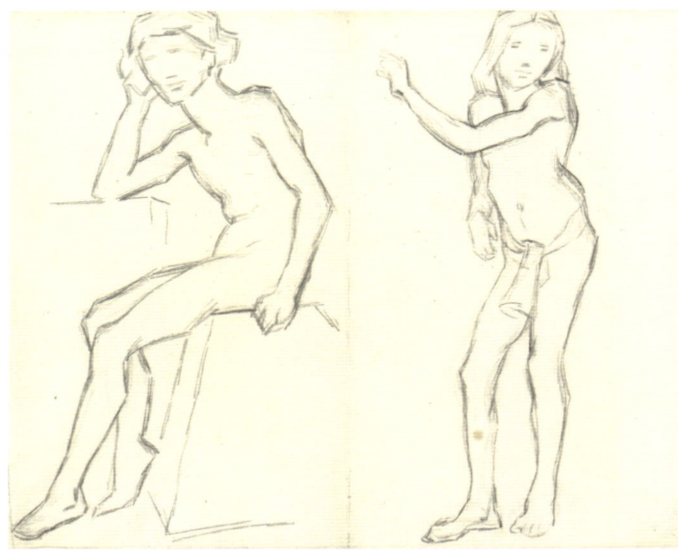

11 *Standing and Sitting Male Nude (after Bargue)*, June 1890. Pencil on paper, 44.6 × 54.6 cm (17⅝ × 21½ in.). VAN GOGH MUSEUM, AMSTERDAM

of Georges Mathieu-Meusnier), *Le Fusain sans maître* (Charcoal for Beginners; 4th edn, 1879), which incorporated information from the earlier accounts given by Auguste Allongé (for example, his *Collection de 30 paysages au fusain* (A Collection of 30 Landscapes in Charcoal) of 1877). For anatomy, help was to hand in Albert von Zahn's *Esquisses anatomiques à l'usage des artistes pour servir aux études d'après nature et d'après l'antique* (Anatomical Diagrams for the Use of Artists for Studies from Life and the Antique; 1865) or *Anatomy for Artists* by John Marshall, the professor of anatomy at the Royal Academy in London, first published in English in 1878 and translated into French as *Esquisses anatomiques à l'usage des artistes* in 1883.

As much as these titles may today seem academic, overly theoretical or plain dull, they were of immense practical significance for Van Gogh, and he referred to them constantly throughout his working life. For instance, arriving in Auvers-sur-Oise on his return to the north from Provence in 1890, a few months before his death, he immediately wrote to Theo asking him to send urgently a copy of Bargue's *Exercices au fusain* so that he could reacquaint himself with drawing the nude and studying proportions (Fig. 11).

A second way of learning for Van Gogh was to make copies after artists whose work he sought out as a guide. Foremost for him in this respect was Millet, on whom, in many ways, he wanted to model himself. Although born in the hamlet of Gruchy near Cherbourg, on the coast of northern France, Millet was most closely linked with the Barbizon School of painting associated with the Forest of Fontainebleau, to the south-east of Paris. His reputation was established by his depiction of scenes of peasant life, such as *The Angelus* (1857–59) and *The Gleaners* (1857), both now in the Musée d'Orsay in Paris. These works viewed the peasant in an heroic light and, when first exhibited, were considered to be radical, although not long after the artist's death they came to be interpreted as sentimental. Apart from the subject matter, Van Gogh particularly admired Millet for his drawings, including pastels, which were often on a large scale (Fig. 12). Such works were frequently commissioned and collected within the artist's lifetime. Van Gogh was able to see the large collection of ninety-five pastels formed by the collector and dealer Émile Gavet that was sold at the Hôtel Drouot in Paris

12 Jean-François Millet
The Plain of Chailly with Harrow and Plough, c. 1862–66.
Pastel on paper, 70 × 94 cm (27⅝ × 37⅛ in.).
THE BURRELL COLLECTION, GLASGOW

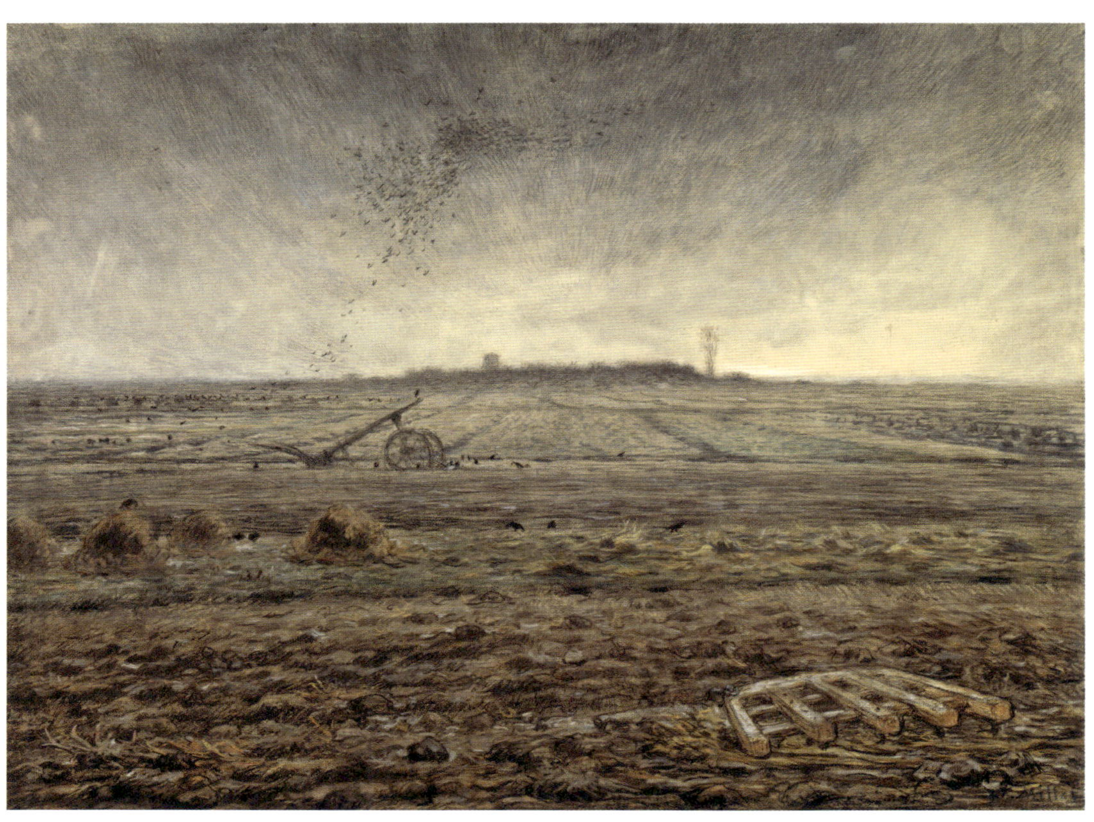

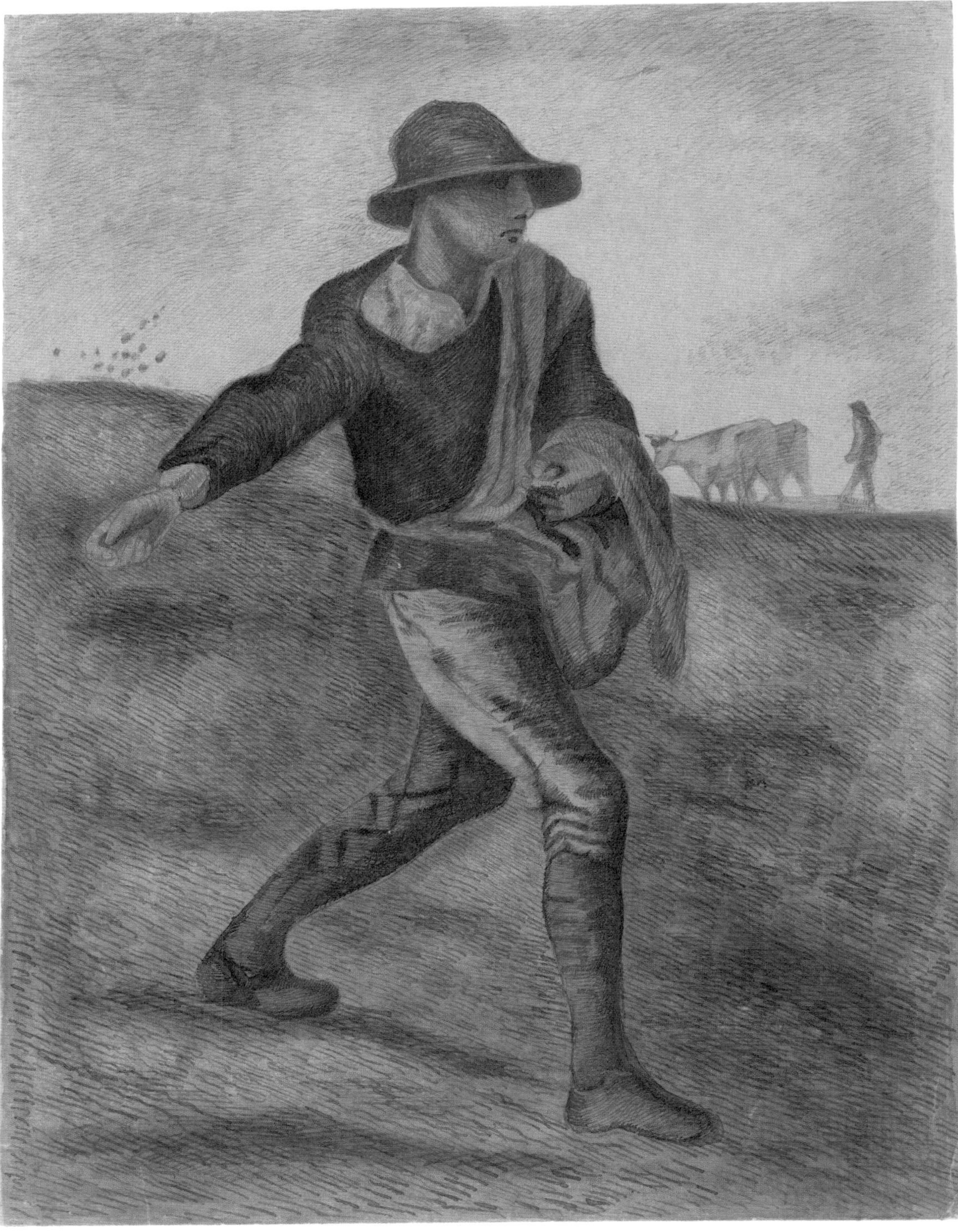

in 1875 (11–12 June), and this inspired him to write to Theo, 'When I entered the room . . . where they were exhibited, I felt something akin to: Put thy shoes from off thy feet, for the place whereon thou standest is holy ground' (36).

Van Gogh himself collected reproductions after Millet's work, especially the series of prints by Adrien Lavieille (1848–1920), published in *L'Illustration* and known as *The Labours of the Fields* (1853) and *The Four Times of Day* (1873), as well as photographs and independent prints. He began to make drawn copies after Millet's work during the summer of 1880 when in Belgium, and it was a practice that he returned to often (Fig. 13). These were the kind of images that prompted Van Gogh to write to Van Rappard that 'Millet is above all, and more than anyone else, the painter of *mankind*' (325).

Van Gogh's principal source for knowledge of Millet's life and work was the illustrated biography written by Alfred Sensier and published in 1881, and the artist's work remained a powerful influence. Indeed, even during his time in the asylum at Saint-Rémy, near Arles in Provence, Van Gogh's thoughts once again turned to Millet, and he made painted copies of *The Labours of the Fields*, *The Four Times of Day* and other similar subjects, prompted in parts by his nostalgia for the north (Fig. 14). These copies were made after the black-and-white prints by Lavieille or photographs, which meant that Van Gogh could choose his colours without reference to the original works – a process he described to his brother as 'translating . . . into a different language, the one of colours, the impressions of chiaroscuro and white and black' (839).

Another exemplar for the depiction of rural subjects favoured by Van Gogh was Jules Breton (1827–1906), to whom he made a pilgrimage in 1875, walking most of the way from Cuesmes in Belgium to Courrières in northern France (a distance of some fifty miles or seventy-eight kilometres), in order to pay his respects. Breton was the painter of such successes at the Paris Salon exhibition as *The Gleaners* of 1854 (National Gallery of Ireland, Dublin) and *The Recall of the Gleaners* of 1859 (Musée d'Orsay, Paris), both notable for their grand scale, clear compositions and accurate drawing. An additional attraction was that Breton was also an accomplished poet. Unfortunately, upon arrival, Van Gogh's nerve failed him, and he left Courrières without feeling able to introduce himself to the artist.

The third course of action open to Van Gogh for learning was to consult directly with practising artists. In this he was well placed, since a cousin by marriage, Anton Mauve (1838–1888), was a leading

13 *The Sower (after Millet)*, April 1881. Pencil, pen and brush and ink, watercolour, on paper, 48.1 × 36.7 cm (19 × 14½ in.). VAN GOGH MUSEUM, AMSTERDAM

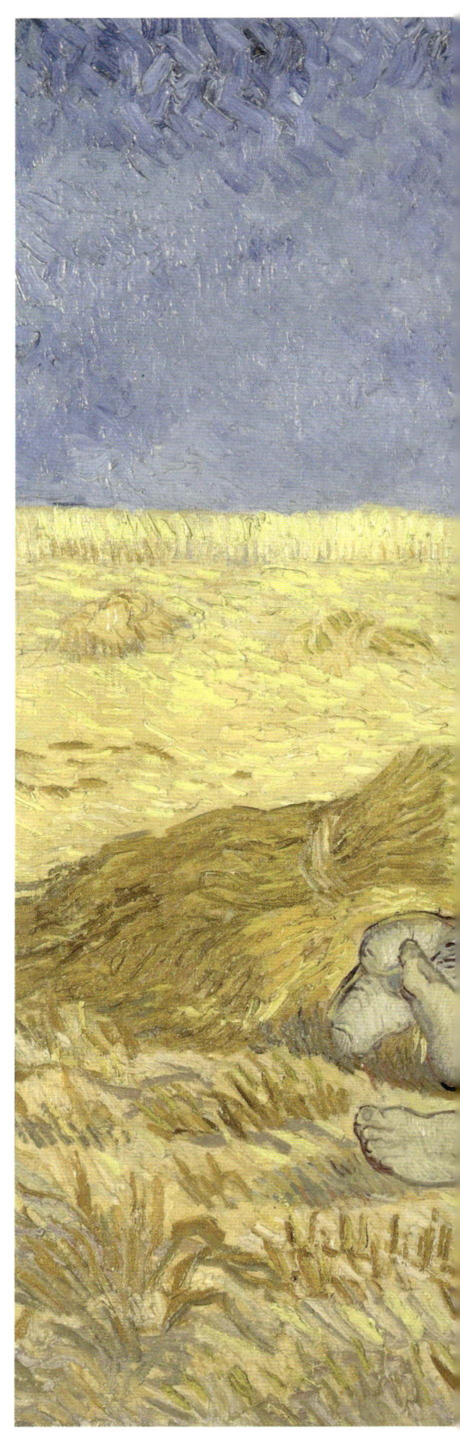

14 *Noon: Rest (after Millet)*, 1890.
Oil on canvas, 73 × 91 cm
(28¾ × 35⅞ in.).
MUSÉE D'ORSAY, PARIS

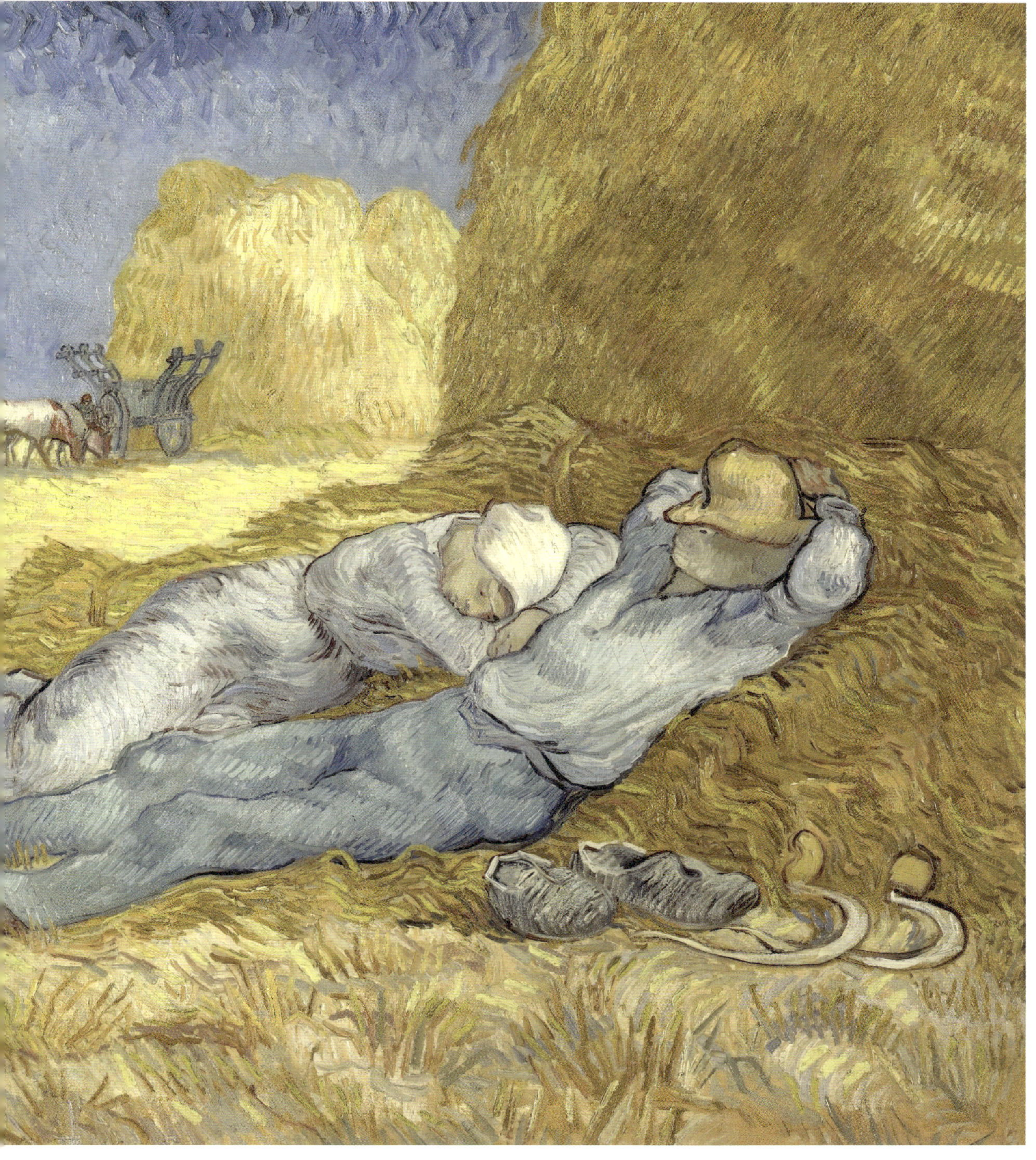

member of the Hague School and influential in such organizations as the Pulchri Studio (founded in 1847), a society based in The Hague that organized exhibitions, and the Hollandsche Teekenmaatschappij (the Dutch Drawing Society, founded in 1876). Artists of the Hague School were recognized as the successors of the Golden Age of Dutch painting in the seventeenth century and specialized in landscapes, marine subjects and domestic genre scenes. Their paintings and watercolours combine technical competence with well-organized compositions, good drawing and muted colours, counterbalanced by convincing evocations of mood and atmosphere (Fig. 15). Van Gogh was well acquainted with their work, because many of the painters were represented by Goupil & Cie when he was employed there. As well as Mauve, he particularly admired Jozef Israëls (1824–1911), Jacob Maris (1837–1899), Hendrik Willem Mesdag (1831–1915) and Jan Weissenbruch (1824–1903).

15 **Anton Mauve**
Fishing Boat on the Beach at Scheveningen, 1876.
Oil on canvas, 78.5 × 113 cm (31 × 44½ in.).
DORDRECHTS MUSEUM, DORDRECHT

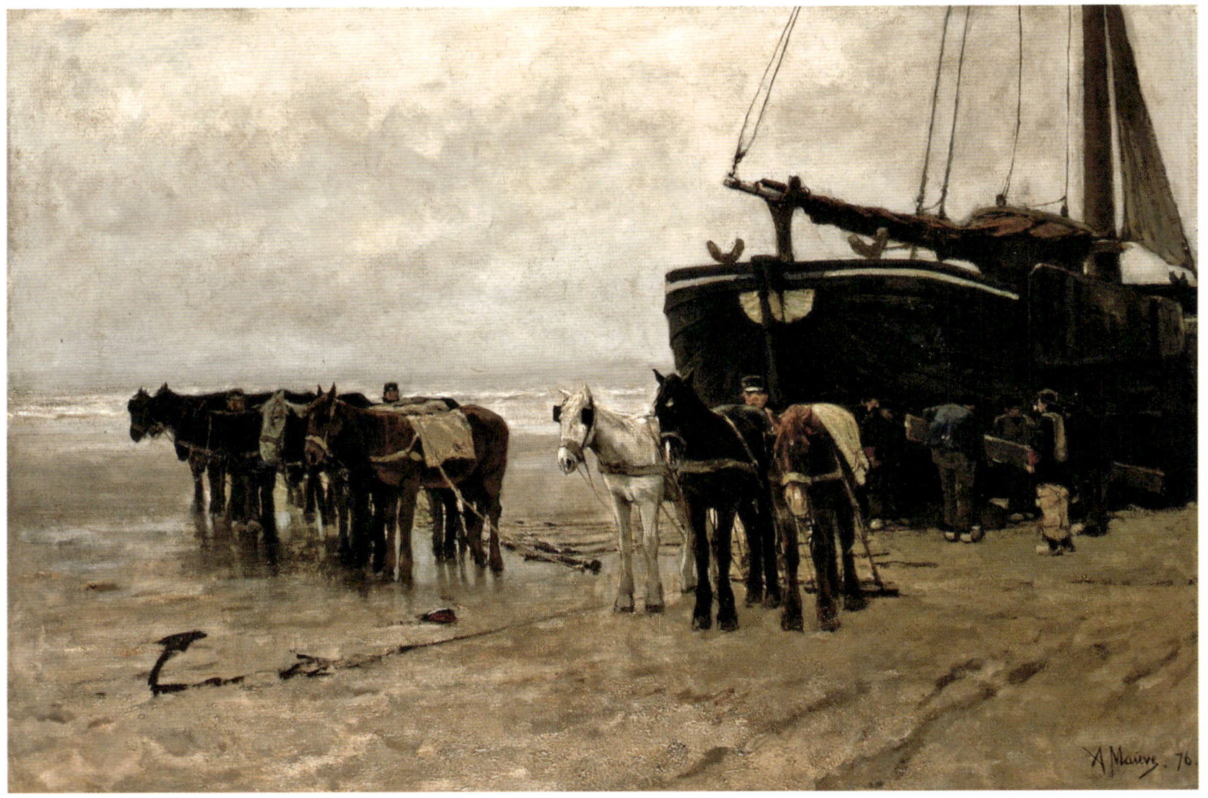

In the summer of 1881, Van Gogh first contacted Mauve, who gave him several lessons and acted as an adviser. The benefits for him were considerable: he was motivated to make drawings from life as opposed to copying, he learnt about the technique of using watercolour and he was introduced to the rudiments of painting in oil. It was not all straightforward, however: Van Gogh, although keen as always to learn, was not readily open to criticism or correction. The situation was also complicated by the fact that Mauve suffered from considerable ill health and, in fact, died in the same month that Van Gogh left for Arles in 1888. *Pink Peach Trees* was painted in recognition of their friendship soon after his arrival in the south (Fig. 16).

Of his younger contemporaries, Van Gogh's closest contact was with Anthon van Rappard, whose family belonged to the lower ranks of the Dutch aristocracy. They met in Brussels in 1880 and formed a friendship based on a shared interest in depicting scenes relating to working life (Fig. 17) and an appreciation of a similar kind of landscape, such as the province of Drenthe in the north-eastern part of the Netherlands where many Dutch and German artists went on painting campaigns. Van Rappard was trained within the traditional academic system and encouraged Van Gogh to study the same curriculum. Both had a catholic taste in art and enthusiastically collected and exchanged prints and reproductions of works by the numerous artists they admired. They frequently visited one another and, when apart, they maintained a warm and informed correspondence. But differences of opinion emerged over the treatment of subject matter, and the friendship only just survived Van Rappard's severe criticism of *The Potato Eaters* (1885), which was Van Gogh's first major painting (Fig. 48). Van Rappard led a more secluded life following his marriage in 1889 and died aged thirty-three of the effects of pneumonia, not long after Van Gogh.

The unusual start to Van Gogh's career as an artist, allied to his strong personality, helped to create the uncompromising and passionate character of his work, which is apparent in equal measure in the intensity of both his paintings and drawings. The governing style of the works on paper, often made with complex combinations of mixed media and sometimes heavily worked, is always energized and forceful. The early choices of materials for making his drawings are an indication of exactly how independent Van Gogh was prepared to be as an artist and to what lengths he was prepared

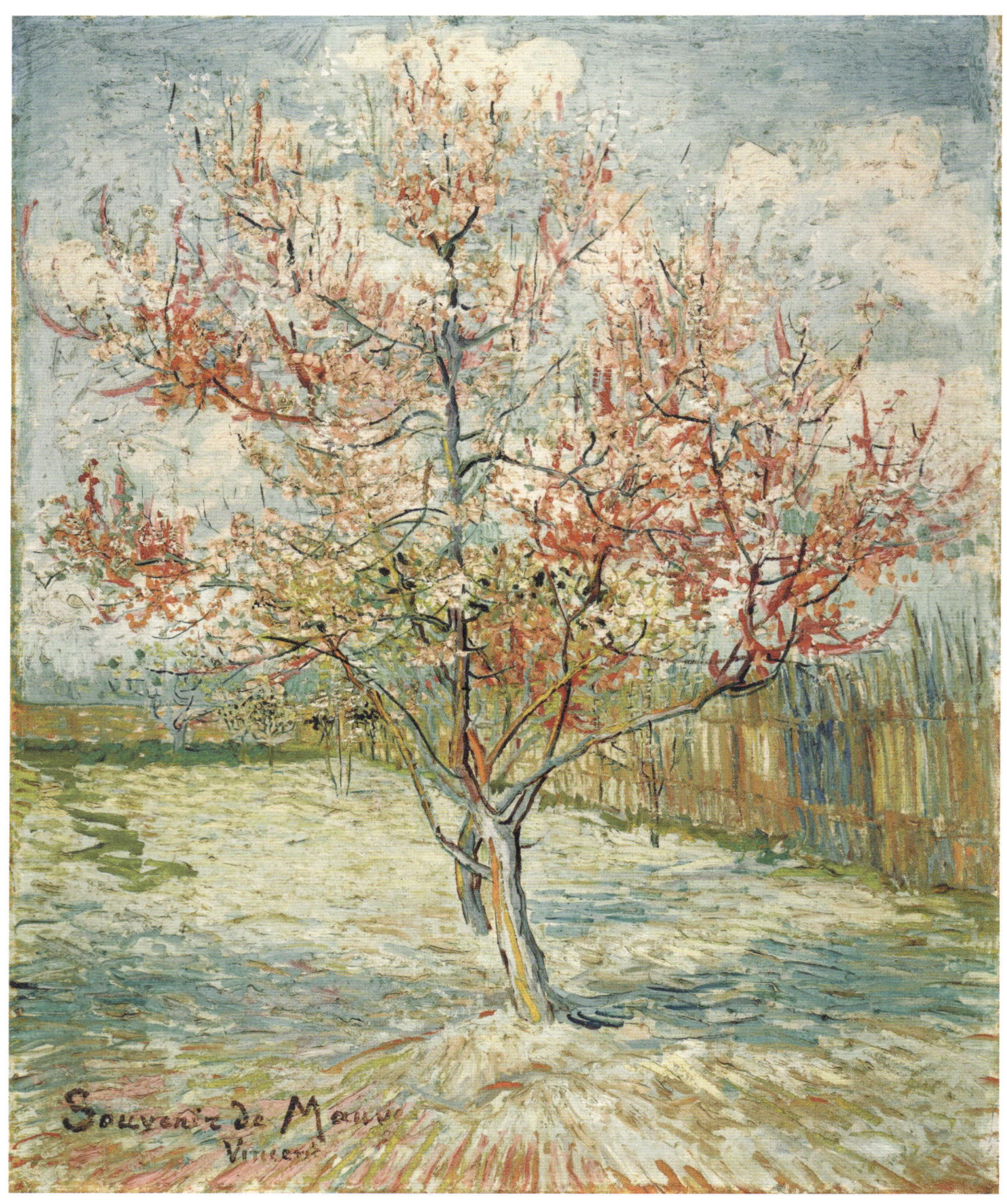

16 *Pink Peach Trees (Souvenir de Mauve)*, *c.* March 1888.
Oil on canvas, 73 × 60 cm (28¾ × 23⅝ in.).
KRÖLLER-MÜLLER MUSEUM, OTTERLO

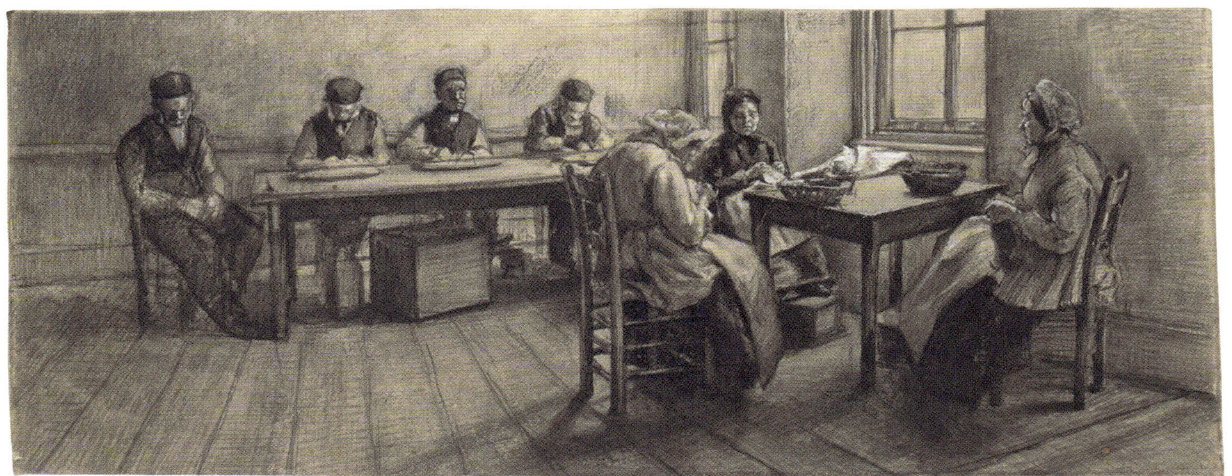

17 Anthon van Rappard
Hall in an Institution for the Blind in Utrecht, 1882–83. Pencil, ink, watercolour, heightened with white, on paper, 20.6 × 50.8 cm (8⅛ × 20 in.).
CENTRAAL MUSEUM, UTRECHT

to go in order to achieve the results he wanted. From the start, he was not afraid to experiment and act independently, endlessly seeking the most effective means of direct expression. It is no exaggeration to say that he adapted or improvised upon nearly all the traditional techniques of drawing and, in the process, became acutely conscious of the visual impact and physical properties of pencil, pen, brush, ink, charcoal, chalk and watercolour. For example, he had at various times a preference for carpenter's pencil over ordinary Faber pencil because it could produce delicate lines as well as broad strokes; early on he selected greasy lithographic crayon and natural (or Italian) chalk over standard manufactured black chalk, charcoal or Conté; he found specially cut quill pens or reed pens preferable to steel nibs; inks of varying hues and liquidity such as printer's ink or autograph ink held sway over bistre or sepia; and he exploited the opaque qualities of watercolour over the more usual transparent effects of the medium. The brush was frequently used to add heightening in either watercolour or opaque white.

There was an ongoing concern also over the actual application of media – how was it best to hold the instrument in the hand; with what pressure should it be applied; how durable was the medium itself and what was its visual impact. Van Gogh often agonized over the appearance of a finished drawing, conscious of avoiding deadening or flattening effects on the surface so that the visual impact of the image was comparable with and as fulsome as a painting. Of particular interest is his habit of fixing drawings with milk (sometimes diluted with water) as a way of unifying the surface, but also as protection against subsequent rubbing or wear. This fixative would be loosely brushed on or sometimes flicked over the surface with the fingers. The resulting stain or tidemark left on the surface can often be detected, particularly on the figure studies executed in the softer media (Fig. 18).

Choice of paper was as important as the selection of medium. Van Gogh frequently discusses in his letters matters relating to tone, luminosity, absorbency, weight and texture – all of which ultimately affected the appearance of a drawing. He tended to describe the papers he used generically as 'Ingres' or 'Arches', which denoted quality, but, in fact, he favoured a whole variety of watermarked papers, among them Berville, Dambricourt Frères, Glaslan, Hallines, Harding, Henig, Lalanne, Michallet, Torchon and Whatman. Only towards the end of his life did he tend to use coloured papers (pink, blue, cream) instead of his usual off-white-toned examples comparable with unbleached cotton or linen.

Like many of his contemporaries, Van Gogh kept sketchbooks to hand for recording momentary observations that might later be developed as proper compositions. Ready-made sketchbooks could be obtained from commercial suppliers of artists' materials, but Van Gogh also made his own by folding large sheets of paper several times into smaller divisions or signatures. When trimmed and stitched together, these signatures could amount to many pages. The surviving evidence for Van Gogh's sketchbooks is fragmentary, owing to dismemberment or loss. Seven are preserved in the Van Gogh Museum in Amsterdam of which only four remain in their original covers. The three others have been broken up and can be only partially reconstructed. When assessed as a group, however, one of the main advantages of the sketchbooks is that they have a broad chronological span extending from the artist's time in Nuenen to Auvers-sur-Oise,

A surprising element of Van Gogh's practice is his dependency on aids to drawing, such as the specially designed perspective frames he made for himself at different stages of his career and on which he relied for many years, often only cursorily removing from the paper the guidelines that such a method required (Figs 19 and 85). He also pinned sheets of paper to boards and assessed the visual effect of a drawing in progress by viewing it through a temporary passepartout frame.

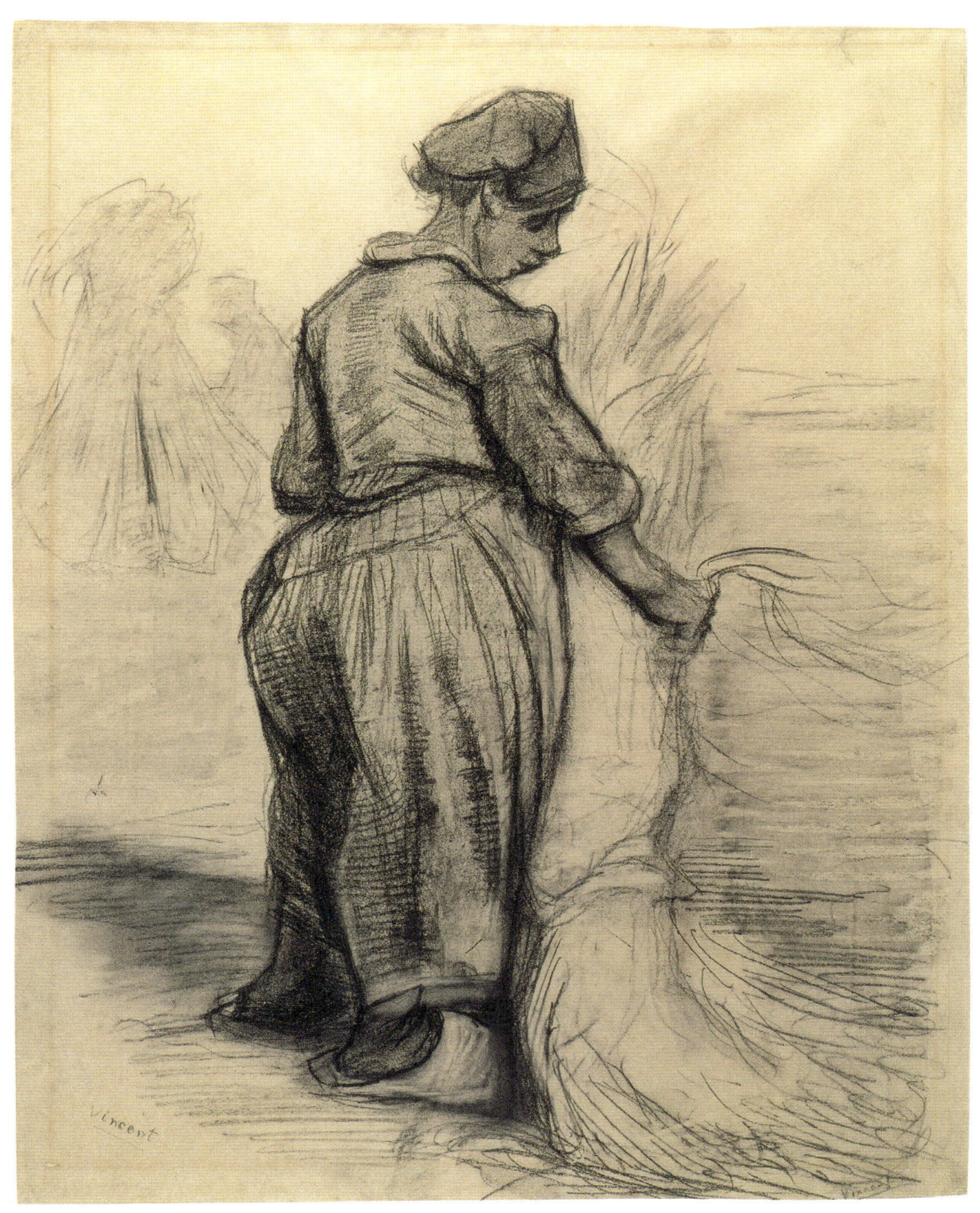

18 *Peasant Woman Binding Wheat Sheaves*, July–August 1885. Black chalk and traces of milk fixative, on paper, 55.4 × 43.4 cm (21⅞ × 17 in.).
KRÖLLER-MÜLLER MUSEUM, OTTERLO

Waarde Theo,

In myn vorigen brief zult ge een krabbeltje gevonden hebben van dat bewuste perspectiefraam. Daar net kom ik van den smid vandaan die yzeren punten aan de stokken heeft gemaakt en yzeren hoeken aan het raam.

Het bestaat uit twee lange palen:

met sterke houten pennen gaat het raam daaraan vast. / zy 't in de hoogte / zy 't in de breedte. —

Dit maakt dat men op 't strand of op 't weiland of op een akker een kykje heeft als door 't venster. De loodlynen & waterpaslynen van 't raam verder de diagonalen & het kruis — of anders een verdeeling in kwadraten geven vast & zeker eenige hoofdpunten waardoor men met vastheid een teekening kan maken die de groote lynen & proporties aangeeft. Dan ten minste wanneer men gevoel heeft voor de perspectief en begrip van de reden waarom en de wyze waarop de perspectief de lynen een schynbare verandering van rigting & de vlakken & de massa's een verandering van grootte geeft. Zonder dat helpt het raam niets of byna niets en duizelt men als men er door kykt.

My dunkt gy zult wel voelen dat het een heerlyk ding is dit vizier te braqueeren op de zee op de groene velden — of s'winters op de besneeuwde vlakte of in den herfst op het grillig netwerk van dunne & dikke takken & stammen, of een stormlucht.

19 Letter from Vincent van Gogh to Theo van Gogh, 5 or 6 August 1882 (Letter 254), with sketches of *Post for Perspective Frame*, *Peg for Perspective Frame* and *Perspective Frame*. Pen and ink, on paper, 20.9 × 13.2 cm (8¼ × 5¼ in.). VAN GOGH MUSEUM, AMSTERDAM

Everywhere in Van Gogh's works on paper, the viewer is aware of the actual physical act of drawing. Apart from the mark-making itself, there is often evidence of scraping, scumbling, rubbing, scratching, erasing, fixing and dampening. Drawing at the best of times was a fractious and totally committed affair or, at worst, an assault. Even so, any judgment on his technique needs to be tempered, on account of the lyrical way in which he could describe the raw materials that he held in his hand, such as his reference to natural chalk as having 'the colour of a ploughed field on a summer evening' (325). It should be remembered that the artist was always short of money and at times relied completely on Theo for supplies and replacements. The materials even for drawing, let alone painting, were expensive and not always available when Van Gogh was working in isolation. Models, too, needed to be paid and sometimes provided with costumes or props. Accordingly, Van Gogh often had to compromise, but this made him only more determined and also more inventive. Such were the circumstances, however, that enabled one of the most naturally gifted draughtsmen in European art to flourish, even if during his own lifetime he was unable to prosper.

Chapter 2

Figures

Given his upbringing and early experiences of life, it is hardly surprising that the principal theme of Van Gogh's art should be the human predicament. As he wrote to his brother Theo from The Hague in 1882,

> Life is the same as drawing: sometimes one has to act quickly and resolutely, tackle things with willpower, take care that the broad outlines appear with lightning speed. It's no use hesitating or doubting, and the hand may not tremble and the eye may not wander but must remain fixed on one's purpose. And one must be so engrossed in it that something quickly takes shape on the piece of paper or the canvas, where at first there was nothing, so that later one hardly knows how one tossed it off. The time of reasoning and reflecting must precede the decisive action. While *doing* it there's little space for reflecting or reasoning. (226)

Such was the commitment and passion that gripped Van Gogh following his decision to become a fully fledged artist. His first efforts were concentrated on learning to draw, but this he soon found to be 'a hard and difficult struggle' (160). The usual practice would have been to attend an academy of fine art, where teaching was directed towards producing artists who could paint subjects acceptable to the more traditional sections of the exhibition-going public – subjects based on historical, religious and mythological sources, as well as genre scenes or landscapes. The principal outlets for such works were the official exhibitions organized by state or municipal authorities where success was measured by the rewarding of medals or the winning of commissions.

Van Gogh was encouraged to take advantage of academic teaching on two occasions – first in Brussels, where he was admitted

Peasant Woman Carrying Wheat in her Apron, July–August 1885 (detail of Fig. 36).

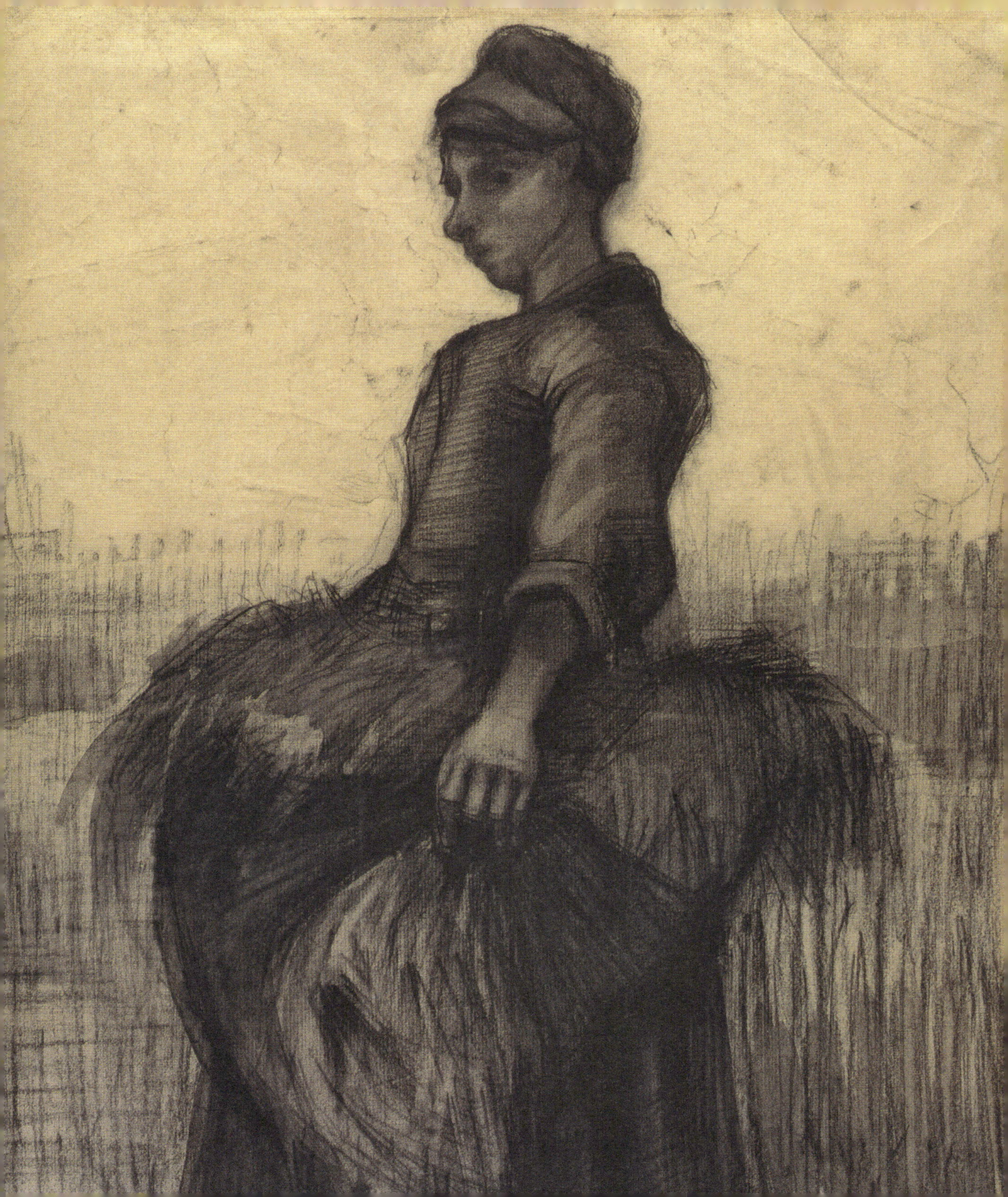

to the Royal Academy of Fine Arts on 15 December 1880, and second in Antwerp, where he attended the Royal Academy of Fine Arts irregularly from 18 January 1886 for about a month. Significantly, both these occasions were after he had begun to teach himself to draw. Even though the curricula at such academies as these were occasionally under review, the teaching programme was long established and universally applied. At a preliminary stage, this involved copying compositions by older artists from prints before undertaking studies after plaster casts of antique sculpture and eventually graduating to life drawing from posed models. The Royal Academy in Brussels, which Van Gogh was encouraged to attend by the Hague School painter Willem Roelofs (1822–1897), did not impress him, and he dismissed the teachers – some of them distinguished artists – as 'pedantic people who could be called the Pharisees of art' (178).

On the other hand, almost six years later, he seems to have been more prepared to seize the opportunity of testing out his drawing skills at the Royal Academy in Antwerp, under the director, Karel Verlat (1824–1890), and the specialists Franz Vinck (1827–1903) and Eugène Siberdt (1851–1931). Recognizing that he lacked the necessary knowledge about proportions and had virtually no experience of modelling, Van Gogh set about making copies from plaster casts of antique sculpture as the first stage in treating the nude convincingly. However, *The Discus Thrower* (Fig. 20), which is thought to have been drawn in Antwerp, reveals the artist's distinctly unorthodox approach to this formal exercise: the viewpoint is unusual and the finish uneven, particularly in the reinforced outlines and the treatment of the vibrant chiaroscural effects, with the figure set against the dark background on the left. This dramatic style was more suited to the drawing clubs that he attended in the evenings in Antwerp than to the strictly controlled classes at the Academy. Van Gogh concluded that, whereas others might have a greater technical understanding of drawing the nude, with a smoother finish, he preferred working directly from nature. This meant, he wrote perceptively, that he 'may perhaps be more daring than many others in dashing things off and tackling a group of things' (565).

Even when Van Gogh left the Netherlands at the end of February 1886 and went to Paris, where Theo was now ensconced as a manager at the headquarters of Goupil & Cie, he tried once again to test his drawing skills against the standards required for academic

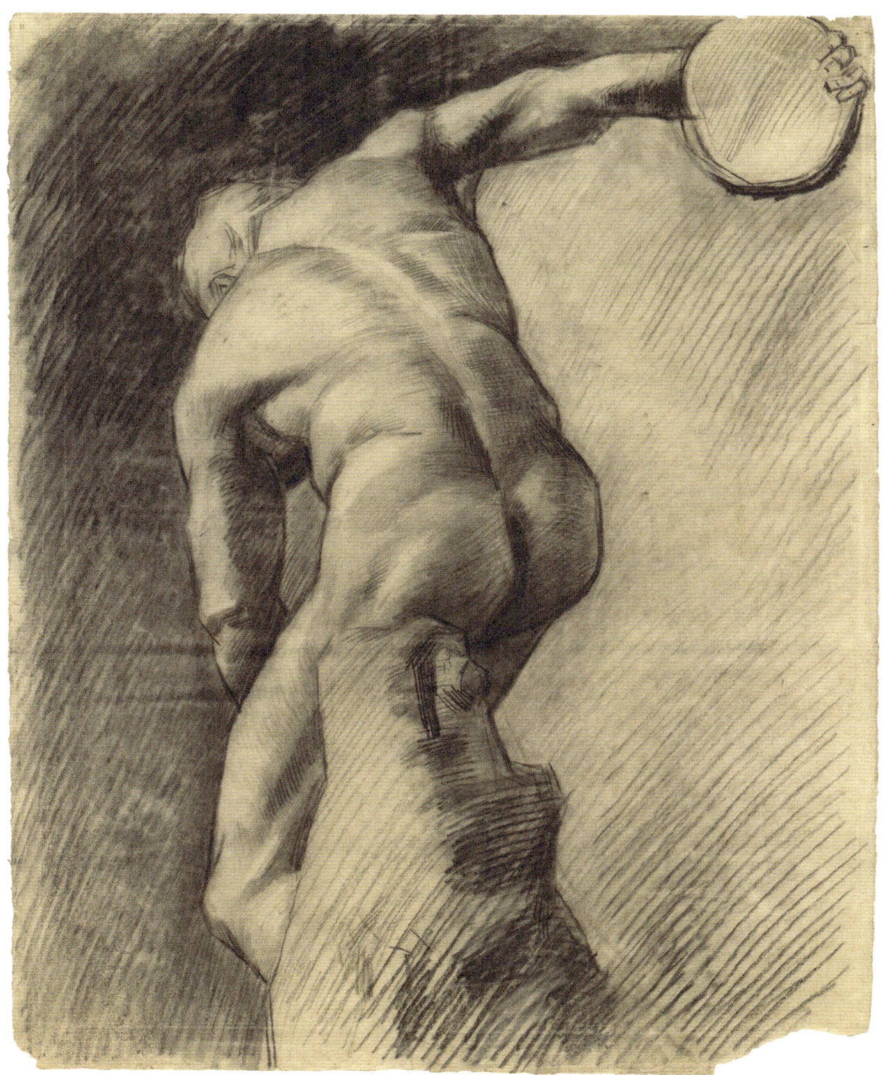

20 *The Discus Thrower*, February 1886. Chalk on paper, 56.2 × 44.3 cm (22¼ × 17½ in.). VAN GOGH MUSEUM, AMSTERDAM

success. This nagging concern continued, in fact, for a year after the completion of his first major figure painting, *The Potato Eaters* of 1885, which, in subject and treatment, was as far removed from academic practice as possible (Fig. 48). For three months while in Paris, he attended the studio run by Fernand Cormon (1845–1924) where students were prepared for the examination for admission to the prestigious École des Beaux-Arts, which was answerable to the influential Académie des Beaux-Arts, founded in 1648 and reconstituted after the French Revolution of 1789. Van Gogh had heard of Cormon's reputation while still in Antwerp and was aware of his freer interpretation of the academic drawing style. He duly set about making copies after plaster casts of antique sculpture (Fig. 21) and drawing the nude from posed models (Fig. 22). These exercises vary in quality. There is a firm grasp of the principles of modelling, but the proportions are often awry.

If anything, the time spent in Cormon's studio only reinforced the limitations that Van Gogh had already detected in the academic

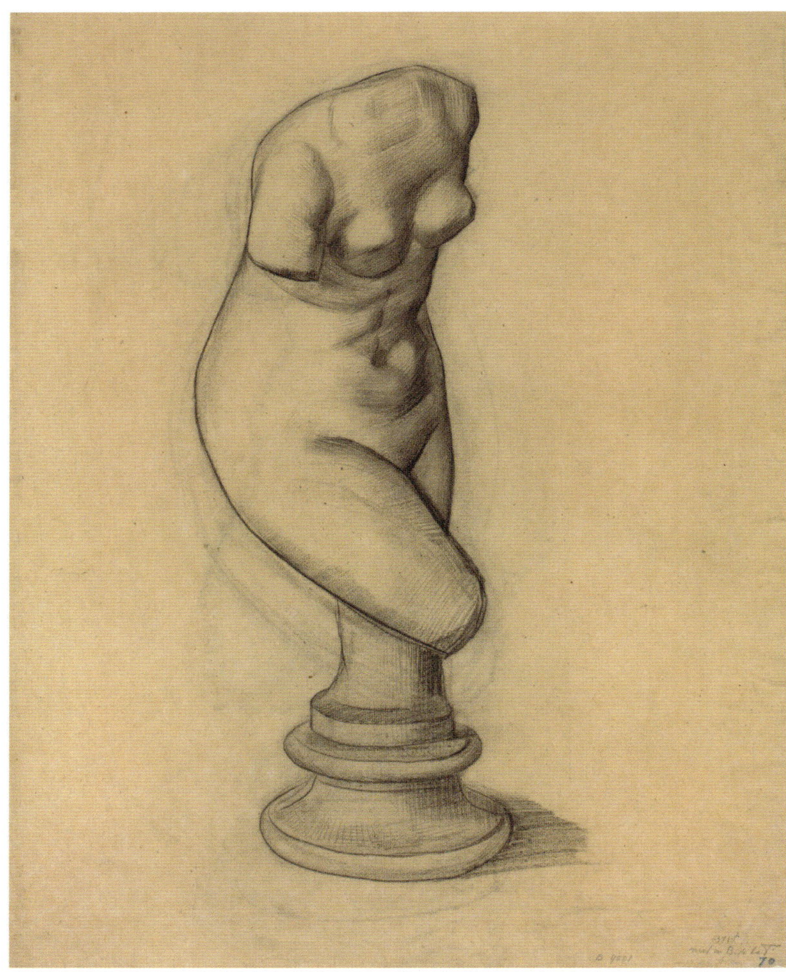

21 *Torso of Venus*, March–May 1886. Chalk on paper, 61.1 × 45.5 cm (24 × 18 in.). VAN GOGH MUSEUM, AMSTERDAM

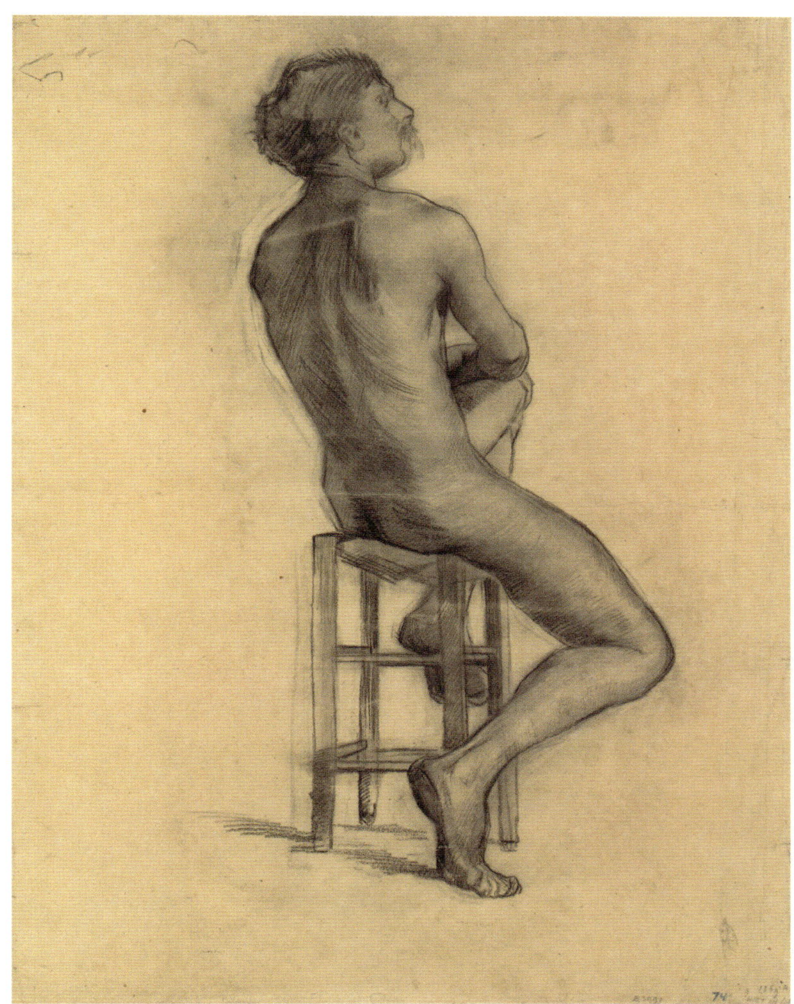

22 *Seated Male Nude Seen from the Back*, March–May 1886. Chalk on paper, 61.7 × 48.2 cm (24⅜ × 19 in.). VAN GOGH MUSEUM, AMSTERDAM

system. Direct copying was restricting, whereas drawing from life, or better still from memory, was liberating; neat outlines were prescriptive, whereas breadth of conception was an indication of originality. Coming from outside the academic system, Van Gogh felt that the students there 'who've never been anywhere else but at academies and studios' were lacking 'that view of reality in which they live, and finding subjects' (558). Nevertheless, being in Paris, the centre of the art world at that time, was sufficient compensation. The city offered so much more than drawing classes, and he realized that he could learn just as much independently by visiting the Musée du Louvre and numerous other galleries owned by dealers or exhibition spaces run by independent organizations. But, most of all, he could now see at first hand, with Theo's help, the work of the Impressionist and Post-Impressionist artists, who were identified as the avant-garde and against whom Van Gogh could measure his true worth.

From the start, Van Gogh recognized the importance of the figure in his art. In fact, inspired by the collection of prints he had formed from such publications as *L'Illustration*, *The Graphic* and the *Illustrated London News*, he felt inclined to become an illustrator himself. He was particularly struck by the skill of the many wood-engravers – English, French, American – who depicted those social realist subjects with which he could readily identify. Among the English wood-engravers for whom he had unreserved admiration were Hubert von Herkomer (1849–1914), Frank Holl (1845–1888), Frederick Walker (1840–1875) and Luke Fildes (1843–1927), whose work (Fig. 23) he went so far as to compare

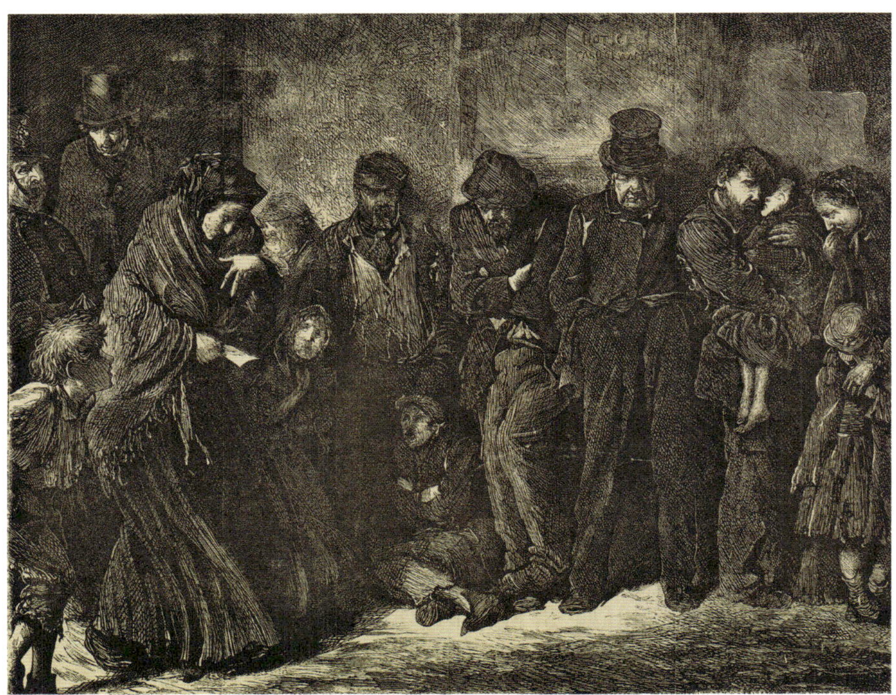

23 Luke Fildes
Houseless and Hungry, 1869 (from *The Graphic*, 4 December 1869). Wood engraving, 18.3 × 23 cm (7¼ × 9⅛ in.). TATE, LONDON

with the novels of Dickens and Eliot, and who, 'on account of their Monday morning-like sobriety and deliberate austerity and prose and analysis, continue to attract me as something solid and firm which gives one something to hold onto on days when one is feeling weak' (274). Although he did not become an illustrator, he was attracted to many of their realist themes, which he had already witnessed in everyday life. Such compositions in whatever medium needed to include figures, which is why, right from the beginning of his career, he put great emphasis on drawing the figure, declaring that 'the basis for everything is knowledge of the figure' (322).

Using Charles Bargue's manuals as his main guide, therefore, Van Gogh began by making several studies from anyone who would pose for him. The fact that many of these comparatively early drawings are signed demonstrates that, even at this stage, they were intended for sale. In *Boy with a Sickle*, the figure, which fills almost the whole sheet of paper, reflects the scale of the reproductions in Bargue's *Exercices au fusain*. The visual impact of the overall image is almost overpowering, but, on the other hand, the details are easily legible (Fig. 24). This study was made in Etten using Piet Kaufmann, a young clog-maker and sometime gardener for the Van Gogh family, as the model. The figure is drawn in chalk with touches of charcoal. The foreground and backdrop resemble a stage set, confirming that the model was specially posed. The challenge for the artist lay in making the tight, contorted pose look convincing. Yet, while the outlines are securely drawn and the watercolour highlighting the clothes and shoes is carefully laid in, the head seems too large for the body, and the positioning of the left leg, rather awkward. The figure does not seem solidly positioned on the ground and looks as though it might topple over.

Woman Sewing, which was drawn at the same time and is also in mixed media, is posed in an interior (Fig. 25). The facial features are sympathetically handled, and the concentration of the sitter on sewing is well observed, but the hands seem too big and the legs too long. The perspective of the table and the view through the window read well, but the chair is somewhat precarious.

As Van Gogh eventually recognized, part of the problem with *Boy with a Sickle* and *Woman Sewing* is that he was positioning himself too close to the models, thereby compressing the space in which the figures are being observed. A watercolour of a similar subject and date to *Woman Sewing* shows the model positioned further away in a more enclosed and less elaborate interior, but the problem here

24 *Boy with a Sickle*, October–November 1881. Black chalk, charcoal wash and opaque watercolour, on paper, 46.6 × 60.4 cm (18⅜ × 23⅞ in.). KRÖLLER-MÜLLER MUSEUM, OTTERLO

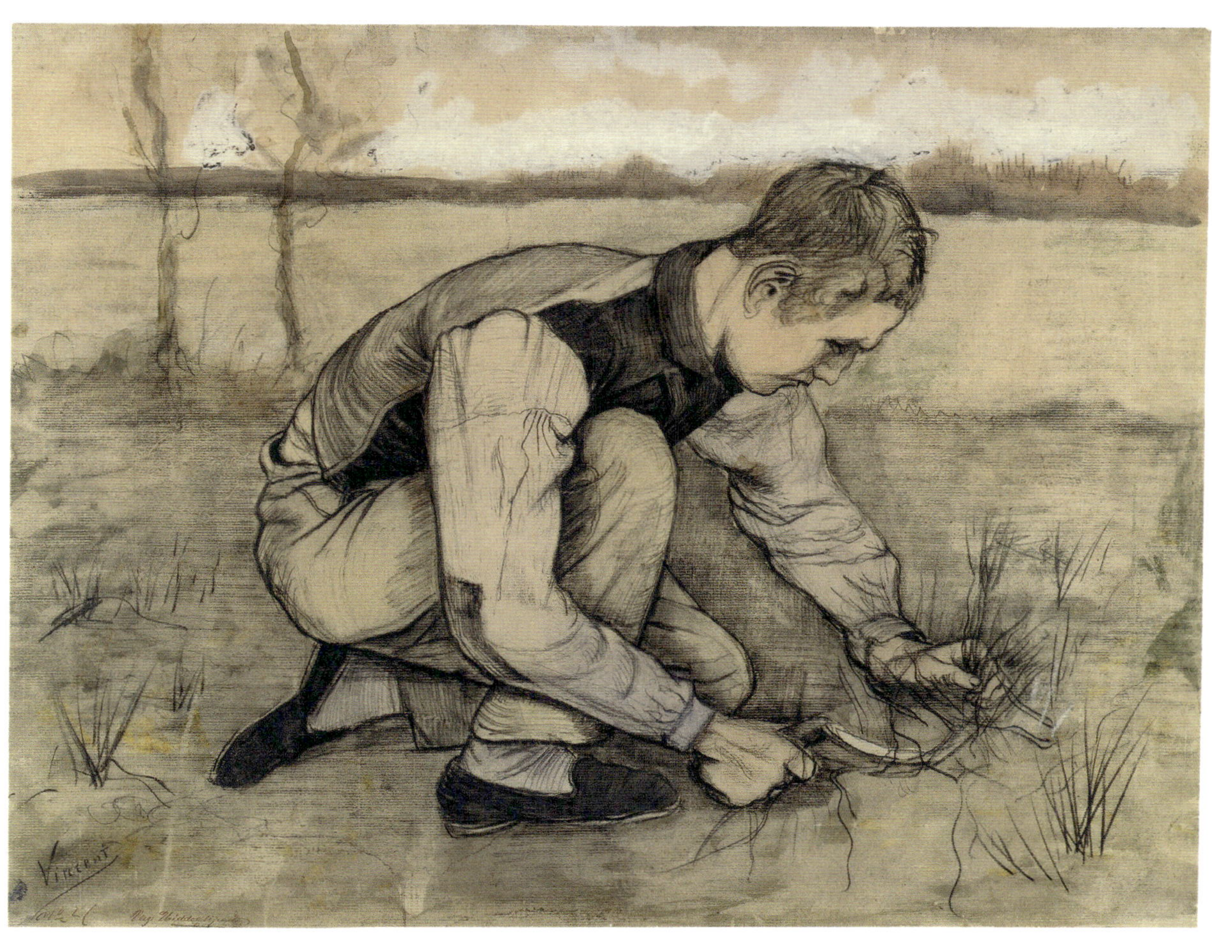

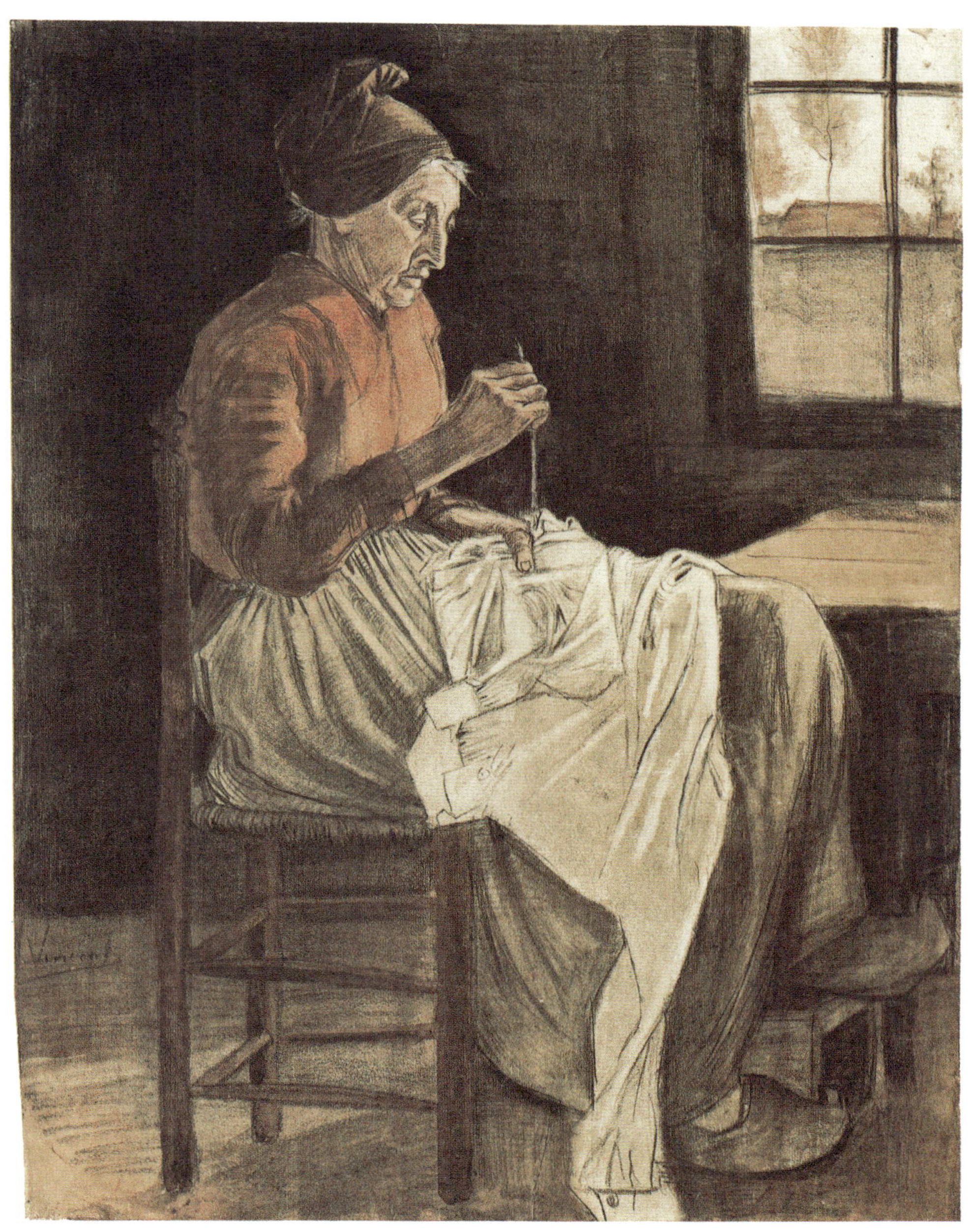

25 *Woman Sewing*, October–November 1881.
Black, red and brown chalk, wash, opaque and transparent watercolour, on laid paper, 62 × 47.2 cm (24½ × 18⅝ in.).
KRÖLLER-MÜLLER MUSEUM, OTTERLO

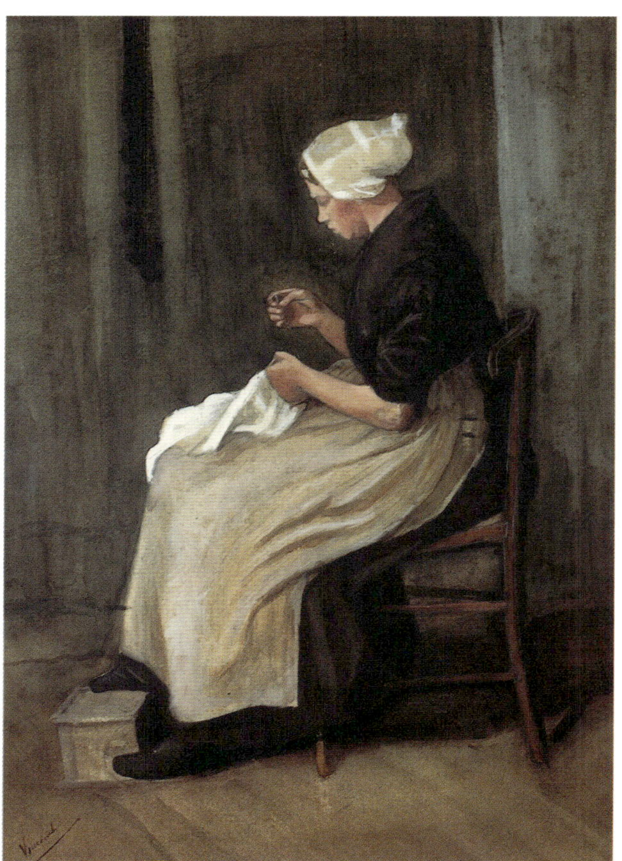

26 *Scheveningen Woman Sewing*, December 1881. Watercolour on paper, 48 × 35 cm (19 × 13⅞ in.). P. AND N. DE BOER FOUNDATION, AMSTERDAM

is that the artist has found it difficult to render the folds of the apron credibly in watercolour (Fig. 26).

With Van Gogh's move to The Hague over Christmas 1881, more possibilities presented themselves for the study of the figure. He had a ready supply of sitters from the Dutch Reformed Old People's Home in their distinctive uniforms of whom one, Adrianus Jacobus Zuyderland, was the most prominent (Fig. 27). The medium here is carpenter's pencil, with milk being used as a fixative while the work was in progress. This had the added effect of toning down the reflective quality of the surface, and, by using his perspective frame, Van Gogh found it easier to fix the poses. The titles of many of the studies based on these sitters (for example, *Worn Out* or *Sorrowing Woman*), as well as their poses, suggest an implied narrative, indicating that Van Gogh was keen to avoid any form of straightforward portraiture. Indeed, the striking *Old Man with a Top Hat*, based, no doubt, also on a resident of the Dutch Reformed Old People's Home, belongs to a group of studies in pencil and lithographic crayon entitled 'Heads of the People', which the artist developed while he was in The Hague (Fig. 28).

The idea for this group of drawings was inspired by a series devised by British artists that had been published in *The Graphic* in 1876, one that Van Gogh had recently added to his collection

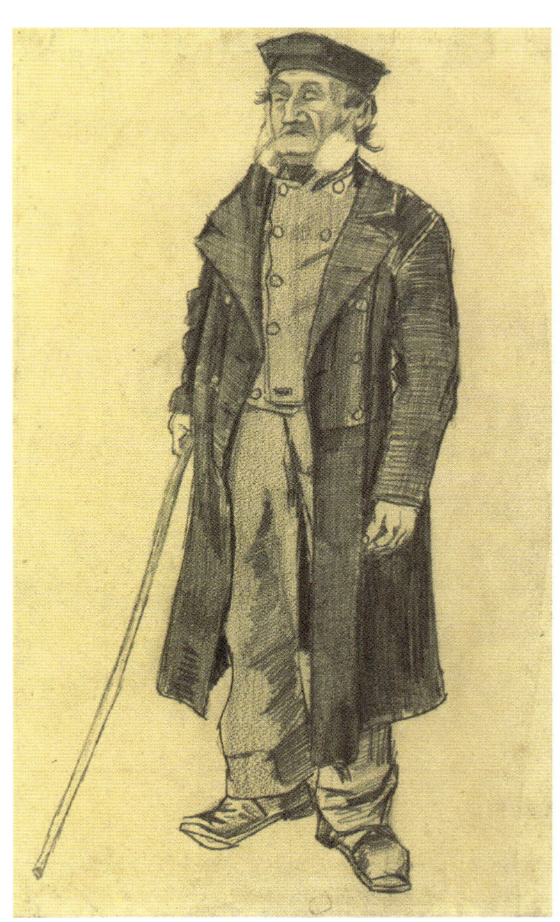

27 *Old Man with a Stick*, September–November 1882. Pencil on paper, 50.4 × 30.2 cm (19⅞ × 12 in.). VAN GOGH MUSEUM, AMSTERDAM

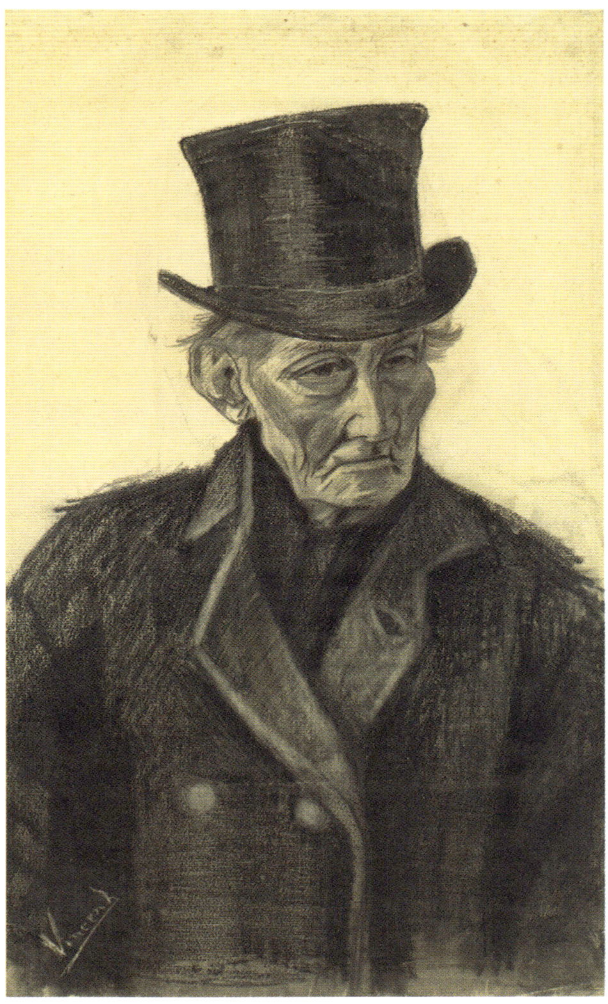

28 *Old Man with a Top Hat*, December 1882–January 1883. Pencil, lithographic crayon, pen and brush and ink, on paper, 60 × 36 cm (23⅝ × 14¼ in.). VAN GOGH MUSEUM, AMSTERDAM

(Fig. 29). He depended on numerous models for his series, often observing them at work or putting them into character with clothes or items he had specially obtained for the purpose (Fig. 30). Particularly significant in this respect is the involvement of the former prostitute Clasina Maria Hoornik (known as Christien or Sien) and her family, who, at the time, were living with Van Gogh in The Hague. Perhaps because of their personal significance, these last drawings all combine remarkable vigour without loss of sensitivity (Fig. 31). Throughout the series there is a sense in which the influence of the broader and more caricatural style of French illustrators, such as Honoré Daumier (1808–1879) and Gustave Doré (1832–1883), can be detected. Gradually, in his turn, Van Gogh was building up a gallery of types that could be incorporated into any future composition on demand, while also holding out the possibility of their being published in their own right as a 'gallery'. In December 1882, he proposed in a letter to Theo just such a

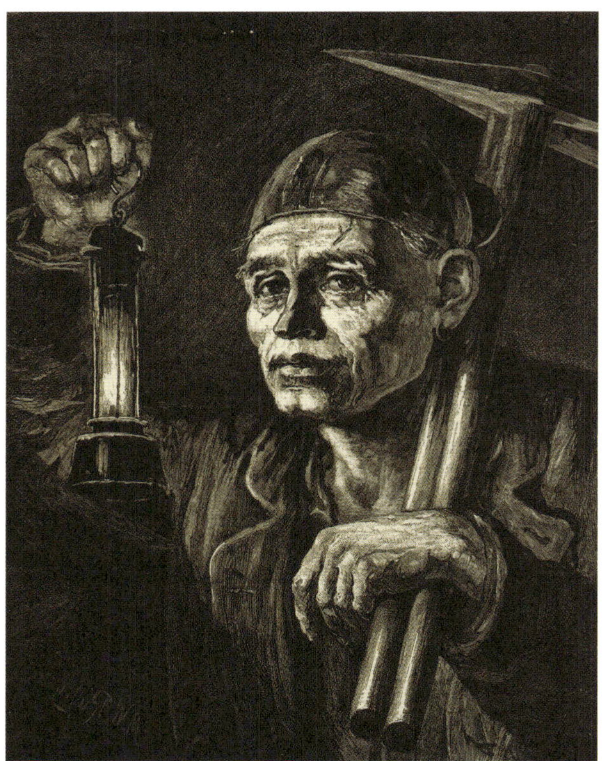

29 Matthew Ridley
Heads of the People: The Miner, 1876 (from *The Graphic*, 15 April 1876). Wood engraving, 29.3 × 22.5 cm (11⅝ × 8⅞ in.).
WITT LIBRARY, COURTAULD INSTITUTE OF ART, LONDON

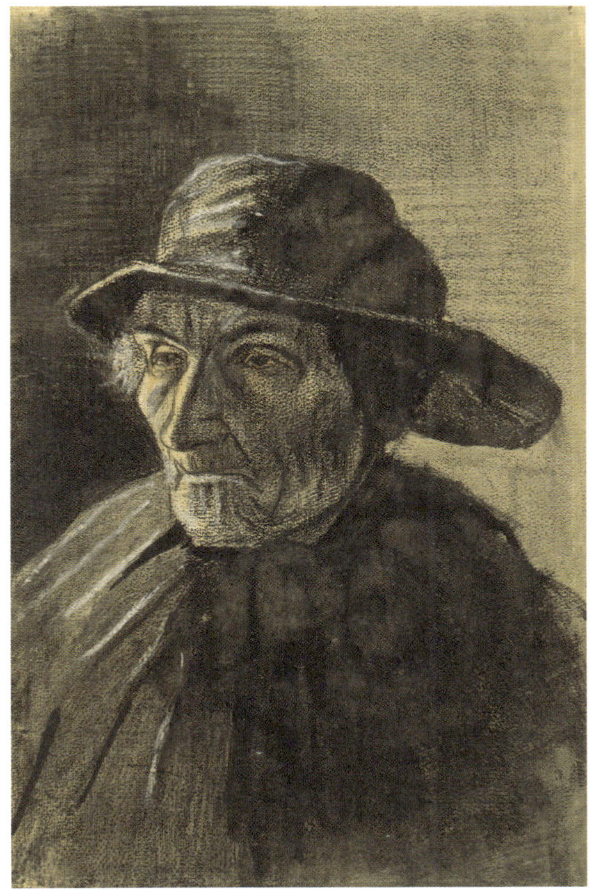

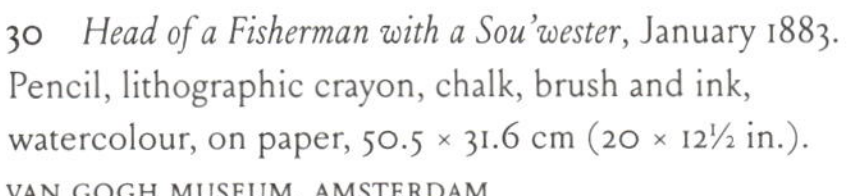

30 *Head of a Fisherman with a Sou'wester*, January 1883. Pencil, lithographic crayon, chalk, brush and ink, watercolour, on paper, 50.5 × 31.6 cm (20 × 12½ in.). VAN GOGH MUSEUM, AMSTERDAM

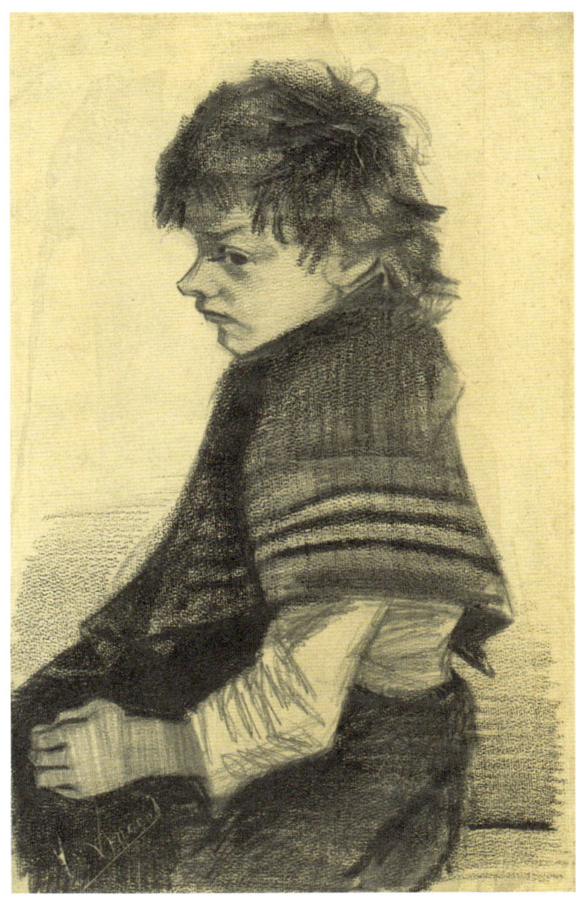

31 *Girl with a Shawl (Maria Wilhelmina Hoornik?)*, December 1882–January 1883. Pencil, lithographic crayon, on paper, 51 × 31.3 cm (20⅛ × 12⅜ in.). VAN GOGH MUSEUM, AMSTERDAM

publishing venture – to make prints of these drawings which would be sold in portfolios, each of thirty items, comprising 'Working types, say – sower, digger, woodcutter, ploughman, washerwoman, plus on occasion a cradle or orphan man [a resident of the Dutch Reformed Old People's Home], in short the whole vast field lies open, there's an abundance of fine material – an enterprise like that – may one undertake it or may one not? It goes even deeper: is it a duty and just, or is it wrong? That is the question' (289).

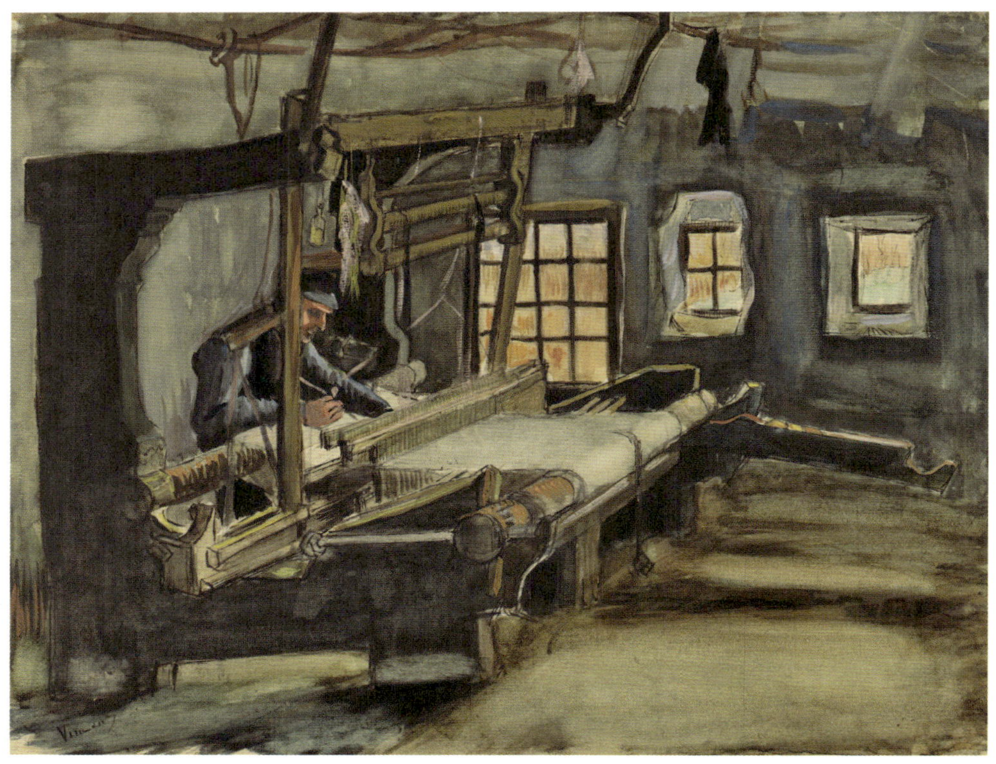

32 *Weaver*, December 1883–August 1884. Pencil, watercolour, pen and ink, on paper, 35.5 × 44.6 cm (14 × 17⅝ in.). VAN GOGH MUSEUM, AMSTERDAM

In the same letter, Van Gogh hopes that these prints would decorate 'workers' dwellings, farmhouses, in a word, for every working man'. It was an idealistic enterprise inspired by both the artist's financial needs and his social principles. Or, as he put it a few days later, 'The idea of drawing types of working man from the people for the people, and circulating them as a popular publication, seeing the whole thing as necessarily being an affair of duty and charity' (291). This particular venture came to nought, but the artist's next move, in December 1883, to Nuenen in North Brabant, where his parents were now living, proved to be more fruitful.

North Brabant was one of the main textile-producing areas in the Netherlands, with the town of Tilburg at the centre of the industry. Although the growth of industrialization was a threat to traditional weaving methods, there were as many as four hundred working looms in and around the village of Nuenen alone when Van Gogh went to live there. He immediately felt that the subject of weavers at work was worth pursuing both in drawings and paintings. This presented a new challenge, as the figure could not be isolated but had to be seen in relation to the complicated machinery being operated in a confined space. Quite apart from the intricacies of the loom itself, there were problems of perspective and lighting. These Van Gogh only partially overcame, but, nonetheless, the drawings of weavers made in mixed media in 1884 reveal a considerable technical advance (Fig. 32).

A similar increase in confidence can be detected in the numerous studies of male and female workers executed in black chalk at Nuenen. Some of those done in the early summer of 1885 are on a small scale, with the figures filling the sheet (Fig. 33). These represent a different approach to the drawing of the figure.

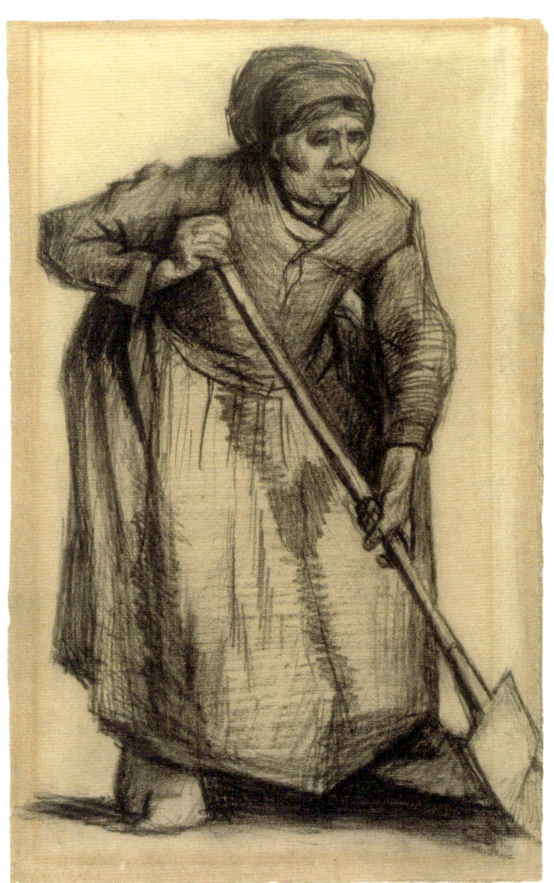

33 *Woman with Shovel*, May–June 1885. Black chalk on laid paper, 34.7 × 21.5 cm (13¾ × 8½ in.). KRÖLLER-MÜLLER MUSEUM, OTTERLO

Van Gogh followed the system adopted by Delacroix about which he had read in the book by Gigoux, *Causeries sur les artistes de mon temps*, published in the same year: instead of beginning the figure with the contours, this method involved working outwards from the centre, building up the mass with a series of spherical forms before enclosing it with the outlines. Van Gogh applied this system in the series of squat, compact figures observed at work. The exploratory nature of these drawings is apparent in the pronounced facial features and large hands, as well as the exaggerated accessories, such as hats, clogs and implements. The modelling throughout is strong and insistent.

The series of fifty or so large figure studies in horizontal and vertical formats made slightly later in 1885, during harvesting, is one of the high points in Van Gogh's graphic oeuvre. He spent time in the fields drawing on the spot as the harvesters worked for long hours. The figures are viewed from all angles, with only brief indications of a setting (Fig. 34). The strength of these drawings lies in their directness: the poses are natural, with no attempt to 'improve' upon life (Fig. 35). In all cases, the energy exuded by the figures is matched by the rhythm and directional flow of the individual strokes of black chalk (Fig. 36). However, the artist was eventually told by 'the reverend gentlemen of the priesthood' (531) that, by merely observing them at work, he was being too familiar with his models, and so, by early September, he had to do without them.

These fine studies rival those of Van Gogh's main guides to the depiction of scenes of rural labour – Millet, Charles Jacque (1813–1894), Breton and Léon Lhermitte (1844–1925). No doubt he had it in mind to follow in their footsteps and create large, painted compositions of rural scenes, but this did not ensue, and it is probable that Van Gogh was temporarily satisfied with what he had achieved in these drawings. For in them he has, indeed, fulfilled a declaration that he had written two years earlier: 'My aim is to do a drawing that not exactly everyone will understand, the *figure* expressed in its essence in simplified form, with deliberate disregard of those details that aren't part of the true character and are merely accidental. . . . Speaking of expression in a figure, I'm becoming more and more persuaded that it lies not so much in the features as in the whole manner' (361).

34 *Reaper*, July–August 1885. Black chalk, grey-white opaque watercolour, on paper, 56.2 × 37.8 cm (22¼ × 15 in.). KRÖLLER-MÜLLER MUSEUM, OTTERLO

The temptation is to compare these works on paper by Van Gogh with drawings by his contemporaries, such as Edgar Degas (1834–1917),

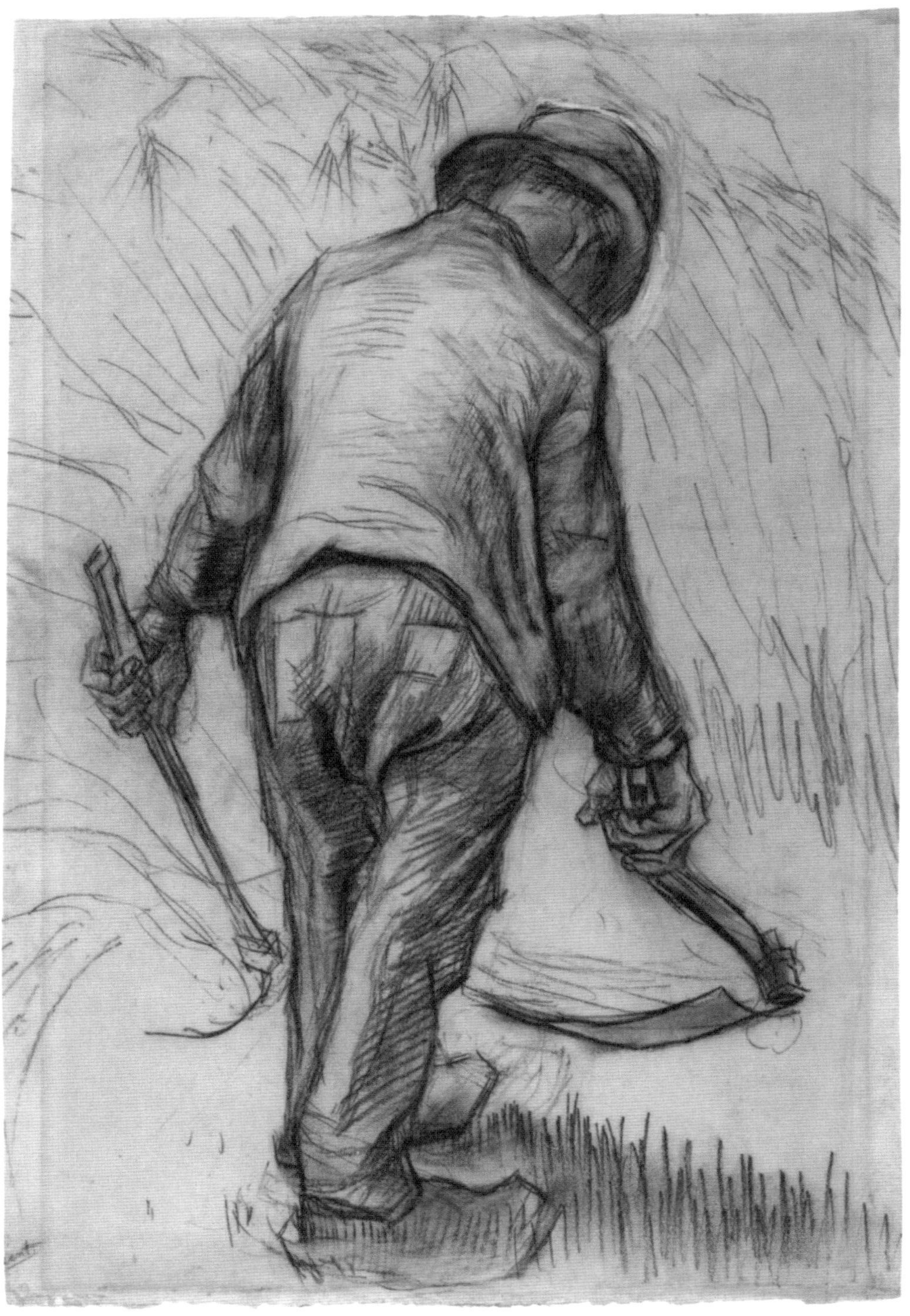

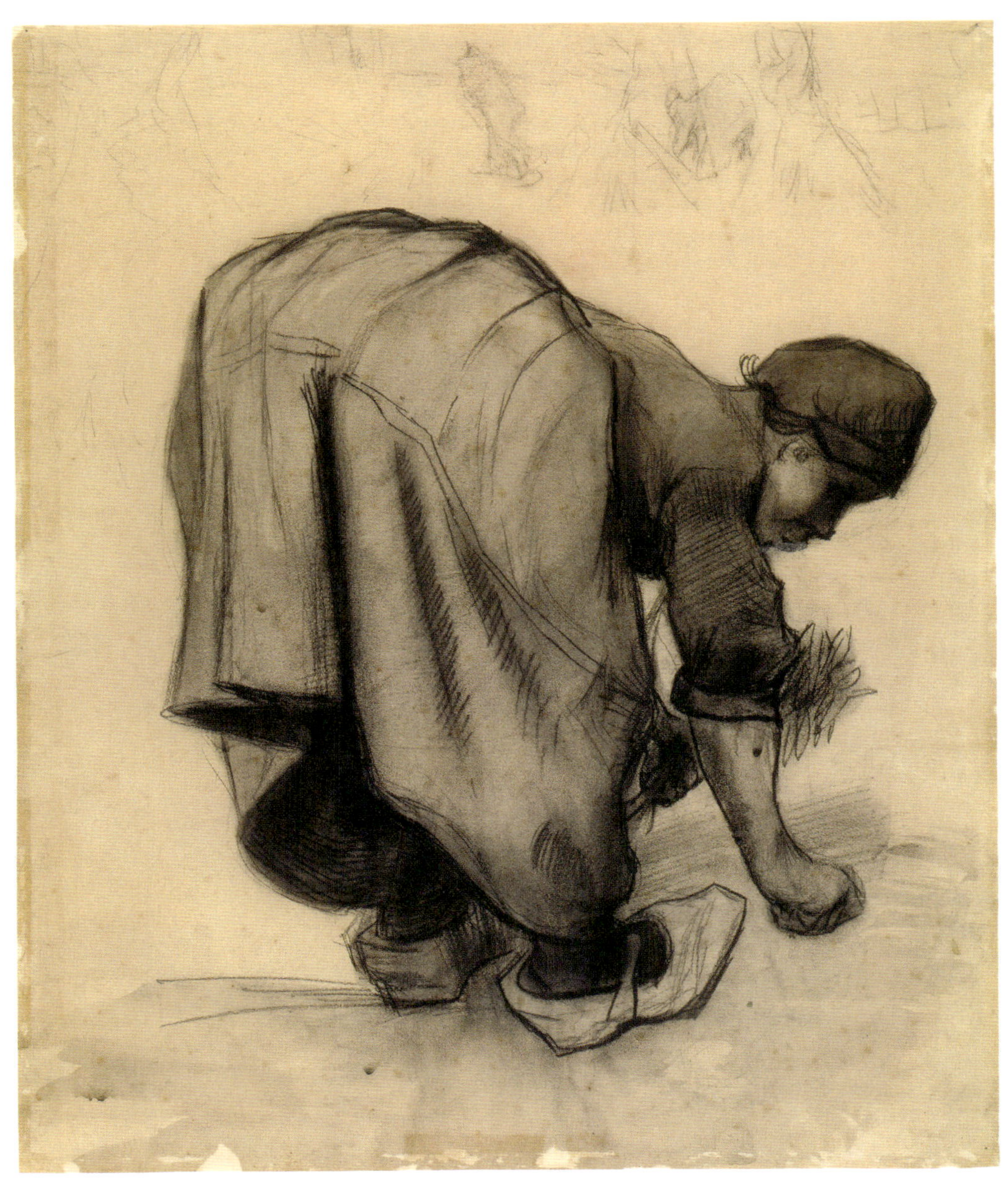

35 *Peasant Woman Gleaning*, July–August 1885. Black chalk, grey wash, white opaque watercolour, traces of milk fixative, on paper, 52.2 × 43.2 cm (20⅝ × 17⅛ in.). KRÖLLER-MÜLLER MUSEUM, OTTERLO

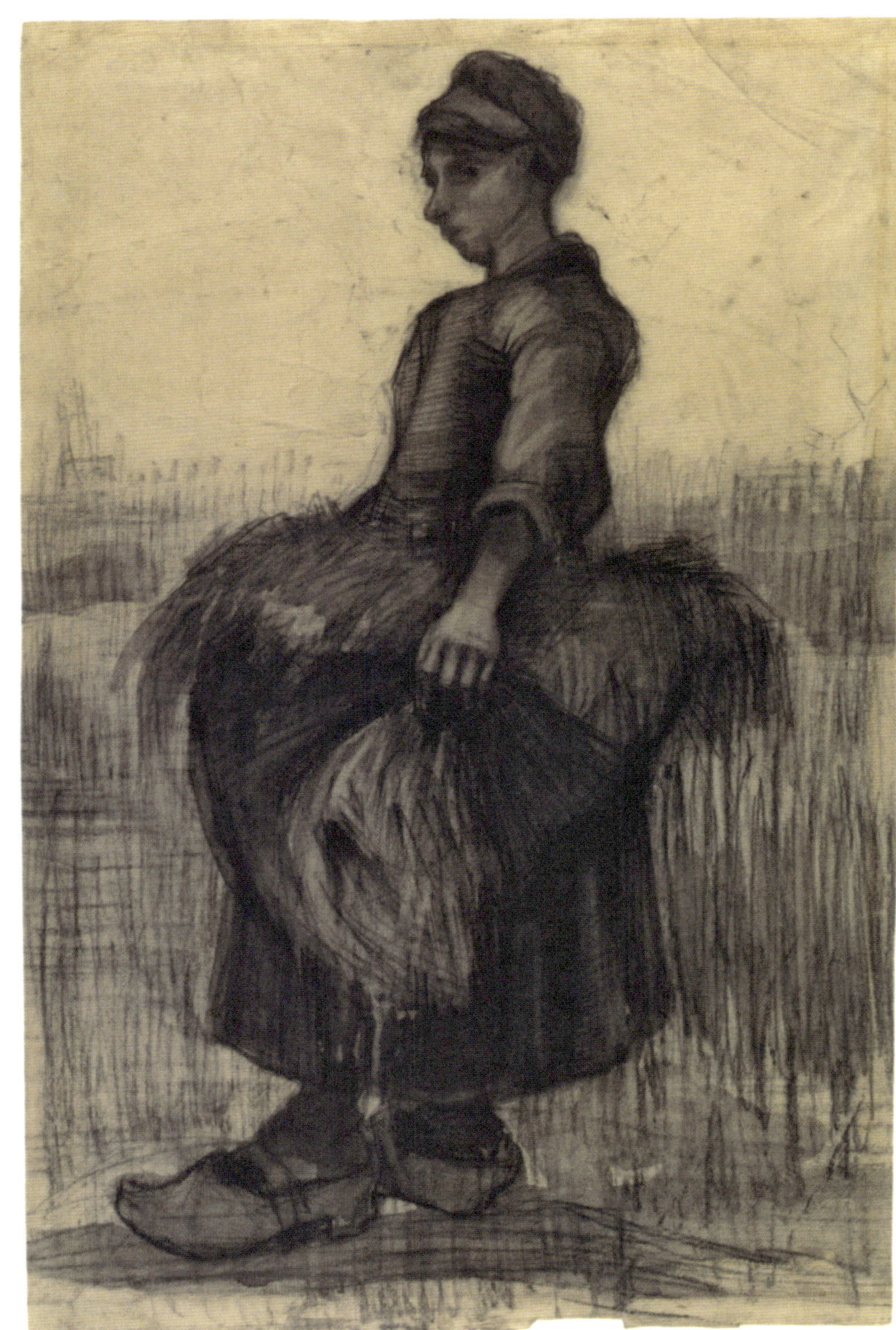

36 *Peasant Woman Carrying Wheat in her Apron*, July–August 1885. Black chalk, grey wash, grey opaque watercolour, on laid paper, 58.2 × 38 cm (23 × 15 in.). KRÖLLER-MÜLLER MUSEUM, OTTERLO

Camille Pissarro (1830–1903) and Gauguin. But, in fact, he had little knowledge of their work at this stage of his life. For expressive line and technical finesse, a more accurate comparison should be made with earlier, north European draughtsmen – Dürer, Matthias Grünewald (*c.* 1470–1528), Rembrandt, Rubens. Among Van Gogh's contemporaries, only Adolph Menzel (1815–1905), who painted and drew every aspect of modern life in Berlin, reached a comparable degree of fluency.

On leaving North Brabant in 1885 and travelling first to Antwerp and then, in 1886, to Paris, Van Gogh became fully aware for the first time of the most recent developments in art about which, while in the Netherlands, he had heard only from a distance. This resulted in his investigating new kinds of brushwork (Pointillism) and new theories of colour (Divisionism). Through Theo, he met Impressionist and Post-Impressionist artists and saw their work at exhibitions and with dealers. At Cormon's studio, he fraternized with Henri de Toulouse-Lautrec (1864–1901), Émile Bernard and Louis Anquetin (1861–1932) and by such means began an association with the avant-garde. Van Gogh most certainly did not give up drawing at this crucial point in his development, but, in general terms, there was greater emphasis on compositional studies either for or related to paintings inspired by life in Paris. He did, however, produce a number of urban views in watercolour and began to show an interest in portraiture.

There was to be yet another change of emphasis when, in February 1888, Van Gogh travelled south to Provence, where, beginning in Arles, a better balance between painting and drawing was maintained. Only after he was admitted in May 1889 to the psychiatric asylum of Saint-Paul-de-Mausole at Saint-Rémy, some seventeen miles (twenty-seven kilometres) to the north-east of Arles, does the artist begin to make figure drawings again in earnest, but these are surprisingly different in style and manner from anything so far encountered in his oeuvre. The reasons for this can be found in the letters written to Theo and his now-widowed mother. A plangent note is introduced into the correspondence, with references to the past. Thus, in September 1889, he writes to Theo, 'I have a terrible desire that comes to me to see my friends again and to see the northern countryside' (801), and he expresses the hope of sharing 'our far-off memories of youth in Holland' (829). By April of the following year, he was beginning to translate his yearning into visual forms by undertaking what he referred to as 'reminiscences of the north' (863). In another letter, written on the same day to his mother and his sister Willemien, he refers more specifically to his having painted from memory 'a reminiscence of Brabant', which he described to them as 'cottages with mossy roofs and beech hedges on an autumn evening with a stormy sky, the sun setting red in reddish clouds. And a turnip field with women lifting turnips in the snow' (864). These mental images were in contrast to the paintings and drawings he was making at the same time from life of the wheatfields, gardens, sunflowers and olive trees at Saint-Rémy. To underscore this longing, he wrote to Theo,

> Please send me what you can find of *figures* among my old drawings. I'm thinking of redoing the painting of the peasants eating supper, lamplight effect [*The Potato Eaters* (Fig. 48)]. That canvas must be completely dark by now, perhaps I could redo it entirely from memory. You must above all send me the women gleaning and diggers, if there are any left. (863)

Detailed compositional drawings for a new version of *The Potato Eaters* were undertaken but remained undeveloped.

Van Gogh made the same request to his mother and sister: 'Do you still happen to have any of my old studies and drawings? Even if they're no good in themselves, they can refresh my memory and provide information for new work, but I don't, for instance, need the ones you have hanging up. They're much more likely to be scratches of peasant figures' (864). In the end, the paintings and drawings of northern themes that he produced in Saint-Rémy were, indeed, done from memory or recreated in his imagination, which explains why he combines landscape features from both north and south and sometimes gives northern subjects a southern setting. Apart from seeing them as an exercise in nostalgic recollection, he may have regarded the drawn studies as preparatory to paintings that he might undertake sometime in the future. But if this was the case, such ideas were not pursued.

The fact that Van Gogh was reverting to old themes did not imply any comparable reversal of style in the sixty or so drawings with figures that he made during his time at Saint-Rémy. Rather, the opposite is the case. Predominantly drawn in black chalk or pencil in improvised sketchbooks, the figures seem surprisingly agitated while pursuing a variety of rural pursuits in almost

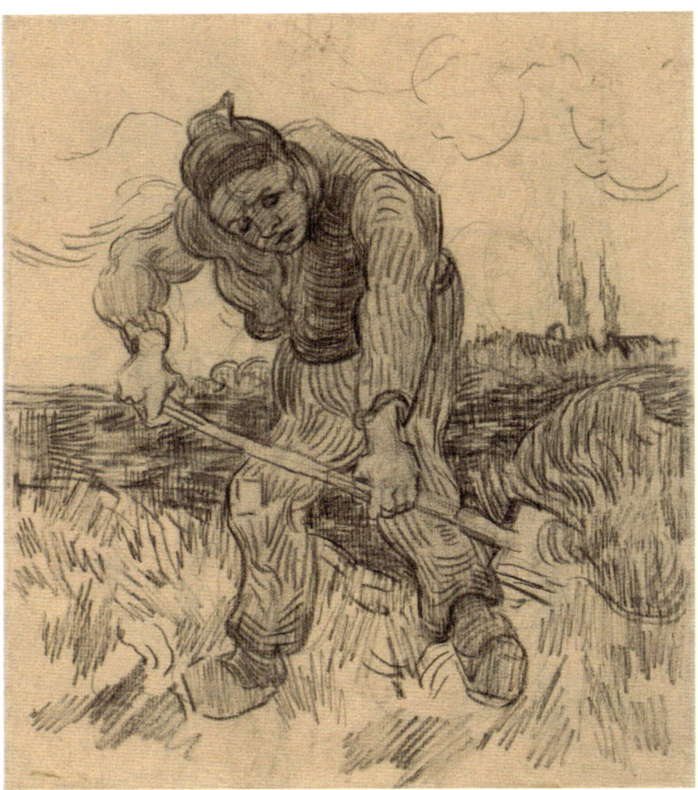

37 *Peasant Digging*, March–April 1890. Black chalk on pink paper, 28.2 × 23.9 cm (11⅛ × 9½ in.). VAN GOGH MUSEUM, AMSTERDAM

balletic poses (Fig. 37). Some of the drawings are more complete than others and can be directly related to paintings, but most of these late figure studies on paper have a febrile quality – people seem to be hyper-active, whether walking up a road, digging in a field, pushing a wheelbarrow, planting or picking crops. In addition, the weather in the settings ranges dramatically, from snow to bright sunshine.

A feature of these late figure drawings is the uniformity of the highly rhythmical style, comprising an abundance of short, repeated strokes, broken contours, curvilinear swoops and sudden jabs. Figures and landscape are conjured out of swirling, almost abstract patterns emphatically and speedily drawn. There is a dynamism that perhaps stems from the fact that the images are recalled from memory. Some of the faces are often featureless and the bodies, boneless. The figures resemble puppets answerable to an unseen power and often treated on an enlarged scale that invites comparison with caricature. As with Daumier, the characterization is broad and would be humorous if the surroundings and circumstances were different. Van Gogh here pushed the style of his figure drawing to its limits, which might be said, in some ways, to anticipate the comic strip (Fig. 38).

What was begun in Saint-Rémy was continued some twenty-five miles (forty kilometres) to the north-west of Paris at Auvers-sur-Oise, where, under the care of Dr Paul-Ferdinand Gachet and the watchful eye of his brother Theo, Van Gogh passed the last two months of his life. Here he investigated a place that several other artists – Charles-François Daubigny (1817–1878), Daumier, Pissarro, Paul Cézanne (1839–1906) – had already explored and had observed the figures working in the fields, moving along the roads or tending their gardens. The thatched roofs, the 'pretty middle-class country houses' (874), the river and the rolling hillsides seem to have suited Van Gogh's mood after his homecoming to the north.

The broad style of curved and hatched lines adopted in Saint-Rémy remains, but it is carried out with even greater exuberance and

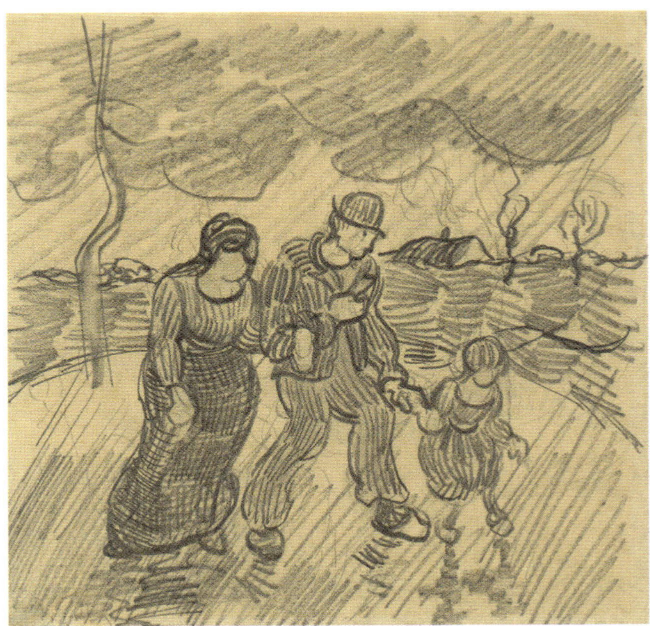

38 *Couple with Child, Walking in the Rain*, March–April 1890. Pencil, on paper, 24.4 × 25.3 cm (9⅝ × 10 in.). VAN GOGH MUSEUM, AMSTERDAM

a wider variety of media, including coloured chalks, watercolour and even, on two occasions, oil. Many of these works are once more drawn from life in improvised sketchbooks that the artist carried with him, and the figures seem less spectral. On balance, the figure in Van Gogh's art by this late stage of his career was making its curtain call, and in many works it is absent from images that are instead filled with a desperate feeling of emptiness and loneliness that can only reflect the artist's state of mind. Indeed, the drawing *Old Vineyard with Peasant Woman* is comparable with the swirling, invigorated brushstrokes in Van Gogh's contemporary pictures, thereby eliminating any hierarchical distinction between painting and drawing (Fig. 39). The figure is so perfectly assimilated within the setting that the viewer has to work hard to see her in the lower-right corner. In *Cottages with a Woman Working in the Middleground*,

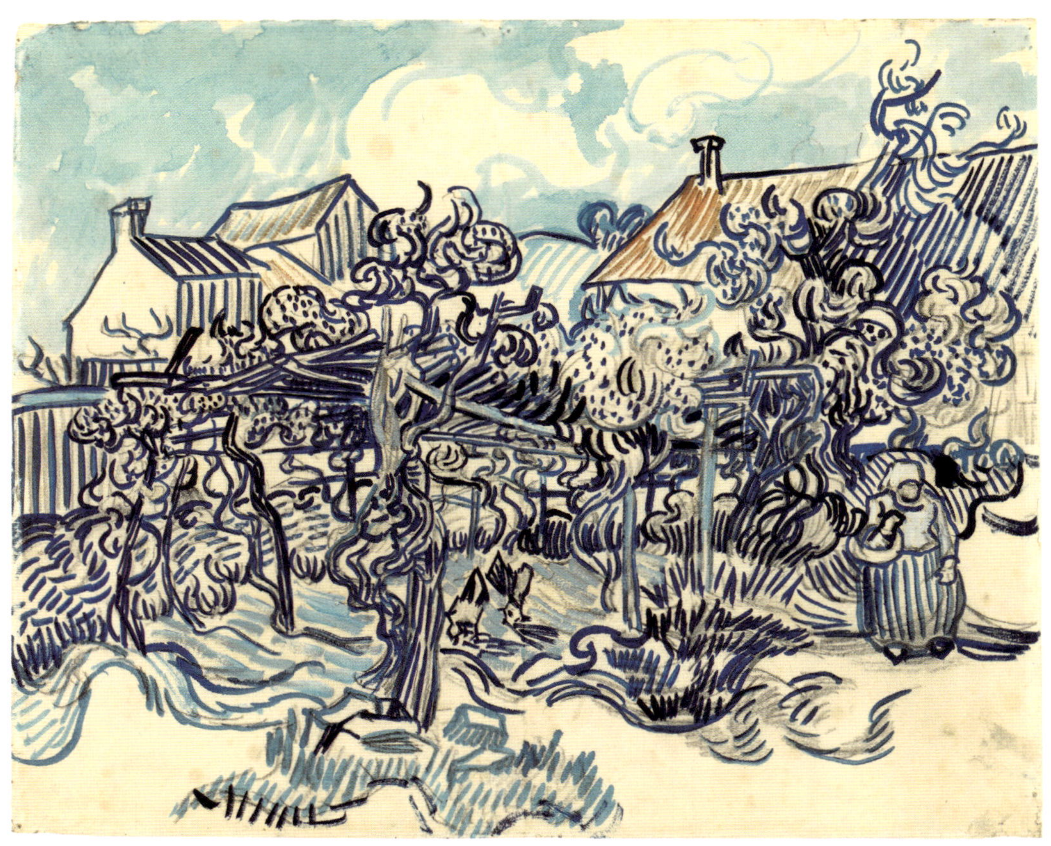

39 *Old Vineyard with Peasant Woman*, 20–23 May 1890. Pencil, brush and oil paint and watercolour, on paper, 44.3 × 54 cm (17½ × 21⅜ in.). VAN GOGH MUSEUM, AMSTERDAM

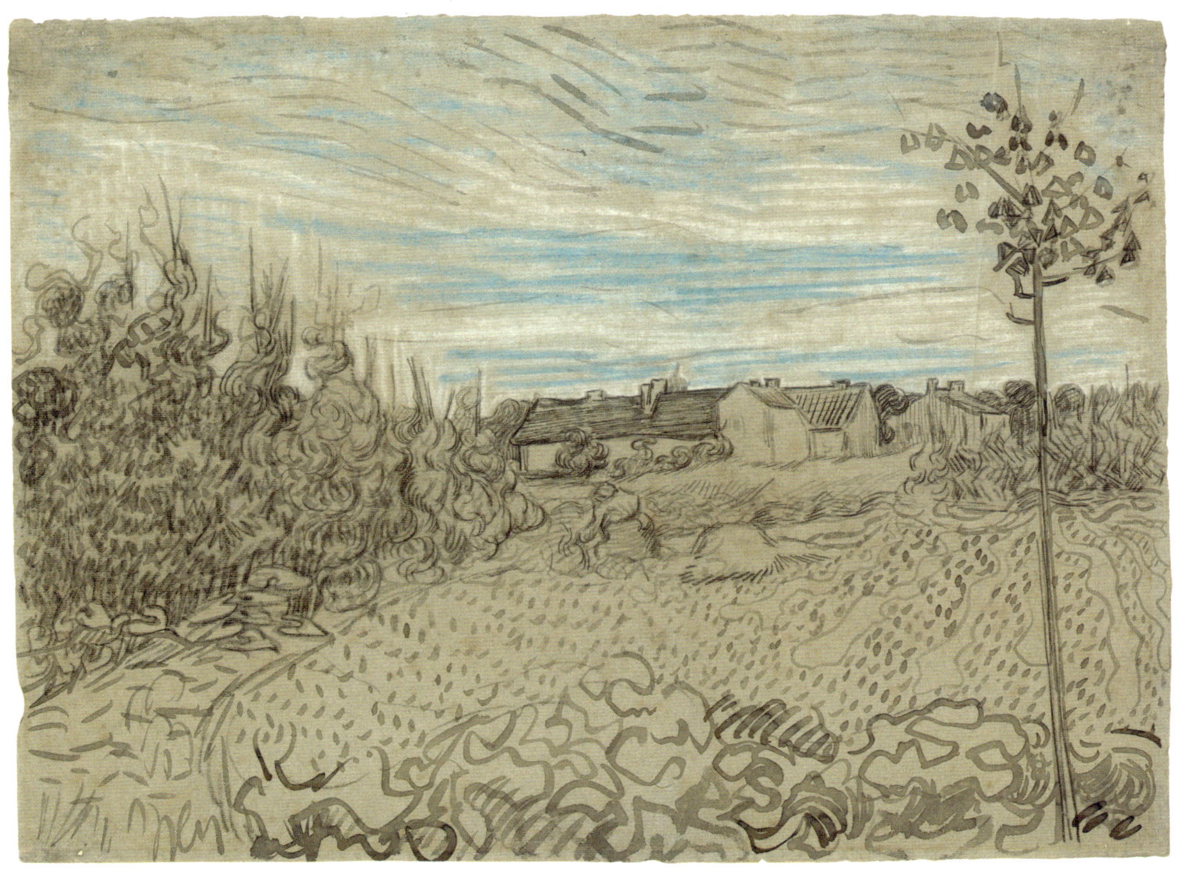

40 *Cottages with a Woman Working in the Middleground*, May 1890. Charcoal, reed pen and black ink, blue pastel, and white chalk on blue-gray laid paper, 47.3 × 62.2 cm (18⅝ × 24½ in.). THE ART INSTITUTE OF CHICAGO

the figure is even more closely integrated, almost to the point of invisibility (Fig. 40). Pictorial coherence of this sophistication unites Van Gogh's skill as both a figurative artist and a landscapist, but it also reveals his ability to create compositional unity. As Mauve so presciently observed in 1882, '*Vincent, when you draw you're a painter*' (208).

Chapter 3

Compositional Drawings

Figures and Landscapes

Van Gogh's independent spirit and his belated start meant that his immediate challenge was to produce a range of work that could bring him an income, so that he could sustain himself as an artist. At first, in the light of his enthusiasm for works by illustrators of popular journals, he considered pursuing a number of socio-realist themes prompted by his own personal experiences. Eventually, however, after being persuaded and cajoled by Theo, Van Gogh moved towards depicting more popular, general subjects, in watercolour and ultimately oil, that were more likely to appeal to collectors. The examples most readily to hand were the paintings and watercolours done by members of the Hague School, with some of whom Van Gogh was already in touch and whose current work could easily be seen in exhibitions. Beyond the technical challenges in drawing that still confronted him, the principal skill he needed to address was how to devise multi-figured compositions.

Van Gogh had little difficulty in finding narrative subjects that interested him. The sights he witnessed when working as an evangelist in the Borinage in southern Belgium certainly impinged on his social conscience if not his artistic instincts. Writing to Theo from Cuesmes in 1880, he reported on the plight of the industrial poor:

> The miners and weavers are something of a race apart from other workmen and tradesmen, and I have a great fellow-feeling for them and would count myself happy if I could draw them one day, so that these types, as yet unpublished or almost unpublished, could be brought to notice. The man from the bottom of the abyss, 'de profundis', that's the miner; the other one with a dreamy, almost pensive, almost a sleep-walker's air, is the weaver. And now it's roughly 2 years that I've been living with them, and to some extent I've learned to know their original character, mainly that of the

Beach at Scheveningen, 1882 (detail of Fig. 46).

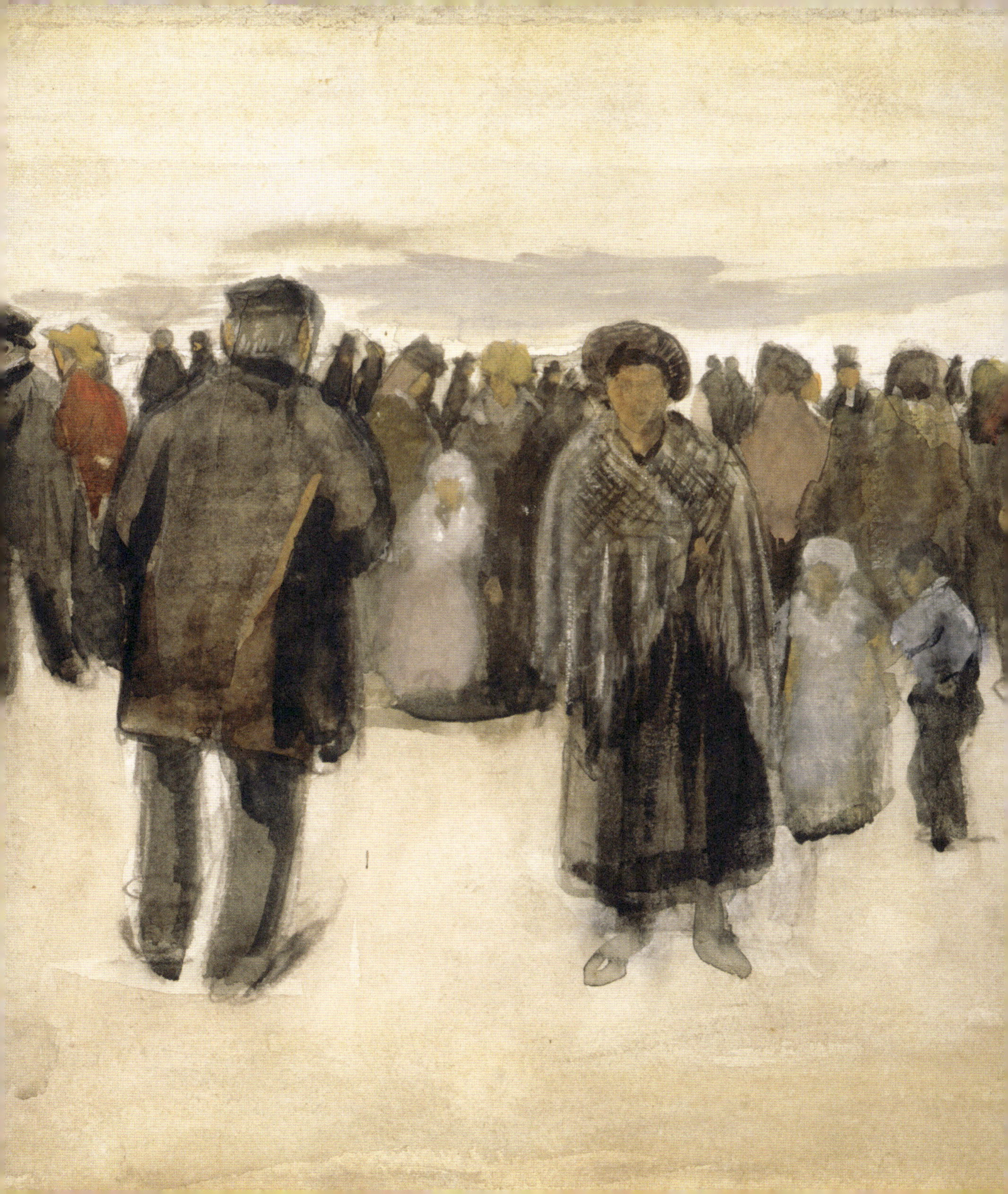

> miners at least. And more and more I find something touching and even heart-rending in these poor and obscure workers, the lowest of all, so to speak, and the most looked down upon, which one usually pictures through the effect of a perhaps vivid but very false and unjust imagination as a race of criminals and brigands. There are criminals, drunkards, brigands here as elsewhere, but that's not at all the true type. (158)

Van Gogh responded to these challenges early on, by depicting a mining scene (*The Bearers of the Burden*) while living between Brussels and Etten in 1880–81 and then by tackling the weavers in Nuenen in 1884–85.

The Bearers of the Burden was the artist's own choice of title, written in English (now hardly visible) on the drawing itself at lower right (Fig. 41). It is an enterprising work in both its aim and execution, undertaken before the publication of Émile Zola's novel about mining, *Germinal* (1885), which the artist later read and admired. The medium of pen and ink over pencil was one with which Van Gogh would accomplish a great deal at the start of his career, but the choice of subject was especially poignant, and it is interesting that in his treatment he hesitates between realism and symbolism, the latter hinted at in the lamp being carried by the leading miner on the left and the crucifixion fixed to the tree on the right. The miners (all women), bent double under the weight of their sacks, move from right to left in the foreground. In this way they resemble the figures on an antique sarcophagus. Although the paper is damaged, the network of tiny cross-hatched lines in the foreground gives way to lighter areas as the eye takes in the full extent of the coal mine, its machinery and the village beyond. The etiolated figures seem disproportionately large, yet there is a sense of shape and form beneath their clothes.

A year later, in 1882, having settled in The Hague, Van Gogh returned to the same subject in *Women Carrying Sacks of Coal in the Snow*, using opaque watercolour over chalk (Fig. 42). The background shows a mining community not dissimilar to that in *The Bearers of the Burden*, but the solidity of the figures is truer to life. The artist likened the poses of these women to figures by Millet in such paintings as *The Gleaners*. Not only is the bleak wintery scene wonderfully realized, with scavenging birds overhead on the left, but the women are strongly characterized, even though seen from the back. Their bodies bent low under the weight of the sacks, the faces of the three closest to the viewer are only glimpsed, and there is a keen sense of the ponderous movement of the group as a whole making its slow, painful way along the tree-lined road. In *The Bearers of the Burden* Van Gogh oscillates between realism and symbolism, but here he begins to balance realism with abstraction.

Van Gogh's employment of models was always dependent on his financial circumstances and also, of course, on the availability of the models themselves, assuming that he could persuade them to pose for him. An observation made in life had to be developed and perfected in the studio. As he admitted to Theo in a letter written early in 1882, 'I don't yet draw as fast as more practised draughtsmen, and actually have to work my drawings out in more detail for them

41 *The Bearers of the Burden*, April 1881. Pencil, pen in brown and black ink, white and grey opaque watercolour, on (originally) blue paper, 47.5 × 63 cm (18¾ × 24⅞ in.). KRÖLLER-MÜLLER MUSEUM, OTTERLO

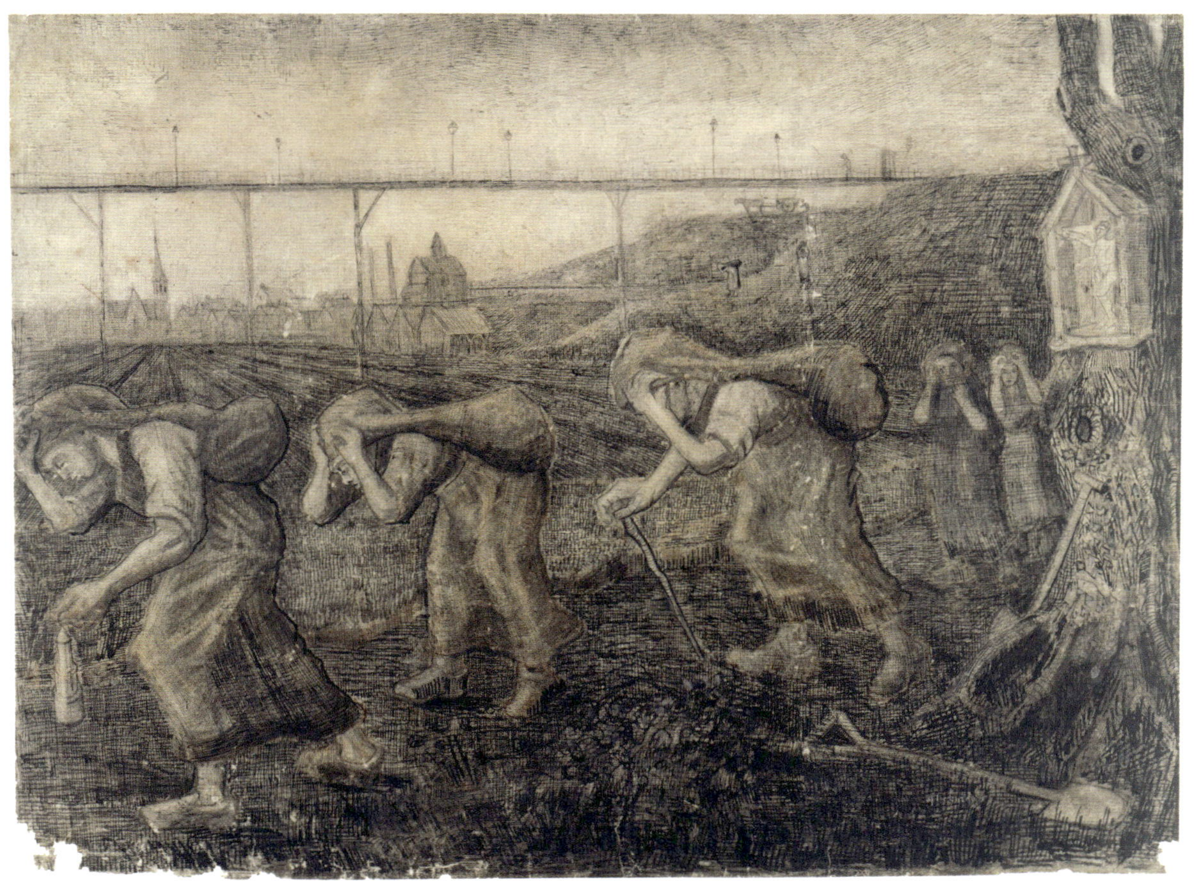

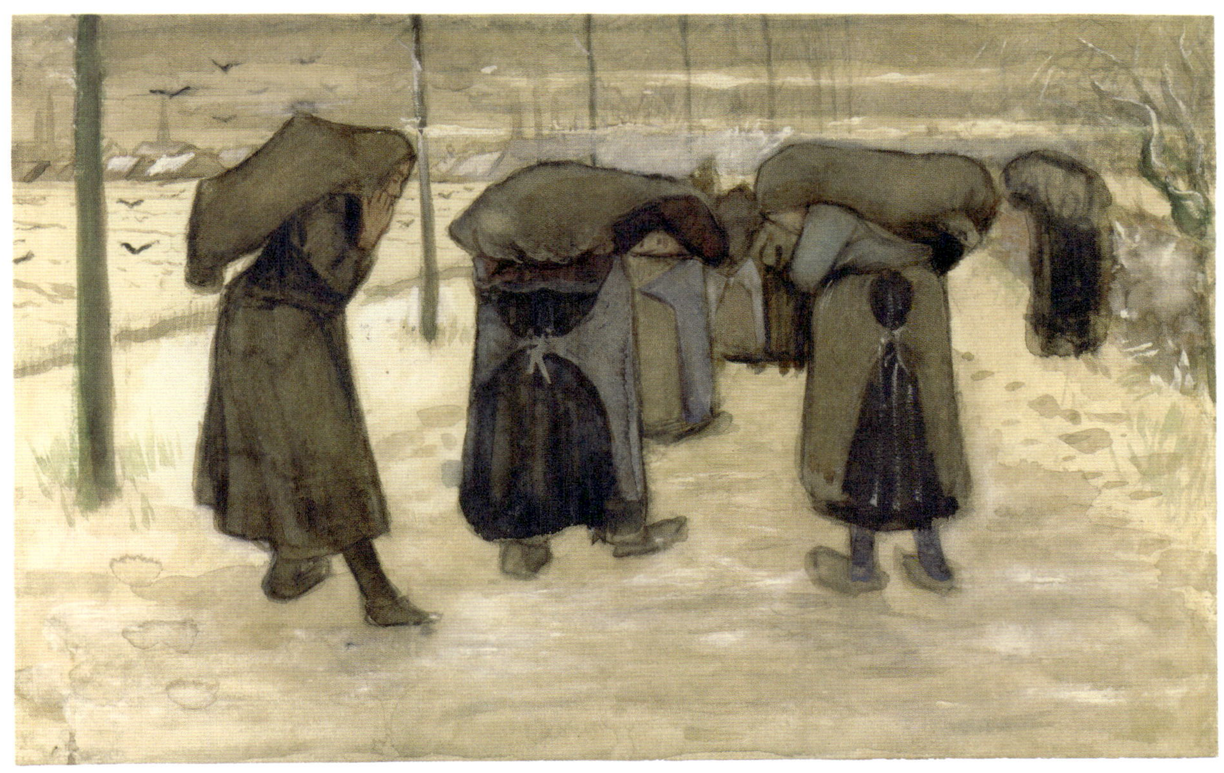

42 *Women Carrying Sacks of Coal in the Snow*, November 1882. Chalk, brush in ink, opaque and transparent watercolour, on paper, 32.1 × 50.1 cm (12¾ × 19¾ in.). KRÖLLER-MÜLLER MUSEUM, OTTERLO

to be of any use to me' (200). At this early stage, Van Gogh relied on individual drawings of models to create his compositions, fitting the different parts together for the final work. As he explained to Theo in March of the same year,

> The reason I'd like to keep them [the studies from models] is simply this: when I draw individual figures it's always with an eye to making a composition with a number of figures, for instance a 3rd-class waiting room or a pawnshop or an interior. But those larger compositions must ripen gradually, and *for a drawing with 3 seamstresses, for example, one must draw at least 90 seamstresses*. That's how it works.' (207)

His accumulation of figure studies was motivated either by an idea that he had for a specific composition already in mind or by the desire to keep them in stock for future use. This, for example, is the way the compositional drawing *Roadworks in Noordstraat* of 1882 (Fig. 43) evolved: notably, the figure that appears in *Old Woman with a Shawl and a Walking Stick* (Fig. 44) has been transplanted to the carefully constructed, although not very convincingly realized, setting of the larger work. Van Gogh may have been considering including the drawing of roadworks in Noordstraat in the group of cityscapes of The Hague commissioned by his uncle Cornelis ('Uncle Cor') in 1882, but he seems to have abandoned the idea, probably because it was too obviously a composite.

Even with the help of Mauve and examples by other members of the Hague School, Van Gogh found it difficult to create unified compositions, confessing to Theo, 'I'm writing to you in great haste, I can assure you that there's a lot involved in compositions with figures, and I'm very busy. It's like weaving: you have to give it all your attention to keep the threads apart; you must control and keep an eye on several things at once' (271). However, his aptitude for handling crowded compositions began to assert itself during the same month that he wrote this letter. Two examples are *The Poor and Money*, which is a depiction of the lottery office in The Hague (Fig. 45), and *Beach at Scheveningen*, which is probably a scene witnessed at that fishing village close to The Hague (Fig. 46). In these drawings, and in *Lumber Sale* and *A Wood Sale of Building Scrap* done two years later in Nuenen – all four executed in opaque watercolour – Van Gogh demonstrates considerable skill in the grouping of figures, without their losing their individuality, which is made evident through the poses, deportment, gestures and dress, even though the facial features are somewhat generalized. In devising the compositions, Van Gogh was particularly conscious of the difficulties of showing a group of figures en masse. Describing the effect of seeing people from the back when grouped together, he coined the term *moutonne*, suggesting the herding of sheep – an effect that he hoped to avoid.

A drawing to which Van Gogh paid careful attention was *Soup Distribution in a Public Soup Kitchen* (Fig. 47). For this interior composition he had his companion, Sien Hoornik, and her family to hand as models. Furthermore, he was able to 'stage' the scene in his own studio. As a result, the composition is satisfyingly symmetrical and solidly structured: the two women (Sien on the right and possibly her sister on the left) stand on either side of the serving hatch, while two girls are in the centre, with the older one looking

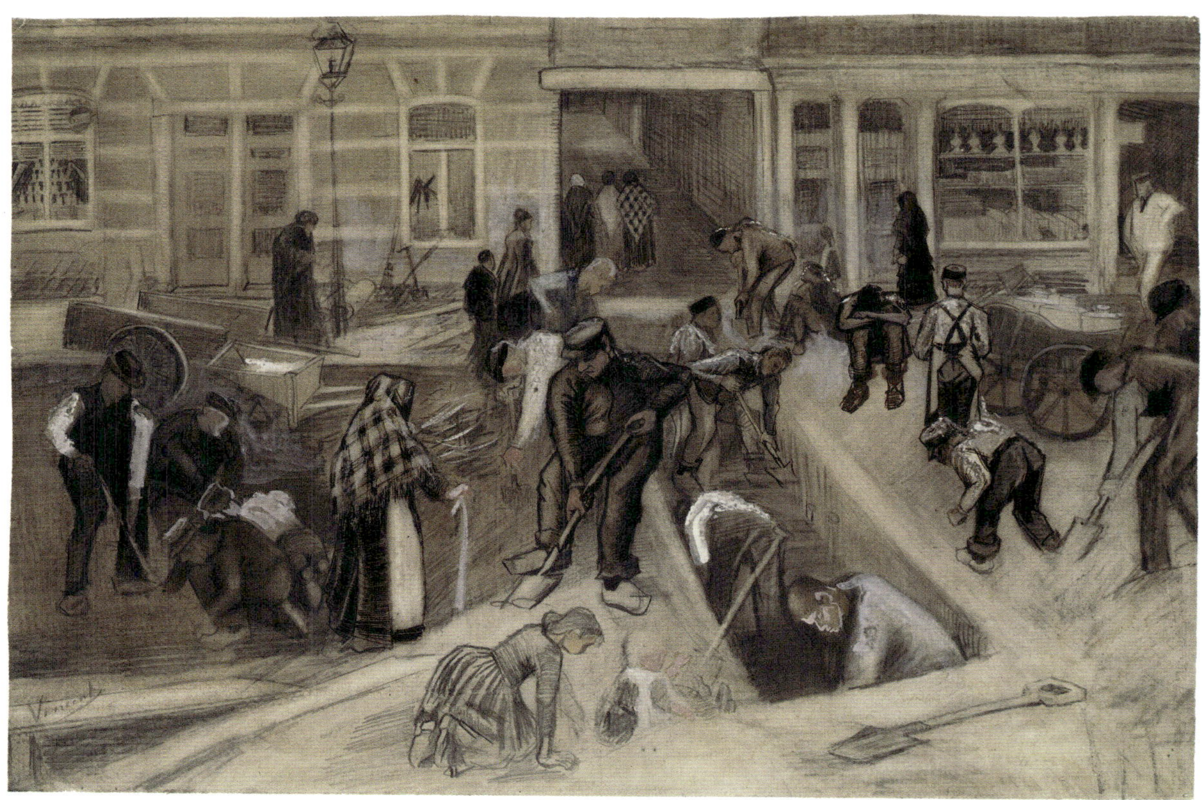

43 *Roadworks in Noordstraat*, April 1882. Pencil, pen, heightened with white colours, watercolour, on paper, 43 × 63 cm (17 × 24⅞ in.). KUPFERSTICHKABINETT, STAATLICHE MUSEEN, BERLIN

through the hatch into the kitchen and the younger one holding a jug and moving towards the viewer. Several studies, some with more figures, preceded this strong drawing, but the present, pared-down version is a powerful statement that Van Gogh obviously hoped would be published as a print or sold as a work in its own right.

Gradually, as the artist gained confidence in his compositional skills, he was emboldened to undertake a major figure painting that he hoped would bring him recognition. Thoughts about *The Potato Eaters* (Fig. 48) seem to have begun towards the end of 1884 and to have come to fruition by the spring of the following year. The preparatory process was elaborate and methodical, deliberately emulating the academic system of preparation for a painting. No part of the composition was untested, and numerous studies, both painted and drawn, were made in connection with its evolution. An oil sketch (Van Gogh Museum, Amsterdam) with only four figures seated around the table in the interior of a peasant cottage prepared the way. This was then expanded with the addition of an extra figure into a preliminary painted study on a larger scale (Kröller-Müller Museum, Otterlo), which was made into a lithograph to help promote the eventual sale of the painting.

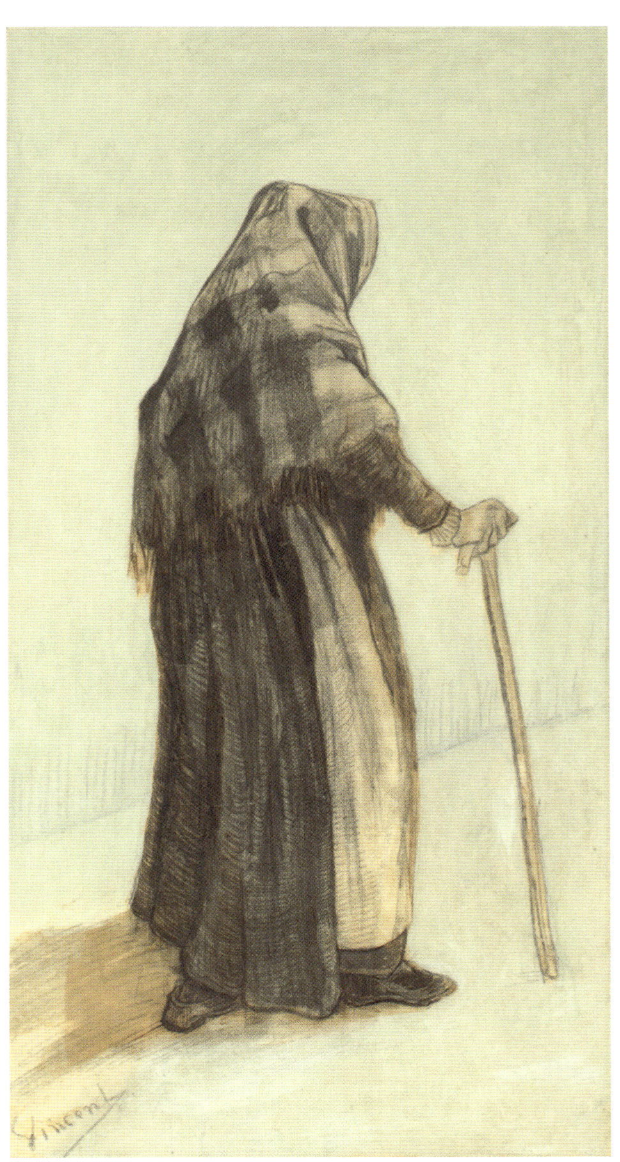

44 *Old Woman with a Shawl and a Walking Stick*, March 1882. Pencil, pen and ink, watercolour, on paper, 57.4 × 32 cm (22⅝ × 12⅝ in.). VAN GOGH MUSEUM, AMSTERDAM

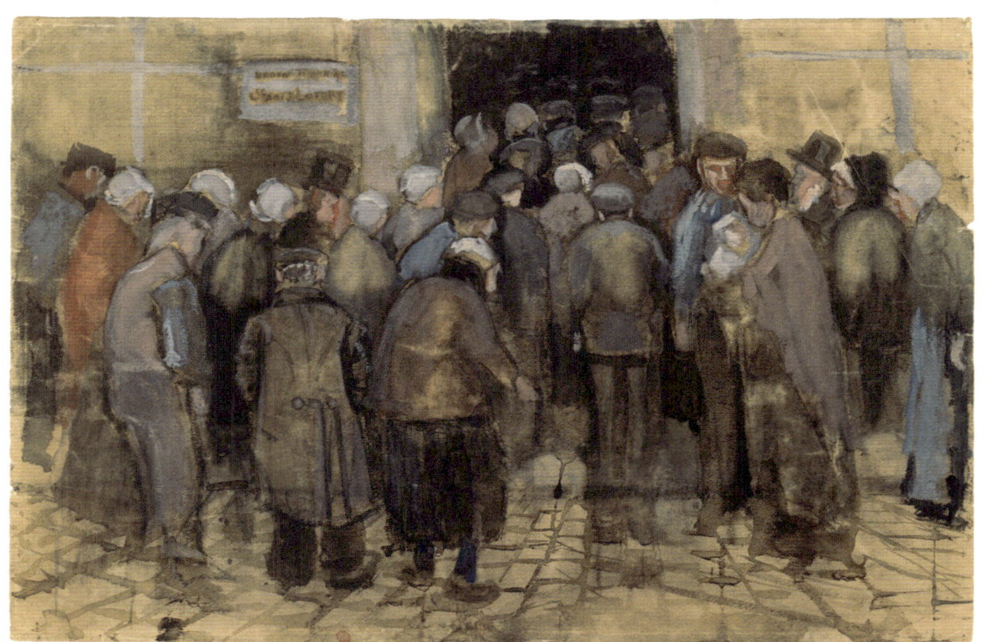

45 *The Poor and Money*, September–October 1882. Chalk, watercolour, pen and ink, on paper, 37.9 × 56.6 cm (15 × 22⅜ in.). VAN GOGH MUSEUM, AMSTERDAM

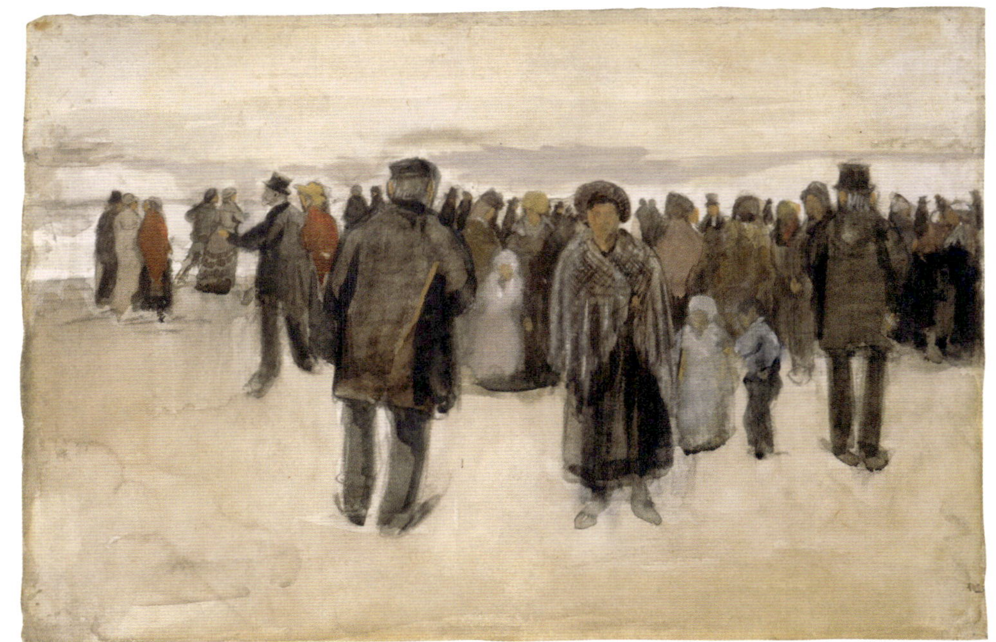

46 *Beach at Scheveningen*, 1882. Transparent and opaque watercolour with charcoal, on light-brown paper, 34.3 × 51.4 cm (13½ × 20¼ in.). THE BALTIMORE MUSEUM OF ART

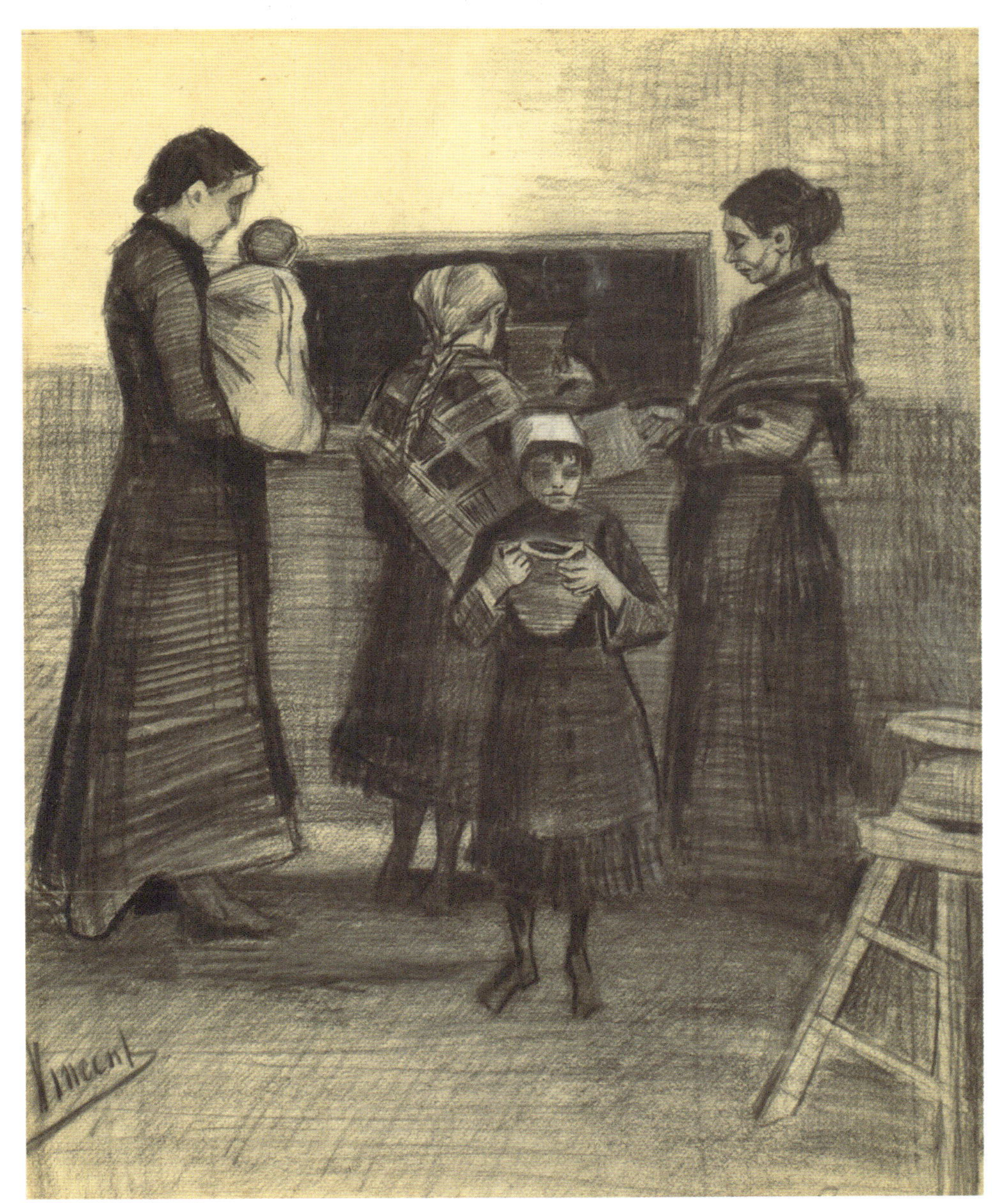

47 *Soup Distribution in a Public Soup Kitchen*, March 1883. Natural black chalk, brush and black paint, opaque white watercolour with scratched highlights and traces of squaring, on paper, 56.5 × 44.4 cm (22¼ × 17½ in.). VAN GOGH MUSEUM, AMSTERDAM

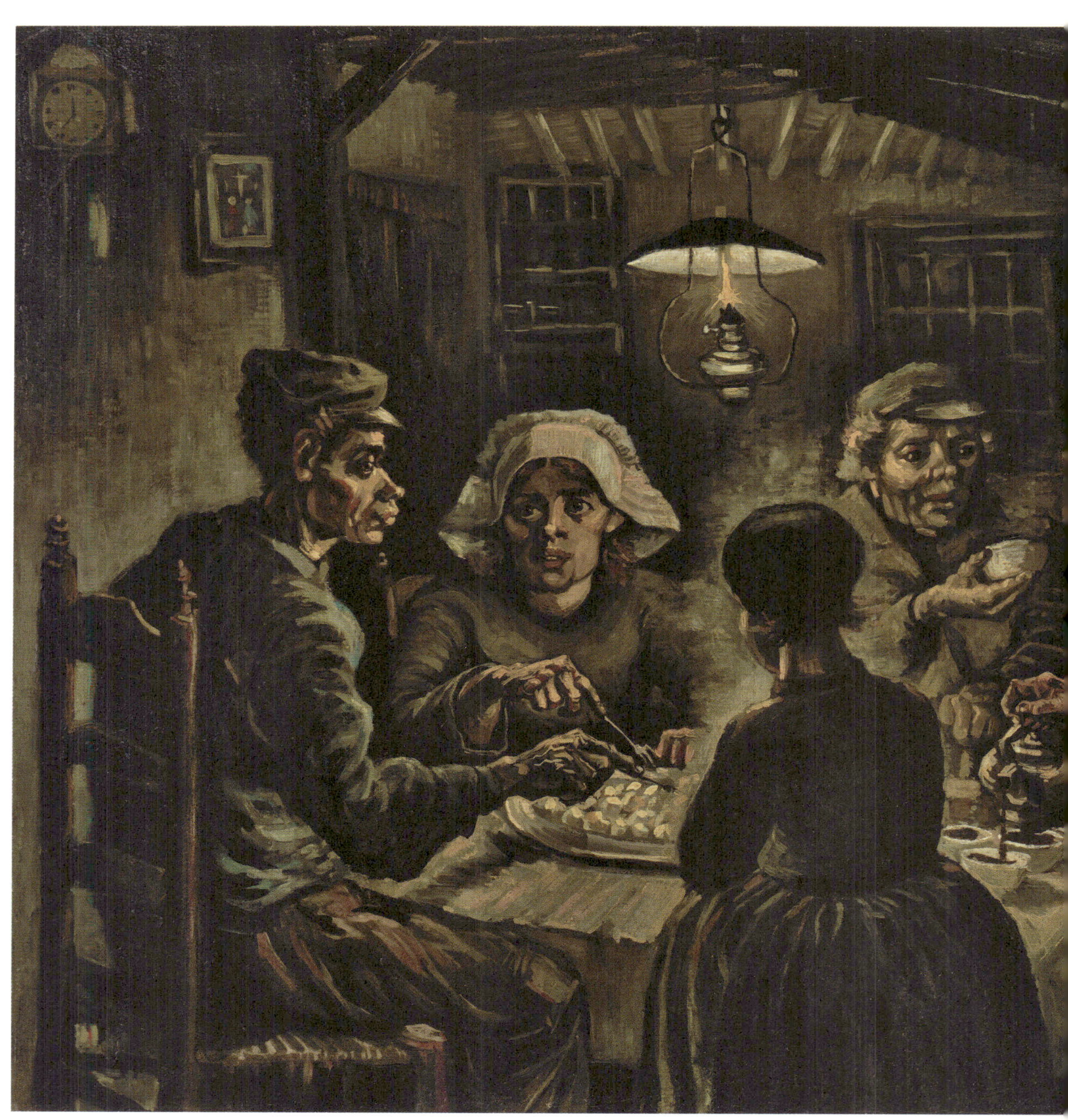

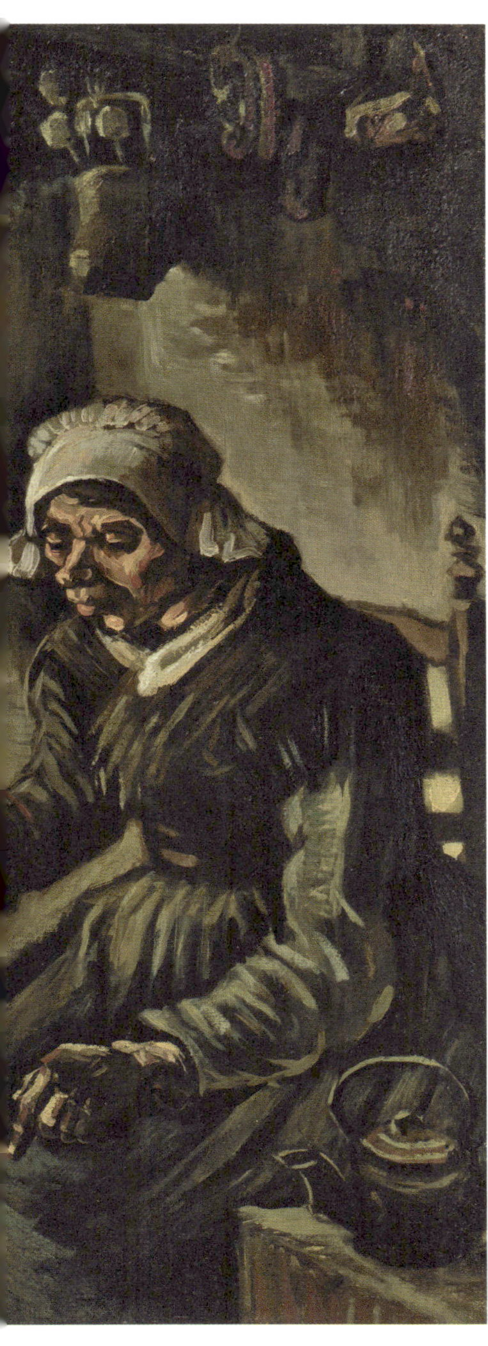

48 *The Potato Eaters*, April–May 1885.
Oil on canvas, 82 × 114 cm (32⅜ × 45 in.).
VAN GOGH MUSEUM, AMSTERDAM

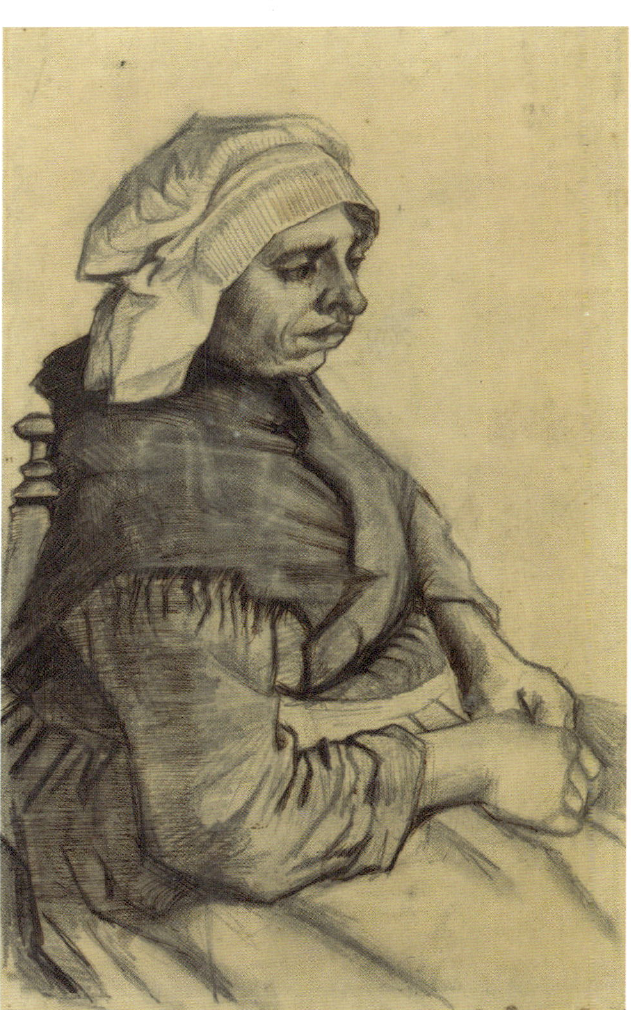

49 *Seated Woman*, February–May 1885. Pencil, pen and ink, on paper, 34.5 × 21.2 cm (13⅝ × 8⅜ in.). VAN GOGH MUSEUM, AMSTERDAM

The preliminary drawings were wide ranging and extended from individual studies and groups of figures seated at the table to details of heads, hands, utensils and the interior of the cottage (Figs 49–51). The preparatory period was intense, and, as Van Gogh wrote to Theo, 'Although I'll have painted the actual painting in a relatively short time, and largely from memory, it's taken a whole winter of painting studies of heads and hands' (497). The finished work was painted for the most part on site in the cottage of the De Groot family, who presumably appear in the picture itself but whose images in this context should be interpreted as types rather than portraits as such. The style of these head studies is workmanlike and strongly focused on the use of chiaroscuro to evoke the ethos of peasant life (Fig. 49). *The Potato Eaters* is not just the climax of the first part of Van Gogh's career, it is also a manifesto. While working on it, he described himself to Theo as 'a peasant painter', adding, 'I've become so absorbed in peasant life by continually seeing it at all hours of the day that I really hardly think of anything else' (493).

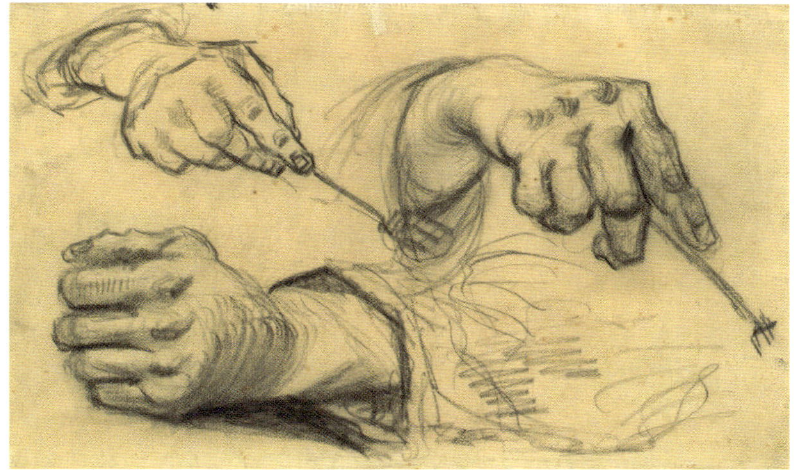

50 *Three Hands, Two Holding Forks*, March–April 1885. Chalk on paper, 21.3 × 34.6 cm (8½ × 13⅝ in.). VAN GOGH MUSEUM, AMSTERDAM

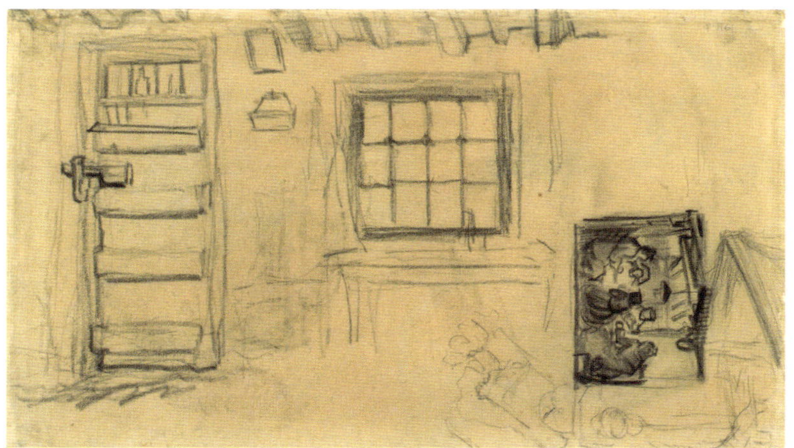

51 *Studies of the Interior of a Cottage, and a Sketch of 'The Potato Eaters'*, March–April 1885. Chalk on paper, 21.3 × 34.6 cm (8½ × 13⅝ in.). VAN GOGH MUSEUM, AMSTERDAM

His commitment was such that, in the context of *The Potato Eaters*, it is possible to speak of Van Gogh as a political painter. He defended his position at considerable length to Theo:

> You see, I really have wanted to make it so that people get the idea that these folk, who are eating their potatoes by the light of their little lamp, have tilled the earth themselves with these hands they are putting in the dish, and so it speaks of MANUAL LABOUR and – that they thus honestly *earned* their food. I wanted it to give the idea of a wholly different way of life from ours – civilized people. . . . And it might well prove to be a REAL PEASANT PAINTING. *I know that it is*. But anyone who would rather see insipidly pretty peasants can go ahead. For my part, I'm convinced that in the long run it produces better results to paint them in their coarseness than to introduce conventional sweetness. . . . No – one must paint the peasants as if one were one of them, as feeling, thinking as they do themselves. . . . I so often think that the peasants are a world in themselves, so much better in many respects than the civilized world. (497)

In taking so much trouble over painting *The Potato Eaters*, Van Gogh clearly hoped that he was producing an exhibition picture that would win critical approbation and enhance his reputation as an artist. The choice of subject recalls the work of seventeenth-century Dutch artists such as Adriaen and Isaac van Ostade (1610–1685 and 1621–1649) (Fig. 52) or Cornelis Pietersz. Bega (1631/32–1664) and was perhaps more immediately inspired by the examples of Jozef Israëls and Charles Degroux (1825–1870). In fact, *The Potato Eaters* was not so much a triumphant success as an ignominious disaster. Theo remained loyal to his brother's ambitions and worked hard to interest dealers in the picture and to find a buyer, but Van Rappard, among others, dismissed both the subject and the treatment as incomprehensible and repellent. On the basis of seeing only the lithograph, Van Rappard wrote a detailed critique of the poses and the lack of compositional cohesion, ending, 'Come on! Art is too important, it seems to me, to be treated so cavalierly' (503). The paradox of *The Potato Eaters* is that the subject matter was somewhat retardataire, while the style was assertively modern. Since the

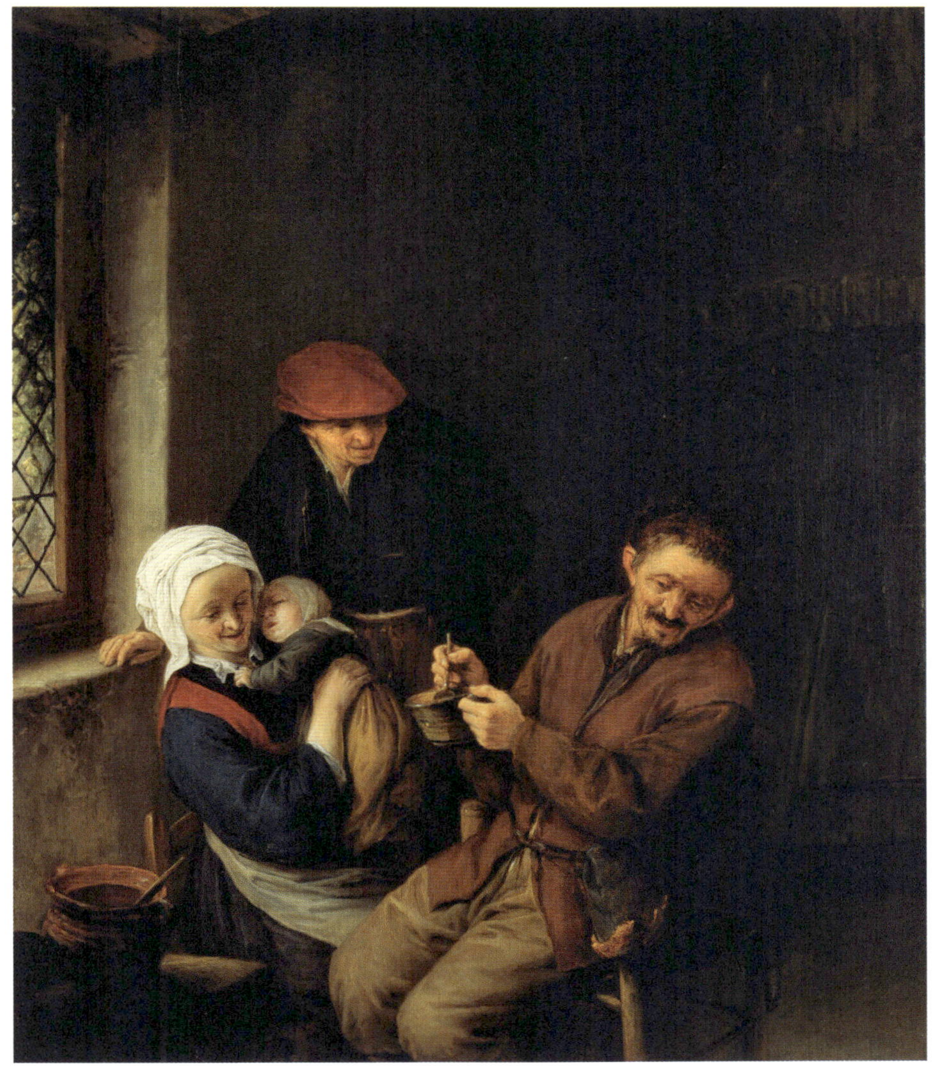

52 Adriaen van Ostade
Interior of a Peasant's Cottage: A Child about to be Fed, 1651.
Oil on panel, 46.7 × 41.6 cm (18½ × 16½ in.).
ROYAL COLLECTION TRUST, LONDON

artist had not yet had the opportunity to make a proper assessment of avant-garde painting, he was unaware of any ambiguity, which explains why no buyer was forthcoming. Today, the painting is an iconic image of Van Gogh's years in the Netherlands, and it is so well known that it comes into the category of one of those works of art that is often used as the basis for politically inspired cartoons. In many ways, *The Potato Eaters* was a coming-of-age work for

Van Gogh, and Theo tacitly acknowledged this by hanging the canvas over the mantelpiece of his apartment in Paris after failing to find a buyer for it or even a dealer interested in promoting the picture. Yet the significance of the painting and what it represented for the artist himself is such that, while he was in the asylum at Saint-Rémy, he contemplated making a reprise of it.

A year after completing *The Potato Eaters*, Van Gogh went to join his brother in Paris and never returned to the Netherlands. Even so, as he had written to Van Rappard shortly after their first meeting in 1881, 'The more we know about what's happening abroad the better, but we mustn't forget that our roots are in Dutch soil' (176). Paris provided plentiful opportunities for Van Gogh. He was at the centre of the art world where ancient shibboleths were being challenged and new subjects and styles essayed in the creation of fresh and stimulating criteria for art. Van Gogh entered this world with an open mind, but was equally prepared to stick to his own principles, which had been so hard won. There are few compositional drawings dating from the two years he spent in Paris, but the emphasis on drawing remains steadfast, to the extent that it is from this time that most of the finished sheets have equal status with the paintings.

A comparison between the *Study for 'Reclining Female Nude'* and *Restaurant de la Sirène at Asnières* might be said to give a true representation of the ways in which Van Gogh's world had changed by his coming to Paris. *Study for 'Reclining Female Nude'* (Fig. 53) is one of the very rare occasions on which the artist depicted the female nude, and it is as though with one bound he is taking on Titian (*c.* 1485/90–1576), Goya (1746–1828), Velázquez (1599–1660) and Édouard Manet (1832–1883). The figure lies on a bed wearing only stockings. The splash of pencil strokes denotes different textures of fabrics, skin and hair. Sharper, more accented lines emphasize the heavy facial features, the breasts and the pudendum. Cleverly, the reinforcing of the body's outline serves to suggest the indentation in the bedclothes made by the weight of the model. The drawing relates very closely to a painting in the Barnes Foundation in Philadelphia in which more is made of the setting. Yet, although the drawing may have been intended as a study for the painting, it has the appearance of a finished work of art in its own right.

A similar compositional affinity exists between the drawing *Restaurant de la Sirène at Asnières* (Fig. 54) and one of two paintings that Van Gogh made of the restaurant near the Pont d'Asnières in the suburbs to the north-west of Paris. For this view of the restaurant, Van Gogh was standing with his back to the River Seine (a mooring post is visible in the lower-right corner). The architecture comprises a series of deftly delineated horizontals and verticals anchoring the building in the top half of the sheet, but the broad verge in the foreground, the trees and the façade of the restaurant are rendered with vigorously hatched strokes and agitated flurries of shading. Although this is strictly speaking not a preparatory study for either of the paintings (Musée d'Orsay, Paris, and Ashmolean Museum, Oxford), it formed part of the process of familiarization with the motif. More remarkably, it matches the loose handling of the paintings, as all three share a notational equivalence.

Similar juxtapositions can be found among the views Van Gogh explored in the area of Montmartre, not far from where he and Theo

53 *Study for 'Reclining Female Nude'*, January–June 1887. Pencil on paper, 24 × 31.6 cm (9½ × 12½ in.). VAN GOGH MUSEUM, AMSTERDAM

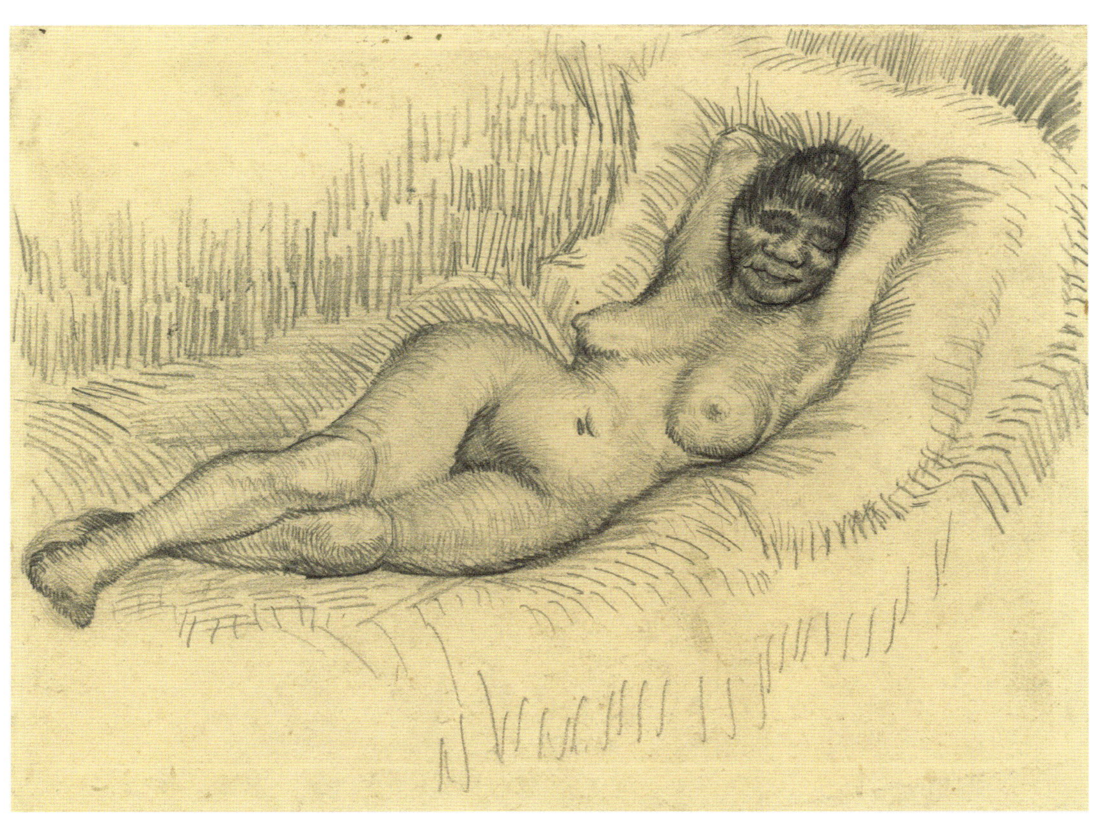

shared an apartment on the rue Lepic. *A Guinguette* shows the garden of a bar with outdoor seating and enough space for dancing (Fig. 55). Such establishments flourished as Montmartre became a place for public entertainment. The related painting (Musée d'Orsay, Paris) is more elaborate, with many changes, and was clearly made at a different time of year, but this highly finished drawing would have formed part of the process of assimilation that would have occurred while Van Gogh was thinking of depicting motifs associated with Montmartre. As such, it was a saleable commodity in its own right.

For several of the drawings made in Paris Van Gogh used coloured chalks, which he applied with the utmost delicacy. The old windmills situated on the Butte Montmartre had been depicted by artists throughout the nineteenth century, as the area developed

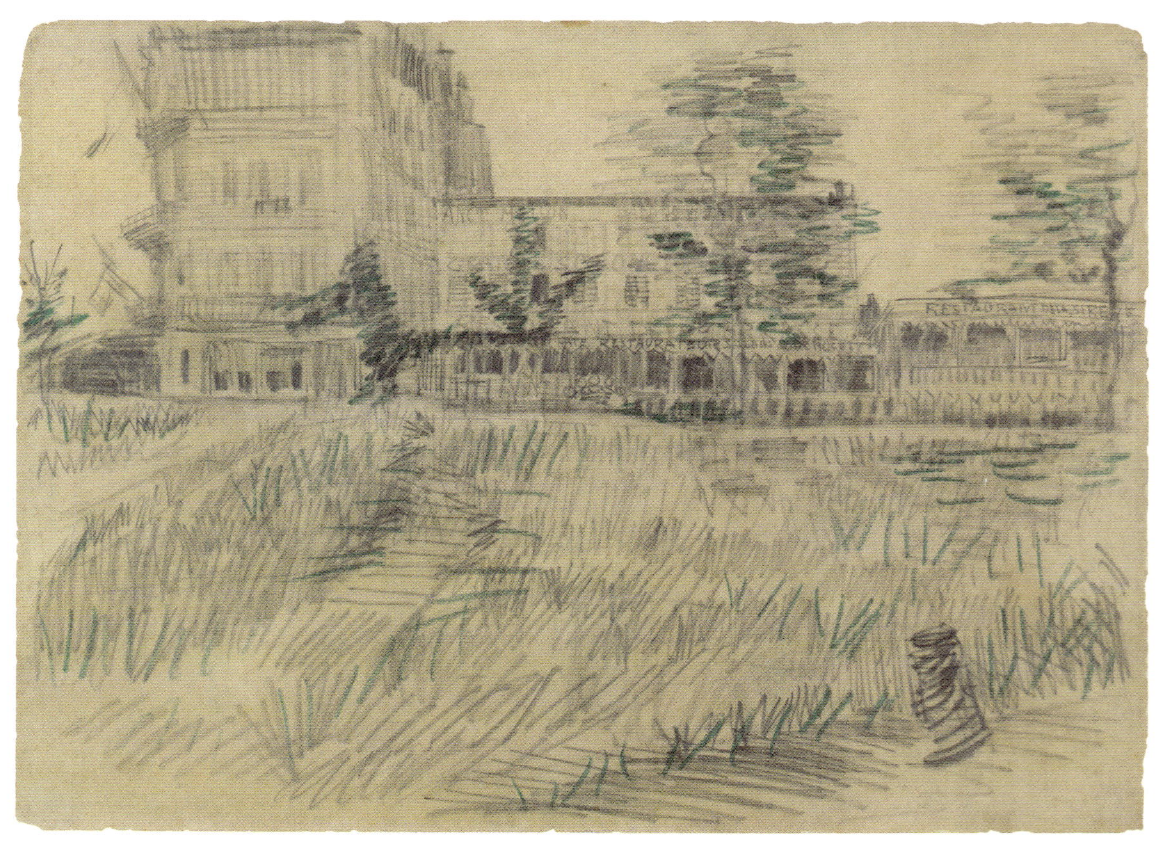

54 *Restaurant de la Sirène at Asnières*, June–September 1887. Pencil and chalk, on paper, 39.8 × 53.8 cm (15¾ × 21¼ in.). VAN GOGH MUSEUM, AMSTERDAM

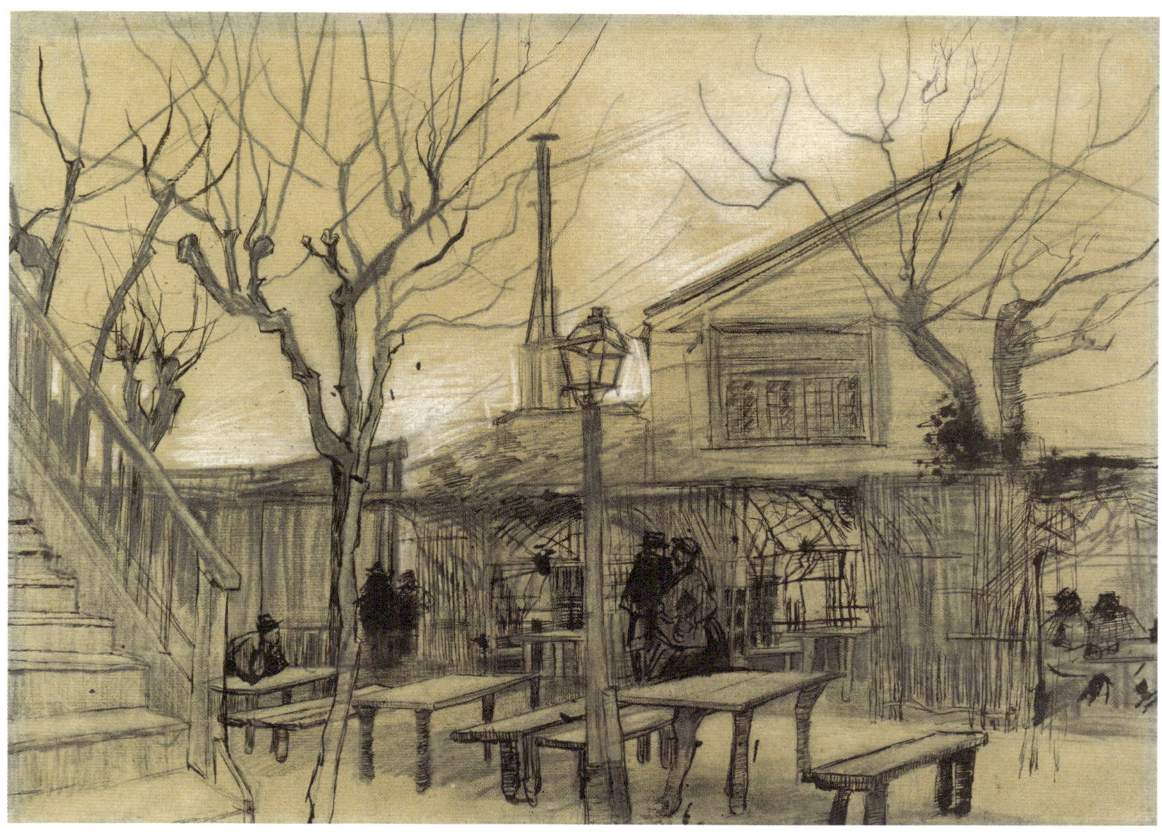

55 *A Guinguette*, February–March 1887. Pencil, pen and brush and ink, chalk, on paper, 38.7 × 52.5 cm (15¼ × 20¾ in.). VAN GOGH MUSEUM, AMSTERDAM

into a tourist attraction and was often photographed. The three remaining windmills and the surrounding gardens and quarries came to symbolize the traditional rural features of this part of the city, which was starting to be overrun by the growth of the suburbs and other such modernizations. Not surprisingly, given his origins, Van Gogh was strongly attracted to the site and made several paintings and drawings of the windmills (Fig. 56). As part of his strategy of surveying the Butte Montmartre, he often depicted the Blute-Fin windmill with the specially built viewing platform to one side and garden sheds on the slope below – a view that is, in fact, seen from the same angle but from further away in a painting with a different format in the Carnegie Museum of Art, Pittsburgh.

The priority given to drawing over painting in the first part of Van Gogh's life became more balanced after he left the Netherlands and as his confidence in the handling of oils increased. The output of works on paper continued steadily alongside that of paintings, and there were sudden bursts of activity when he prioritized one over the other. This was particularly the case when he moved in February 1888 to Provence in the south of France, basing himself in Arles. It was from there that Van Gogh bombarded Theo and his friends with numerous independent images on paper. The dependency of a painting on a drawing had only rarely been a feature of his artistic practices so far, and while in the south he came increasingly to regard painting and drawing as equals. Thus, many of the motifs that are shared between paintings and drawings were the result of separate visual assessments rather than part of a process of sequencing.

Even those few drawings that could be described as preparatory, in so far as they are closely related to paintings, are sufficiently precise and detailed to entice potential buyers. *Landscape with Path and Pollard Willows* (Fig. 57), *Field with Farmhouses* or *Farmhouse in a Wheatfield*, all done shortly after Van Gogh's arrival in Arles, are neatly drawn and carefully observed compositions serving as works of art in their own right. As in Rembrandt's landscape drawings, the economy of style belies the directness of the observation and the sheer accumulation of visual information (Fig. 58). *View of Arles with Irises in the Foreground* was more problematic compositionally, with the corner of the field, which protrudes like an arrowhead pointing at the viewer, dramatically placed in the foreground (Fig. 59). This effect was reduced in the related painting, but, nonetheless, it is the variety of the penwork that gives the drawing its truly outstanding quality in successfully mapping out the changing topography of the view.

Similar refinements between drawing and painting were made in the powerful rendition of *Street in Saintes-Maries-de-la-Mer*, a Mediterranean pilgrimage village that the artist visited in late May and early June 1888 (Fig. 60). The emphatic strokes used for the houses on the left were made with a heavily inked and broadly cut reed pen pressed and dragged across the surface of the paper. Such passages are as powerful as any brushstrokes in Van Gogh's paintings, in the same way as the ebb and flow of the lines of the foliage on the right have a complementary force and variety.

Perhaps the most striking alliance between painting and drawing dating from the months in Arles is *Café Terrace on the place du Forum* – a night-time scene (Fig. 61). The rippling penwork,

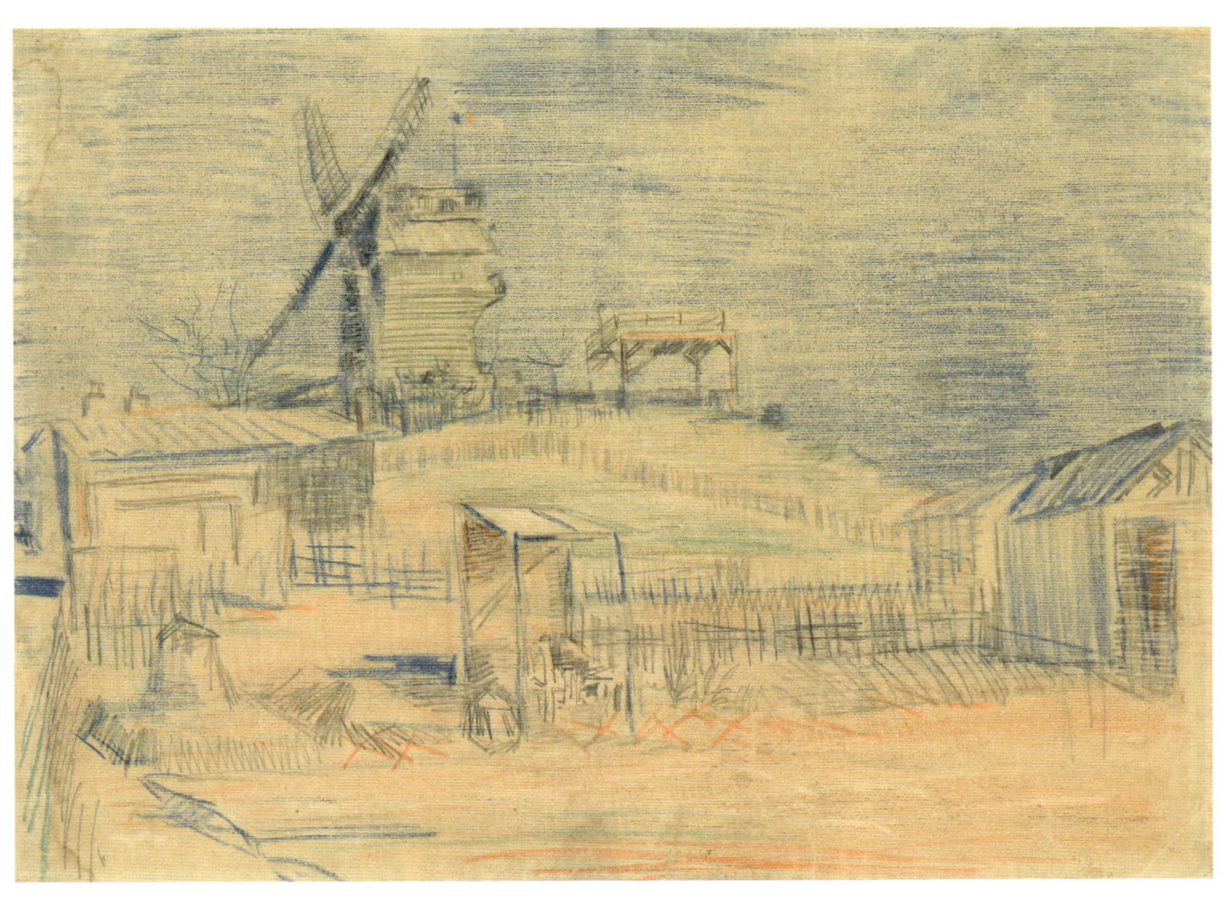

56 *Gardens on Montmartre and the Blute-Fin Windmill*, February–March 1887. Pencil, chalk, on paper, 39.8 × 53.8 cm (15¾ × 21¼ in.). VAN GOGH MUSEUM, AMSTERDAM

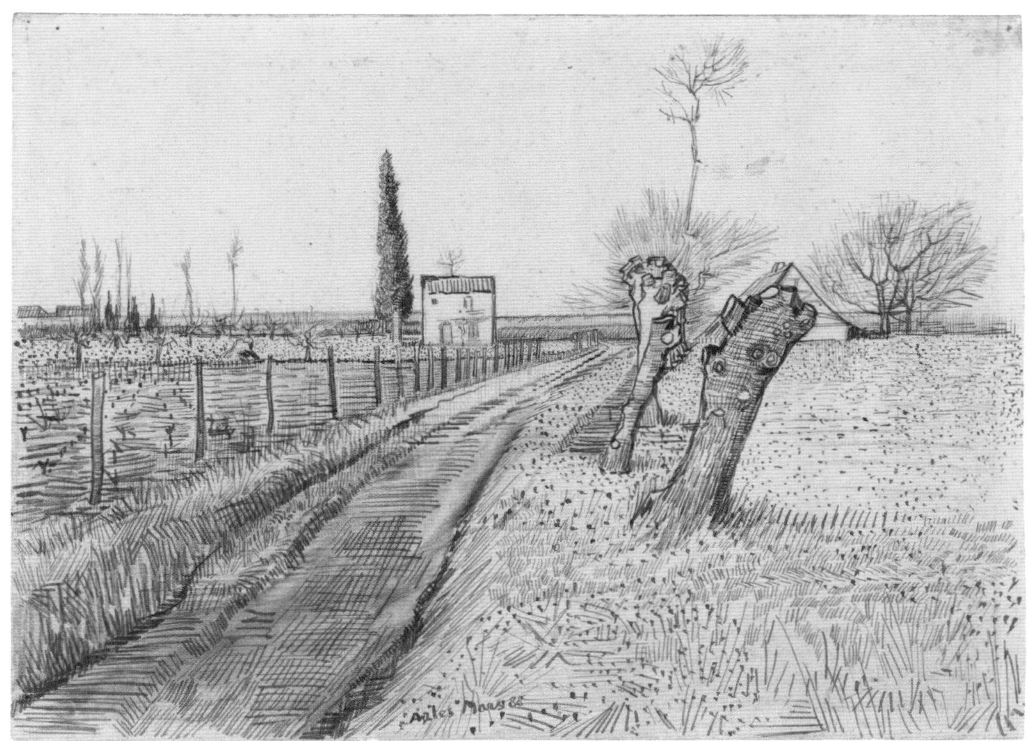

57 *Landscape with Path and Pollard Willows*, March 1888. Pencil, pen and reed pen and ink, on paper, 25.8 × 34.7 cm (10¼ × 13¾ in.).
VAN GOGH MUSEUM, AMSTERDAM

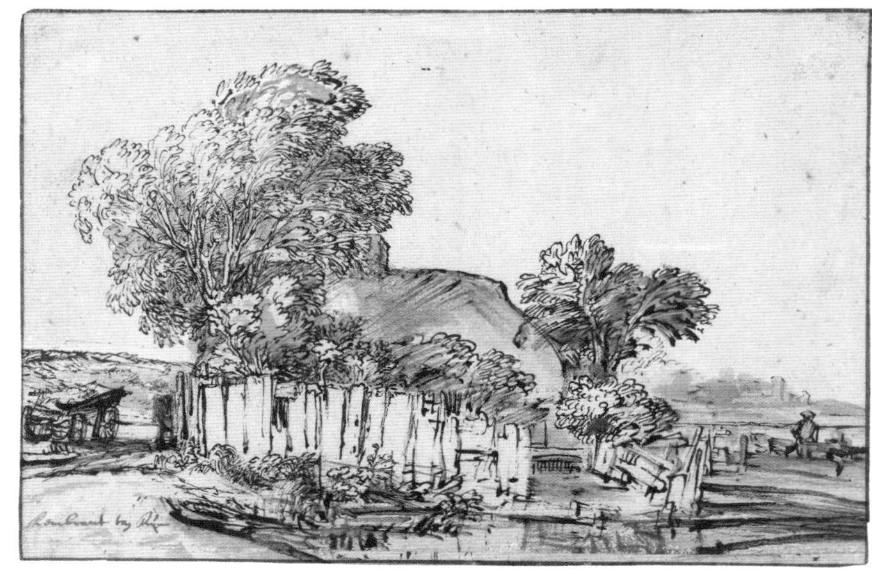

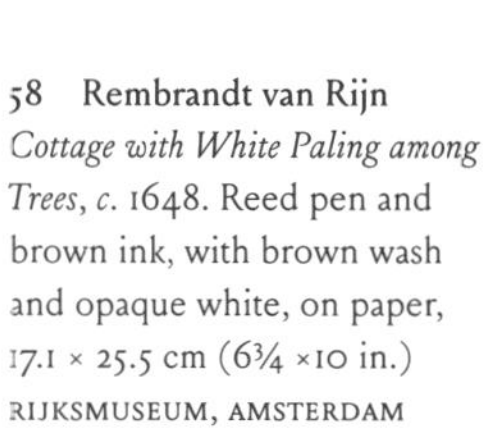

58 Rembrandt van Rijn
Cottage with White Paling among Trees, *c.* 1648. Reed pen and brown ink, with brown wash and opaque white, on paper, 17.1 × 25.5 cm (6¾ ×10 in.)
RIJKSMUSEUM, AMSTERDAM

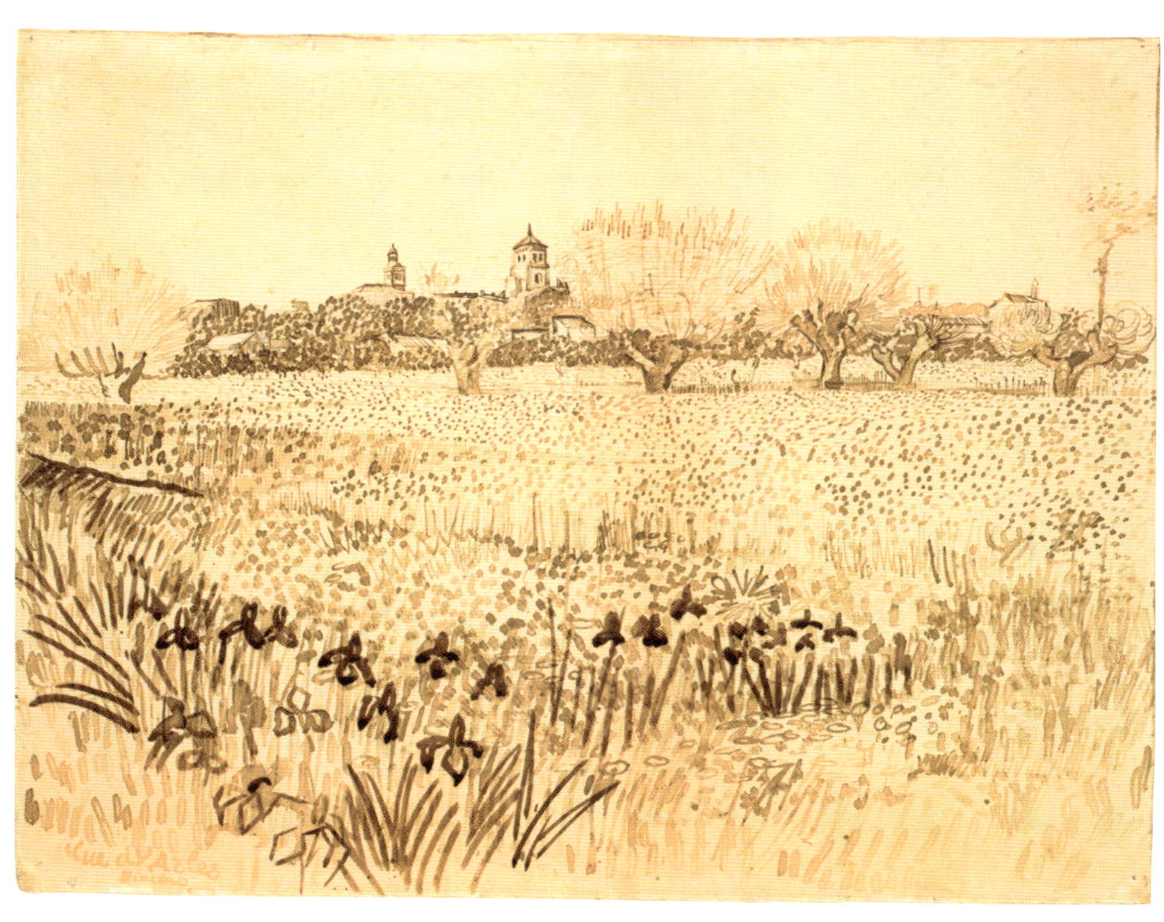

59 *View of Arles with Irises in the Foreground*, first week of May 1888. Reed pen, pen, ink and wash over pencil, on paper, 41.5 × 55.5 cm ($16\frac{3}{8} \times 21\frac{7}{8}$ in.). RISD MUSEUM, PROVIDENCE, R.I.

comprising a plethora of often accented short lines, loops, curlicues, zigzags and curves, is combined with pencil in the shadowy areas under the awning. The reed pen is handled with the dexterity of a fencer. Yet, however animated in style, the intense lighting of the scene is skilfully suggested by the areas of blank paper seen in contrast with the animated night sky. This drawing is like a reconnaissance raid on a scene that Van Gogh suddenly came across and then returned to regularly at different times of day and night as an habitué in order to become more familiar with it. His performance in both the drawing and the related painting is nothing less than a totally virtuosic display.

Arriving back in the north of France at Auvers-sur-Oise in May 1890, Van Gogh immediately set about finding motifs for painting and drawing. He liked the gentle hilly landscape, the river and the thatched houses that characterize the area. Furthermore, he could watch people going to and from the fields, as well as observing those working in them. These were not unanticipated pleasures. It was a sort of homecoming, and the lyricism with which both paintings and drawings are executed is surely a form of celebration for the artist. *Dead-End Street with Houses* is immaculately

60 *Street in Saintes-Maries-de-la-Mer*, *c.* 30 May–5 June 1888. Reed pen and ink over pencil, 30.5 × 47 cm (12⅛ × 18⅝ in.). PRIVATE COLLECTION, ON DEPOSIT AT THE MORGAN LIBRARY & MUSEUM, NEW YORK

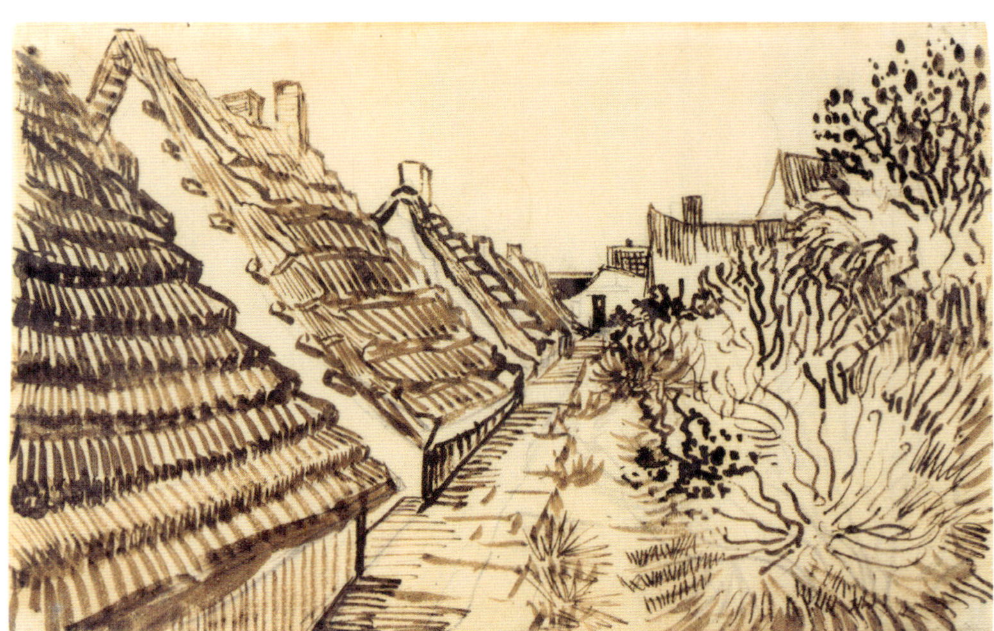

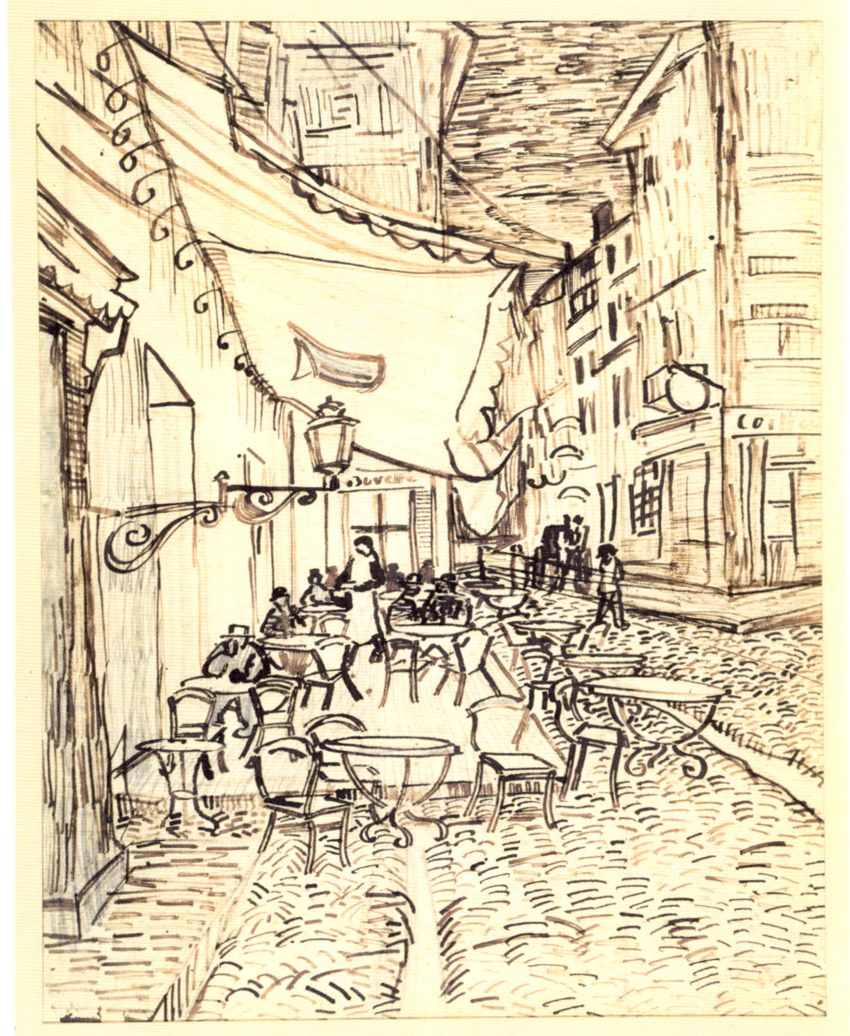

61 *Café Terrace on the place du Forum*, early September 1888. Chalk, ink and pencil, on laid paper, 62 × 47 cm (24½ × 18⅝ in.). DALLAS MUSEUM OF ART

drawn in every detail (Fig. 62). Outlined in pencil first, it is the penwork that is the most striking feature. Sinuous, snake-like lines lead the eye down the cart tracks in the centre, but the outburst of hatched lines on the right, suggesting the shape and rustling of the branches of the chestnut tree at the height of summer, are particularly apt. For the architectural features and the ruts in the track approaching the house, the paper is left untouched. The only

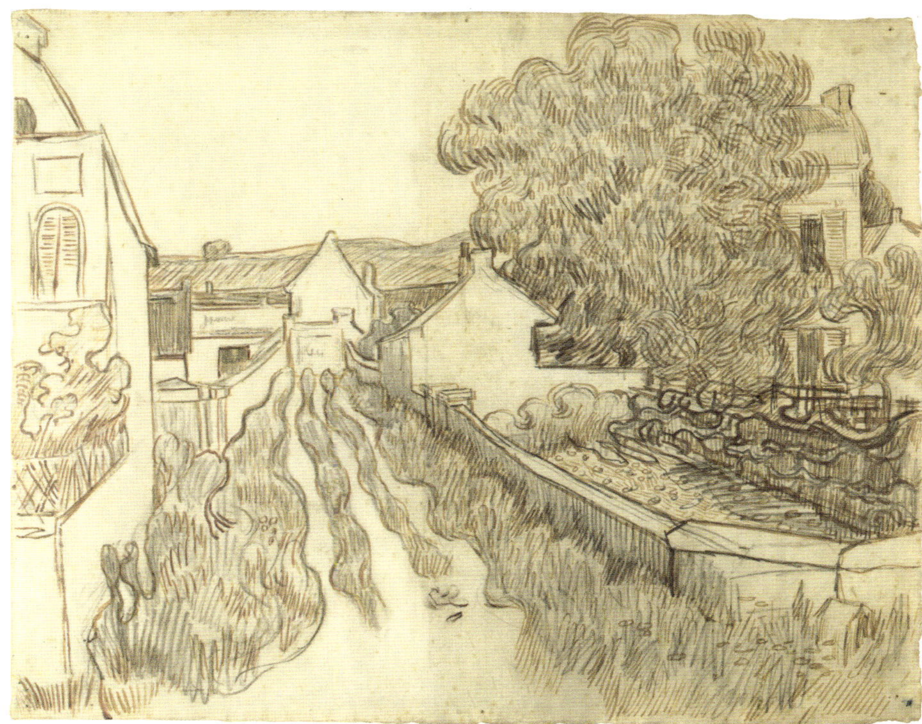

62 *Dead-End Street with Houses*, May–June 1890. Pencil, pen and ink, on paper, 45 × 55.6 cm (17¾ × 22 in.). VAN GOGH MUSEUM, AMSTERDAM

difference between the painting of this subject (private collection) and the drawing is a slight shift in viewpoint, but in every other way there is parity.

The agreement that Van Gogh, in his fragile mental state, should be watched over by Dr Gachet, an art lover, collector and part-time artist as well as a homeopathic doctor recommended by Pissarro, was providential. The rapport between them was good, and being overseen by someone in the medical profession gave Van Gogh the necessary freedom and confidence to keep working. The artist had always liked to paint portraits of those he saw regularly and befriended, whatever their station in life, and he painted Dr Gachet first in June 1890. At the end of the month, he began a portrait of the doctor's daughter, Marguerite, playing the piano (Kunstmuseum, Basel). Probably because, for him, it was an unusually contrived subject, he thought it necessary to make a preparatory study, which appears to have been done at speed, judging by the force of the hatched lines and the stippled background (Fig. 63). The study establishes the pose without worrying about anatomical accuracy, with the result that the hands are clearly too long. Yet, beyond the essentials, it is the details that count: the concentration of the player reading the sheet music in front of her, the foot on the pedal and the long protruding leg of the piano stool. It is an intimate drawing revealing the very essence of a gifted and highly emotional artist in the company of someone with whom he feels empathy. The following month Van Gogh would kill himself.

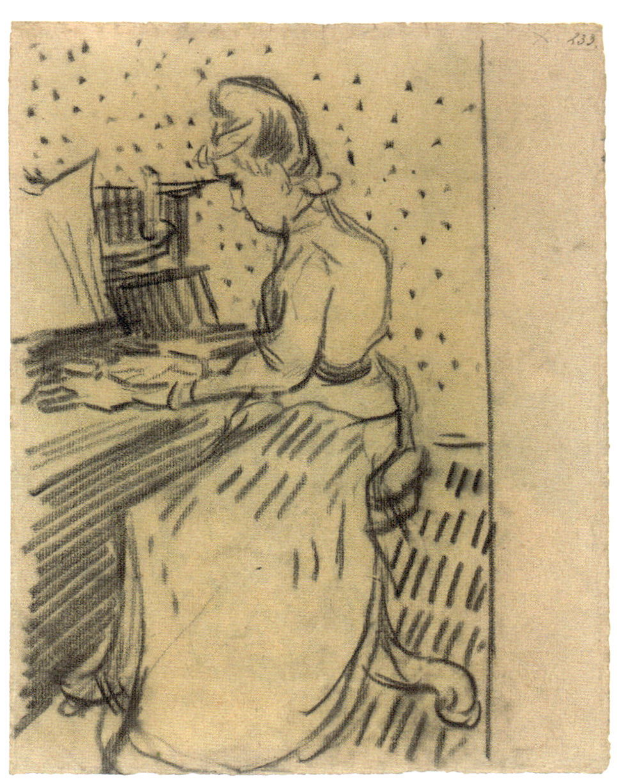

63 *Marguerite Gachet at the Piano*, June 1890. Chalk on paper, 30.5 × 23.8 cm (12⅛ × 9⅜ in.). VAN GOGH MUSEUM, AMSTERDAM

Chapter 4

Place

Van Gogh had an acute and highly developed sense of place. His letters include vivid descriptions of his surroundings, often based on the contrast between north and south or city and country. Frequently, his concept of place arose from personal associations or was prompted by flights of fantasy. As an artist, he did not shy away from depicting scenes of modernization or industrialization, but this was balanced by a sympathetic feeling for nature, which, on occasions, he interpreted as an expression of human emotions, in the same way that, at the beginning of the nineteenth century, such northern Romantic painters as Caspar David Friedrich (1774–1840) in Germany or John Constable in England viewed the landscape in terms of what John Ruskin (1819–1900) later called 'the pathetic fallacy'. In Van Gogh's art, every aspect of the subjects he chose to depict was as important as the manner in which he carried out the work. Indeed, the special quality of his oeuvre lies in its fusion of realism with symbolism, as conveyed, for example, by his rendition of trees – the willow in the Netherlands, the olive in Provence – the sun, the stars and the night sky.

This emotional response to his surroundings was intensified by Van Gogh's deep knowledge of literature and his profound appreciation of art in all its guises. He tended to see people and places through the eyes of writers whose themes and subjects coincided with his own social conscience and of artists whose motifs and strategies stimulated him. On a purely practical level, even the weather played a role in his art. The cold often precluded him from working outside during the winter months in the north, while in the south the combination of the heat, mosquitoes and the mistral regularly posed problems.

Van Gogh's memories of places were often awakened by separation. When first taken ill in Arles in December 1888 and January 1889, he wrote to Theo and recalled his birthplace: 'During my illness I again saw each room in the house at Zundert, each path, each plant in the garden, the views round about, the

Boulevard de Clichy, February 1887 (detail of Fig. 72).

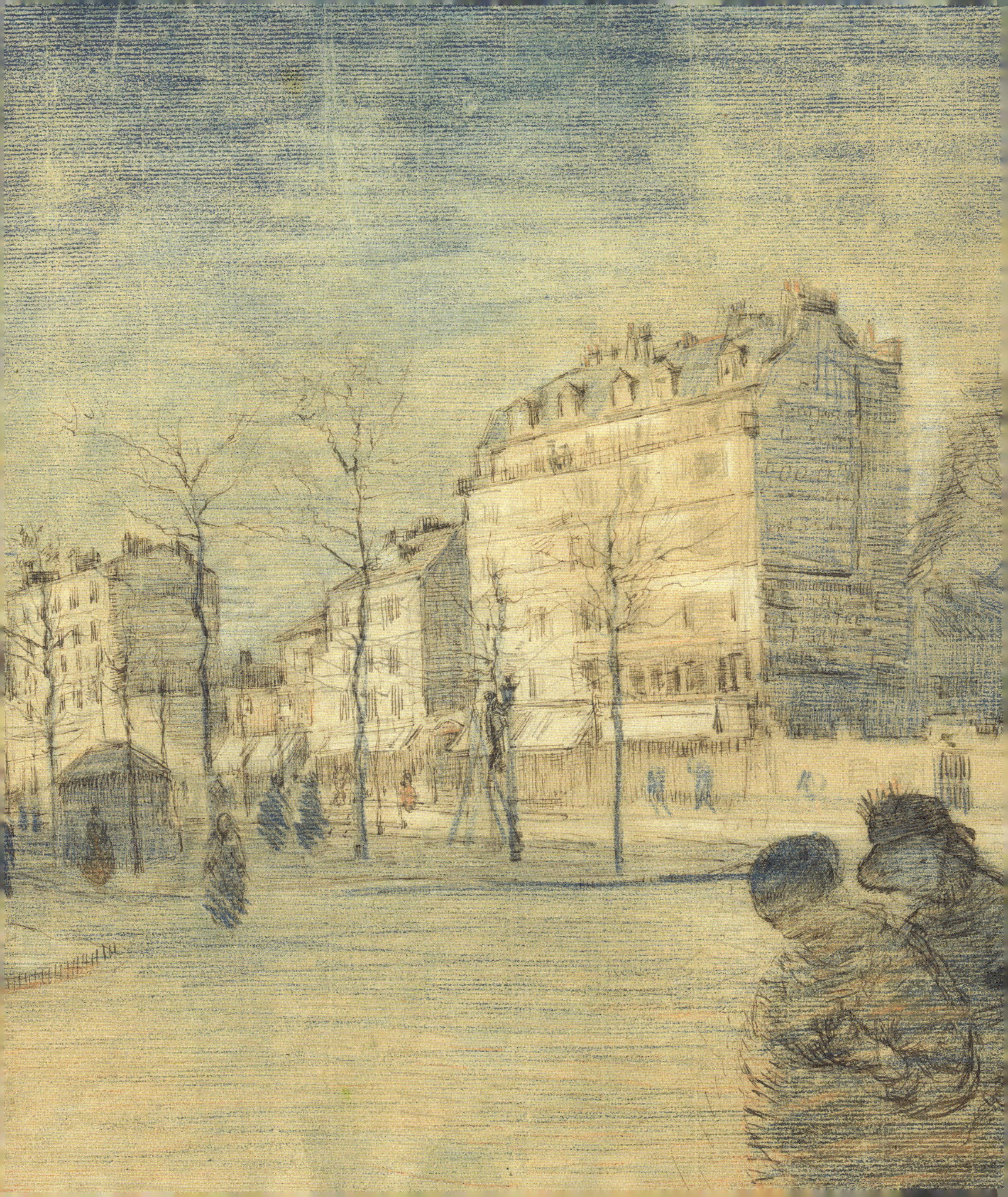

fields, the neighbours, the cemetery, the church, our kitchen garden behind – right up to the magpies' nest in a tall acacia in the cemetery. That's because I still have the most primitive memories of all of you, of those days, to remember all this there's only Mother and me' (741). No drawings of Zundert survive, because, of course, during those years, from 1853 to 1871, Van Gogh had not yet become an artist. The visual evidence is also thin for the time during which his parents lived in Helvoirt (1871–75) and only partial for the years in Etten (1875–82, Fig. 64). But the next move his father made was to Nuenen, where the artist lived with his parents from December 1883 until leaving for Antwerp in November 1885, shortly after his father's death. It was a time that was punctuated by family disagreements and misunderstandings, but, nonetheless, it was a

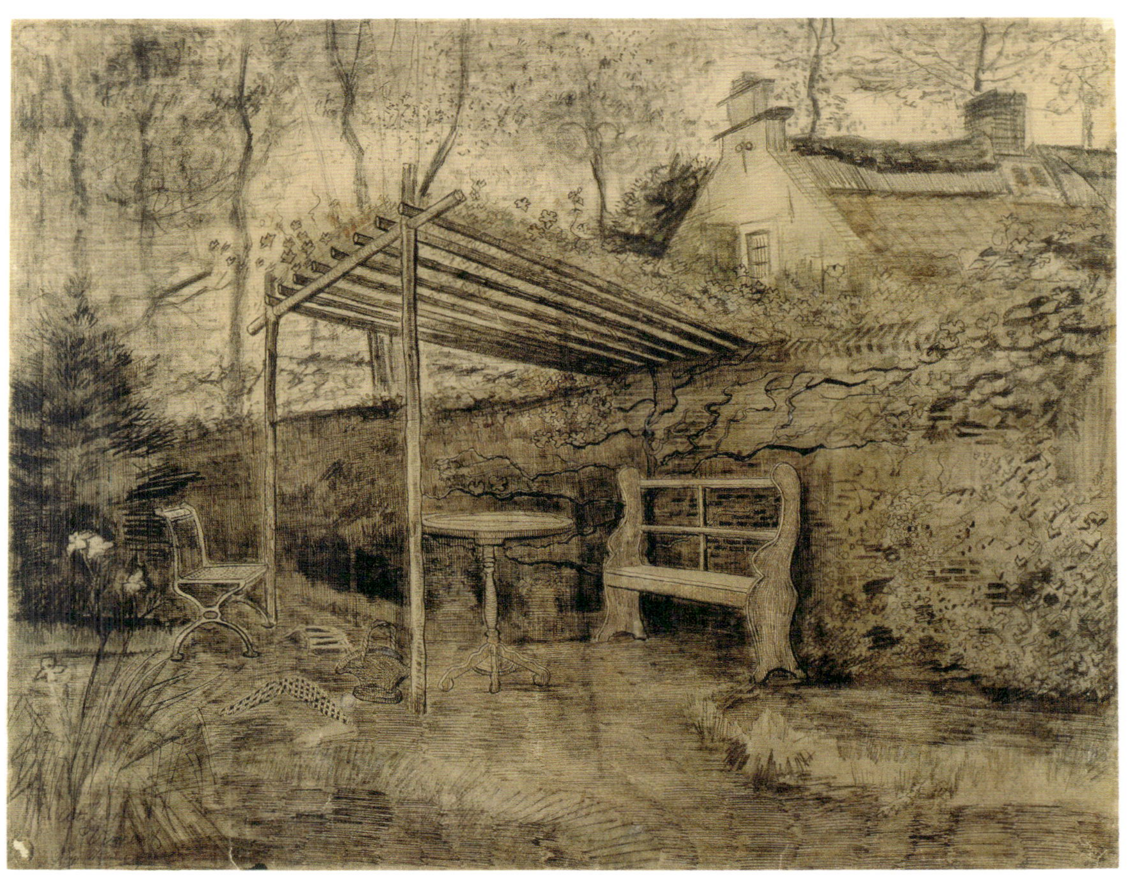

64 *Corner of a Garden, Etten*, June 1881. Pencil, pen and black ink, transparent watercolour, on laid paper, 44.5 × 56.7 cm (17⅝ × 22⅜ in.). KRÖLLER-MÜLLER MUSEUM, OTTERLO

place that left a deep impression on him and resulted in some of his most memorable drawings. As he recalled in a letter to his mother, written while he was in the asylum at Saint-Rémy, 'Then here one also never sees the mossy peasant roofs on the barns or cottages like at home, and no oak coppices and no spurry and no beech hedges with their red-brown leaves and whitish tangled old stems. Also, no proper heathland and no birches, which were so beautiful in Nuenen' (788).

The vicarage garden at Nuenen and its vicinity inspired a suite of six drawings by Van Gogh, undertaken during the spring of 1884. It is one of his greatest achievements as a draughtsman. Using combinations of pencil and pen and ink, each drawing is intensely worked and immensely detailed. In *Pollard Birches, Nuenen*, thinly hatched pen strokes represent the spindly branches sprouting from the pollarded trees and the grass below; more rounded pen strokes circumscribe the gnarled trunks (Fig. 65). The rich tonal quality is derived from the interaction between pencil and ink. The mood is one of transience as the seasons change, with winter retreating and spring arriving. A feeling of hope replaces a mood of resignation, while renewal presides over decay. The processional feeling of the trees is reflected by the woman with a rake over her shoulder on the left and the shepherd tending his flock on the right. Both figures are seen from the back, and both are at one with nature, their dignity representing the good in humankind. Clearly, Van Gogh is at peace with this scene, which exudes personal contentment, inspired in part by a spirit of pantheism and underscored by his love of literature.

Van Gogh's reactions to city life were almost certain to be idiosyncratic. Such places were not his usual habitat, and he therefore had to adapt to a different way of life, which, in his case, was dogged by extreme poverty and complicated by a growing sense of social injustice. Although no stranger to cities in the north, having lived in London (then the largest city in the world) and visited Amsterdam and The Hague at intervals during the 1870s, it was as a burgeoning artist that he engaged with Brussels (1880–81), The Hague (1881–83), Antwerp (1885–86) and Paris (1886–88).

The most sustained examination of an urban space during these early years was of The Hague, which came about as the result of a commission from his uncle the art dealer, Cornelis van Gogh ('Uncle Cor'), based in Amsterdam. In March 1882, Cornelis asked his nephew for twelve small views of The Hague which,

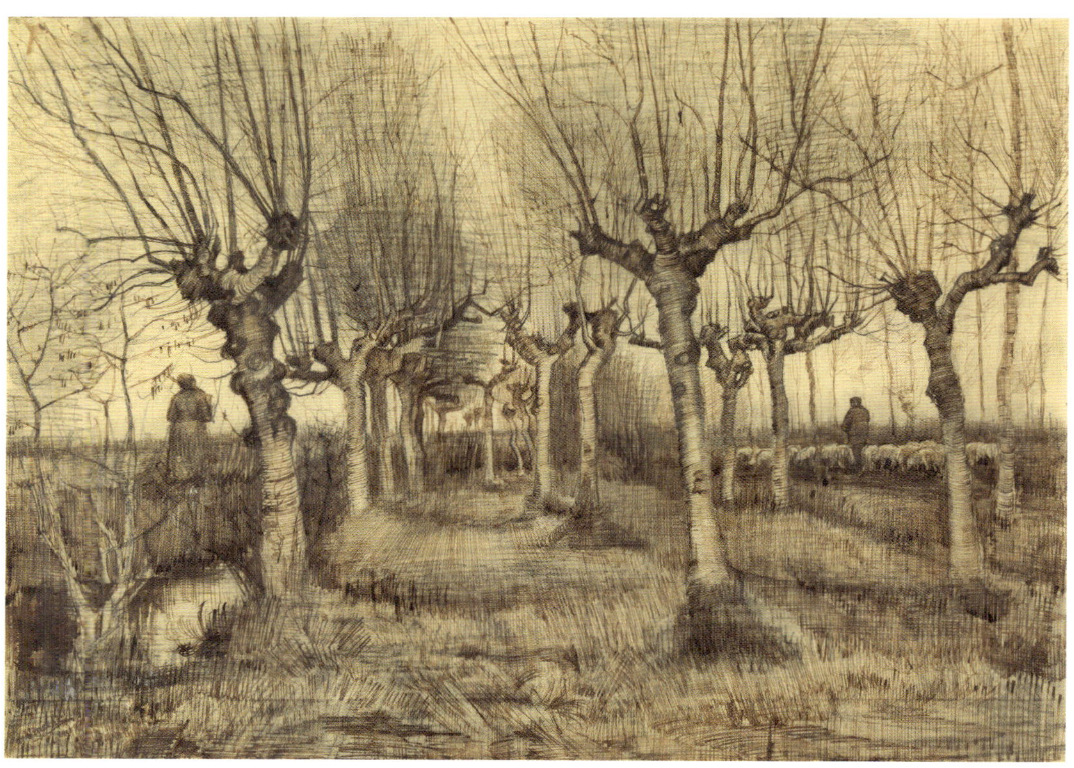

65 *Pollard Birches*, March 1884. Pencil, pen and ink, watercolour, on paper, 39.5 × 54.2 cm (15⅝ × 21⅜ in.). VAN GOGH MUSEUM, AMSTERDAM

if they proved to be successful, would be followed by a further commission. The idea was to encourage Van Gogh to produce work that would appeal to the general collector, and no doubt Uncle Cor was expecting his nephew to depict the main sites of the city, in accordance with a well-established topographical tradition – the royal palace, government buildings, churches, canals, markets and parks. But Van Gogh did not adopt this approach and, furthermore, preferred to make the drawings in mixed media instead of the more pleasing watercolour that topographical artists usually employed. No doubt such decisions disconcerted Uncle Cor, and he was at first hesitant in accepting the particular views that his nephew had selected.

Van Gogh's choice of subjects was certainly unusual and included the pawn shop, the gasworks and the railway station, which were not exactly picturesque sites. The only conformist view he made was *Bridge and Houses on the Corner of Herengracht-Prinsessegracht*

(Van Gogh Museum, Amsterdam). Two factors probably dictated Van Gogh's approach to the project. The first was that he was living in the outskirts of The Hague on the Schenkweg, on the eastern side of the city where there were several new urban developments. The second factor was his friendship with George Breitner (1857–1923), whose studio in the centre of The Hague was in the poor district known as the Geest. There were several shared interests between Van Gogh and Breitner, especially at this early stage of their careers, and together they explored the Geest and other central areas searching for subjects representing everyday life and in pursuit of suitable models. Although the drawings made for Uncle Cor show a real advance in Van Gogh's skills as a draughtsman, as was intended, they were not wholly satisfactory (Fig. 66). The handling of the medium was impressive, but, as the artist confessed, he deliberately set himself the task of perfecting the use of perspective. Evidence of grid lines on the paper show that for this purpose a specially made perspective frame was used. This ensured that the sightlines of the architecture were correctly recorded, although, in the present

66 *The Entrance to the Pawn Bank, The Hague*, March 1882. Pencil, pen and brush and ink, watercolour, on paper, 23.9 × 33.7 cm (9½ × 13⅜ in.). VAN GOGH MUSEUM, AMSTERDAM

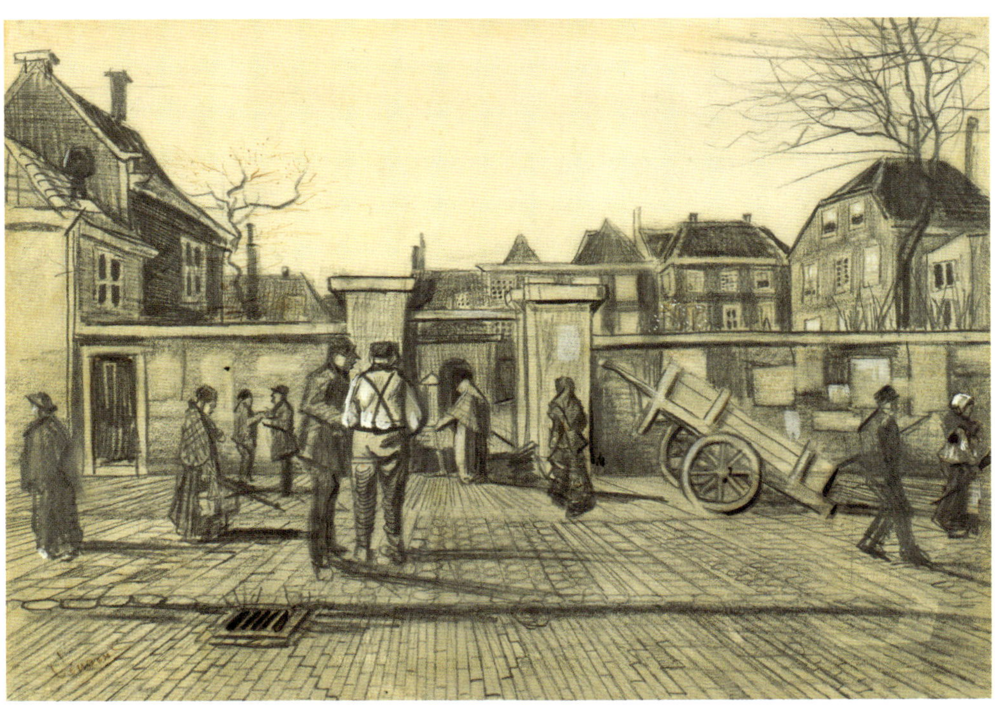

67 *Carpenter's Yard and Laundry*, late May 1882. Pencil, black chalk, pen and brush in black ink, brown wash, opaque watercolour, scratched, and traces of squaring, on laid paper, 28.6 × 46.8 cm (11⅜ × 18½ in.). KRÖLLER-MÜLLER MUSEUM, OTTERLO

68 *Dab-Drying Barn in Scheveningen*, late May 1882. Pencil, pen and brush in black iron gall ink (faded to brown in places), white opaque and transparant watercolour and traces of squaring on laid paper, 29 × 45.4 cm (11½ × 17⅞ in.). KRÖLLER-MÜLLER MUSEUM, OTTERLO

instance, the stilted movement of the figures and their relationship to the buildings are not completely successful. However, the suite of drawings as a whole is undoubtedly impressive, particularly since he completed all twelve in two weeks.

The delay in agreeing to a second commission perhaps reflects Uncle Cor's disquiet at what he had received in response to his first request. This time, in April 1882, he asked for only six 'detailed, specific city views', but these should be larger, and the artist would be paid as much as he was for the twelve drawings in the original commission. There is greater variety in this second group in the selection of subjects and the choice of media. The compositions are more detailed, sometimes complex, incorporating more daring viewpoints. Even so, again technically, the drawings did not really fulfil Uncle Cor's expectations. On at least one occasion, Van Gogh simply depicts the view out of his studio window (*Carpenter's Yard and Laundry*; Fig. 67); others are of motifs close by (*Nursery on the Schenkweg*; Metropolitan Museum of Art, New York) or those of personal significance (*The Back Garden of Sien's Mother's House*; Norton Simon Museum, Pasadena). He also chose to leave The Hague and search for motifs in the nearby coastal resort of Scheveningen, which was the *locus classicus* for painters belonging to the Hague School. Here he made *Dab-Drying Barn in Scheveningen* for the series (Fig. 68). After completing this second commission for his uncle, Van Gogh moved between The Hague and Scheveningen during the summer, producing some outstanding independent drawings with a remarkable eye for detail and an increasing willingness to exploit colour, as in *The Fish-Drying Barn at Scheveningen* (private collection) and *Rooftops*, which was a view from the window of his rooms in The Hague (Fig. 69).

A similar advance in Van Gogh's art took place during the two years, from 1886 to 1888, that he was in Paris, where he encountered avant-garde art for the first time. By attending Cormon's studio, he was completing the academic training that he had been encouraged to pursue while in Brussels and Antwerp, whereas coming into contact with the art of Impressionist and Post-Impressionist artists encouraged him to explore new ways of making art. The paintings and drawings that Van Gogh made in Paris show him coming to terms with new aspects of composition, facture and colour, as well as subject matter. This had the dramatic effect of turning him into a modern artist – a spectrum exemplified by Manet, Auguste Renoir (1841–1919), Degas, Pissarro, Claude Monet (1840–1926), Gustave

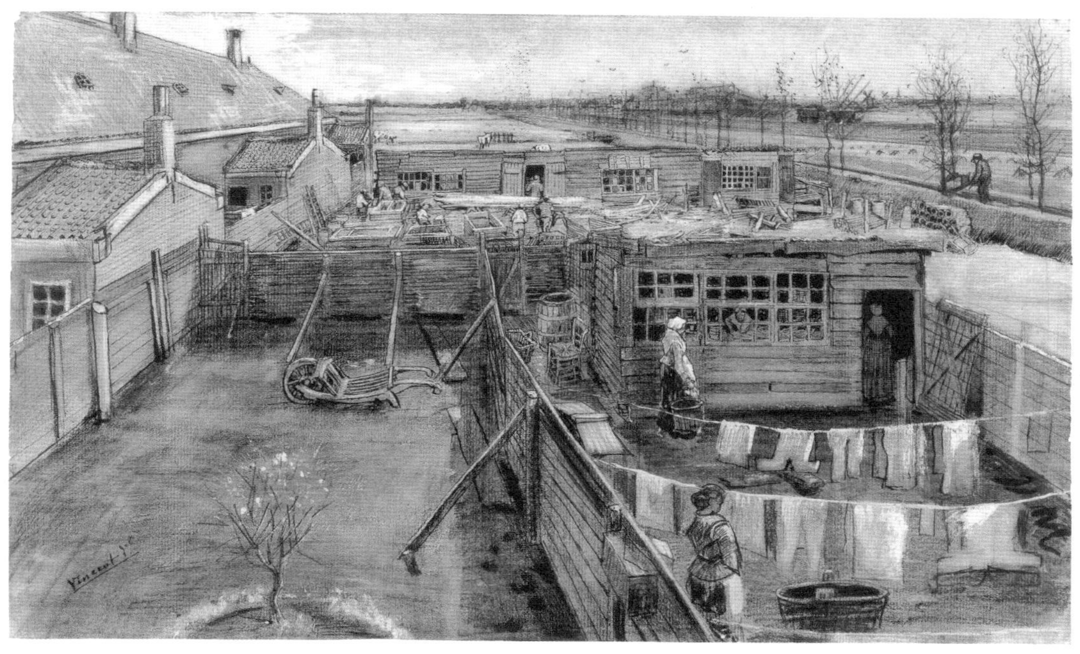

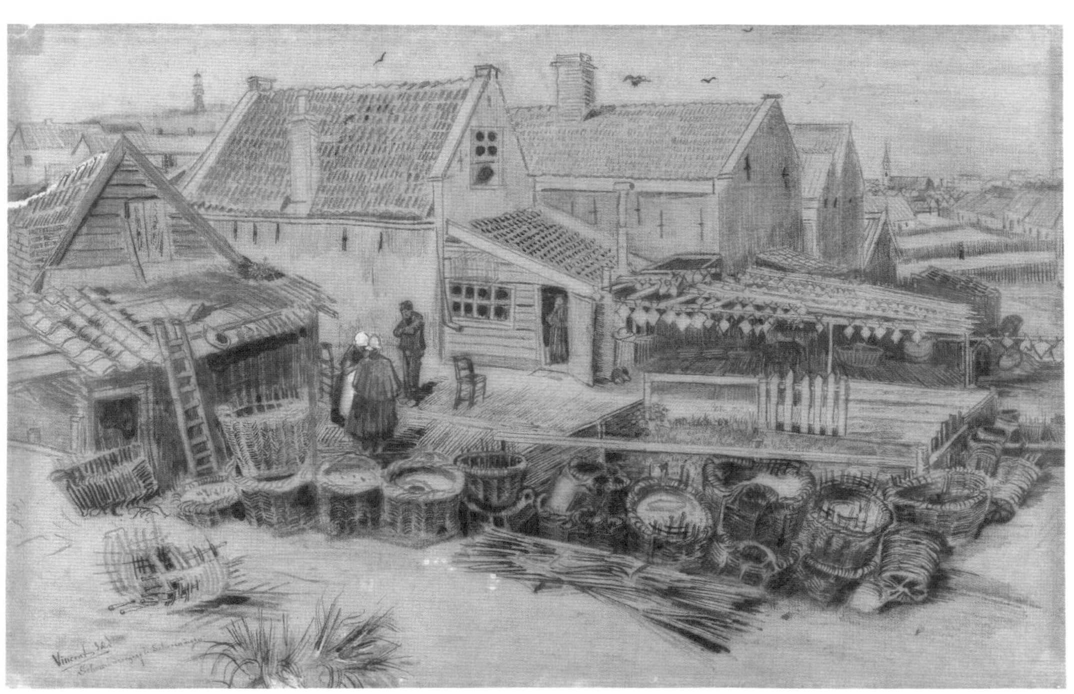

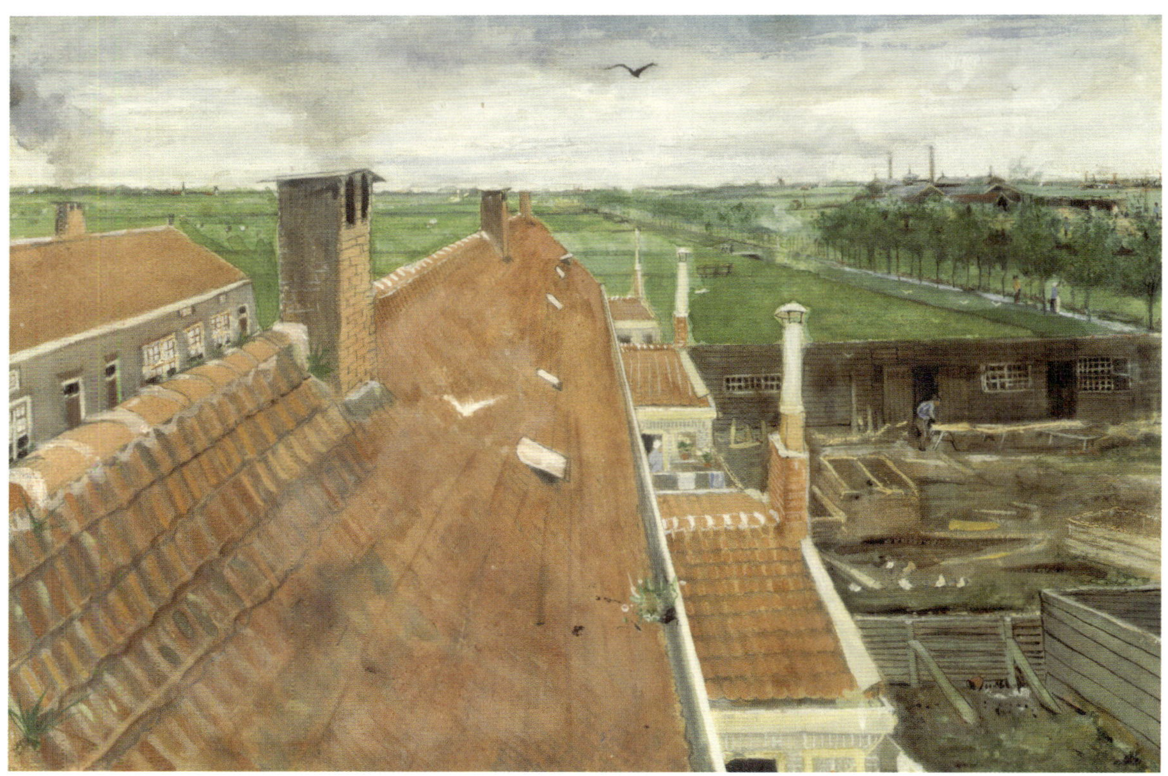

69 *Rooftops*, 21 July 1882. Watercolour and gouache, on paper, 39 × 56.5 cm (15⅜ × 22¼ in.). PRIVATE COLLECTION

Caillebotte (1848–1894), Georges Seurat (1859–1891) and Paul Signac (1863–1935).

The panoramic cityscapes made by Van Gogh from the Butte Montmartre, near where he was living with Theo on the rue Lepic, literally set the scene for this transformation (Fig. 70). These drawings show remarkable economy of means in the arrangement of the numerous buildings silhouetted against the sky or floating above the miasma created by the urban turmoil below. The panoramas include distinctive features of the Paris skyline, but, characteristically, as in The Hague series, Van Gogh never concentrates exclusively on any one of the iconic historic buildings for which the city was famous. Some of these panoramic views were made from the apartment itself and resemble snapshots taken from a concealed position, more akin to a side-long glance over the city. In *View from the Apartment on the rue Lepic, Paris* (Fig. 71), the bold repoussoir

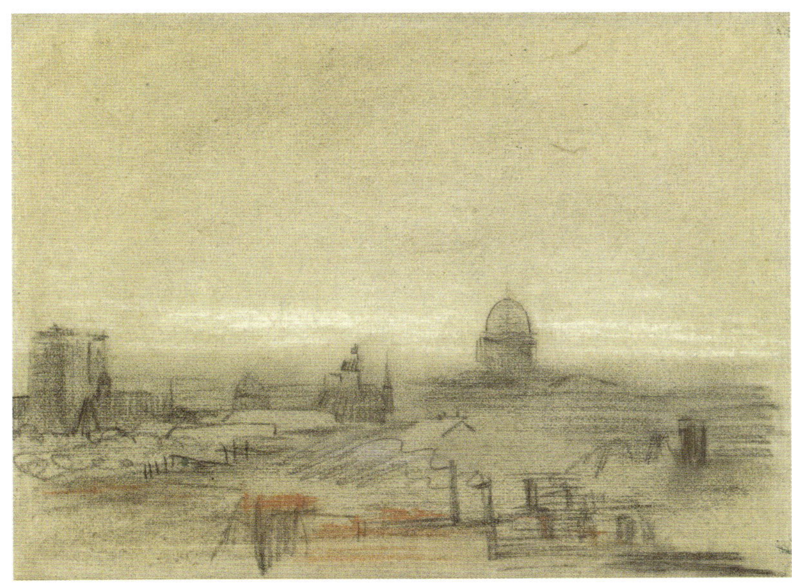

70 *View of Paris with Notre-Dame and the Panthéon*, March–May 1886. Chalk on paper, 22.7 × 30.2 cm (9 × 12 in.).
VAN GOGH MUSEUM, AMSTERDAM

71 *View from the Apartment on the rue Lepic, Paris*, February–March 1887. Pencil, charcoal, pen and ink, on paper, 39.5 × 53.9 cm (15⅝ × 21¼ in.).
VAN GOGH MUSEUM, AMSTERDAM

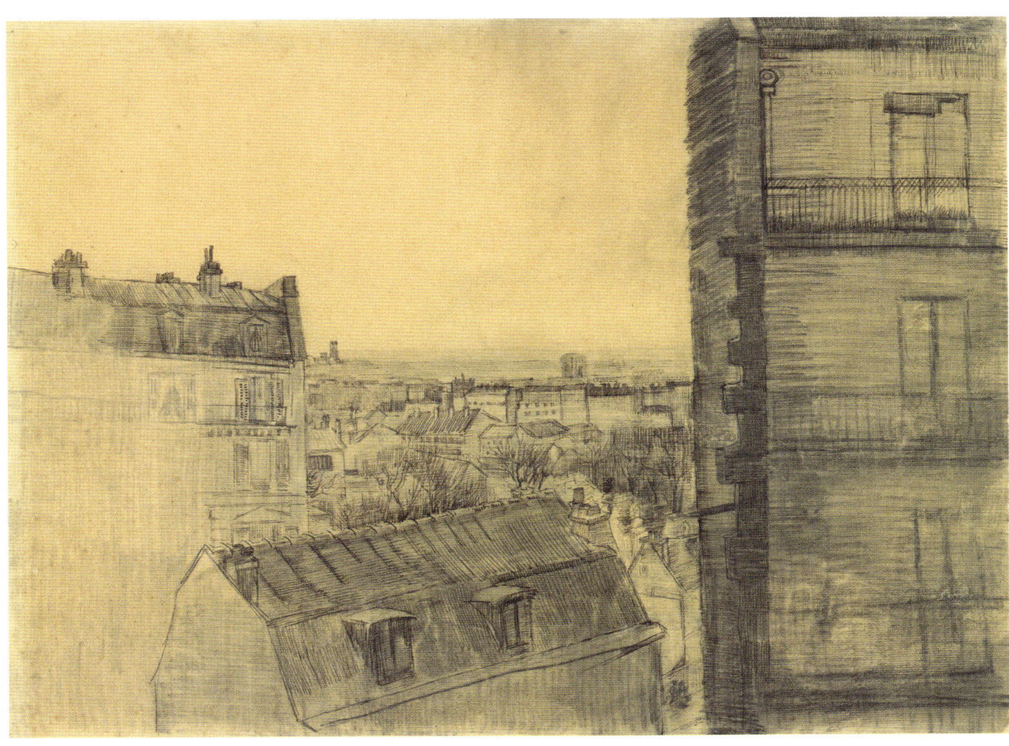

effect created by the tall apartment block on the right works like a drawn curtain, around and below which the city is glimpsed.

Van Gogh fleetingly observes people in the parks or walking in the streets and records musicians at *cafés-concerts*, but he chooses not to develop them. The only exception in this respect is the highly finished drawing *Boulevard de Clichy*, dating from February 1887, which is a scene shown at street level on the place Blanche, where the rue Fontaine joins the boulevard (Fig. 72). The foreground is empty apart from two figures in the lower-right corner, establishing a diagonal that leads the eye towards the centre of the composition. The imposing buildings on either side of the boulevard flank the saplings and the tiny human figures (some twenty or so) as though enclosing them within brackets. The combination of strokes made with pencil, pen and coloured chalk is applied with the utmost

72 *Boulevard de Clichy*, February 1887. Pencil, pen and ink, chalk, watercolour, on paper, 40.1 × 54.4 cm (15⅞ × 21½ in.). VAN GOGH MUSEUM, AMSTERDAM

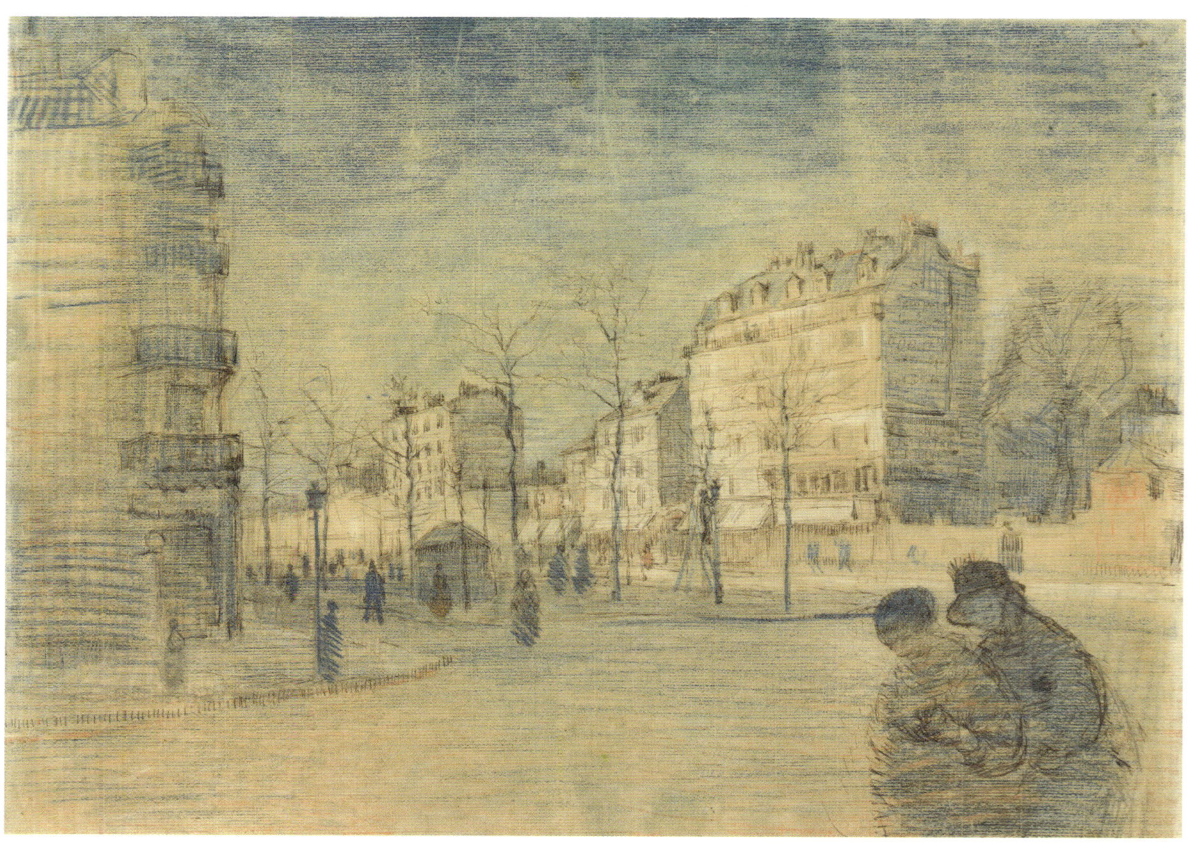

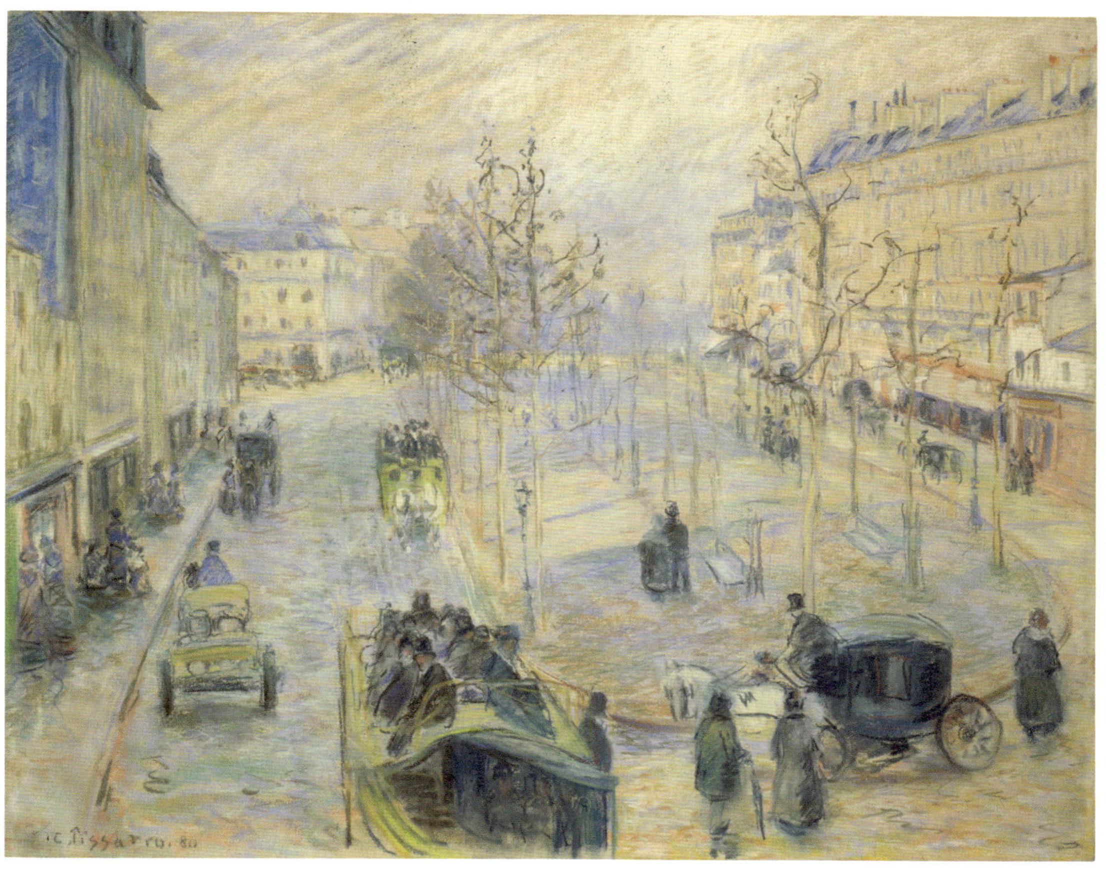

73 Camille Pissarro
Boulevard Rochechouart, 1880.
Pastel on paper, 59.9 × 73.5 cm (23⅝ × 29 in.).
CLARK ART INSTITUTE, WILLIAMSTOWN, MASS.

refinement, so that the scene is observed as though suffused through a piece of gauze. Compared with Pissarro, whose pastel of a similar view of the same area from 1880 was included in the sixth Impressionist exhibition of 1881 (Fig. 73), Van Gogh seems reluctant to evoke the rumbustiousness and vitality of Parisian street life.

Significantly, the artist preferred to depict scenes on the periphery of the city. His one panoramic view from Montmartre is a heavily worked watercolour that looks away from the centre of Paris towards such north-western industrialized suburbs as Saint-Ouen, Saint-Denis and Asnières (Fig. 74). Two other watercolours, however, explore the more decorative features of Montmartre in addition to the windmills and were presumably intended for sale on the tourist market. Less obviously attractive for potential buyers

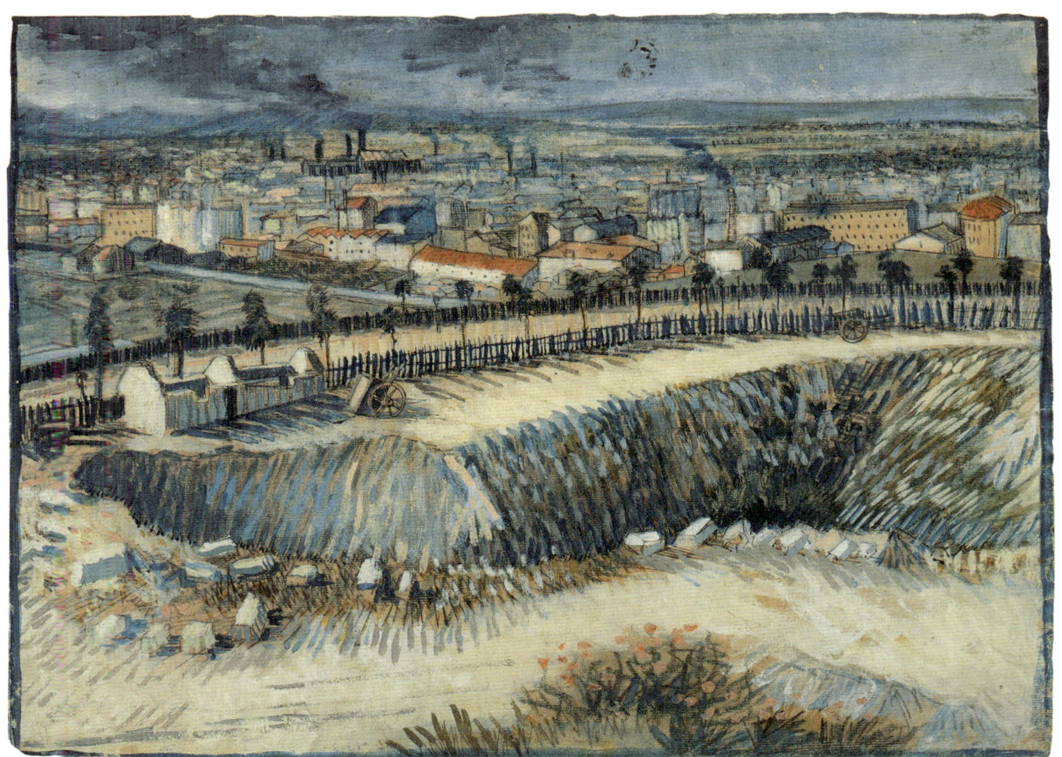

74 *View from Montmartre*, June–September 1887. Opaque watercolour, coloured chalk, pen and ink, oil paint and pencil, on paper, 39.5 × 53.5 cm (15⅝ × 21⅛ in.).
STEDELIJK MUSEUM, AMSTERDAM

were the four watercolours of the fortifications of Paris (Fig. 75). The city was at this time encircled by a defensive wall extending for some nineteen miles (thirty kilometres). The wall was punctuated by ninety-four bastions, twenty or so of which had military barracks attached. There were fifty-two gates in the ramparts for entry to the capital. Parallel to the fortifications was a canal, beyond which was a swathe of barren land roughly 980 feet (300 metres) wide. Although built between 1841 and 1845, the ramparts were obsolete by 1880, and their main use had become recreational, particularly for the poorer classes living in outlying areas of the city. Essentially a wasteland frequented by wayfarers, criminals and prostitutes, such areas were described by the writer Octave Mirbeau as 'no longer city and . . . not yet countryside where nothing ends and nothing begins, where people [are] the flotsam of social misfortune'.

Perhaps inspired by the work of Jean-François Raffaëlli (1850–1924), an artist much admired by Van Gogh, he adopted the fortifications as one of his main subjects while in Paris. Paradoxically, while other artists working in these same areas chose to highlight the social-realist aspects of the scene, Van Gogh stands further back in *Gate in the Paris Ramparts* and emphasizes the picturesque (Fig. 76). This was partly because he had begun to be influenced by the Japanese *ukiyo-e* prints that he and Theo had started to collect in considerable numbers. Compositional elements with steep perspectives and insistent diagonals, together with the clear demarcation of areas of colour and the profusion of tiny figures, all bespeak the influence of Japanese art.

There is a sense in which Van Gogh could be said to have been only passing through Paris. On arriving in Provence at Arles in the early months of 1888, he felt elated, even though it was unusually cold, with snow on the ground. He wrote to Theo, 'I feel I'm in Japan' (585) and to Bernard, 'this part of the world seems to me as beautiful as Japan for the clearness of the atmosphere and the

75 *Fortifications of Paris with Houses*, June–September 1887. Watercolour and gouache, pencil, on grey paper, 39.5 × 53.5 cm (15⅝ × 21⅛ in.). THE WHITWORTH, MANCHESTER

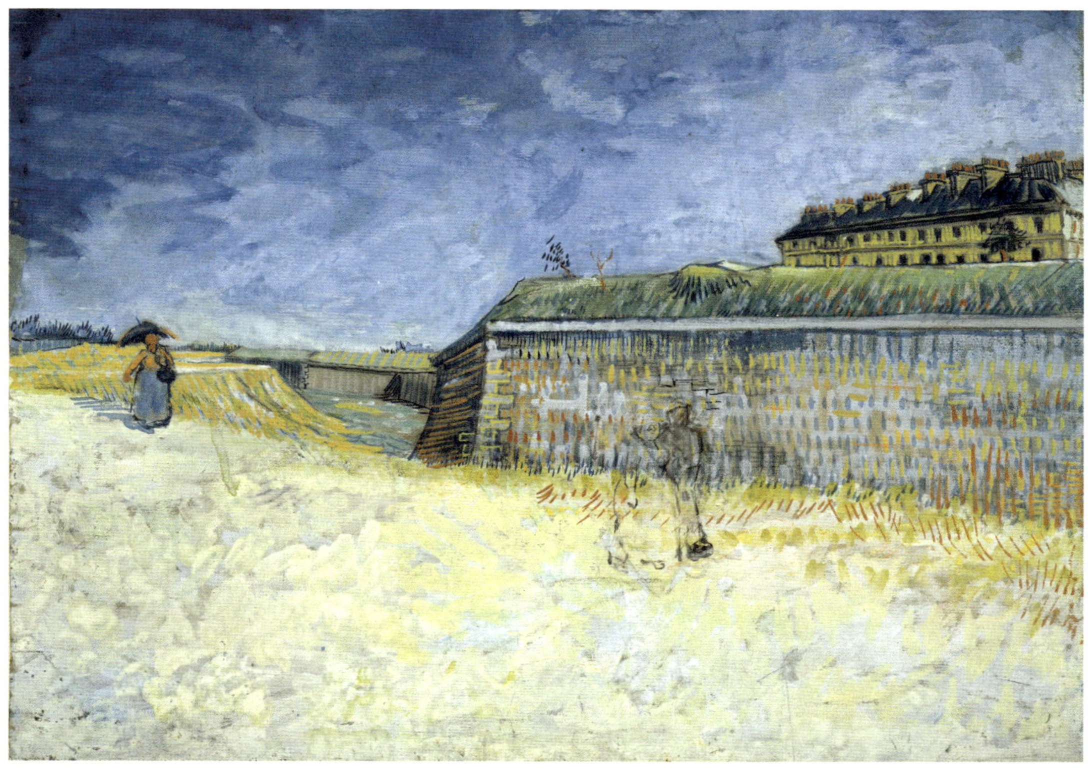

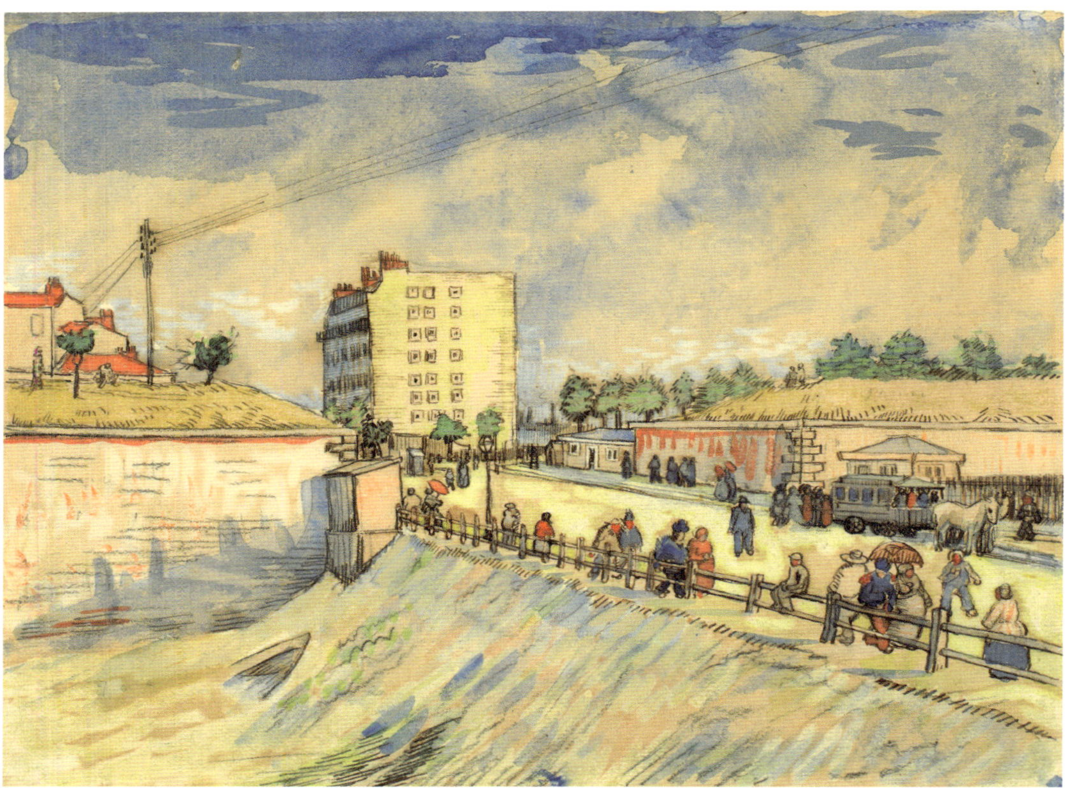

76 *Gate in the Paris Ramparts*, Paris, June–September 1887. Pencil, pen and ink, watercolour, on paper, 24.1 × 31.6 cm (9½ × 12½ in.). VAN GOGH MUSEUM, AMSTERDAM

gay colour effects' (587). Later, recalling his reasons for going to Provence, Van Gogh wrote to his brother while in the asylum at Saint-Rémy of wanting 'to see another light, to believe that looking at nature under a brighter sky can give us a more accurate idea of the Japanese way of feeling and drawing' (801). Provence seemed to him to be a new beginning and where, ultimately, he hoped to establish a colony of artists with like-minded ideas to form a 'Studio of the South'.

The warmth and colour of Provence must have seemed to Van Gogh, a man of the north, like paradise, and he was keen to immerse himself in the area. It seems that there was no clear, overriding reason as to why he chose to settle in Arles, although he already had a number of general points of contact with Provence. For instance, he had read the novels of Alphonse Daudet and Émile Zola, and, equally, he admired the paintings of Monticelli and Cézanne.

He seems, however, to have had no specific knowledge of Arles itself, an important town during the Roman Empire and at one time even designated as the 'little Rome of Gaul'. Notable remains of that period were the arena (the largest in France), where bullfights were staged, and the theatre, as well as the cemetery known as Les Alyscamps (Champs Élysées in Provençal dialect). The most prominent medieval building was the Church of Saint-Trophime in the place de la République, where the seventeenth-century town hall and a famous obelisk were also situated. In the middle of the nineteenth century, the town had had a role in the Provençal Renaissance nurtured by the local Félibrige Society and symbolized by the beauty of its women, known as Les Arlésiennes.

Van Gogh may have intended to settle in a larger place, such as Marseilles, but Arles seems to have answered the artist's immediate expectations of the south. The town is located on the banks of the River Rhône, some twenty-five miles (forty kilometres) inland from its estuary on the Mediterranean. To the south-west is the marshy plain of the Camargue and to the south-east is the stony plain of La Crau. Canals, along with bridges and ditches, were constructed for the drainage and irrigation of these two areas, as well as improving access to the Mediterranean basin. Arles was added to the national railway system in 1848, and heavy industry was introduced in the form of extensive railway workshops. Agriculture, however, was the basis of the local economy – olives, wheat and grapes.

Van Gogh tended to view the town from a distance, usually across fields, meadows and orchards and often from even greater distances (Fig. 77). The principal features and recognizable landmarks, including factory chimneys, are silhouetted against the sky. The fact that, in his depictions of Arles, Van Gogh does not engage directly with any of its historical aspects suggests that he might in some way have equated the town in his imagination with the Celestial City of Bunyan's *The Pilgrim's Progress*. The same might be said of *View of Saintes-Maries-de-la-Mer*, the fishing village on the Mediterranean coast that the artist visited for a week in late May and early June of 1888, only here the allusion to Bunyan is even more pronounced, owing to the appearance of a giant radiant sun (Fig. 78). On the journey from the City of Destruction towards the Celestial City, Bunyan's pilgrims were allowed a glimpse through the gates, where they saw that 'the City shone like the sun: the streets also were paved with gold, and in them walked many men, with crowns on their heads, palms in their hands and

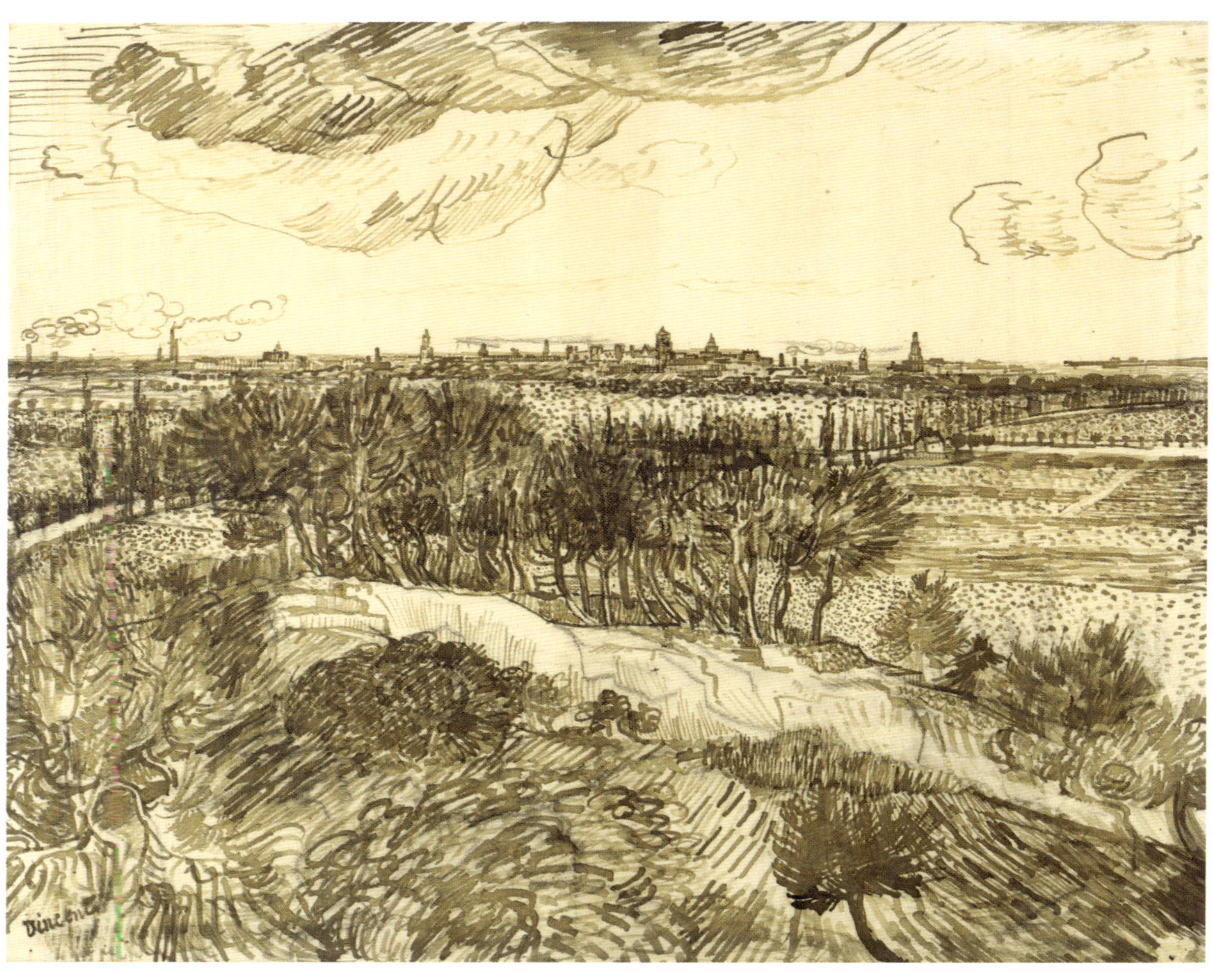

77 *View of Arles from Montmajour*, 27–29 May 1888. Pen and pencil, on paper, 48 × 59 cm (19 × 23¼ in.).
NATIONAL GALLERY, OSLO

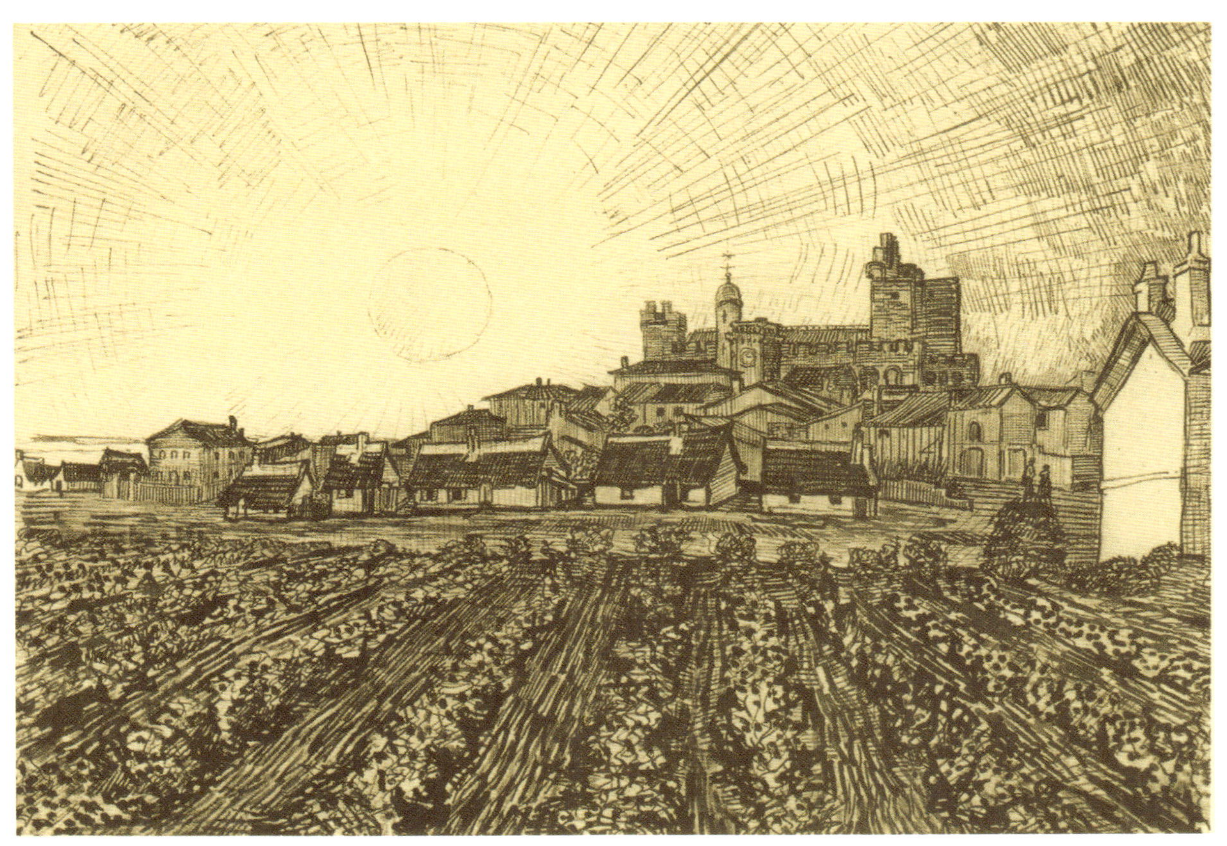

78 *View of Saintes-Maries-de-la-Mer*, 30 May–3 June 1888. Pen and ink, on paper, 43 × 60 cm (17 × 23⅝ in.). OSKAR REINHART COLLECTION 'AM RÖMERHOLZ', WINTERTHUR

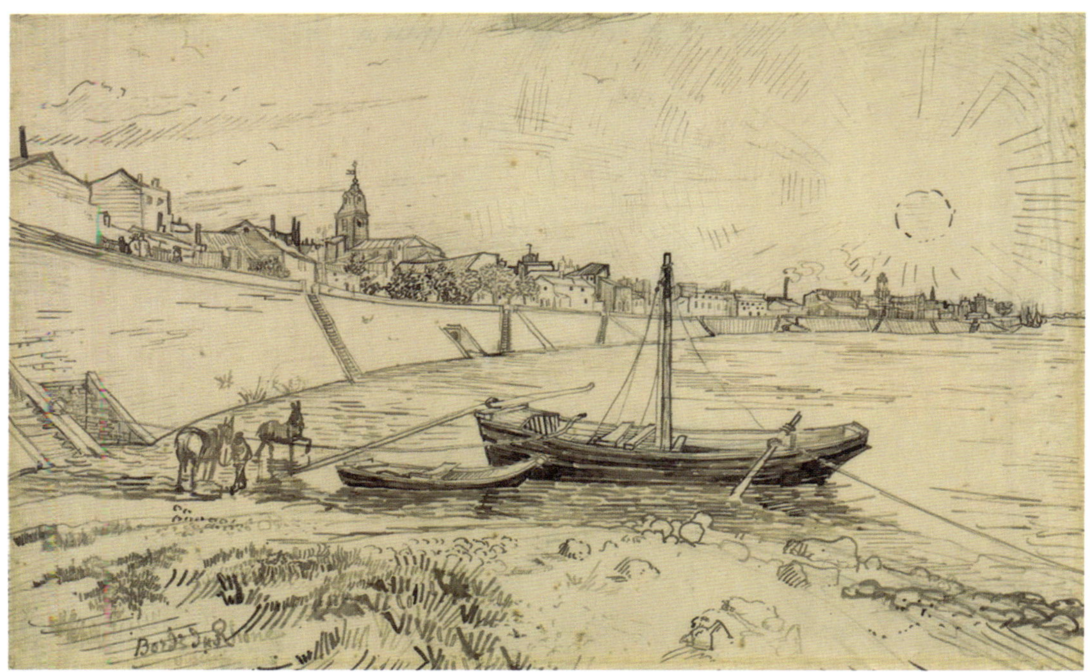

79 *View of Arles on the River Rhône*, April 1888. Pen and brush and brown (originally violet) aniline ink, on paper, 38.5 × 60.5 cm (17 × 23⅞ in.). BOIJMANS VAN BEUNINGEN MUSEUM, ROTTERDAM

golden harps to sing praises withal'. It should be remembered, however, that, whatever private allusions the sun might have had for Van Gogh, several of his avant-garde contemporaries, including the philosophical anarchists Pissarro and Signac, interpreted it differently, using the sun in their art politically, as a symbol of the overthrow of the old order and the creation of a new world.

Rather than concentrating on the historical landmarks of the town, Van Gogh chose to represent in his drawings the more dynamic modern aspects of life in Arles. The activities on and off both the river and the canals – boats, washerwomen, bridges, trains, gasworks, factory chimneys – absorbed his attention (Fig. 79). Balancing these sporadic representations are motifs inspired by the public gardens that had been established in 1872 in the place Lamartine in the north of the town, near the railway station (Figs 80 and 150–52). Here Van Gogh exploits the dynamic of urban versus rural, and he depicts the public gardens either altogether devoid of human interest or populated with strolling figures, which he then allowed his imagination to identify with the spirits of Petrarch, Boccaccio and Dante, whom he associated with the town. Four of the paintings of the gardens were titled in a metaphoric vein *The Poet's Garden* and were intended to decorate Gauguin's bedroom when and if he arrived to join Van Gogh in the 'Studio of the South'.

Van Gogh's wish to establish a 'Studio of the South' was given greater credence by his renting the Yellow House at 2 place Lamartine in early May 1888. He repaired, decorated and furnished the house himself in preparation for the arrival of other artists, particularly Gauguin, who eventually reached Arles in late October 1888 and stayed for nine weeks, until the end of December. At various stages of planning, Émile Bernard and Charles Laval (1862–1894) were expected to join them. Not only was the Yellow House itself a

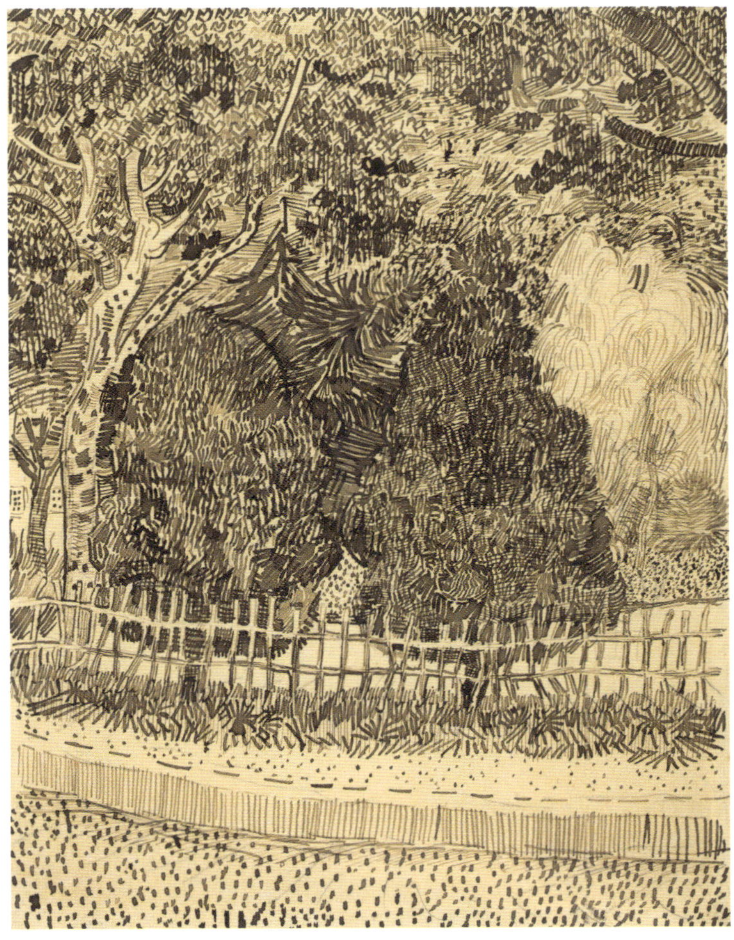

80 *Park with Fence*, September 1888. Pencil, reed pen and ink, on paper, 31.9 × 24.4 cm (12⅝ × 9⅝ in.). VAN GOGH MUSEUM, AMSTERDAM

symbol of Van Gogh's yearning to create an artistic community, but, in the end, as a consequence of the deterioration of his professional and personal relationship with Gauguin, it also signalled the beginning of the decline in his health. Nonetheless, his occupation of the house marked a moment of real independence in Van Gogh's life, giving him security and freedom.

The watercolour Van Gogh made of the Yellow House takes the viewer at last to the centre of Arles and to the heart of his main project there. Proudly, he made both a painting and a watercolour of the house, sending the latter to Theo in early October (Fig. 81). The title is that given by the artist himself. Looking out from one of the public gardens in the place Lamartine, the Yellow House with green door and shutters is centrally placed. The restaurant at which Van Gogh regularly ate is on the left, partly obscured by a tree. The road on the right leading out of town is the avenue de Montmajour. Two railway bridges, the nearest one with a train crossing it, straddle the road. The composition is uncluttered, but the intensity is heightened by the colour contrast of yellow, green and red beneath a canopy of blue sky.

Van Gogh's breakdown in Arles at the end of 1888 led first to his hospitalization in the town, before he admitted himself into the private psychiatric asylum of Saint-Paul-de-Mausole at Saint-Rémy, some seventeen miles (twenty-seven kilometres) to the north-east of Arles, beyond the Alpilles. Although it was not an insignificant place, Van Gogh did not see a great deal of the small town of Saint-Rémy. Severely restricted in his movements at first, he was eventually, if accompanied, allowed to venture further afield, including into the town itself on two occasions. The asylum was a former monastery, dominated by a Romanesque tower and with extensive outbuildings used as wards for the thirty or so men and women undergoing treatment. When Van Gogh arrived, he described the institution as being rather run down. He was assigned two rooms, both on the upper floor but in different wings: one served as a bedroom and overlooked fields and the mountains beyond; the other, as a studio, with a view over the asylum's garden. He was allowed to continue working at the asylum under medical supervision and, while there, created several of his most famous works, including *A Wheatfield, with Cypresses* (National Gallery, London) and *The Starry Night* (Museum of Modern Art, New York).

Van Gogh began working in the overgrown garden of the asylum before moving on to the surrounding wheatfields, olive

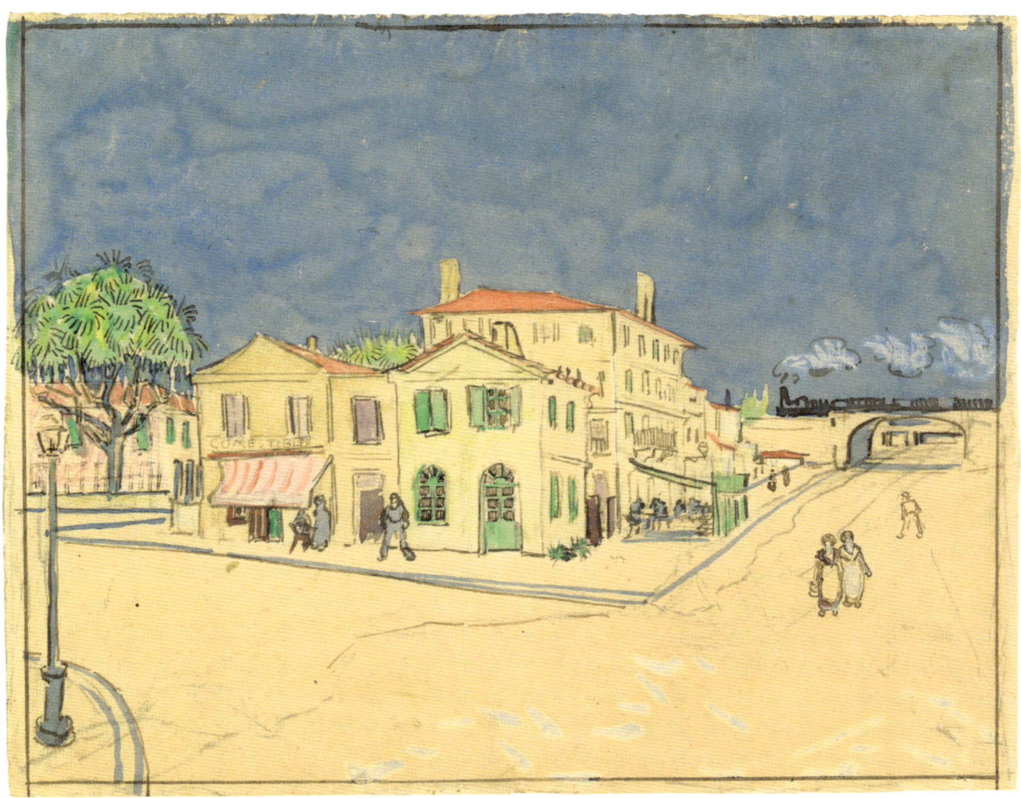

81 *The Yellow House (The Street)*, October 1888. Pencil, reed pen and pen and ink, watercolour, on paper, 25.7 × 32 cm (10⅛ × 12⅝ in.). VAN GOGH MUSEUM, AMSTERDAM

groves, the foothills of the Alpilles and finally into Saint-Rémy itself. But the overwhelming sense of place is best illustrated by the three interior views – *Window in the Studio*, *Vestibule in the Asylum* and *Corridor in the Asylum* – in mixed media of black chalk, brush, oil paint and watercolour (Figs 82–84). *Window in the Studio* (Fig. 82) is an image soaked in the Romantic tradition, as evidenced by comparison with Friedrich's two sepia drawings of 1805/06 of the view from each of his studio windows (Belvedere, Vienna), in which the enclosed space becomes a metaphor for the artist's looking out on the wider world (in Van Gogh's case, from behind bars) in search of the infinite. The bottles and cups on the shelf, the pictures on the wall and the boxes on the table stand in for the artist, as though Van Gogh had just left the room. The view through the window from the studio and the open doors on the ground floor (Fig. 83) are powerful personal reflections on the artist's feeling of

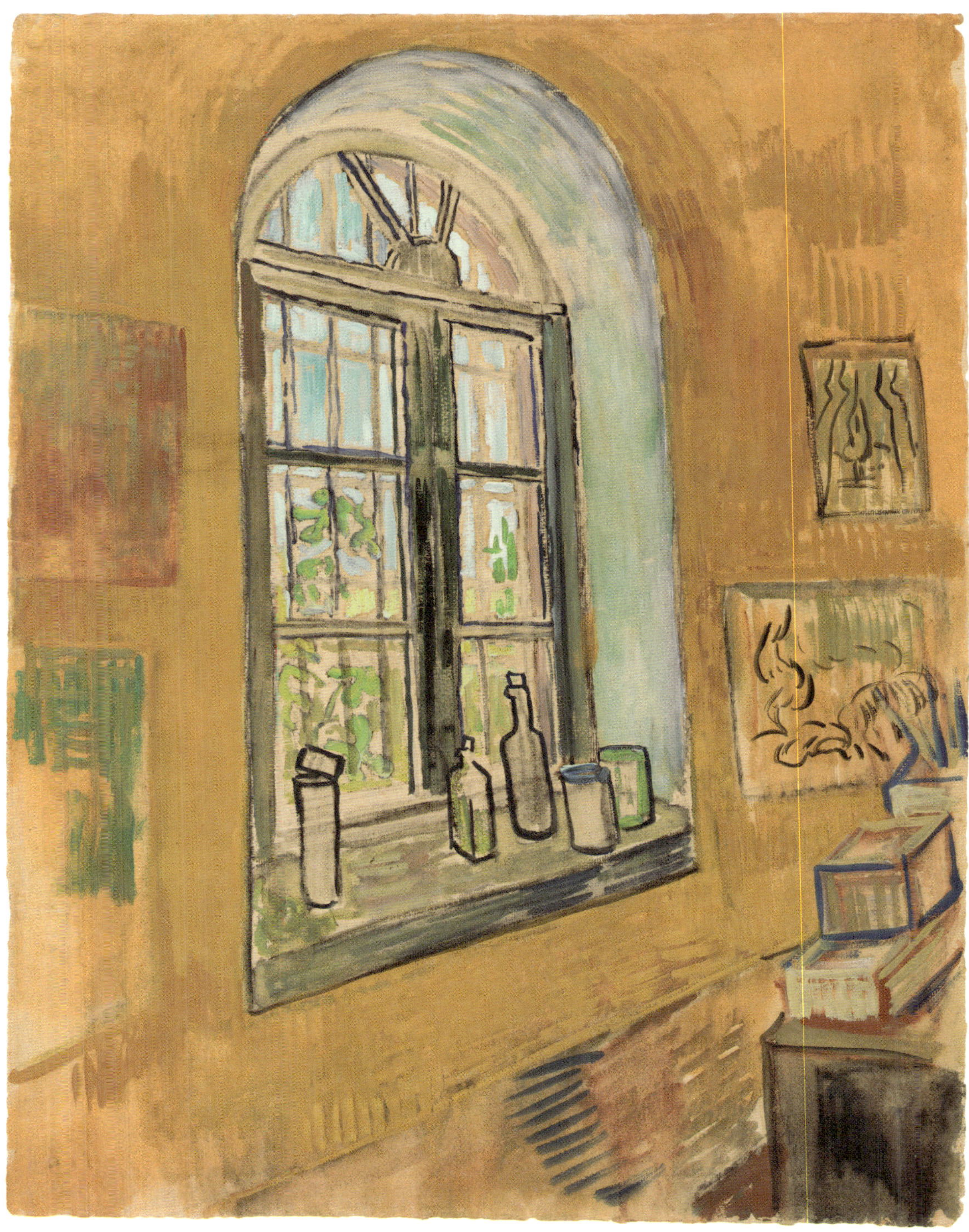

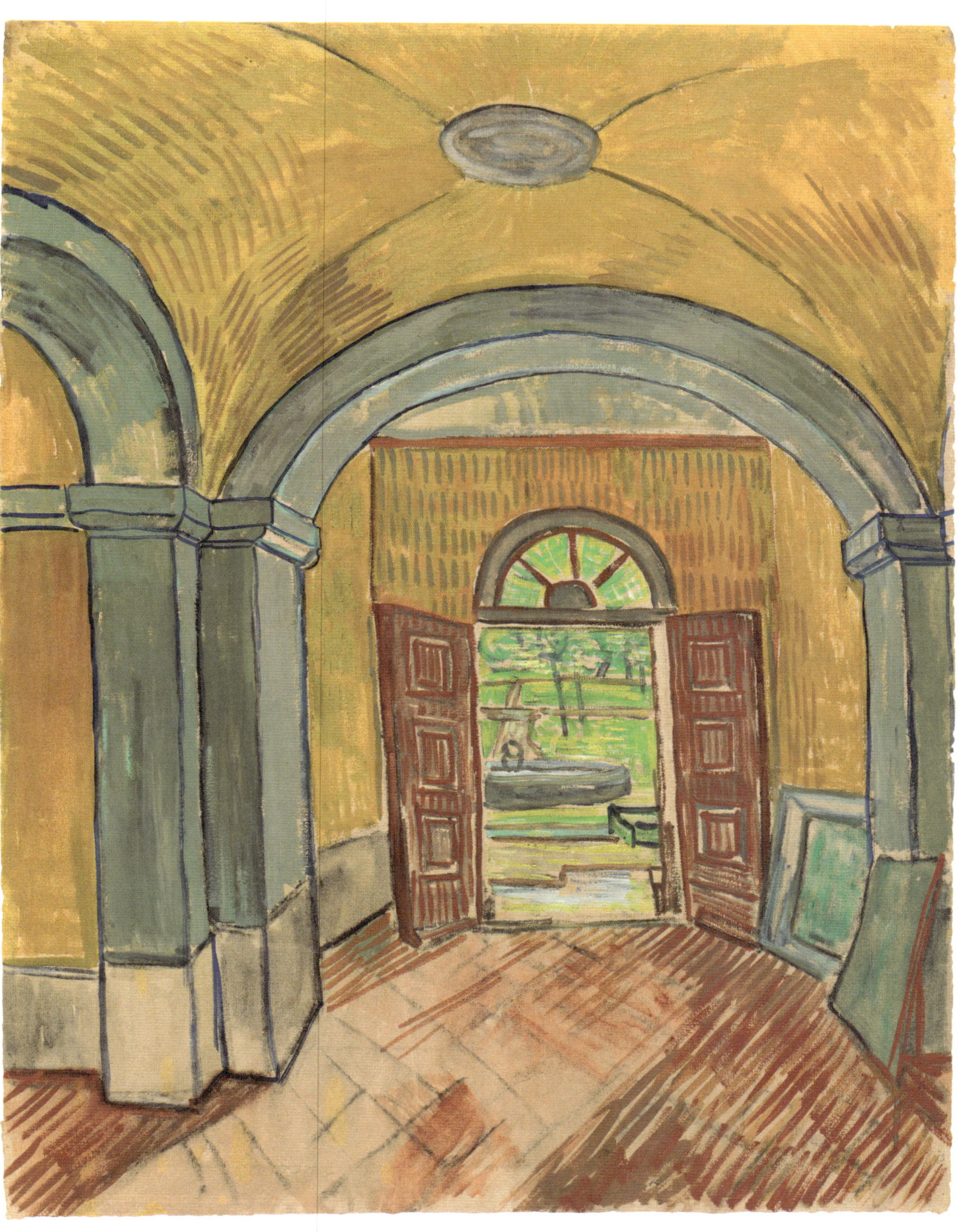

82 (page 11[illegible])
Window in the Studio,
September–October 1889.
Chalk, brush and oil paint
and watercolour, on paper,
62 × 47.6 cm (24½ × 18¾ in.).
VAN GOGH MUSEUM,
AMSTERDAM

83 (page 11[illegible])
Vestibule in the Asylum,
September–October 1889.
Chalk, brush and oil paint,
on paper, 61.6 × 47.1 cm
(24⅜ × 18[illegible] in.).
VAN GOGH MUSEUM,
AMSTERDAM

84 (opposite)
Corridor in the Asylum,
September 1889. Oil paint,
black chalk on pink paper,
61.[illegible] × 47.4 cm (24⅜ × 18¾ in.).
THE METROPOLITAN MUSEUM
OF ART, NEW YORK

confinement – this, after all, is the environment in which he suffered several mental breakdowns during his year's stay. Most evocative is the claustrophobic *Corridor in the Asylum* from which there is no obvious escape (Fig. 84). Indeed, the heavy thick outlines and subdued colour suggest a form of entombment in an enclosed world. It is tempting to interpret these images as an exploration of Van Gogh's own mind, as well as a record of his physical circumstances. Although there are few signs of life, it is not difficult for the viewer to imagine the sounds that echoed in these cavernous spaces. As Van Gogh wrote to his sister Willemien, 'Life isn't always very jolly here, and my companions in misfortune quite often feel bored, but there's a lot of resignation and patience here' (832).

While in the asylum, Van Gogh was more than usually conscious of the rhythm of the day and the cycle of the year. As his condition gradually improved and his thoughts turned towards trying to leave, he began to assess his time in the south: 'My dear brother, I feel I have more confidence in my work than when I left, and it would be ungrateful of me to speak ill of the south, and I confess that it's with great sorrow that I turn my back on it' (870). One of the advantages of having worked in Provence, he felt, was that he would be able to see the north more clearly.

Van Gogh returned to northern France in May 1890. Following Pissarro's advice, he settled in the popular town of Auvers-sur-Oise, close to the larger market town of Pontoise. Paul Alexis a friend of Cézanne, described Auvers-sur-Oise in an article he wrote for *Le Cri du Peuple* (15 August 1887): 'All length, lying along the Oise like a lizard that basks in the sun, set against a long ridge of rocks eaten into by stone quarries, Auvers-sur-Oise . . . extends to some eight or ten kilometres. A large town, with more than two thousand inhabitants in the winter and three thousand each summer, it has nonetheless the general aspect of a small village, thanks to its being spread out.'

Van Gogh found the town pleasing: 'Here we're far enough from Paris for it to be the real countryside . . . there are many villas and various modern and middle-class dwellings, very jolly, sunny and covered with flowers' (875). These, together with the surrounding fields and hillsides, were to be the artist's main subjects in his final frenzy of activity, during the course of which he painted some of his most expressionist works. He lived at the Auberge Ravoux, opposite the town hall. A small drawing of the town hall made in a sketchbook, in preparation for a painting

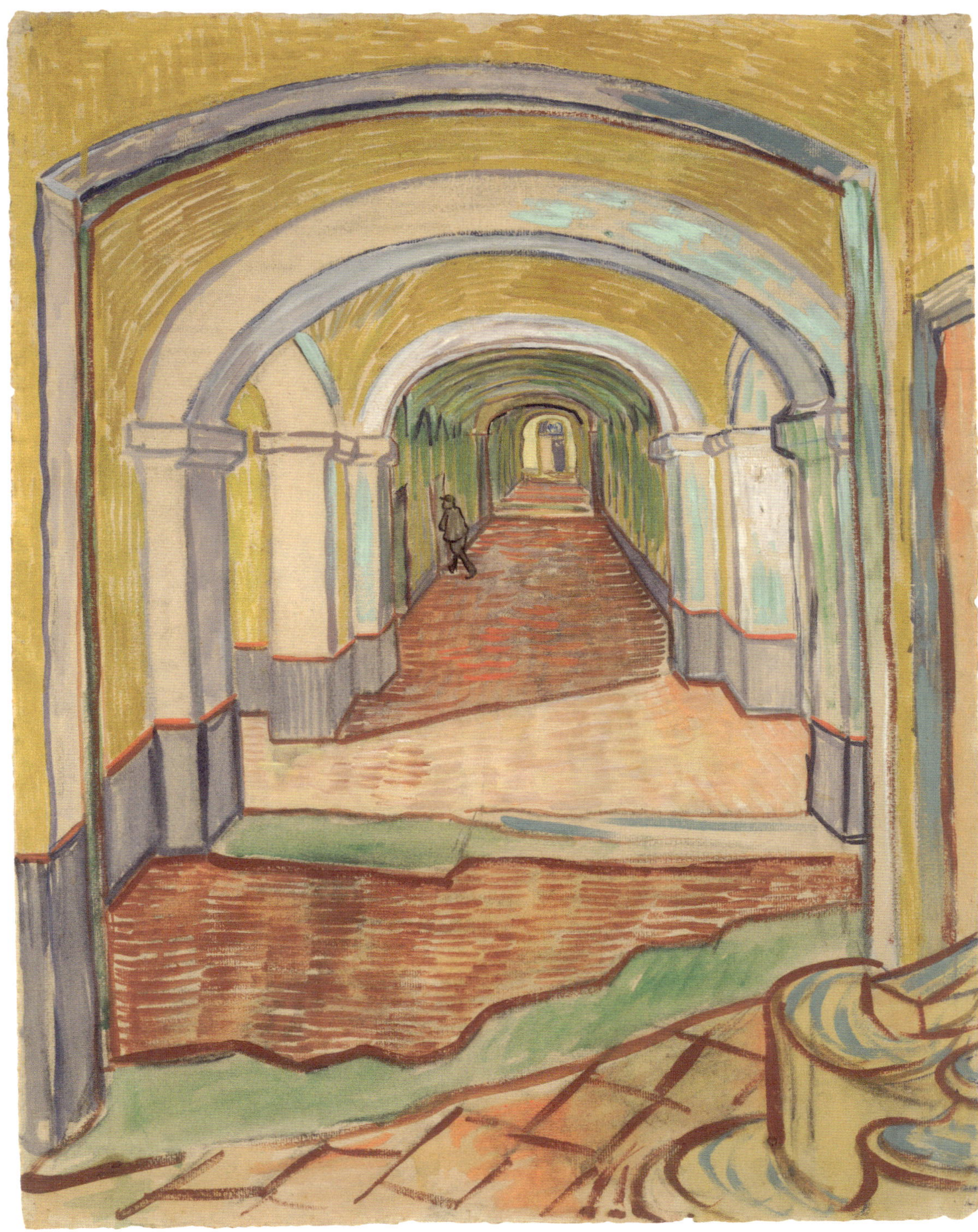

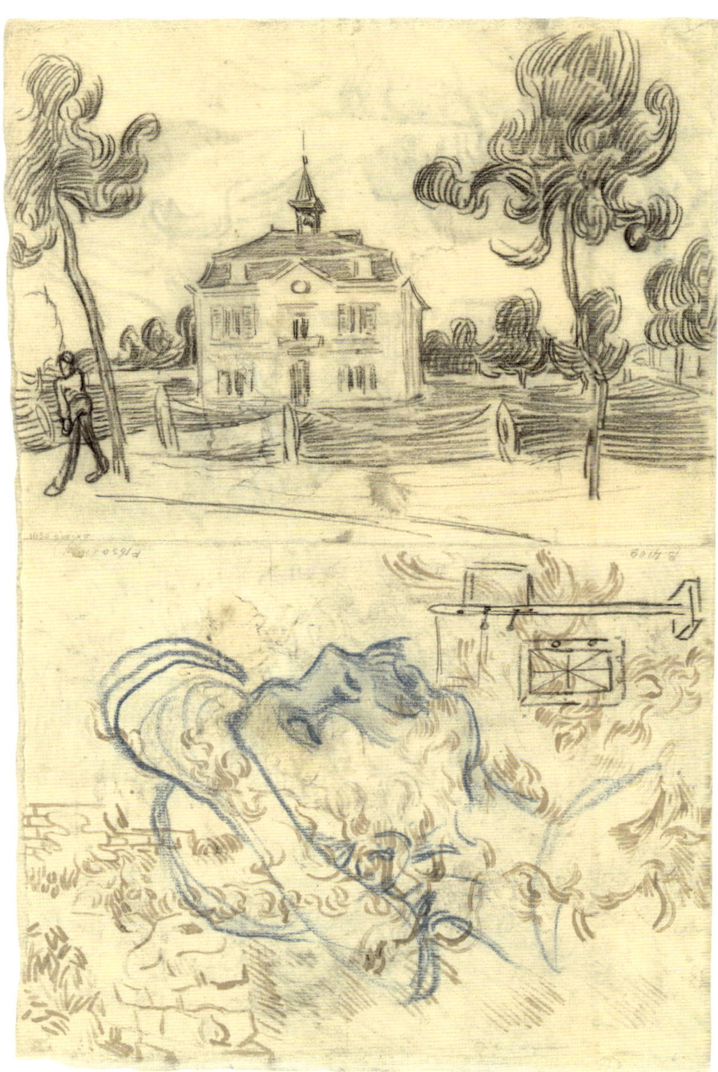

85 *Auvers Town Hall and Head of a Man*, June–July 1890. Chalk on paper, 48.4 × 31.2 cm (19⅛ × 12⅜ in.).
VAN GOGH MUSEUM, AMSTERDAM

(private collection) that shows the building decorated with flags for Bastille Day, is the only acknowledgment the artist made of a public institution in the village (Fig. 85). Far more representative of his time there is *The Oise at Auvers*, a broadly brushed gouache drawing over pencil (Fig. 86). Intensely rhythmical, with flowing horizontal strokes unifying the composition, the scene unfolds across the fields towards the river. A screen of trees in the middle distance obscures the contours of the slopes on the other bank. Yet it is not a completely idyllic scene: an iron suspension bridge, only recently constructed and opened in December 1889, spans the Oise on the right, and behind the trees is a factory. This is not a picturesque view, but a modern one. Furthermore, it is one of the last that Van Gogh looked upon before his death, and it is one that is not far from where he is buried.

86 *The Oise at Auvers*, late May–early June 1890. Pencil and gouache, on paper, 47.8 × 62.8 cm (18⅞ × 24¾ in.). TATE, LONDON

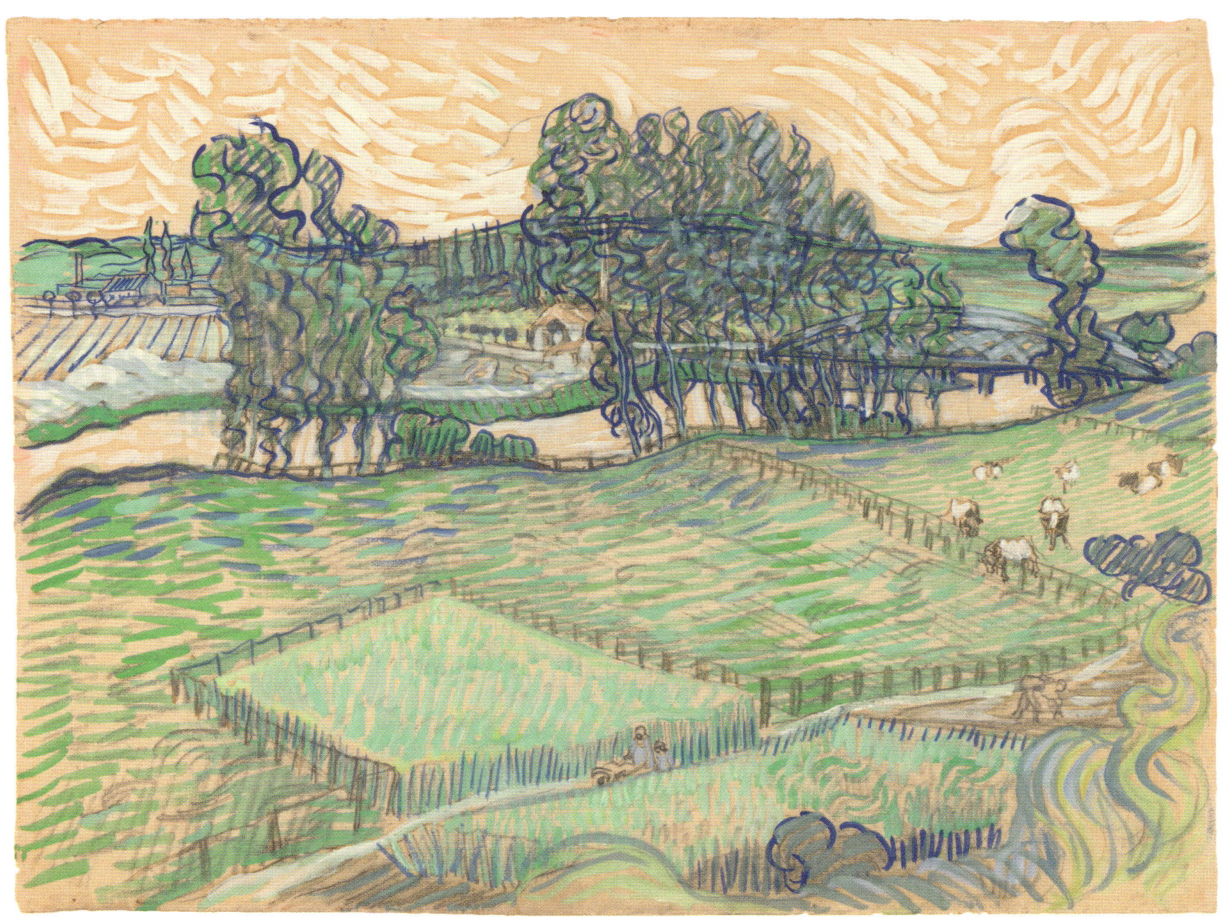

Landscape

Van Gogh was one of the greatest landscape draughtsmen in the history of European art. His skill in depicting nature on paper rivals that of Leonardo, Dürer, Albrecht Altdorfer (*c.* 1480–1538), Pieter Breugel the Elder (*c.* 1525–1569), Rembrandt and Rubens, although sources of inspiration nearer to his own time are to be found among those artists associated with the Barbizon School of painting in France – Millet, Jean-Baptiste Camille Corot (1796–1875), Daubigny, Jacque, Constant Troyon (1810–1865) and Théodore Rousseau (1812–1867). Van Gogh's unique ability was to capture the essence of nature in both northern and southern climes, the differences between them being one of the regular themes of his letters. Also relevant in his letters are the magnificent verbal descriptions of nature and of motifs that he observed in everyday life while in the countryside. Fortunately, in Van Gogh's case, the images he created more than surpassed the words he wrote.

Landscape drawings by Van Gogh form a concerted block of work within his oeuvre. The progress he made in the space of a decade is particularly dramatic, as a straightforward comparison demonstrates. *The Swamp* was drawn when the artist was living in Etten during the early 1880s, while he was receiving some informal instruction from Van Rappard (Fig. 87). For a beginner, such a broad, all-encompassing composition is a brave undertaking, and the determination to succeed is almost palpable. The horizon line divides the scene into two equal parts, which the artist then skilfully unites by the reflections of the sky in the water. The various forms of vegetation are represented by flurries of short pen strokes, with areas of tight cross-hatching. Some of the clouds are curiously shaped, with areas of intermittent cross-hatching. The luminosity of the scene comes from the exposed patches of the paper. Overall, the style of the drawing veers from a rather naive concept of *horror vacui* to dramatic and not unsuccessful attempts at recession and illumination.

By comparison, at the end of his life at Auvers-sur-Oise, Van Gogh often made drawings in the surrounding wheatfields. *Hayricks*

Rock and Ruins, Montmajour, 6–12 July 1888 (detail of Fig. 105).

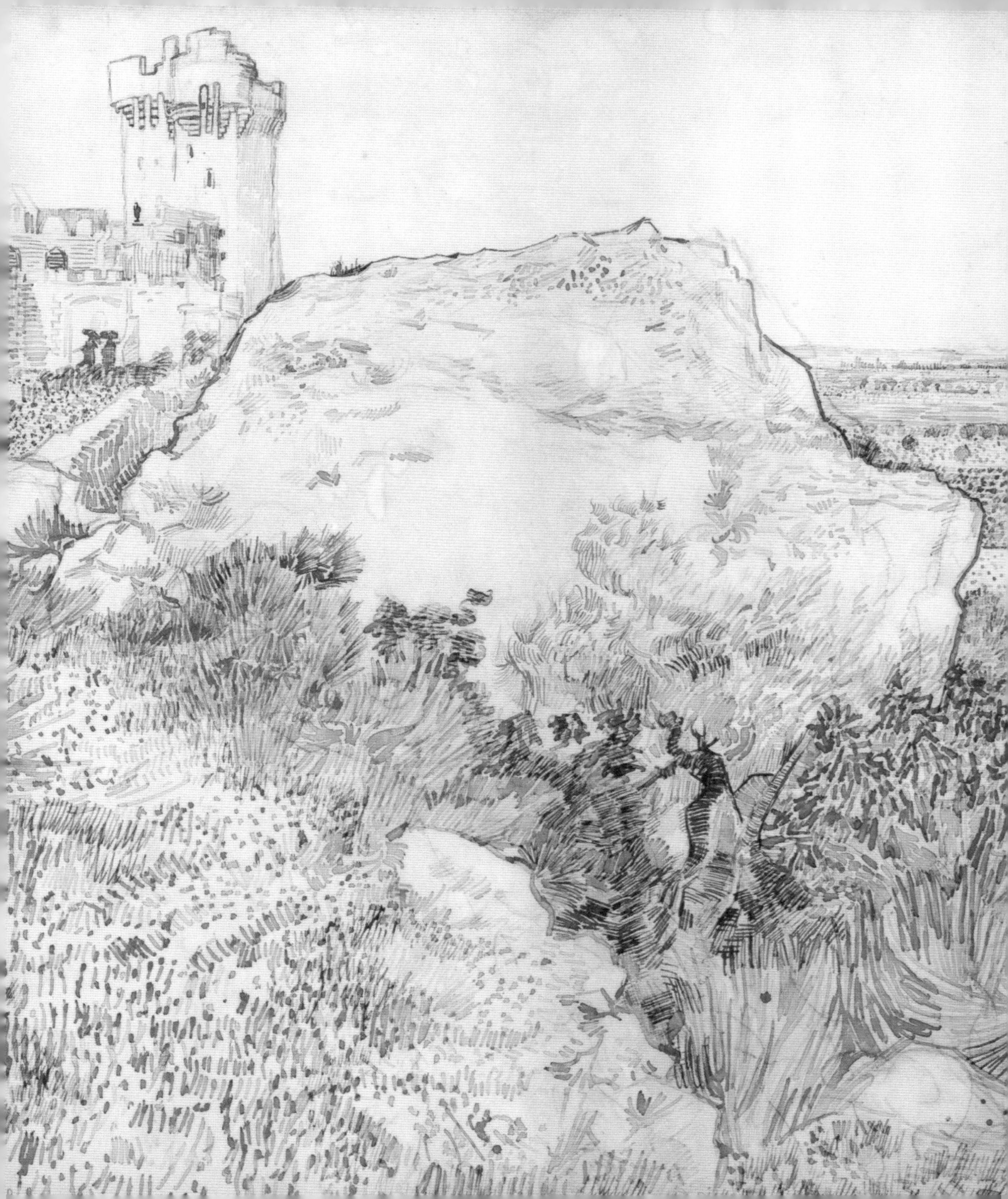

illustrates the extraordinary sophistication that the artist achieved in his final works on paper (Fig. 88). The composition seems to be spontaneous, but it is carefully, even if unconsciously, structured. The hayrick is centrally positioned, although at a slight angle to the picture plane, with the path in the foreground set on a shallow diagonal. The whole is unified by the repeatedly rhythmical pen strokes made with the reed pen – some straight, others curvilinear, but all instinctive and effortlessly flowing. More heavily inked strokes provide accents that recede towards the horizon, above which the top of the haystack is silhouetted. Here, too, the paper has a positive role, suggesting in this case the heat of summer. Just as *The Swamp* reveals a beginner's enthusiasm, so *Hayricks* has a lyricism born of a long and careful examination of nature. Most affecting

87 *The Swamp*, June 1881
Pen and ink, pencil, on paper,
46.3 × 59.[illegible] cm (18½ × 23⅜ in.).
NATIONAL GALLERY OF CANADA, OTTAWA

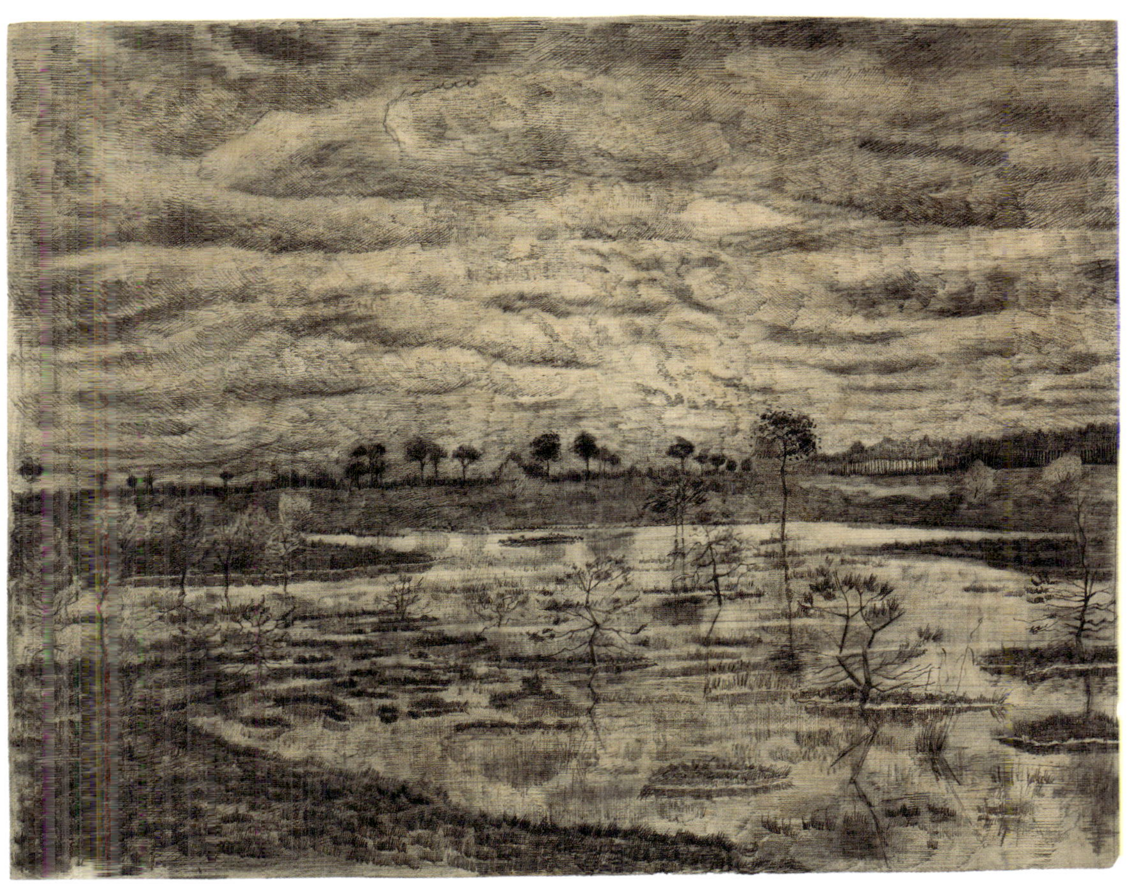

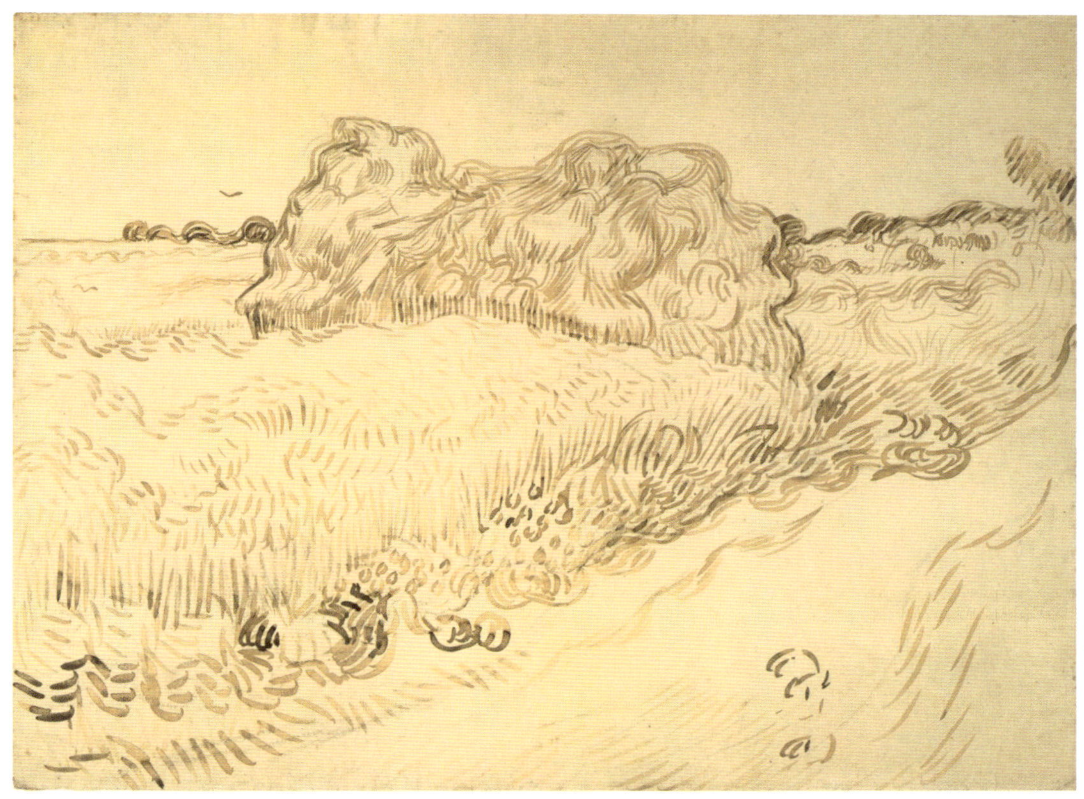

88 *Hayricks*, July 1890. Black chalk, pen and brown ink, on paper, 46.5 × 61 cm (18⅜ × 24⅛ in.).
THE WHITWORTH, MANCHESTER

in *Hayricks,* however, is the feeling of emptiness, which, like the single bird in the sky to the left of the hayrick, might symbolize the artist's sense of loneliness and hopelessness during the final months of his life.

Van Gogh's feeling for nature was such that he became remarkably accomplished as a landscape draughtsman relatively quickly. In August 1881, while travelling by train from Etten to The Hague, he noticed the windmills at Dordrecht, which he thought would be a promising subject for a drawing. When he returned to Dordrecht to pursue the idea, it was a rainy day with an overcast sky. *Windmills at Dordrecht* confirms Van Gogh's skill in judging compositional possibilities and also, again, his preference early on for mixed media (Fig. 89). The foreground is dominated by a curving rustic fence over a ditch. Behind this, across a field, is a path leading to the many windmills spread out along the horizon.

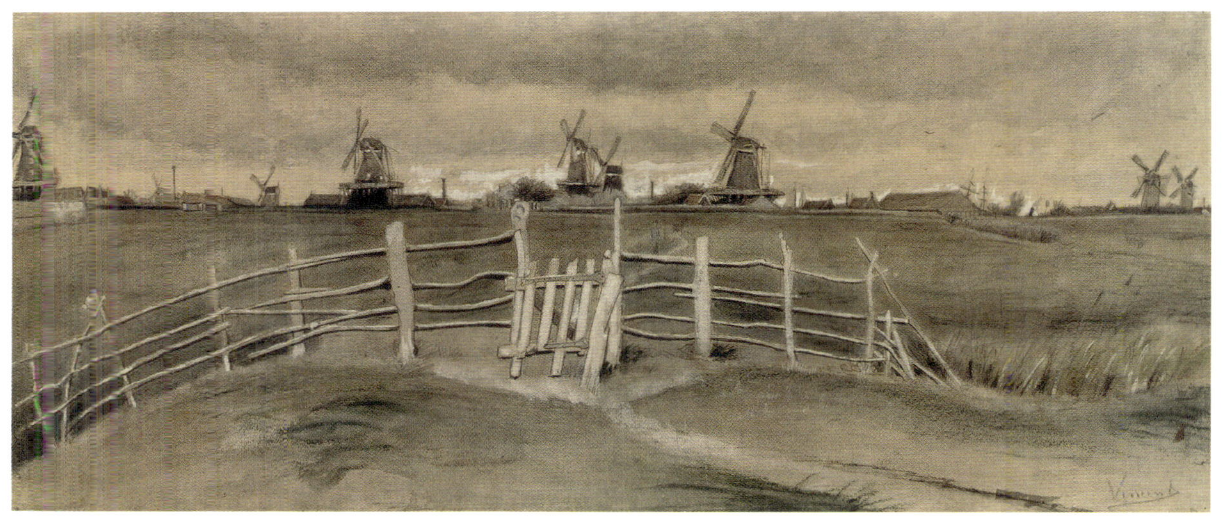

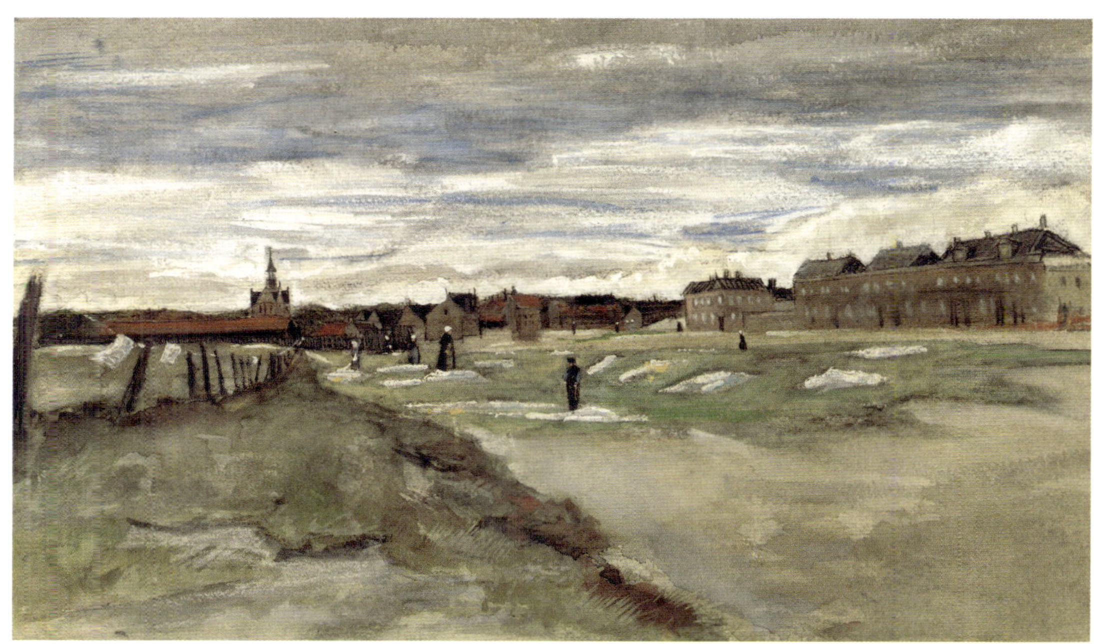

Pencil, combined with pen and ink and black and green chalk, provides the essential outlines, while broader areas of watercolour define the sky, middle distance and foreground. White highlights pick out the fence, the windmills and the distant sky. Van Gogh's facility for controlling wide panoramas, broad masses and minute details is here readily apparent.

The fusion of the various stylistic initiatives taken in Van Gogh's earliest works on paper are developed further in his watercolours dating from his time in The Hague and the province of Drenthe in the north-east of the Netherlands. The increasingly fashionable coastal resort of Scheveningen, close to The Hague, was well known to Van Gogh. The *Panorama* (measuring overall some 46 by 394 feet or 14 by 120 metres) devised by Mesdag and painted in 1880–81 (Museum Panorama Mesdag, The Hague) captures the spirit as well as the physical aspects of the traditional fishing village that was rapidly being transformed into a tourist attraction. Van Gogh's *Bleaching Ground at Scheveningen* depicts a public space in the village set aside for bleaching cloth, with the old church of St Anthony Abbot in the background (Fig. 90). Van Gogh usually favoured opaque watercolour diluted to various strengths rather than transparent watercolour, but here he combines both with great technical dexterity.

During the late summer of 1883, Van Gogh, prompted by Van Rappard, decided to leave The Hague to work in the countryside. The province of Drenthe, close to the German border, was an area notable for its peat bogs and heathland. In winter it presented a particularly bleak and damp landscape in which Van Gogh immersed himself, to the extent that, after only three months, even he was forced to retreat. He lived first at Hoogeveen and then Nieuw-Amsterdam. A long letter to Theo describes the effect that Drenthe had on him: 'When one travels for hours and hours through the region, one feels as if there's nothing but that infinite earth, that mould of wheat or heather, that infinite sky, Horses, people, seem as small as fleas then. One feels nothing any more, however big it may be in itself, one only knows that there is land and sky'. He goes on to describe the end of the day:

> And then, when dusk fell – imagine the silence, the peace of that moment! Imagine, right then, an avenue of tall poplars with the autumn leaves, imagine a broad muddy road, all black mud with the endless heath on

89 *Windmills at Dordrecht*, August–September 1881. Pencil, black and green chalk, wash, pen and brush in ink, and opaque watercolour on laid paper, 25.7 × 59.8 cm (10⅛ × 23⅝ in.). KRÖLLER-MÜLLER MUSEUM, OTTERLO

90 *Bleaching Ground at Scheveningen*, late July 1882. Watercolour heightened with white gouache, on paper, 31.8 × 54 cm (12½ × 21¼ in.). J. PAUL GETTY MUSEUM, LOS ANGELES

91 *Landscape with a Stack of Peat and Farmhouses*, September–December 1883. Watercolour on paper, 41.7 × 54.1 cm (16½ × 21⅜ in.). VAN GOGH MUSEUM, AMSTERDAM

the right, the endless heath on the left, a few black, triangular silhouettes of sod huts, with the red glow of the fire shining through the tiny windows, with a few pools of dirty, yellowish water that reflect the sky, where bogwood trunks lie rotting. Imagine this muddy mess in the evening twilight with a whitish sky above, so everything black on white. And in this muddy mess a rough figure – the shepherd – a throng of oval masses, half wool, half mud, that bump into one another, jostle one another – the flock. You see it coming – you stand in the midst of it – you turn round and follow them.

With difficulty and reluctantly they progress along the muddy road. Still, there's the farm in the distance – a few mossy roofs and piles of straw and peat between the poplars. Again the sheepfold is like a triangle in silhouette. Dark.

The door stands wide open like the entrance to a dark cave. The light from the sky behind shines through the cracks in the boards at the back. The whole caravan of masses of wool and mud disappears into this cave – the shepherd and a woman with a lantern shut the doors behind them. (402)

The watercolour, *Landscape with a Stack of Peat and Farmhouses*, evokes with the utmost conviction the atmosphere of such an evening as described by Van Gogh (Fig. 91). The encroaching darkness, the dampness in the air, the feeling of isolation, the impenetrable silence are all made evident in this broadly brushed, almost saturated sheet.

The penumbral tones of *Landscape with a Stack of Peat and Farmhouses* are in stark contrast with the snow scene of *Drawbridge at Nieuw-Amsterdam*, in which the perspective leads the eye across the empty foreground straight to the drawbridge (Fig. 92). The verticals formed by the single tree on the left and the lamp-post on the right are echoed by the metal posts of the drawbridge, which rises above the roof levels of the houses in the background. The watercolour is sparingly applied throughout, with the foliage that remains on the trees being merely suggested, although the architectural features are more boldly laid in. The spatial intervals are brilliantly implied by the tonal nuances. Not least, there is the lone female figure trudging through the snow in the frosty air, keen to gain the warmth of her

92 *Drawbridge at Nieuw-Amsterdam*, autumn 1883. Watercolour on paper, 40.3 × 82.2 cm (15⅞ × 32⅜ in.). GRONINGER MUSEUM, GRONINGEN

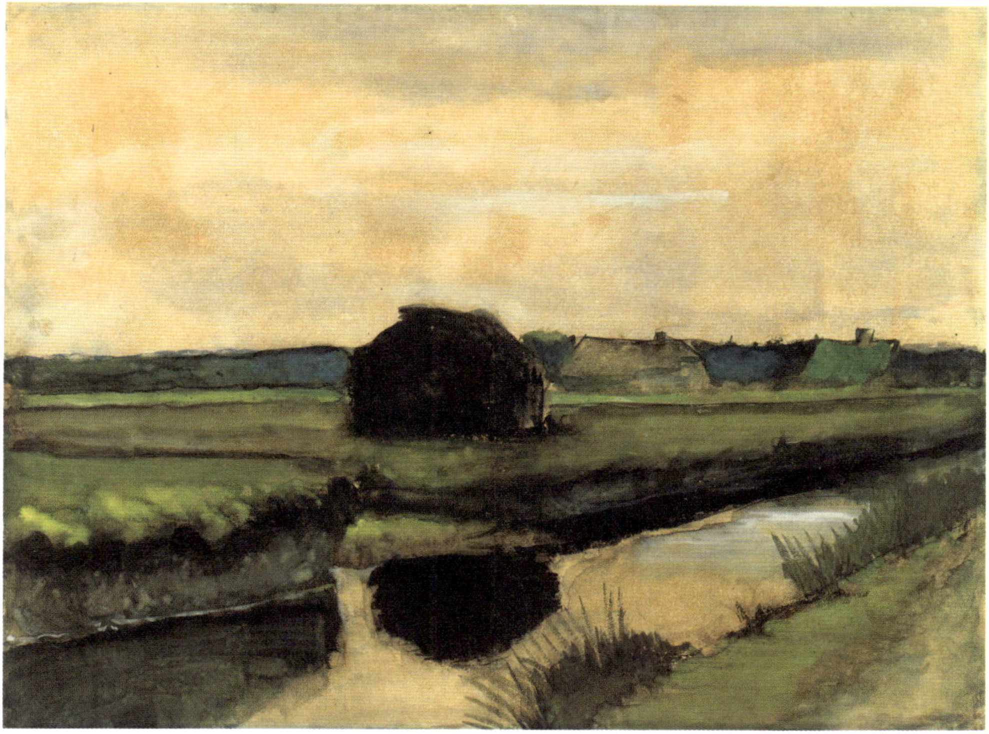

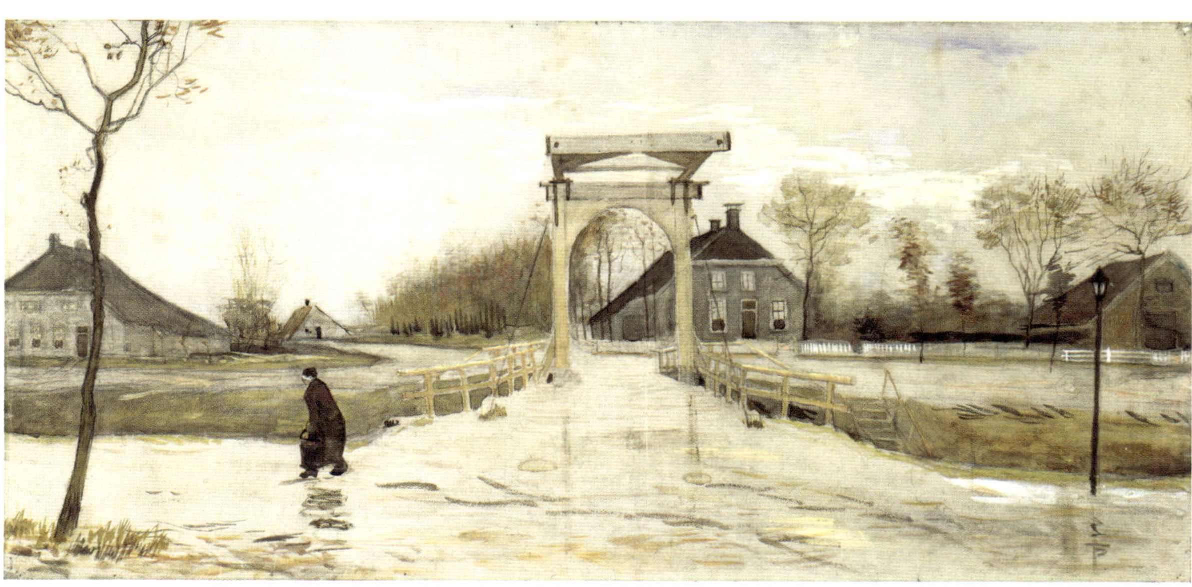

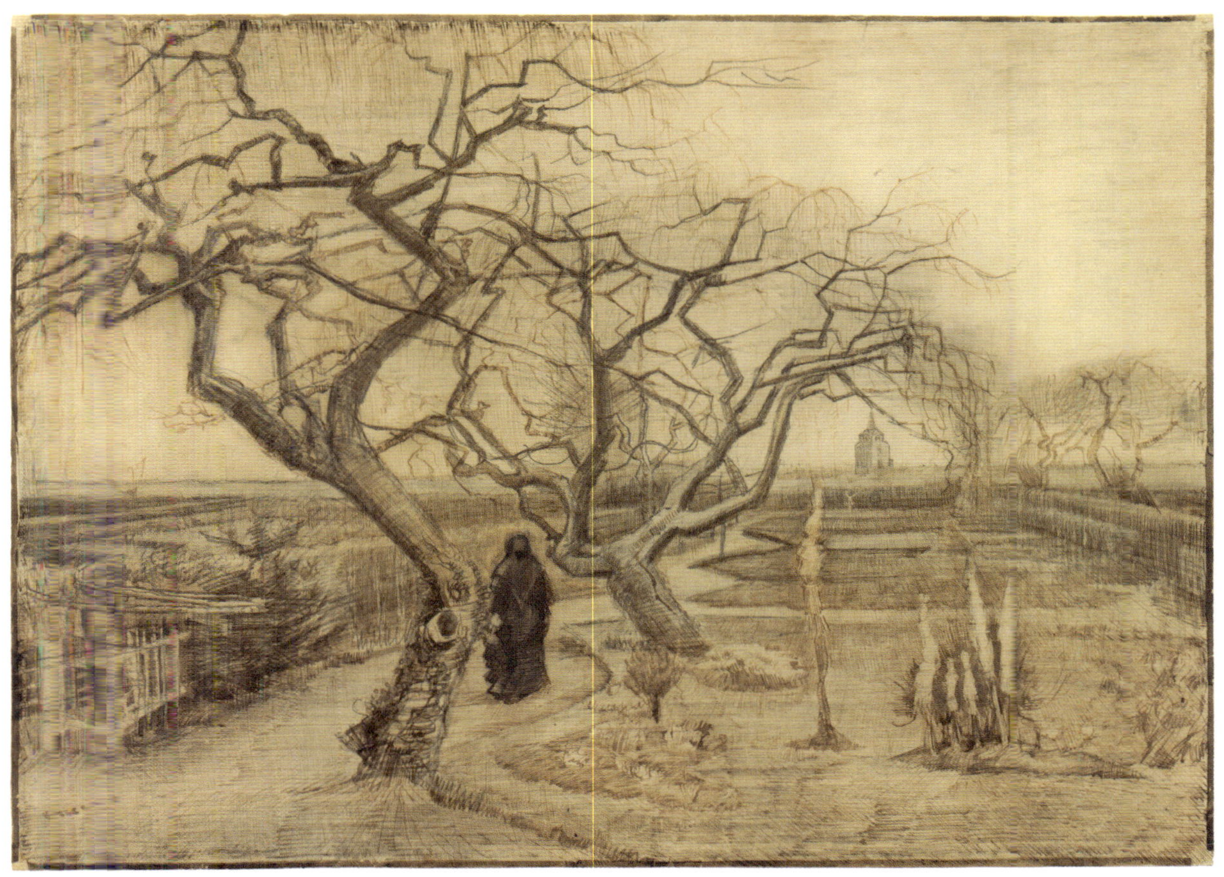

93 *Winter Garden*, March 1884. Pencil, pen and ink, on paper, 40.3 × 54.5 cm (15⅞ × 21½ in.). VAN GOGH MUSEUM, AMSTERDAM

hearth – one of a whole cast in Van Gogh's work of single figures striding along open roads. A recapitulation of the subject of the drawbridge at Nieuw-Amsterdam occurs in Arles, where the artist's fascination with the Langlois Bridge on the south-west side of the town is expressed both in paint and on paper.

The relatively settled period in Nuenen, from December 1883 to November 1885, resulted in one of Van Gogh's most assured series of landscape drawings (probably seven in all), which explored the vicarage garden and surrounding areas (Fig. 93). The drawings are highly finished and deeply committed works, with each composition immaculately wrought and bursting with atmosphere as the season changes from winter to spring. There is immense grandeur in the conception of these drawings, as well as a certain ambiguity in mood, which infuses the images with a literary quality. Even in *The Kingfisher*, where the bird dives into the pond, the viewer is not certain whether the mood is one of melancholy or rapture (Fig. 94). The mesmerising detail in this absorbing series of landscapes is born of meticulous penmanship, and the rich tonal quality is acquired through the commingling of pencil, ink and the restrained use of white heightening. Indeed, the feeling of the rebirth of nature emerging from the iron grip of winter is suggested most acutely in *The Kingfisher* by the delicate flecks of white heightening in the immediate foreground.

The series of landscape drawings done at Nuenen is essentially an expression of Van Gogh's pantheism. He readily acknowledged a close relationship between what he saw in the changing seasons and his own personal feelings. As with the Romantic artists and

94 *The Kingfisher*, March 1884. Pencil, pen and brush in brown ink (originally black), heightened with opaque white paint, on paper, 40.2 × 54.2 cm (15⅞ × 21⅜ in.). VAN GOGH MUSEUM, AMSTERDAM

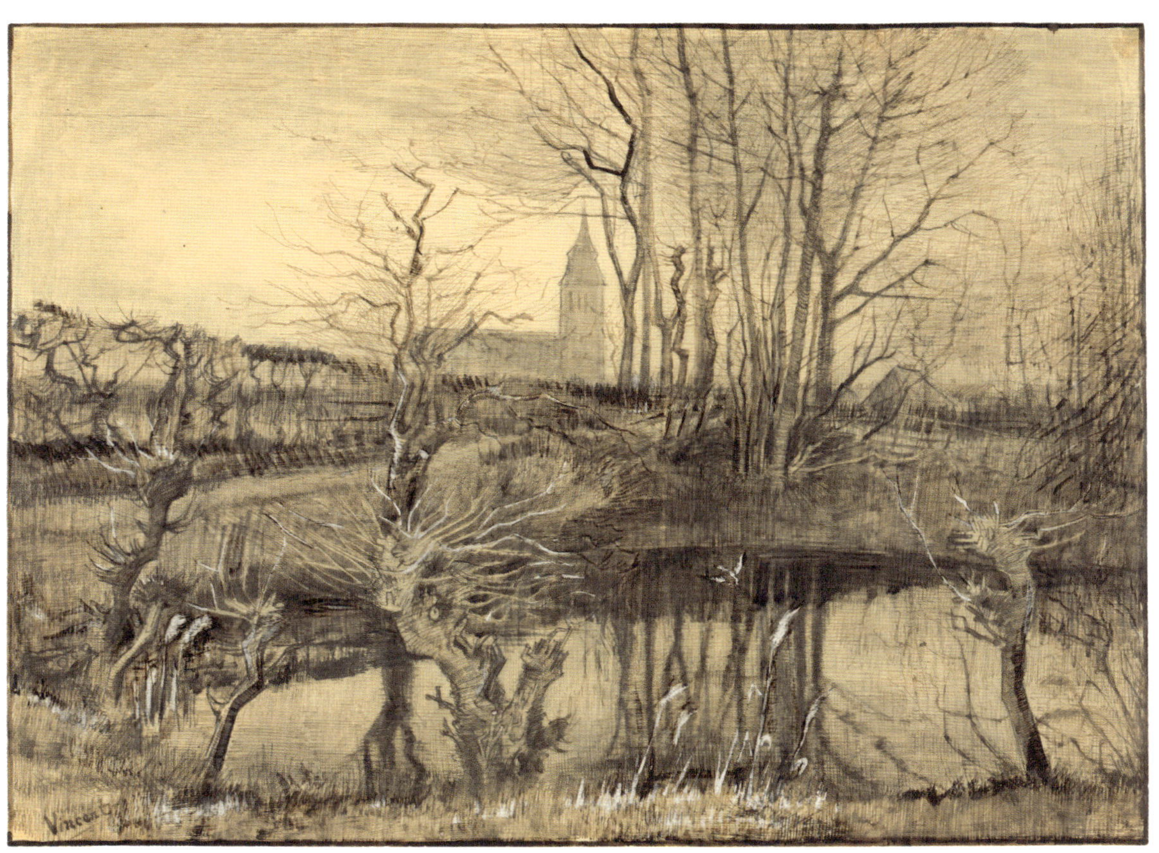

writers at the turn of the eighteenth into the nineteenth century in Europe, Van Gogh empathized so closely with nature that he could impose upon the components of a landscape the emotions of a sentient human being. Some of his drawings of trees, for example, are anthropomorphic, which is a topic that occurs in letters to Theo: 'I feel more and more as time goes on that figure drawing in particular is good, that it also works indirectly to the good of landscape drawing. If one draws a pollard willow as though it were a living being, which it is, then the surroundings follow more or less naturally, if only one has focused all one's attention on that one tree and hasn't rested until there was some life in it' (175). He reiterated this belief a year later, in December 1882, while living in The Hague:

> Sometimes I long so much to do landscape, just as one would for a long walk to refresh oneself, and in all of nature, in trees for instance, I see expression and a soul,

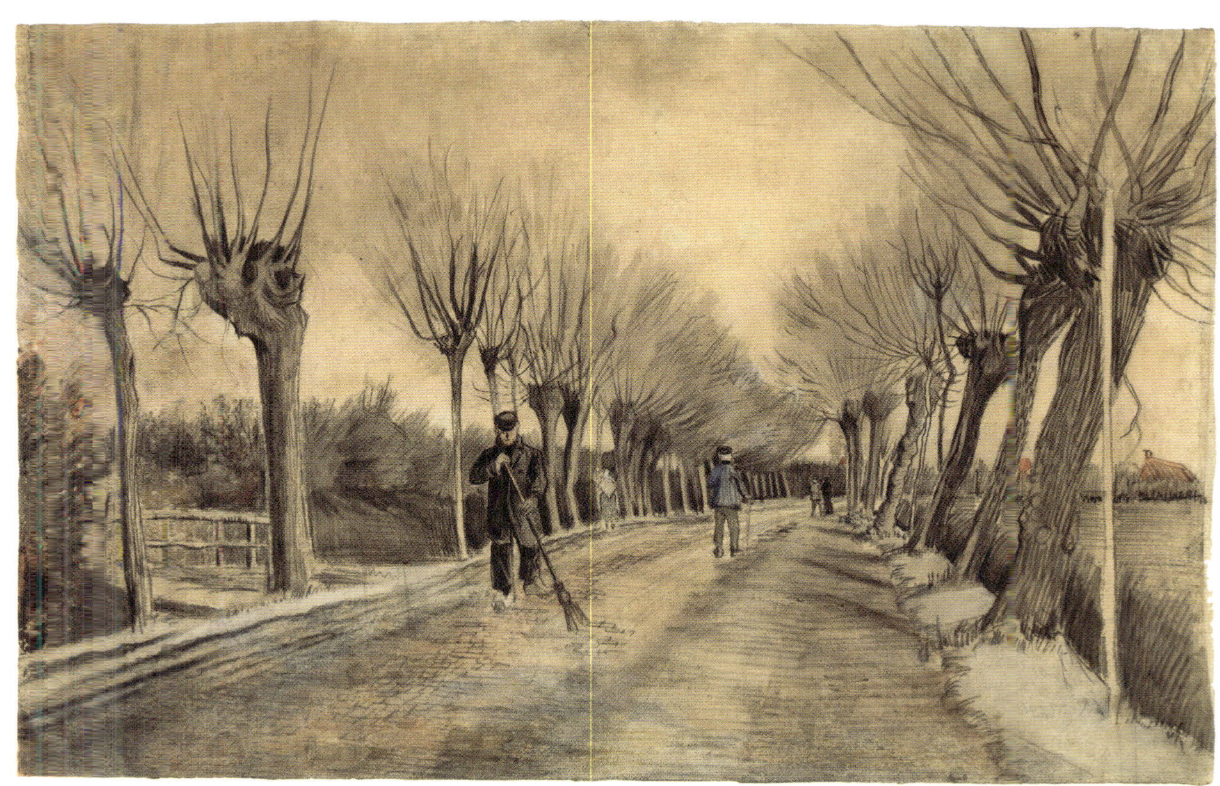

95 *Road in Etten*, October 1881. Black chalk, ink and watercolour over pencil, on off-white paper, 39.4 × 57.8 cm (15½ × 22¾ in.). THE METROPOLITAN MUSEUM OF ART, NEW YORK

as it were. A row of pollard willows sometimes resembles a procession of orphan men [residents of the Dutch Reformed Old People's Home in The Hague].

Young wheat can have something ineffably pure and gentle about it that evokes an emotion like that aroused by the expression of a sleeping child, for example. (292)

An image that reflects the idea of a procession of men resembling a row of pollard willows is *Road in Etten* of 1881 (Fig. 95), but the drawing most obviously related to Van Gogh's ideas about anthropomorphism is *Tree Roots in a Sandy Ground*, a subject that is a visual surrogate for the figure of *Sorrow*, drawn at the same time (Figs 96 and 97). Concerning this juxtaposition he wrote to Theo,

I've tried to imbue the landscape with the same sentiment as the figure.

Frantically and fervently rooting itself, as it were, in the earth, and yet being half torn up by the storm. I wanted to express something of life's struggle, both in that white slender female figure and in those gnarled black roots with their knobs. Or rather, because I tried to without any philosophizing to be true to nature, which I had before me, something of that great struggle has come into both of them almost inadvertently. (222)

The trees in the landscape drawings executed at Nuenen partake of the same thinking, particularly two in the series, both entitled *Winter Garden* (Figs 93 and 98). The branches of the trees bringing new life are not as aggressive as the tentacular shapes in *Tree Roots in a Sandy Ground*, but both human and animal presences and the dilapidated Old Tower in the background underscore the frailty of life and the passing of time. A similar sense of desolation or foreboding is echoed in the early landscape paintings and drawings of Piet Mondrian (1872–1944) (Fig. 99).

The next group of landscape drawings comparable with those done at Nuenen was undertaken in the south of France, in a radically different environment and in entirely different circumstances. It seals Van Gogh's reputation as a landscape draughtsman of the highest calibre and also demonstrates his versatility. In fact, before he experienced the south of France,

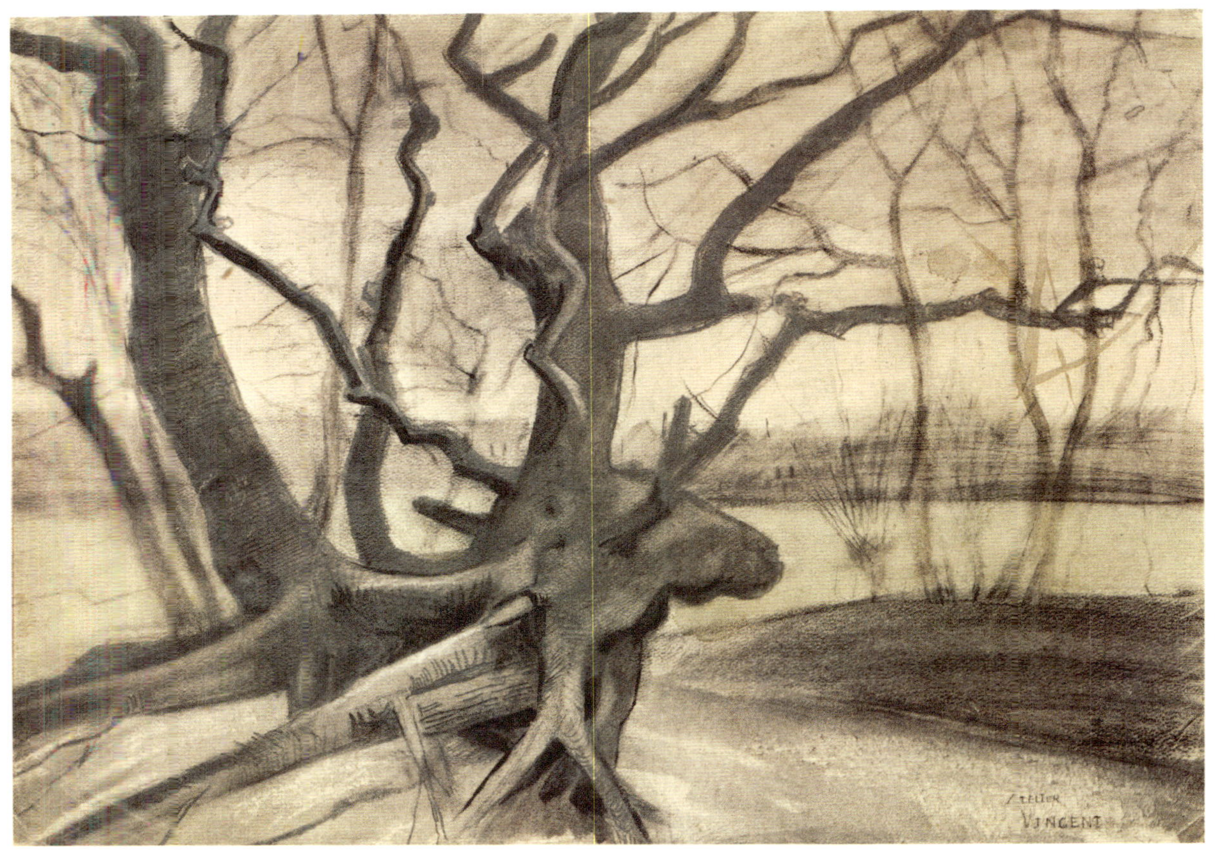

96 *Tree Roots in a Sandy Ground (Les Racines)*, April–May 1882. Pencil, black chalk, brush in ink, brown and grey wash, on paper, 51.5 × 70.7 cm (20⅜ × 27⅞ in.).
KRÖLLER-MÜLLER MUSEUM, OTTERLO

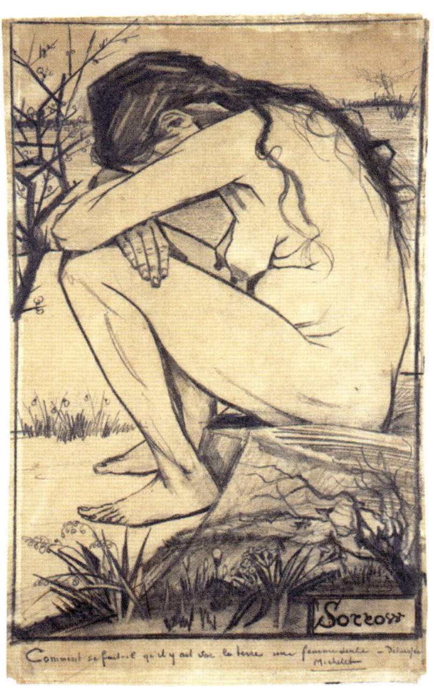

97 *Sorrow*, April 1882.
Pencil, pen and ink, on paper,
44.5 × 27 cm (17⅝ × 10¾ in.).
THE NEW ART GALLERY WALSALL

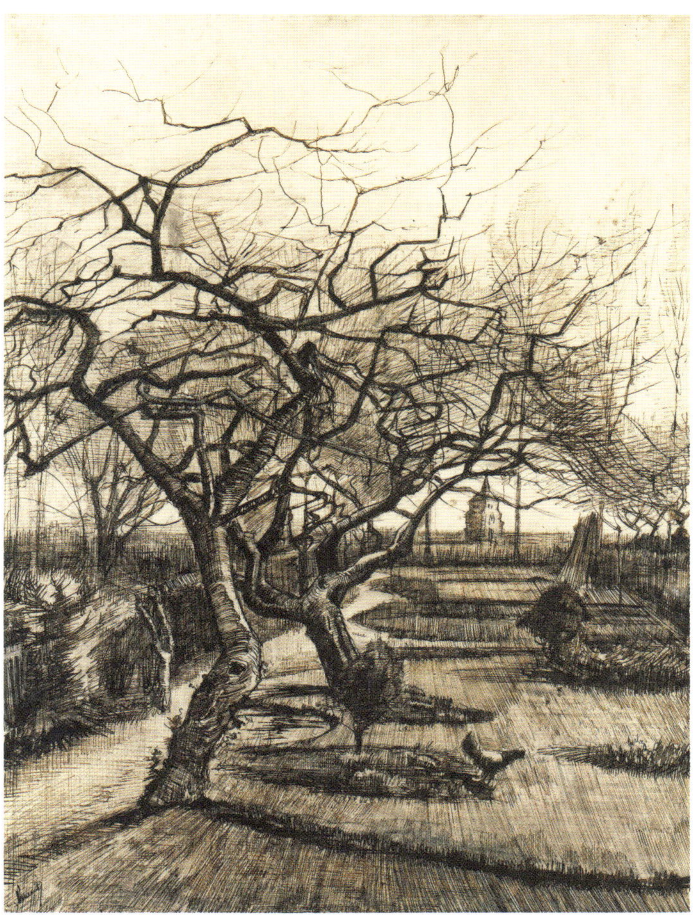

98 *Winter Garden*, March 1884.
Pencil, pen in brown ink
(originally black), on paper,
51.5 × 38 cm (20⅜ × 15 in.).
MUSEUM OF FINE ARTS, BUDAPEST

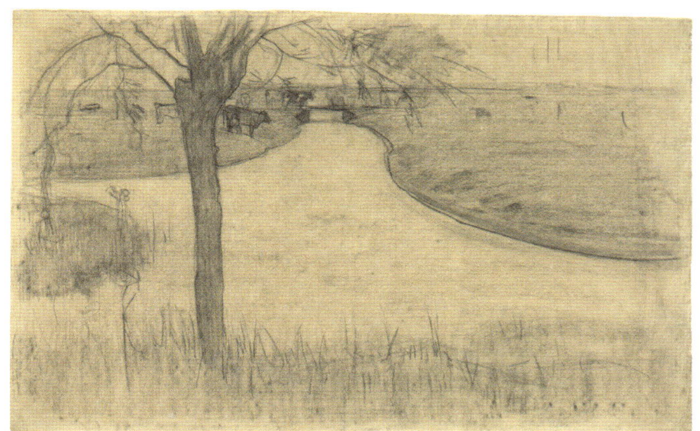

99 Piet Mondrian
Irrigation Ditch with Young Pollarded Willow near Landzicht Farm, 1900. Charcoal on paper,
39.2 × 61.6 cm (15½ × 24⅜ in.).
BRITISH MUSEUM, LONDON,
PROMISED BEQUEST

he had only read about it in the novels of Alphonse Daudet, particularly the humorous adventure stories featuring the hero Tartarin (*Tartarin de Tarascon* of 1872 and *Tartarin sur les Alpes* of 1885). His expectations, therefore, were based on a fictitious character full of bonhomie and optimism. He later described many times the differences between the terrains of the north and the south, as in a reflective letter to his mother, written retrospectively while in the asylum at Saint-Rémy:

> It occurs to me that in the summer it's not much hotter than at home as regards being bothered by it, since the air here is clearer and purer. What's more, we very often have a strong wind, the mistral. I've painted in the wheatfields during the hottest part of the day without it bothering me much. But one can sometimes see that the sun can be quite strong from the way the wheat turns yellow so quickly. But the fields at home are infinitely better farmed, more regularly than here, where the rockiness of the soil in many places means it's not suitable for everything.
>
> There are very beautiful fields of olive trees here, which are grey and silvery in leaf like pollard willows. Then I never tire of the blue sky. One never sees buckwheat or rape here, and generally speaking there's rather less variety than at home. . . .
>
> But what are beautiful in the south are the vineyards, where they're on the flat land or the hillsides. . . . I like to see a vineyard as much as a wheatfield. Then the hills here, full of thyme and other aromatic plants, are very beautiful, and because of the clarity of the air one can see from the heights so much further than at home. (788)

Van Gogh was surprised that there was snow on the ground after his train journey from Paris in February 1888, and a period of adjustment was needed. No doubt this encouraged the internal dialogue he had about the contrast between north and south that persisted throughout his stay in Provence. Four months after his arrival he told Theo, 'Here – except for a more intense colour, it reminds one of Holland, it's all flat – only one thinks more of the Holland of Van Ruisdael and Hobbema and the Ostades rather than the Holland of today. What amazes me is how few flowers there are, so no cornflowers in the wheatfields, seldom any poppies'. Further on in the letter there is a hint of disillusionment: 'I don't find the southern gaiety here that Daudet talks about so much, on the contrary, an insipid affectation, a sordid carelessness, but that doesn't mean that the region isn't beautiful' (630).

At first, Van Gogh tended to translate compositions or themes he had tested out earlier in the north to his new surroundings, as in *The Road to Tarascon with a Man Walking* (Fig. 100), in which a lone figure strides out purposefully along a wide, tree-lined avenue set on a shallow diagonal. Compositional indications have been made in this drawing in pencil, but the penwork in all its variety is predominant and signals the artist's preference in the south for the reed pen. One of the reasons for this preference was that the reeds found in Provence were better suited to Van Gogh's mature style of drawing than those to which he had access in the

100 *The Road to Tarascon with a Man Walking*, April 1888. Pencil, quill and reed pen in brown ink, on paper, 25 × 34 cm (9⅞ × 13½ in.). GRAFISCHE SAMMLUNG, KUNSTHAUS ZÜRICH

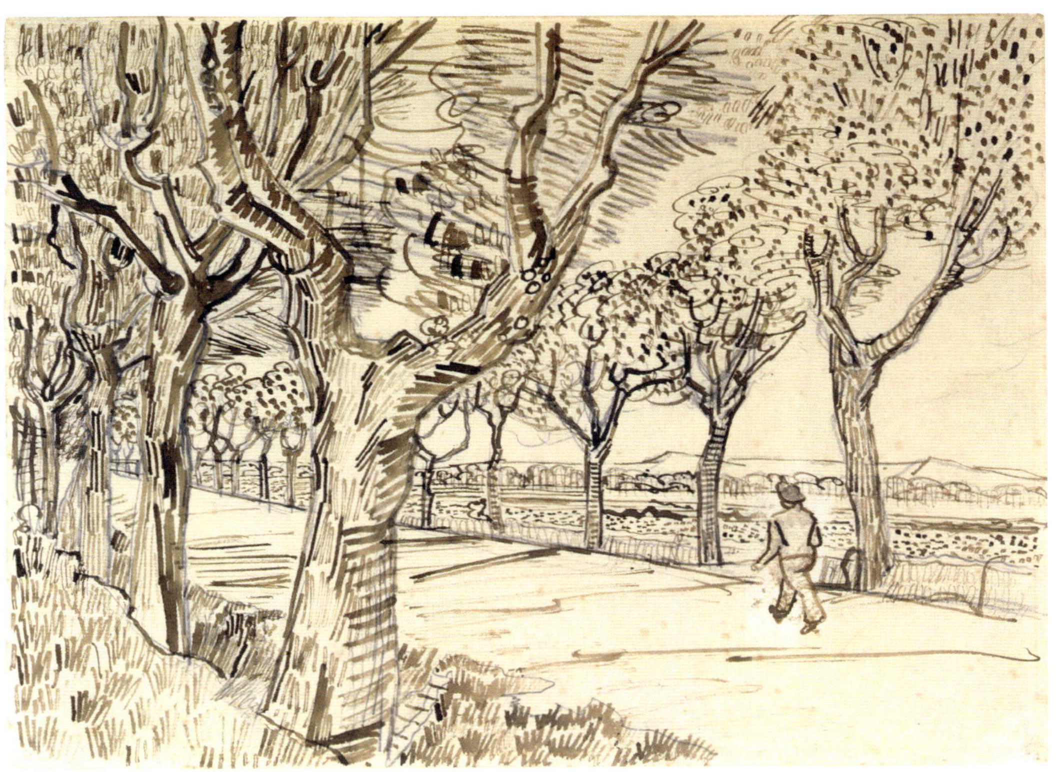

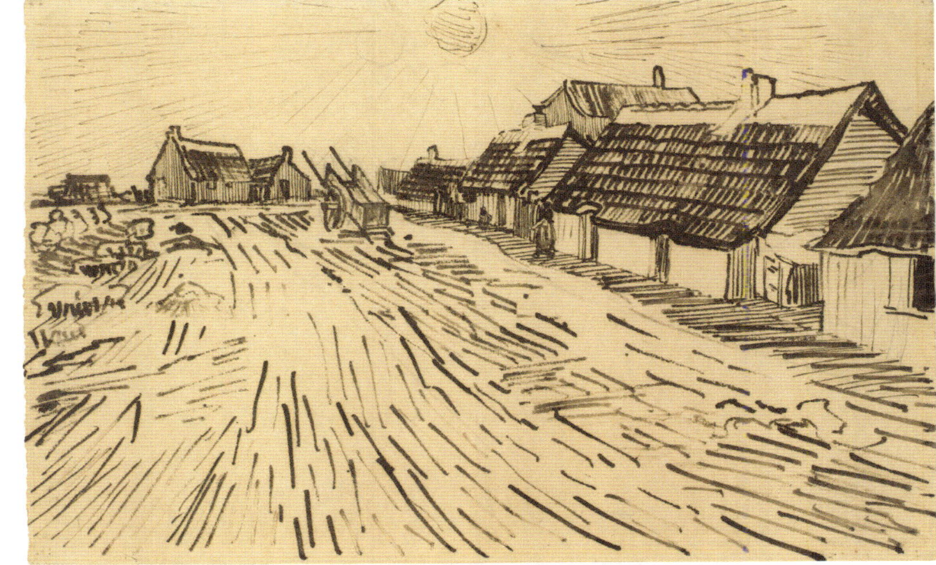

101 *Houses in the Sun in Les Saintes-Maries-de-la-Mer*, May–June 1888. Pencil, pen and reed pen, brush and ink on paper, 30.[illegible] × 47.2 cm (12 × 18⅝ in.)
VAN GOGH MUSEUM, AMSTERDAM

north. The broader points characteristic of reed pens, however, eventually split under pressure, and so only at the start could they be fully controlled by the artist. Although pencil is still evident and undoubtedly remains part of the process, it is the pen – both the reed and the quill – that has the major role during the late 1880s. The drawings made at Saintes-Maries-de-la-Mer (Fig. 101), among many others, testify to this commitment, thereby fulfilling the artist's intention 'to arrive at a more deliberate and exaggerated way of drawing' (617). This aim was pursued systematically while he was in Provence and was determined in part by the policy of producing finished drawings that could be sent to Theo in Paris for sale.

Significantly, the road in Arles that Van Gogh nominates as the road to Tarascon was, in fact, the avenue de Montmajour. This leads across the plain of La Crau to a rocky hilltop with the extensive remains of the Benedictine Abbey of Montmajour dating mainly from the twelfth to the fourteenth centuries. Van Gogh virtually ignored the buildings themselves but admired the site, which afforded wonderful views of the small town of Fontvieille to the north and the larger town of Arles to the south, as well as of the flat expanse of La Crau. When he first discovered Montmajour, the artist reported to Theo, 'I have seen lots of beautiful things – a ruined abbey on a hill planted with hollies, pines and grey olive trees' (583). But, partly owing to the cold, he did not make his first drawings there until May. Seven, of relatively small dimensions (half-size sheets of paper), were made as a start and were originally intended to be presented to Gauguin as a group, in the form of a folded-paper book in the Japanese style. These drawings were made with aniline ink, which is particularly fugitive, and so they are badly faded, but *View of La Crau* is sufficiently well preserved to reveal Van Gogh's skill at capturing the essence of a panoramic view on paper (Fig. 102). The viewpoint is on the slopes of Montmajour, looking south towards the Mont de Cordes, with the plain of La Crau beyond. The variety of pen strokes is prodigious: bold marks emphasize the shrubs and rocks in the foreground; more schematized lines represent the vineyards and fields in the middle distance; tiny blobs with delicate hatching suggest remoter parts. There is a concision and specificity in the style that matches Rembrandt's ability to submit a landscape to close visual analysis.

102 *View of La Crau*, May 1888. Pencil, pen, reed pen and ink, on paper, 30.9 × 47.7 cm (12¼ × 18⅞ in.).
MUSEUM FOLKWANG, ESSEN

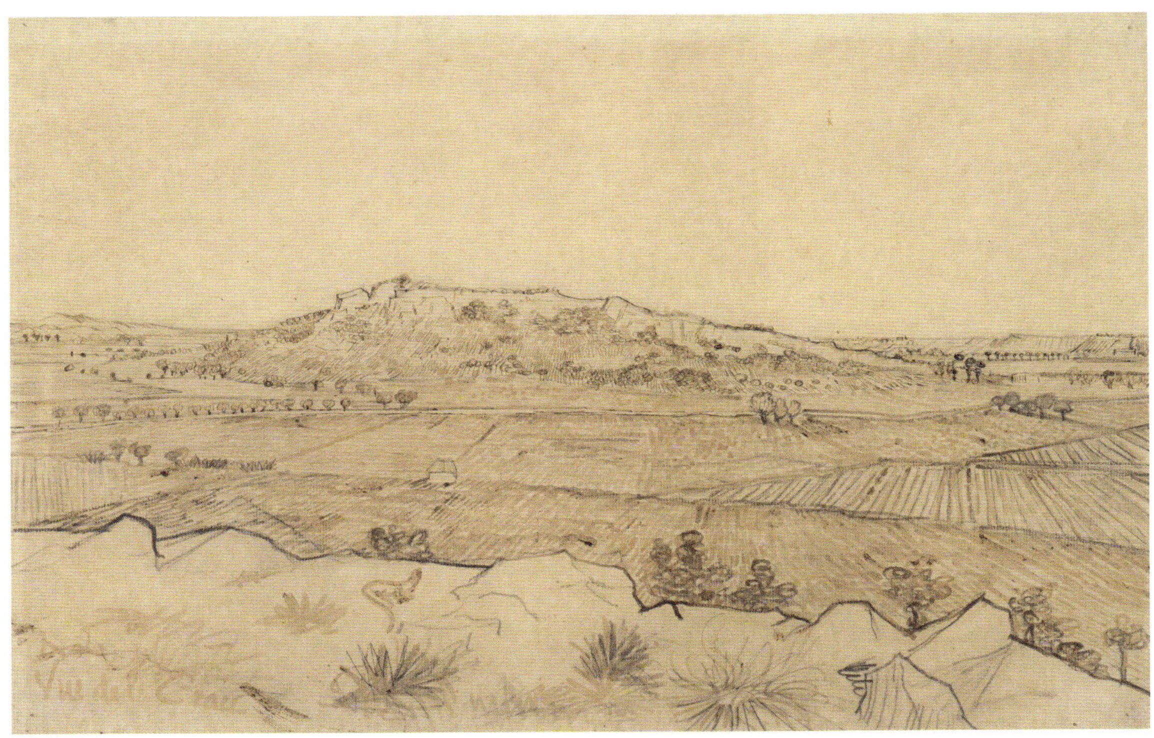

Van Gogh's second and definitive campaign at Montmajour was conducted in early July, when he had to battle against the heat, the mistral and the mosquitoes with only bread and milk for sustenance. There was, in addition, a greater sense of purpose about this series, since Gauguin had confirmed that he would be coming to join the artist in Arles in the near future. If sold, the drawings that Van Gogh now undertook would, therefore, help to fund Gauguin's much heralded trip. In scale and ambition these works amount to surrogate paintings. Within a week, Van Gogh had completed five full-scale drawings (out of a projected group of six), comprising what the artist termed 'the epitome of a really beautiful corner of Provence' (637). These encompass a more thorough examination of Montmajour itself: further exploration of the ruined abbey and its garden had resulted in the discovery of 'tall reeds, grape vines, ivy, fig trees, olive trees, pomegranate trees with fat flowers of the brightest orange, hundred-year-old

103 *The Rock of Montmajour with Pine Trees*, July 1888. Pencil, pen, reed pen and brush and ink, on paper, 49.1 × 61 cm (19⅜ × 24⅛ in.). VAN GOGH MUSEUM, AMSTERDAM

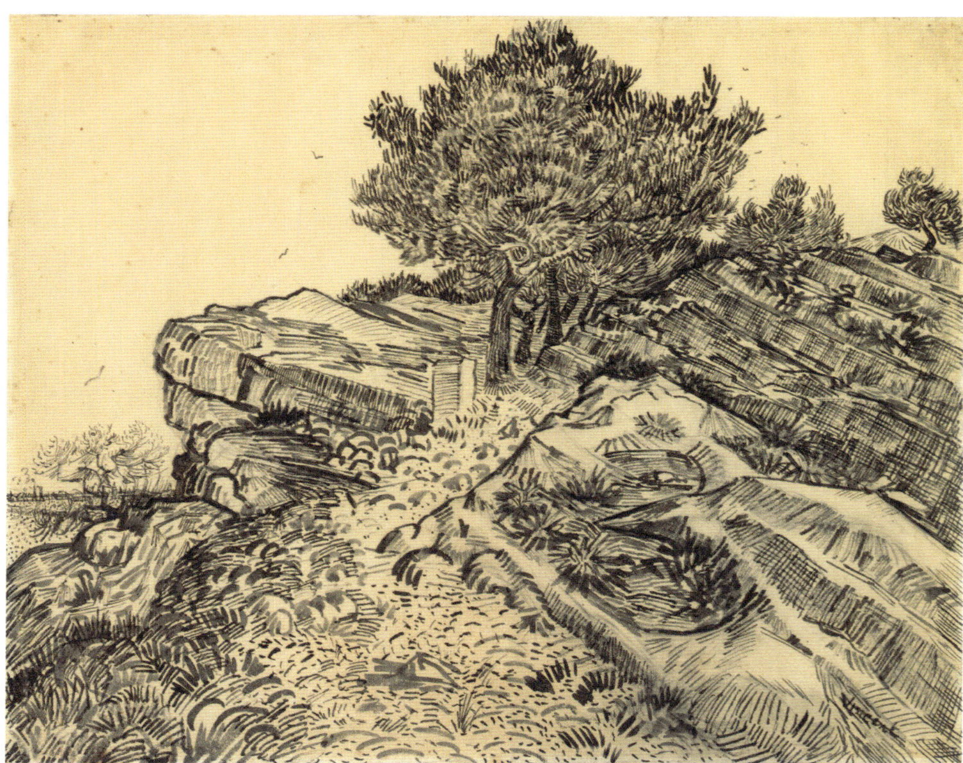

cypresses, ash trees and willows, rock oaks. Half-demolished staircases, ruined Gothic windows, clumps of white rock covered in lichen and pieces of collapsed wall scattered here and there in the undergrowth' (638).

The physical features of the place and the profusion of plant life are apparent in *The Rock of Montmajour with Pine Trees* and *Olive Trees, Montmajour*, which are enclosed compositions where the lines tend to fall into patterns of cross-hatching, notably in the formations of the rocks and the swaying branches of the trees (Figs 103 and 104). *Rock and Ruins, Montmajour* contrasts a view of one part of the abbey with a large rock (Fig. 105). Here firm outlines vie with speckled dots and blobs that recede into the distance. Two tiny figures are silhouetted walking towards the entrance of the tower. Rembrandt could be similarly impressed by historic buildings on a monumental scale, as in his drawing *The Western Gate at Rhenen* of around 1647–48 (Fig. 106).

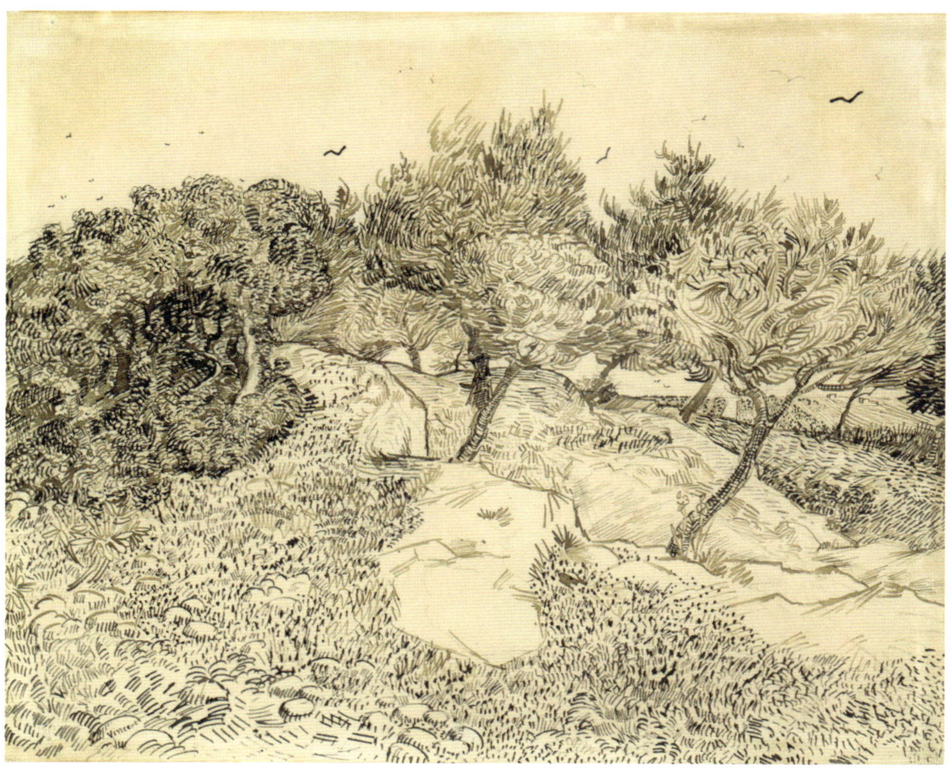

104 *Olive Trees, Montmajour*, 6–12 July 1888. Reed pen and ink, on paper, 48 × 60 cm (19 × 23⅝ in.). MUSÉE DES BEAUX-ARTS DE TOURNAI

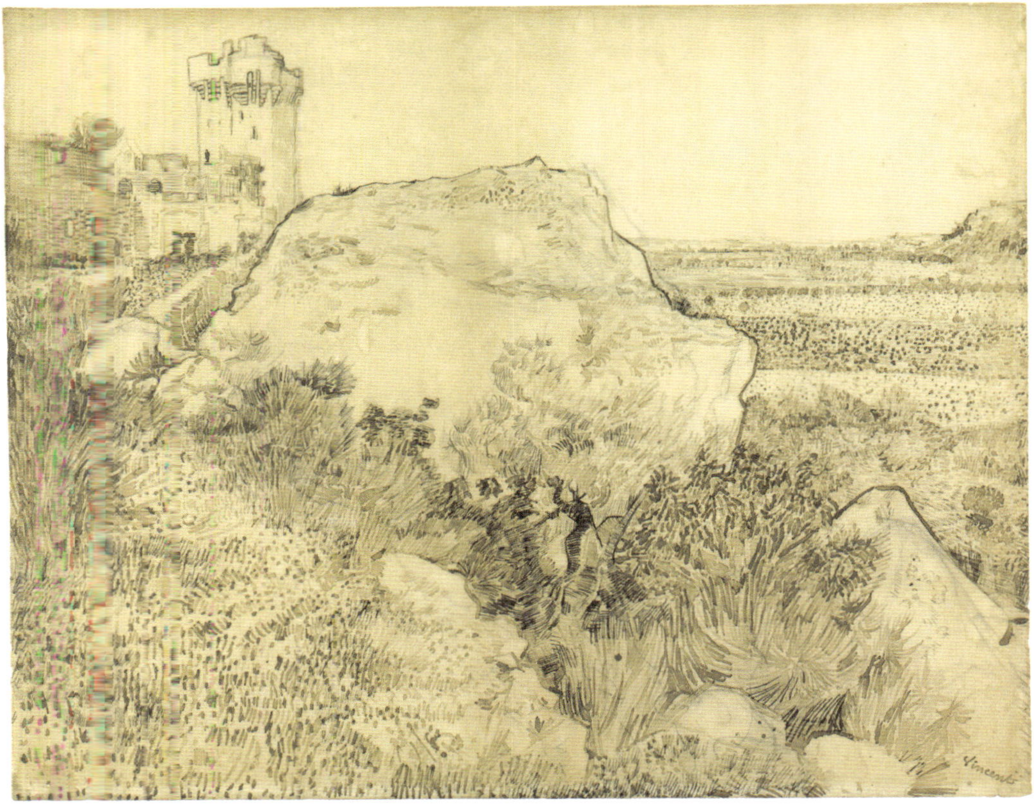

105 *Rock and Ruins, Montmajour*, 6–12 July 1888. Reed pen, quill and ink over pencil, on paper, 47.5 × 59 cm (18¾ × 23¼ in.).
RIJKSMUSEUM, AMSTERDAM

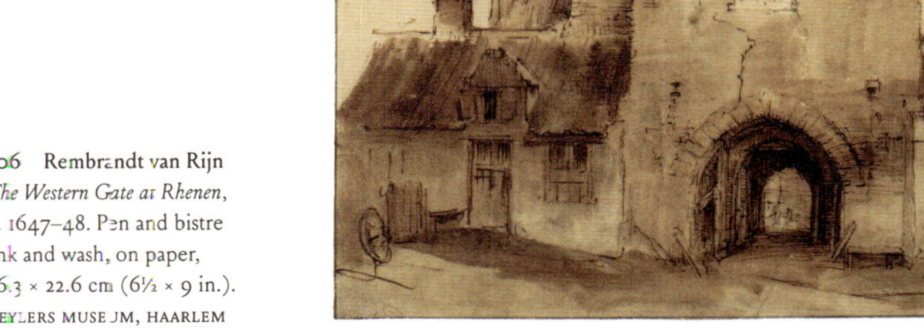

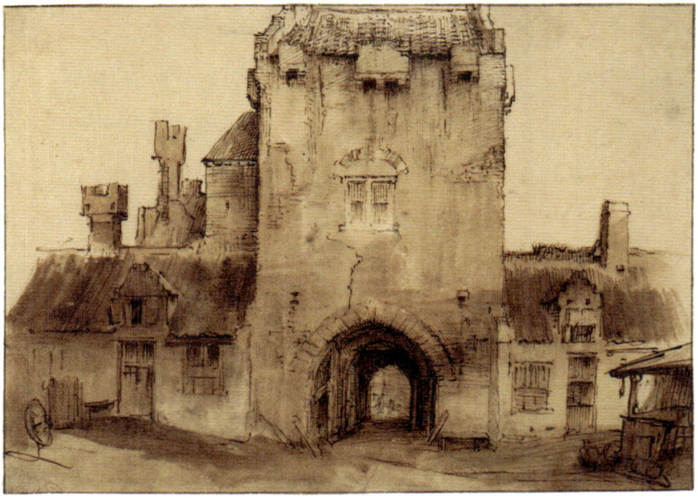

106 Rembrandt van Rijn
The Western Gate at Rhenen, c. 1647–48. Pen and bistre ink and wash, on paper, 16.3 × 22.6 cm (6½ × 9 in.).
TEYLERS MUSEUM, HAARLEM

The final drawings in the sequence, *La Crau Seen from Montmajour* and *The Country on the Banks of the Rhône, View from Montmajour*, depict panoramic views taken from different vantage points looking away from the abbey (Figs 107 and 108). The first looks south-east across La Crau, with a partial view of the Mont de Cordes on the left, and the second looks north-west, in the direction of the River Rhône, with the Alpilles just visible at the upper right and the train heading for Fontvieille in the middle distance. Both these drawings are proudly signed and titled by the artist, and they form part of Van Gogh's contribution to the Dutch tradition of the panoramic vision of landscape, as seen in paintings by so many seventeenth-century artists, such as Jan van Goyen (1596–1656), Van Ruisdael and Philips Koninck (1619–1688).

All the drawings in the sequence were prepared and executed in an orthodox way in front of the motif. Indications in pencil were then worked over in pen and ink, followed by a small amount of retouching or embellishment in the studio in a darker ink. But the results, particularly the panoramic views, are breathtaking – 'the best things I have done with my pen', the artist declared to his brother (639). The world is seen in microcosm – another Dutch trope – rendered in such detail that the viewer craves the use of a magnifying glass, just as the scientist in the laboratory reaches for a microscope. Indeed, the paper on which these drawings were made virtually crawls with life, as though taken over by swarms of insects. Van Gogh himself wrote, 'there's no *effect*, at first sight it's a map, a strategic plan as far as *workmanship* goes' (639). In the same letter, he records walking at Montmajour with a friend, to whom he described the view as being 'as beautiful and infinite as the sea', to which the friend replied that it was '*better* than the sea because it's just as infinite and yet you feel it is *inhabited*'. And Van Gogh does indeed pay great attention to detail, almost combining cartography with art, but without sacrificing the whole. There are clear signs of human activity and modernization in these panoramic landscapes, but they are subservient to the fecundity and omniscience of nature, and even to a higher power.

During the summer of 1888, Van Gogh was affected as much by the harvesting scenes he witnessed around Arles as he had been in the spring by the gardens, meadows and fields. Although drawn a month before the series done at Montmajour, the drawings of the harvest he made in June can be interpreted as a summary of his experiences in the south. For a painter of rural subjects deeply

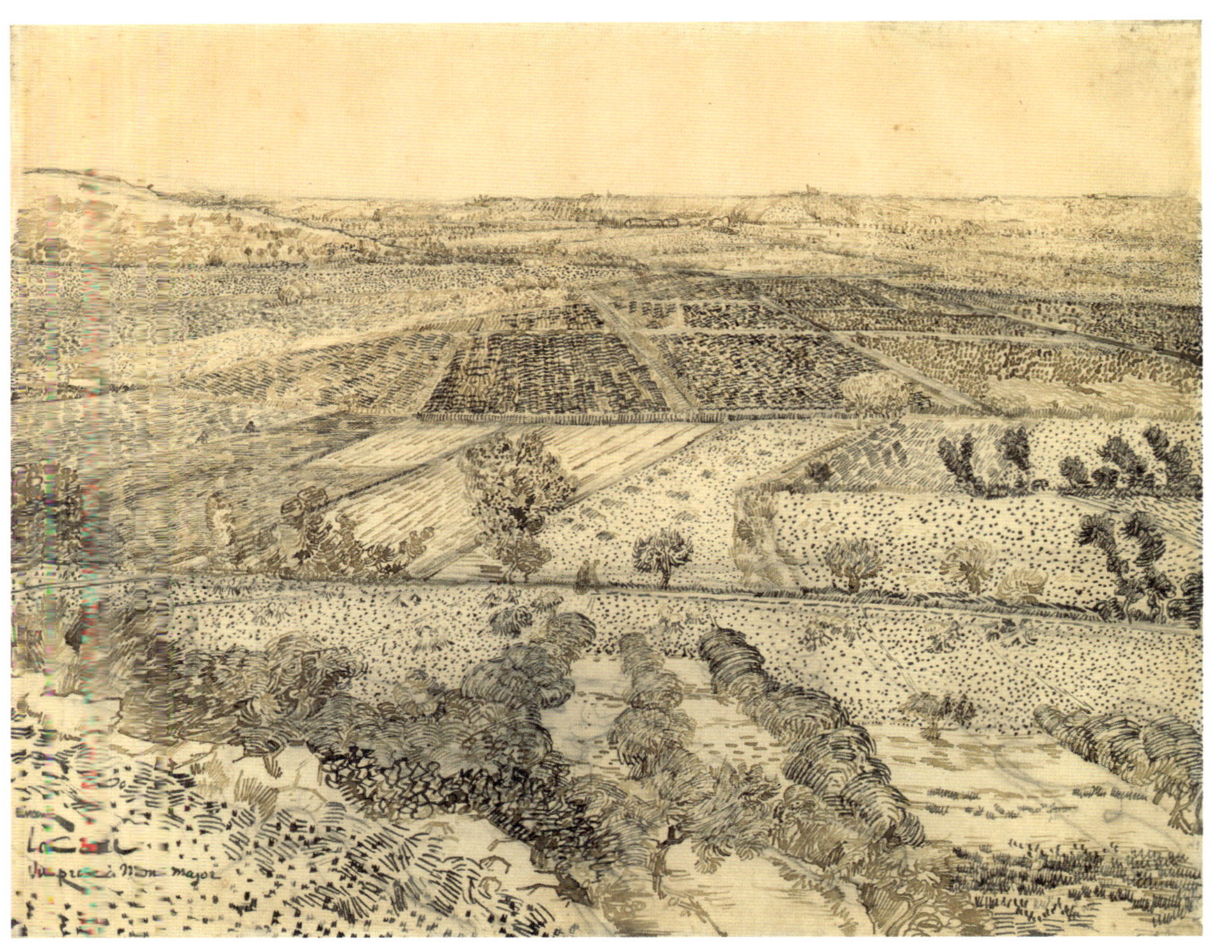

107 *La Crau Seen from Montmajour*, July 1888.
Pencil, pen and reed pen and ink, on paper,
49 × 61 cm (19⅜ × 24⅛ in.).
VAN GOGH MUSEUM, AMSTERDAM

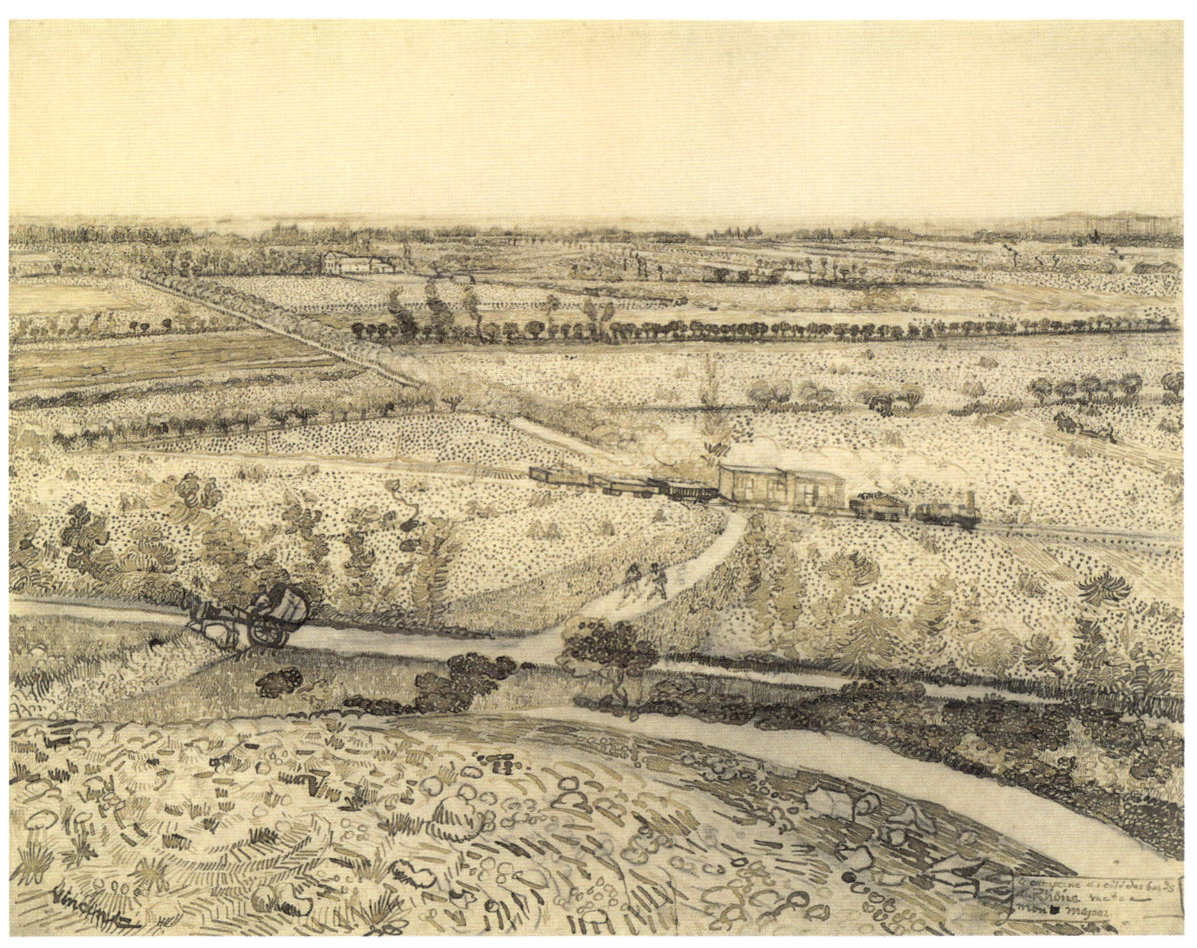

108 *The Country on the Banks of the Rhône, View from Montmajour*, 6–12 July 1888. Reed pen, quill and ink over black chalk and pencil, on paper, 48.7 × 60.7 cm (19¼ × 24 in.).
BRITISH MUSEUM, LONDON

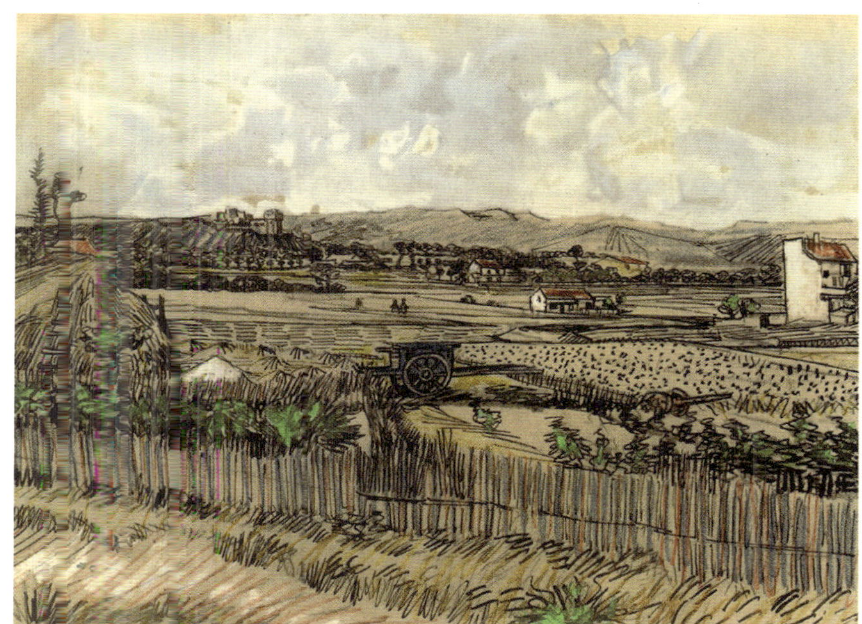

109 *Harvest in Provence*, *c.* 12 June 1888. Reed and quill pen and ink with watercolour, wax crayon and gouache over charcoal, on paper, 50.5 × 61 cm (20 × 24⅛ in.).
PRIVATE COLLECTION

110 *Weeping Tree in a Garden*, early May 1889. Black chalk, quill and reed pen with brown and black ink, on paper, 49.3 × 61.3 cm (19 7/16 × 24 3/16 in.).
ART INSTITUTE OF CHICAGO

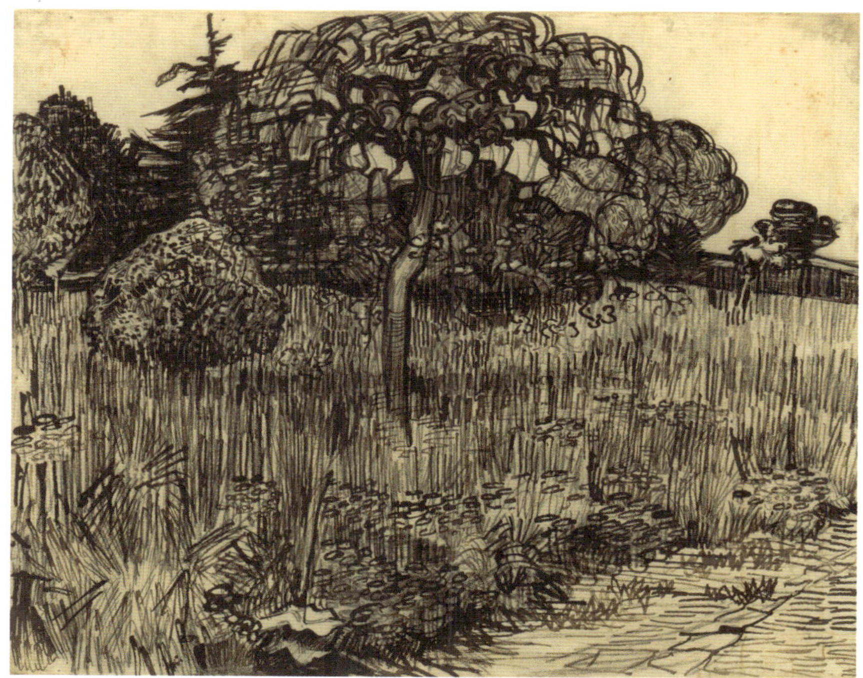

influenced by Millet and Breton, the subject had immense appeal, and the flat terrain of La Crau lent itself to a treatment that again links Van Gogh directly with the seventeenth-century Dutch painters that he admired and emulated. The modernity in Van Gogh rests on his concern to update the tradition into which he was born by harnessing it to what he had seen and learnt in Paris, where he had met avant-garde artists and viewed their work. And to this must be added the state of his increasingly fevered mind.

As a finished drawing, *Harvest in Provence* exists in two versions, both drawn before the painting of the same subject (Van Gogh Museum, Amsterdam). Of the two, the version in the Fogg Art Museum (Cambridge, Mass.) seems slightly more restrained and tentative, with more limited use of watercolour, especially in the sky, and so may have been drawn first. In the second version (Fig. 109), in a private collection, a more comprehensive rendering of the scene shows that the artist is looking north-eastwards from Arles towards Montmajour, which is visible on the left, with the Mont des Cordes and the Alpilles on the horizon. The middle distance is filled with the harvesting scene, while the foreground is demarcated by a wooden fence, as though keeping the viewer at bay. A haycart is symbolically positioned in the centre. The two drawings and the related painting stand as independent works of art in their own right: they are similar in all compositional respects, with only minor changes in the details and very slight shifts of viewpoint. Van Gogh was so proud of his achievement that he sent drawn repetitions of the composition to Émile Bernard and John Russell (1858–1930). He regarded *Harvest in Provence* as one of his most successful compositions, and in discussing it he chose Cézanne as his principal point of reference.

Several of the drawings by Van Gogh made in the public gardens on the place Lamartine or in the park by the Roman arena in Arles reveal new tendencies in his style, as he immersed himself more deeply in the town. It is a moot point as to whether such changes reflect his deteriorating physical condition or his mental state, but the content in the drawings and also the paintings of this period is handled in a more abstract or self-absorbed way. Correspondingly, there is a sense in which mark-making is indulged in for its own sake. Generally speaking, there is a tendency for lines to be less descriptive and to become more decorative. Both *Park with Fence* (Fig. 80) and *Weeping Tree in a Garden* (Fig. 110) display the usual repertoire of flowing lines, dashes, dots, curls, whorls and spirals, but often, now, they are more systematically placed on the sheet and in a more stylized manner. There is a feeling of restlessness or of ceaseless motion that suggests a writhing turmoil of the inner spirit. It is the representation of a fluctuating world, one not quite without a sense of direction but of uncertain outcome. Similar stylistic traits are apparent in the last drawings done in the hospital at Arles and in the garden at Saint-Rémy shortly after his arrival at the asylum.

However, when Van Gogh looked out from his bedroom on the upper floor at Saint-Rémy across the neighbouring fields, he once more became responsive to the real landscape. Indeed, *Enclosed Wheatfield with Sun and Cloud* (Fig. 111) is comparable with the outpouring of drawings done earlier at Montmajour and clearly precedes the related painting in Copenhagen (Ny Carlsberg Glyptotek), which shows the field after the rain clouds have passed. In the drawing, the stormy conditions are emphasized by the contrast between the pen and ink and the

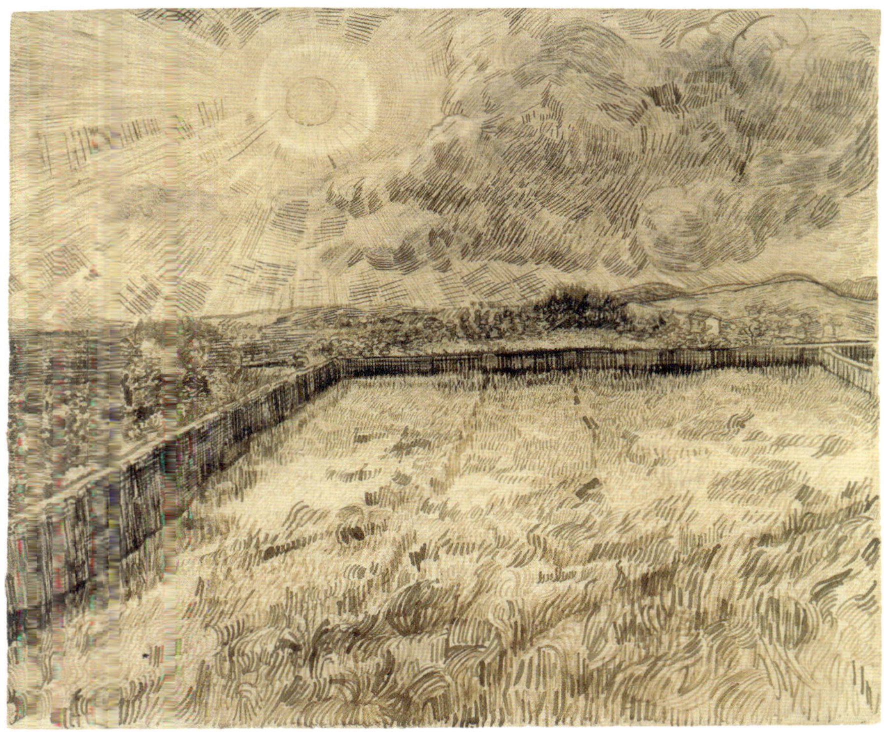

111 *Enclosed Wheatfield with Sun and Cloud*, May–June 1889. Black chalk, reed pen and ink with white opaque watercolour, on paper, 47.5 × 56.6 cm (18¾ × 22⅜ in.). KRÖLLER-MÜLLER MUSEUM, OTTERLO

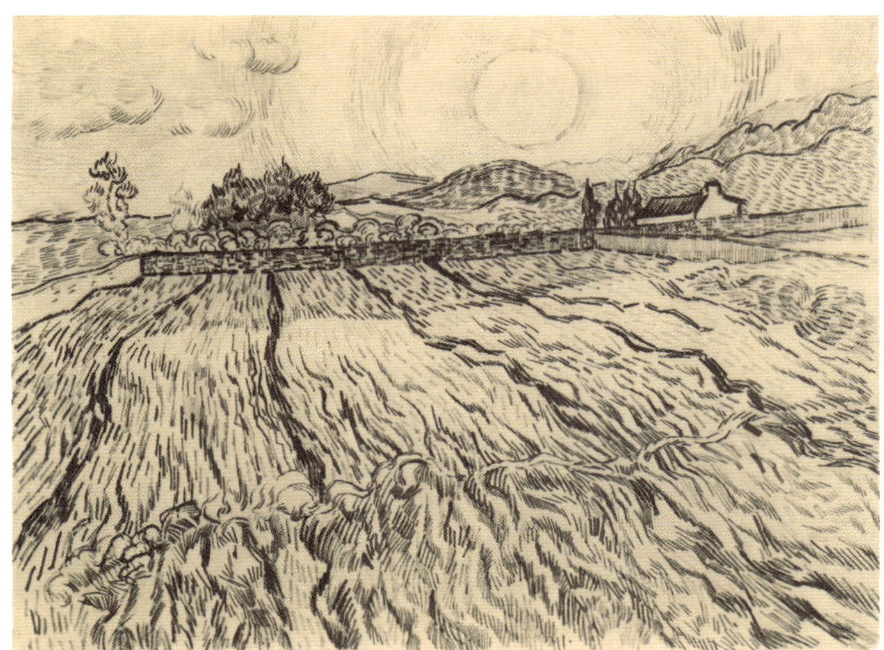

112 *Wheatfield with Rising Sun*, mid-November–mid-December 1889. Black chalk, reed pen, pen and ink on pink laid paper, 47.4 × 62 cm (18⅝ × 24½ in.). STAATLICHE GRAPHISCHE SAMMLUNG, MUNICH

touches of white heightening, which is also used to increase the radiance of the sun.

This view became one of Van Gogh's principal motifs when he was in the asylum. He was able to observe the space through the full cycle of the year – ploughing, sowing, ripening, reaping. The wheatfield was enclosed by walls and faced the Alpilles, which could be interpreted as a further metaphor for the artist's own confinement. But to counterbalance that sense of enclosure, Van Gogh often included the blazing sun rising above the walls. Its radiance is the main feature in a drawing in which the artist has used black chalk and ink in combination, leaving much of the paper in the sky untouched, apart from groups of radial lines (Fig. 112). The sun is low in the sky and the wall at the end of the field casts a lengthy shadow, which has been made on the paper by rubbing the black chalk used in that area. A related painting exists (private collection), but it is not easy to establish the order of precedence. The drawings of this view in Otterlo and Munich are not connected merely on account of their subject matter. The selection and use of media provided the opportunity for Van Gogh to recreate different effects in the weather, but, interestingly, the lines in both are similarly drawn – short, simple strokes varying in thickness, length and direction and spreading over the surface like a spilt box of matches.

While in Provence, Van Gogh, the artist from the north, had become in thrall to the sun, aware of its power and also of it as a source of magic, as it had been for such Romantic artists as J. M. W. Turner (1775–1851). Now, during his illness, he greeted the sun as a symbol of hope and renewal, preoccupied by it in the same way that he had been by sunflowers and stars towards the end of his time in Arles. Another motif visible from the asylum at Saint-Rémy – and of which he had been aware in Arles – assumed new significance, becoming the foremost subject of several paintings and drawings. This is the cypress trees. In June 1889, he wrote to Theo,

> The cypresses still preoccupy me, I'd like to do something with them like the canvases of the sunflowers because it astonishes me that no one has yet done them as I see them.
>
> It's beautiful as regards lines and proportions, like an Egyptian obelisk.
>
> And the green has such a distinguished quality.
>
> It's the *dark* patch in a sun-drenched landscape, but it's one of the most interesting dark notes, the most difficult to hit off exactly that I can imagine.
>
> Now they must be seen here against the blue, *in* the blue, rather. (783)

The painting *Cypresses* in the Metropolitan Museum of Art, New York, painted in the same month as the letter to Theo was written, is of two such trees standing tall against the blue sky with a crescent moon above, on the right. It is heavily worked with strong contrasts of colour. The sense of movement is suggested by the intertwined, twisting brushstrokes. The same stylistic features are present in the related drawing, where colour is implied by tonal differences and thickness of line (Fig. 113). Cypress trees are in almost constant movement, particularly when the mistral blows. It is an unusual tree, in that the trunk is short, extending upwards for only part of the tree. The distinctive height and shape are derived from the fact that the fronds reach upwards in different directions instead of pointing outwards or leaning downwards,

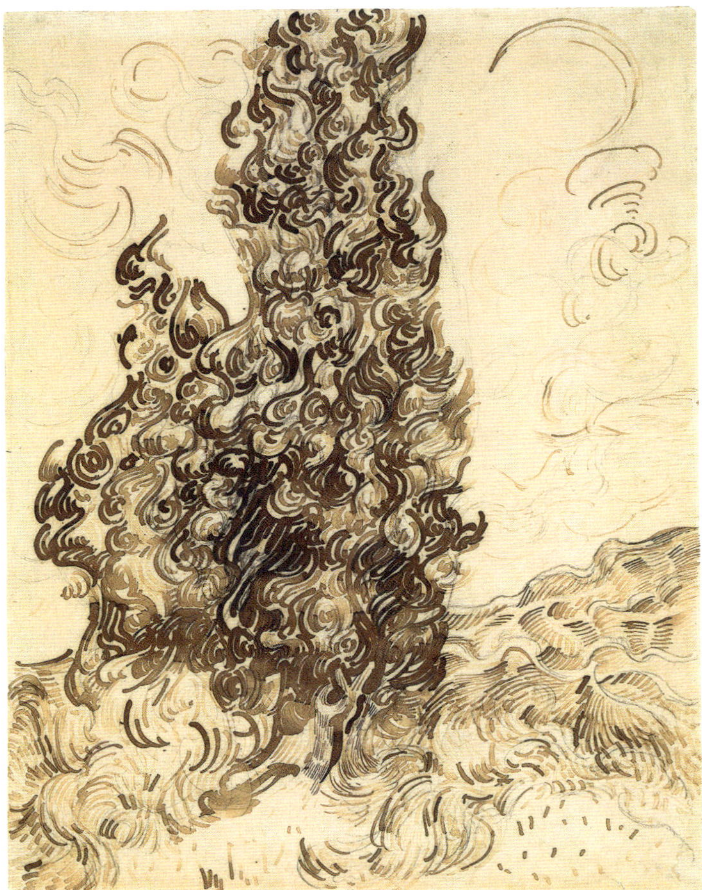

113 *Cypresses* (*Les Cyprès*), 20–25 June 1889. Reed pen and ink, pencil, on paper, 61.9 × 47.3 cm (24⅜ × 18⅝ in.). BROOKLYN MUSEUM, NEW YORK

so that, when the wind blows, the tree seems to shiver as well as to sway. Van Gogh suggests this sense of eternal movement by the oscillation of his pen strokes, as though wrapping them around the tree.

In Mediterranean countries, the cypress tree has been associated since antiquity with death and was often placed in cemeteries, where it came to symbolize life beyond the grave. Van Gogh was clearly conscious of the pictorial and technical permutations presented by the cypress tree, but contained within this fascination there may also have been a degree of prescience.

Chapter 6

Portraits

Numerically there are far fewer painted or drawn portraits in Van Gogh's oeuvre than landscapes or figure compositions. Admittedly, the thirty-five surviving self-portraits constitute one of the greatest personal achievements in the history of art, particularly since, unlike in the cases of Rembrandt, Joshua Reynolds (1723–1792), Courbet or Cézanne, they were done in such a short period. Beyond those self-portraits, however, there are relatively few individual traditional portraits.

Many artists begin by depicting members of their own family, but Van Gogh eschewed this approach. Neither his parents nor his siblings, let alone more distant influential relatives, seem to have sat for him at the start of his career as an artist. The three examples of family portraits that do exist were done from photographs and not from life – two in July 1881 and the third in September–October 1888. Significantly, the later one of these is of his mother and was painted in Arles (Fig. 114). As he wrote to Theo, 'I'm working on a portrait. That's to say, I'm doing a portrait of our *mother* for myself. I can't look at the colourless photograph and I'm trying to do one with harmonious colour, as I see her in my memory' (699). He also wanted to paint a portrait of his father using a similar source, but that never materialized. This development occurred at a time when, in Provence, Van Gogh was beginning to think nostalgically of the north and was writing letters to his mother and his sister Willemien full of reminiscences of his earlier life. It is hardly surprising that two months after painting his mother's portrait she appears again in the foreground of the painting *Memory of the Garden at Etten*, a work in the Symbolist style, influenced by Gauguin and Bernard and done from the imagination (Fig. 115). Van Gogh was disappointed by the result and he told Theo on 1 December that he had 'spoiled' the picture, by which he probably meant that he had overworked it (723).

The ambivalence that Van Gogh experienced about portraiture resulted in part from his own diffidence and in part from his

The Postman Joseph Roulin, early August 1888 (detail of Fig. 130).

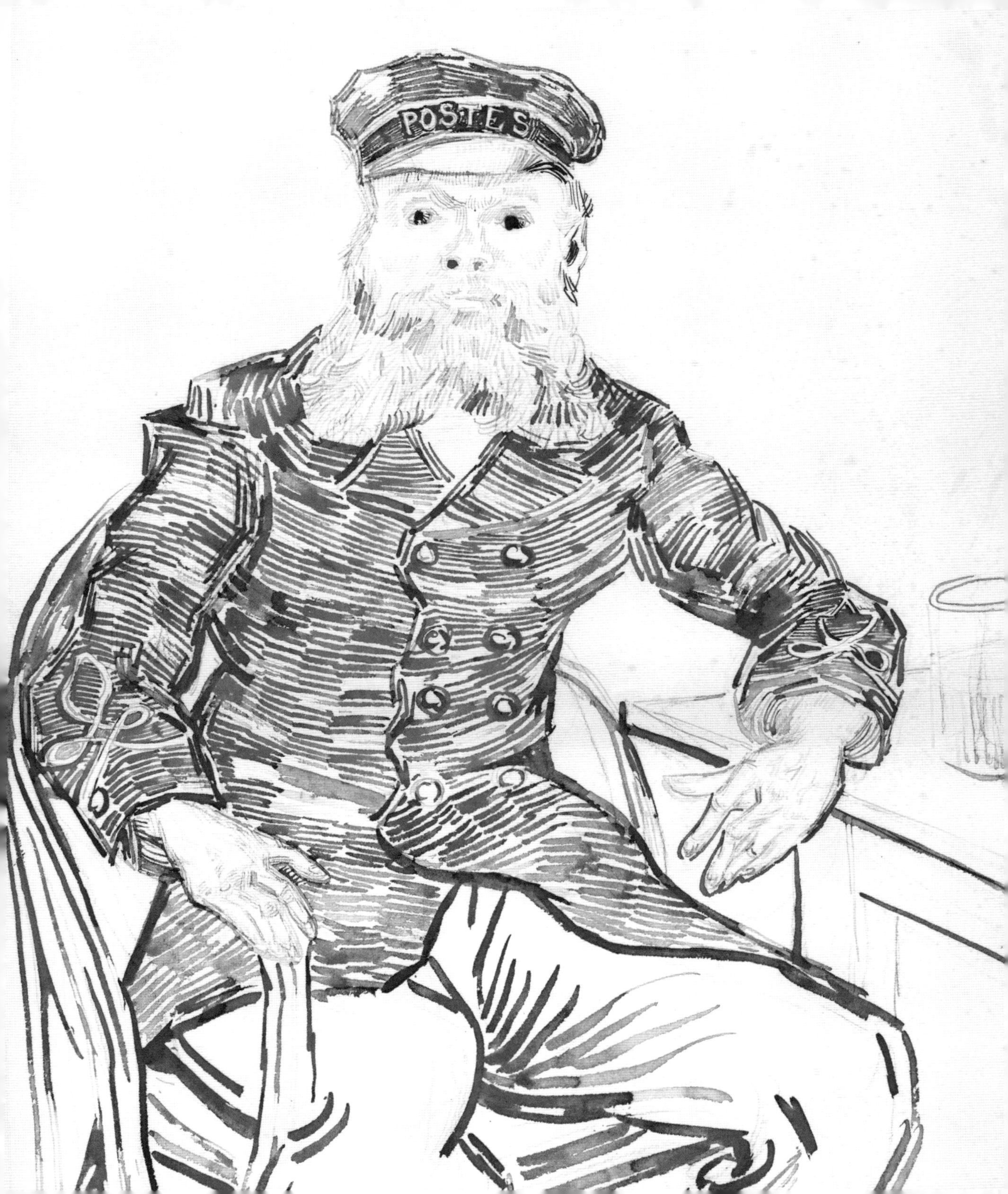
POSTES

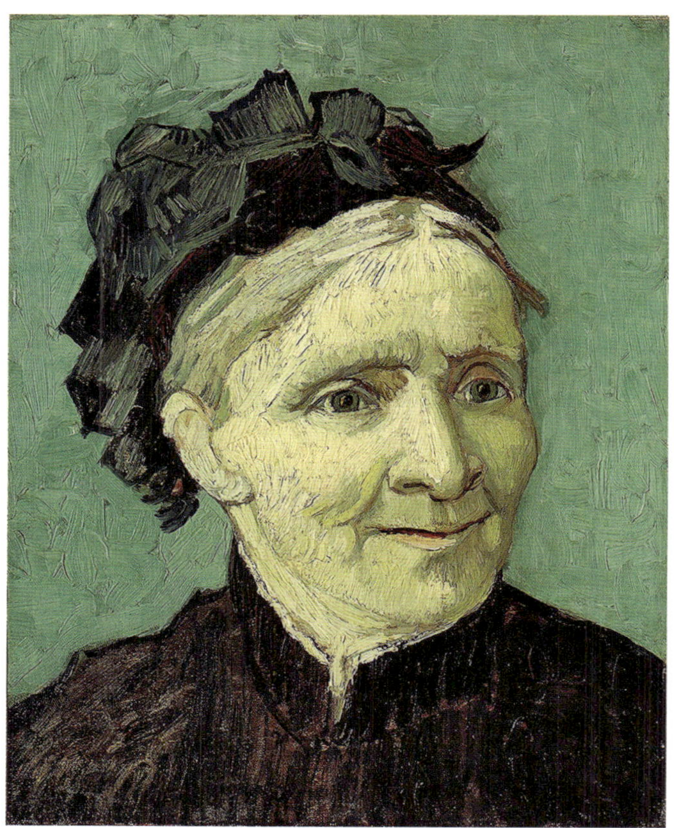

114 *Portrait of the Artist's Mother*, October 1888. Oil on canvas, 40.7 × 32.3 cm (16⅛ × 12¾ in.). NORTON SIMON MUSEUM, PASADENA, CA

nervousness about the reaction of potential sitters. As far as it is known, he was never officially commissioned to undertake any formal portraits. This absence in Van Gogh's oeuvre does not seem to have worried him while he was working in the Netherlands, but, as his view of the world broadened in Brussels, Antwerp and Paris, he began to recognize the potential of portraiture, which would have been one way of increasing his reputation as well as being to his financial advantage. Indeed, it is reasonable to assert that Van Gogh's corpus of painted portraits begins in Paris and is pursued, although intermittently, in Arles, Saint-Rémy and Auvers-sur-Oise.

Even so, Van Gogh clearly had difficulties finding sitters, and it is clear from those that are identifiable that most of these were people he responded to on a personal basis or with whom he formed a strong attachment and found himself in sympathy.

Van Gogh's portraits are rarely if ever spontaneous. They have the air of an extended private dialogue, often exuding an air of mystery, to the extent that the viewer can feel like an intruder. A random sampling of Van Gogh's most important painted portraits includes among his subjects the dealers Père Tanguy and Alexander Reid in Paris; the postal worker Joseph Roulin and his family, the café owner Marie Ginoux ('L'Arlésienne'), the soldier Paul Eugène Milliet, the Belgian painter Eugène Boch and Van Gogh's physician, Dr Félix Rey, in Arles; the chief orderly and his wife (Charles-Elzéard and Jeanne Trabuc) in the asylum at Saint-Rémy; and, finally, Adeline Ravoux, Dr Gachet and his daughter, Marguerite, in Auvers-sur-Oise. These sitters, together with a few others, were people who, in the ordinary

115 *Memory of the Garden at Etten (Ladies of Arles)*, December 1888. Oil on canvas, 73.5 × 92.5 cm (29 × 36½ in.). STATE HERMITAGE MUSEUM, ST PETERSBURG

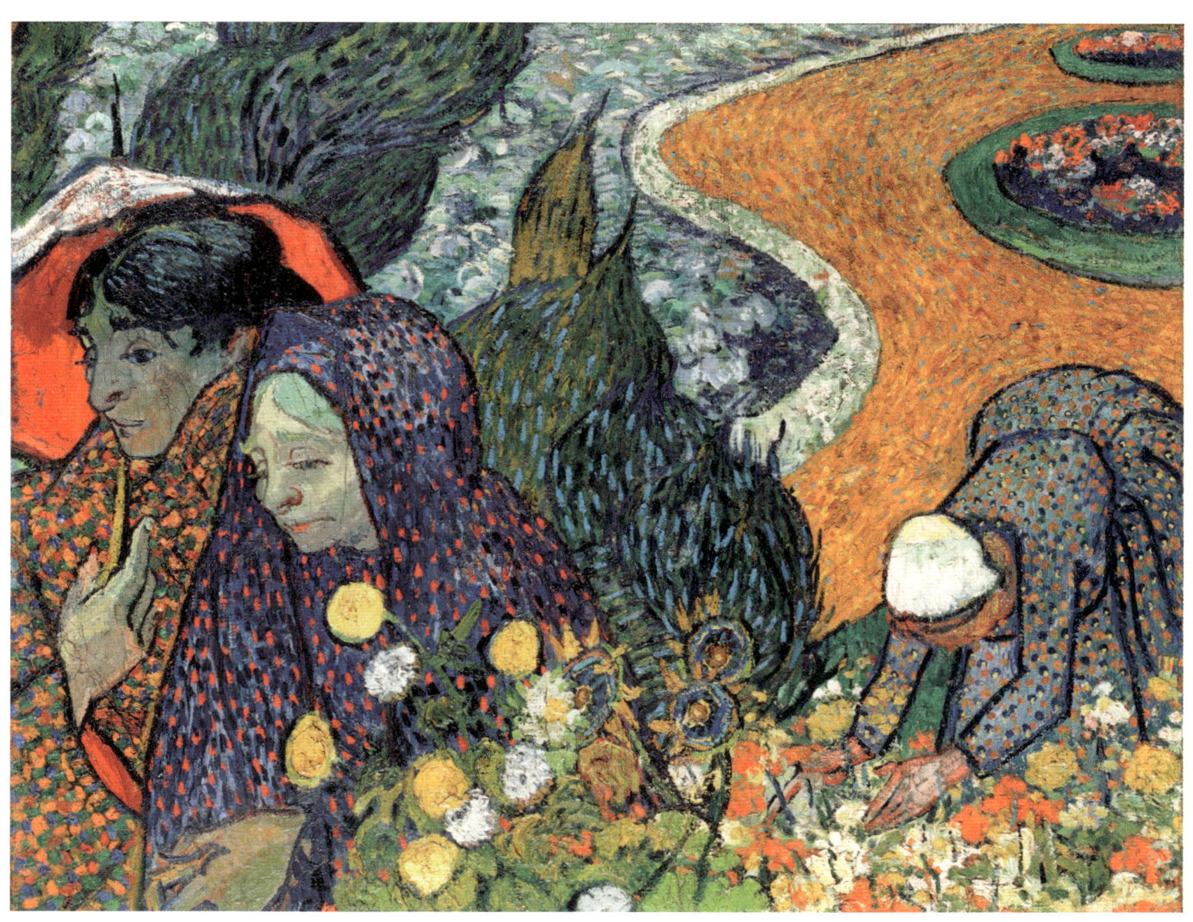

course of affairs, would not have commissioned their own portraits or even have expected to have been recorded for posterity in such a way. Van Gogh's portraits, therefore, are not about status or wealth, but more about the commonplace and the familiar: he does not seek out dignitaries but rewards intimacies. When painting the portrait of one of his fellow inmates in the asylum at Saint-Rémy (*Portrait of a Man*; Van Gogh Museum, Amsterdam), he described the experience to his mother: 'It's strange that when one is with them for some time and is used to them, one no longer thinks about their being mad' (811). The forerunners of this single portrait might be the group of ten portraits by Théodore Géricault (1791–1824) representing some of the inmates of an asylum in Paris and known as 'Portraits of the Insane' (*c.* 1820), some of which belonged to painters of the Barbizon School.

Van Gogh did not distance himself from his sitters either emotionally or socially. In artistic terms, there is a revealing contrast between the unassuming qualities of the subjects portrayed and the audacious manner in which they are depicted. The artist summarized his position when he was painting the *Portrait of Dr Gachet* (private collection) in 1890 (Fig. 116):

> What I'm most passionate about, much much more than all the rest in my profession – is the portrait, the modern portrait. I seek it by way of colour, and am certainly not alone in seeking it in this way. I WOULD LIKE, you see I'm far from saying that I can do all of this, but anyway I'm aiming at it, I *would like* to do portraits which would look like apparitions to people a century later. So I don't try to do us by photographic resemblance but by our passionate expression, using as a means of expression and intensification of the character our science and modern taste for colour. (879)

This was a conclusion he had reached before finding models. As he complained to Theo when in Arles, 'If we painted smoothly like Bouguereau people wouldn't be ashamed to let themselves be painted, but I believe it's made me lose models, that people found that it was "badly done", *it was only pictures* FULL OF PAINTING that I was doing. So the good whores are afraid of being compromised, and that people will laugh at their portraits' (660). Van Gogh sought not just likenesses in his portraits, but the true expression

116 *Portrait of Dr Gachet*, June 1890. Oil on canvas, 67 × 56 cm (26½ × 22⅛ in.). PRIVATE COLLECTION

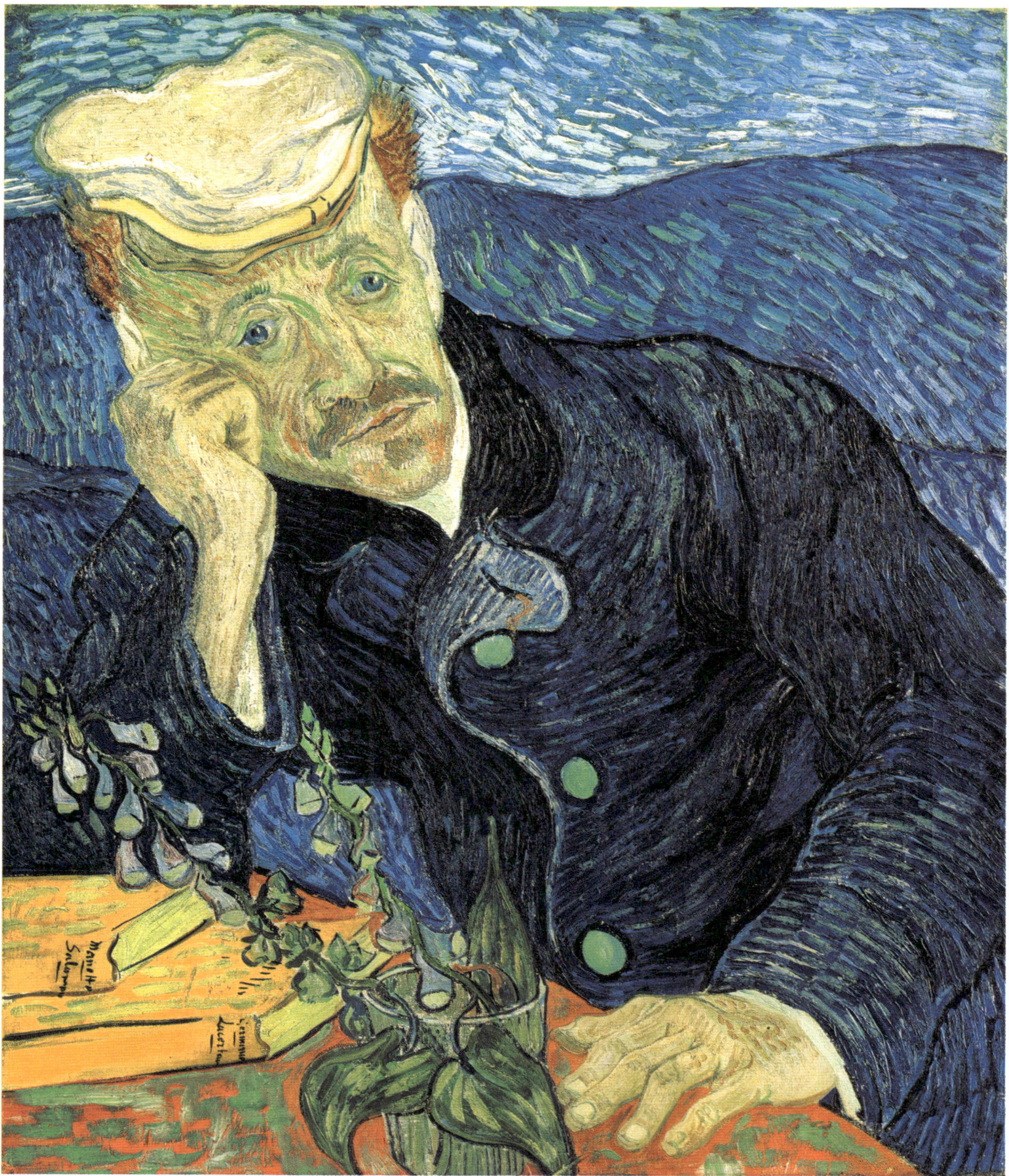
Manette
Salomon

of character achieved not just by line or modelling, but by natural poses, vivid colour and strong brushwork.

It is fair to say that Van Gogh always had an underlying interest in portraiture throughout his working life. After all, he was fully aware of the skill of Hans Holbein the Younger (1497/8–1543) as a portraitist through the copies he had made from Bargue's *Cours de dessin* in 1880–81 (Fig. 10). At the same time, Theo was encouraging him to begin by making portraits from photographs of which two early examples survive – one probably of his younger sister Willemien and the other identified as his grandfather the

117 *Portrait of Vincent van Gogh, the Artist's Grandfather*, July 1881. Pencil, brush and ink and watercolour, on paper, 34.[illegible] × 26.1 cm (13⅝ × 10⅜ in.).
VAN GOGH MUSEUM, AMSTERDAM

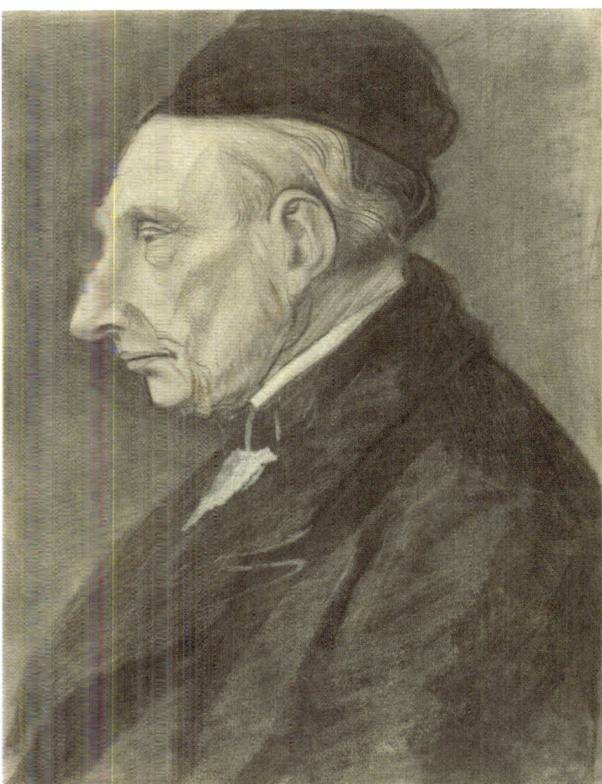

118 *Portrait of Jozef Blok*, November 1882. Pencil, watercolour, lithographic crayon, on paper, 38.5 × 26.3 cm (15¼ × 10⅜ in.)
VAN GOGH MUSEUM, AMSTERDAM

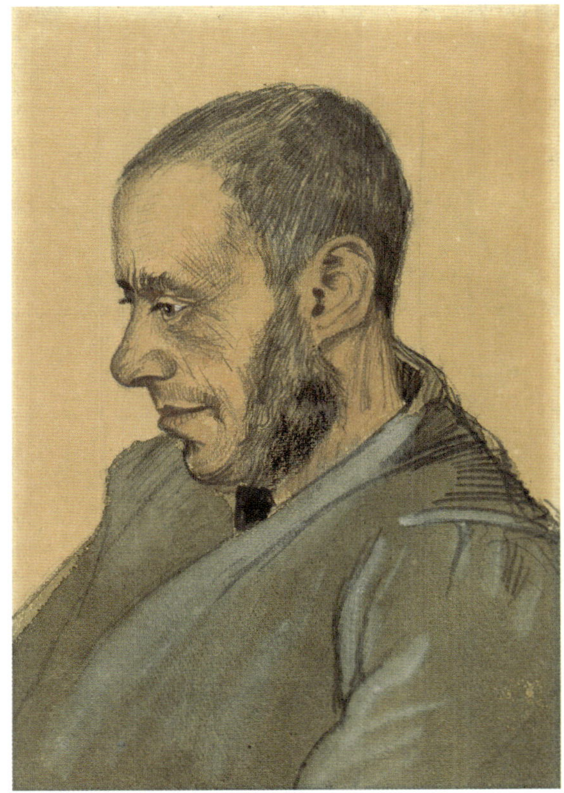

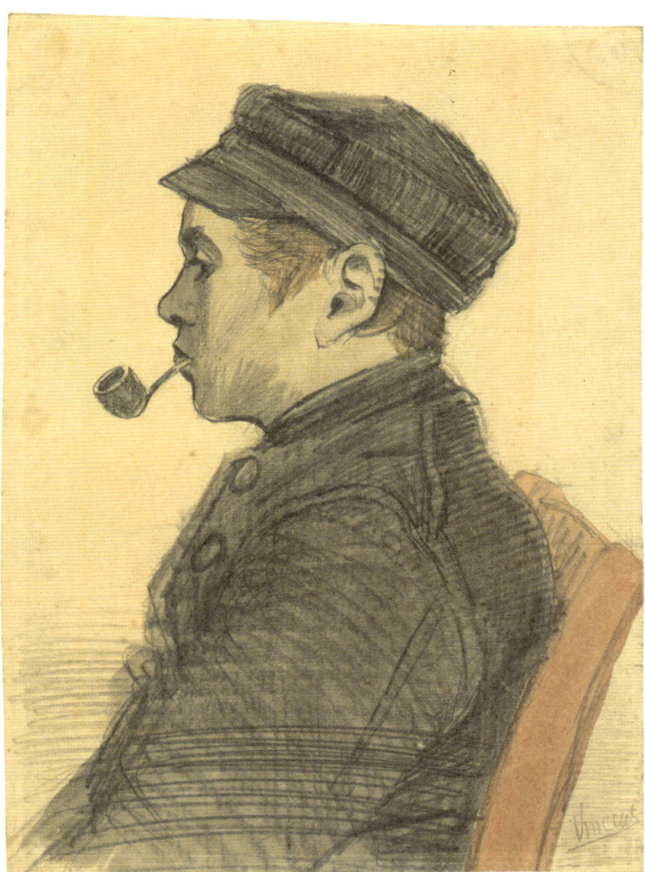

119 *Young Man with a Pipe*, March 1884. Pencil and watercolour, on paper, 39.9 × 28.4 cm (15¾ × 11¼ in.). VAN GOGH MUSEUM, AMSTERDAM

Revd Vincent van Gogh (Fig. 117). By comparison, there are only two drawings that can be described as viable drawn portraits in the whole period leading up to Van Gogh's arrival in Paris. One is *Portrait of Jozef Blok*, which was made on 5 November 1882 in The Hague (Fig. 118). Blok was a bookseller with an open-air stall in the Binnenhof at which Van Gogh bought many of his illustrations from English and French journals. The face is seen not quite in profile and slightly from above. The features are depicted with pencil and lithographic chalk, emphasized in parts with the brush and washed overall with opaque watercolour. Another drawing similarly treated is *Young Man with a Pipe*, dating from nearly two years later (Fig. 119). Both portraits are carefully observed and are drawn with considerable élan.

As he gained in confidence, it would have been perfectly possible for Van Gogh to have made many more portrait drawings of this kind, but his interests lay elsewhere, as is demonstrated by a passage he wrote in a letter to Theo about the portrait of Blok: 'I wish I had more from that family, for they are a true type. It's enormously difficult to get the types one would prefer to have – in the meantime I'm content to draw *what I can get*, without losing sight of the others I would draw if I had the choice' (280). The implication is that Van Gogh's priority during the years in the Netherlands was with types rather than individuality. This suited his agenda of creating an art that concentrated on rural themes

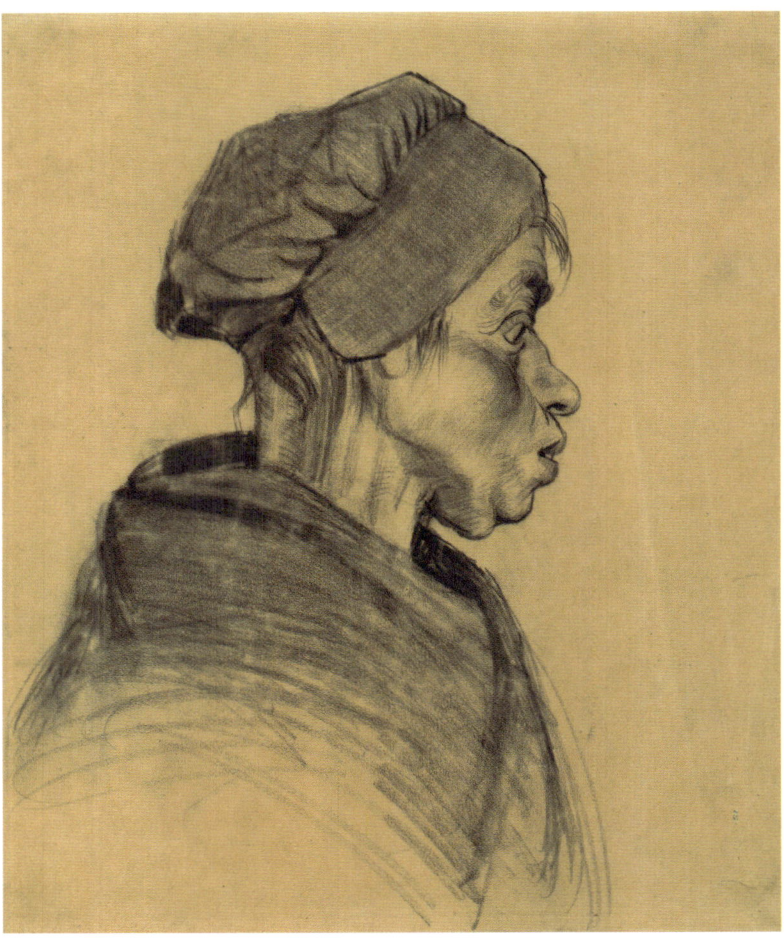

120 *Head of a Woman*, December 1884–May 1885. Chalk on paper, 40.2 × 33.3 cm (15⅞ × 13⅛ in.). VAN GOGH MUSEUM, AMSTERDAM

and urban poverty, which were the two subjects that, at this stage of his life, he could most readily observe at first hand. The studies made in these contexts were of a general typological kind involving the observation of routine occupations either at work or at home. Some of these studies came to fruition as finished drawings and variants with such titles as *Worn Out* (1882) or *Sorrowing Woman* (1883), and later in more elaborate, multi-figured compositions, culminating in *The Potato Eaters* in 1885 (Fig. 48).

As early as 1880, while in Brussels, Van Gogh mentioned, in a letter to Theo, reading Alexandre Ysabeau's *Lavater et Gall: Physiognomonie et phrénologie rendues intelligibles pour tout le monde* (Lavater and Gall: Physiognomony and Phrenology made Intelligible for All) of 1862. Such texts – upheld during the nineteenth century as scientific but now discredited – propounded the view that human character and behaviour were dictated by certain parts of the brain and could be inferred by the shape of the skull or outward physical appearance. When in Nuenen, Van Gogh made an extended study of the peasants at work in the fields, but also a more detailed series of drawings of heads alone, in which he was possibly testing out contemporary ideas about physiognomy.

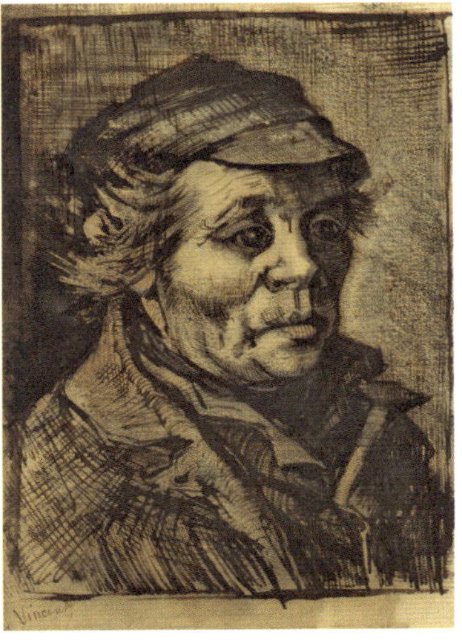

121 *Head of a Man*, December 1884–May 1885. Pencil, pen, brush and ink, on paper, 14.8 × 10.4 cm (5⅞ × 4⅛ in.). VAN GOGH MUSEUM, AMSTERDAM

Two groups of such studies were made amid the long preparations for *The Potato Eaters*: one group in black chalk or pencil (Fig. 120) and the other on a smaller scale in pen and ink (Fig. 121). These he described as 'heads from the people' to differentiate them from the earlier 'Heads of the People' series. Both groups emphasize facial features associated with hard physical work and poverty. These were legitimate 'scientific' investigations of the Brabant peasantry, which Van Gogh treated sympathetically. As Theo wrote to their mother on 19 May 1885, 'Some find great beauty in them, precisely because his characters are genuine. For after all it is true to say, to some extent, that more peasant faces in Brabant display the harsh marks of toil and poverty than there are attractive faces' (*Vincent van Gogh Drawings*, vol. 2: *Nuenen 1883–1885*, Amsterdam and London, 1997, p. 111). Many of these drawings are unabashedly direct and even intimate, but they are not strictly speaking portraits. There is a similar ambivalence about the figures based on the residents of the Dutch Reformed Old People's Home, who posed for the artist in The Hague. Even though the name of the principal model there – Adrianus Jacobus Zuyderland – is known, he is observed objectively in the various poses and clothes that Van Gogh gave him in order to imply a narrative context (Fig. 122).

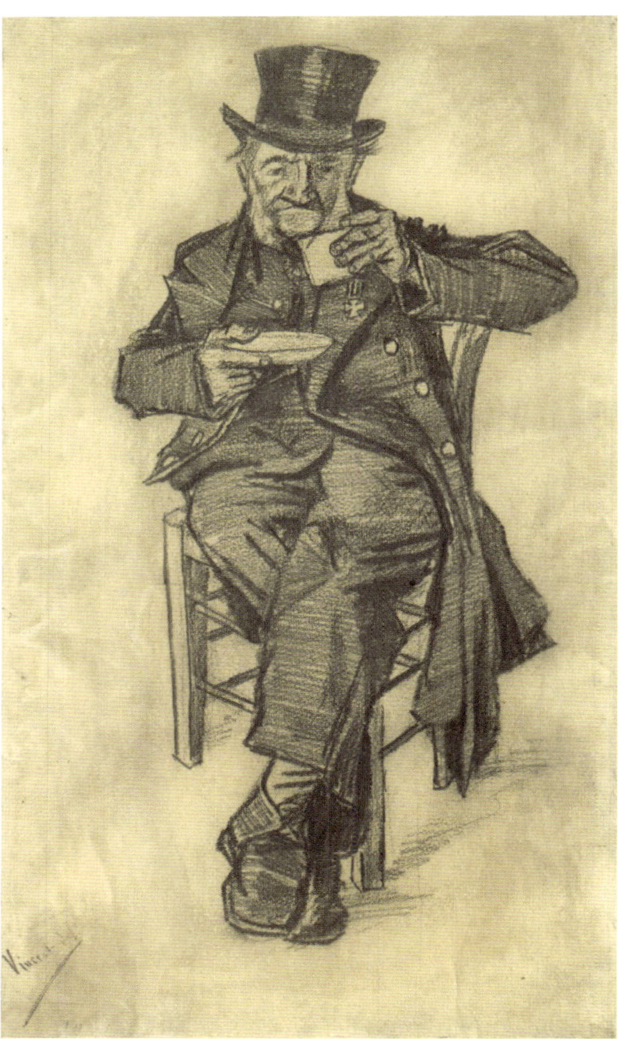

122 *Old Man Drinking Coffee*, September–November 1882. Pencil on paper, 49.4 × 28.6 cm (19½ × 11⅓ in.). VAN GOGH MUSEUM, AMSTERDAM

Among the drawings Van Gogh made in The Hague are those of his companion, Sien Hoornik, who began to model for him early in 1882 and who moved in with the artist in July of the same year, together with her daughter, Maria Wilhelmina. Sien was a former prostitute who had been brought up in the poor area of The Hague known as the Geest. Her mother also became part of Van Gogh's household, although she lived independently, as perhaps did a younger sister. While living with Van Gogh, Sien gave birth to

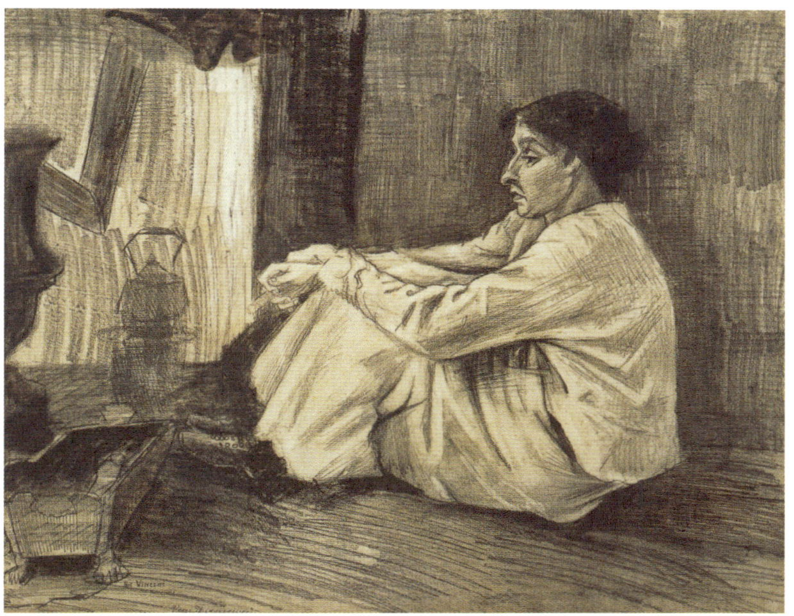

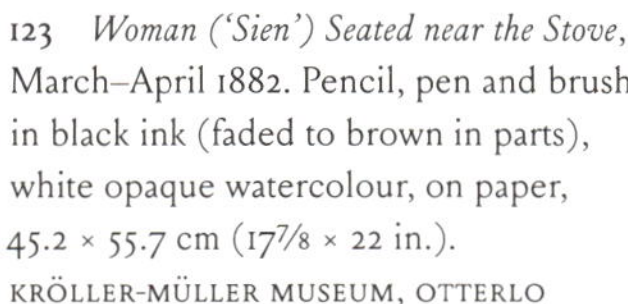

123 *Woman ('Sien') Seated near the Stove*, March–April 1882. Pencil, pen and brush in black ink (faded to brown in parts), white opaque watercolour, on paper, 45.2 × 55.7 cm (17⅞ × 22 in.). KRÖLLER-MÜLLER MUSEUM, OTTERLO

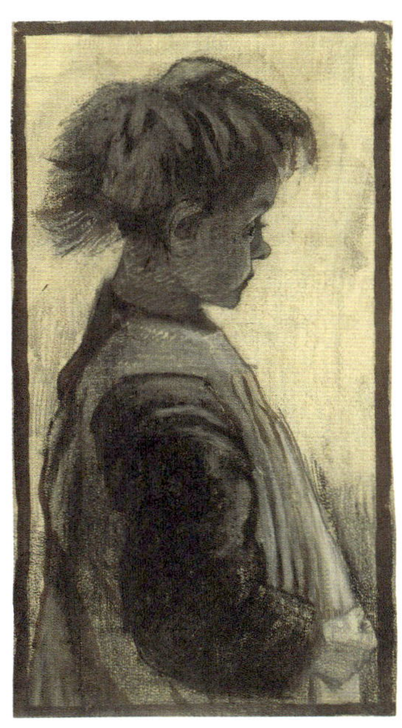

124 *Girl with a Pinafore (Maria Wilhelmina Hoornik)*, December 1882. Black crayon, iron-gall ink (with pen and brush), charcoal, graphite, opaque white watercolour, on paper, 48.6 × 25.6 cm (19⅛ × 10⅛ in.). MUSEUM OF FINE ARTS, BOSTON

a boy (Willem) by another man. The artist's intentions at this stage were purely philanthropic, somewhat to the dismay of his family and friends such as Van Rappard. In fact, the relationship lasted only until September 1883, when the artist made the difficult decision to leave The Hague for Drenthe alone. Although Sien was an omnipresent model, some of the drawings he made of her, her mother and her daughter do enter the realm of portraiture (Figs 123 and 124). The difference between a posed study and a portrait is a narrow one, but essentially it lies in the approach: for Van Gogh, a true portrait is more direct, more spontaneous; it is the product of improvisation, as opposed to contrivance.

From the moment Van Gogh moved to Paris, he seems to have rejected his notion of drawing types and embraced proper portraiture. There was, of course, a promising array of potential

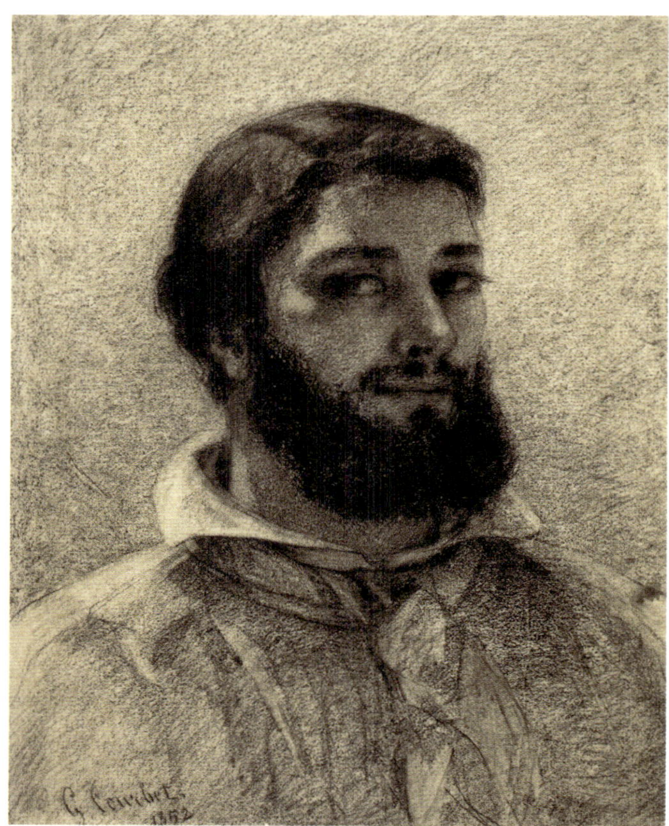

125 Gustave Courbet
Self-portrait, 1852. Black chalk and charcoal on paper, 56.6 × 45.1 cm (22 3/8 × 17 7/8 in.).
BRITISH MUSEUM, LONDON

sitters in the city who recognized the importance and value of portraiture, although since the artist was not known for his output in this field, he was forced to rely on people who may have been only humouring him in this respect. The majority of Van Gogh's painted self-portraits date from his two years in Paris, from 1886 to 1888. This may not signify his failure to attract sitters, nor is it necessarily simply an exercise in introspection; rather, it may be the artist's proving his own worth as a portraitist by depicting himself in the same way as had Dürer, Titian, Rubens, Anthony van Dyck (1599–1641), Rembrandt, Reynolds, Courbet (Fig. 125) and Cézanne. There are, however, also two drawn self-portraits in this Parisian sequence. The more interesting of the two sheets dates from the first half of 1887 and originally formed part of a large, single piece of paper, which the artist divided into four areas (Fig. 126).

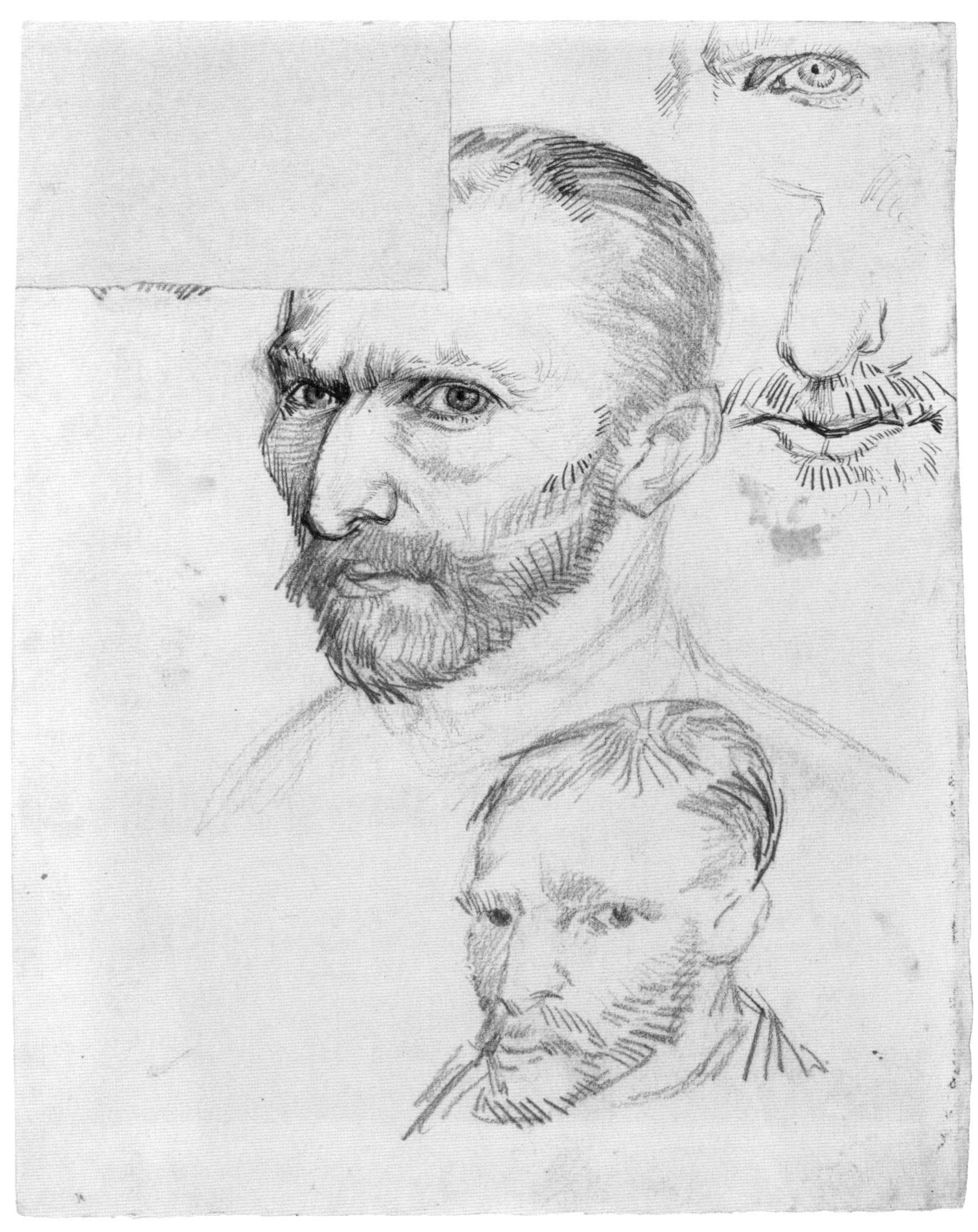

126 *Self-portrait*, January–June 1887.
Pencil, pen and ink, on paper,
31.1 × 24.4 cm (12¼ × 9⅝ in.).
VAN GOGH MUSEUM, AMSTERDAM

On this sheet Van Gogh depicts himself three times. The more finished, detailed head in the upper half is drawn in pencil with touches of pen and ink. It is a firmly structured likeness with due attention being paid to the features, particularly the eyes. Behind this face are less fully realized renderings of nose, mouth and eye, combining pencil with pen and ink, and seen in close up. Below is a more hastily drawn view of the whole head. The juxtaposition of these heads suggests the theme of the Three Ages of Man, but this is emphatically not Van Gogh's purpose here, even if the thought might have occurred to him as he was making the drawing. What he has achieved is a montage of his face and even of his moods, in preparation, possibly, for the self-portrait in oil either in the Art Institute of Chicago or in the Kunstmuseum in The Hague. Cézanne, in the privacy of his sketchbooks,

127 Paul Cézanne
Self-portrait, c. 1880.
Pencil on paper,
30 × 25 cm
(11⅞ × 9⅞ in.).
MUSEUM OF FINE ARTS, BUDAPEST

accumulated information about his own face in a comparable way: the viewer is teasingly confronted with a presence that seems to come and go like a mirage (Fig. 127).

On leaving Paris and moving to Arles, Van Gogh's principal goal became the establishment of a 'Studio of the South', to which he would invite other artists to work alongside him. The focus of such a project would be on producing paintings, but, when Van Gogh arrived alone in February 1888, he divided his time equally between painting and drawing. The original idea of inviting or enticing other artists to join him, particularly Gauguin, progressed slowly over the summer months and involved him in concentrated bouts of drawing. The much-delayed arrival of Gauguin in October, however, meant that Van Gogh became at that juncture more concerned with painting than drawing, and it was only after Gauguin's departure in December 1888 that he returned to his usual practice of pursuing both painting and drawing.

During the months that Van Gogh spent in Arles waiting for Gauguin to make up his mind, or, indeed, to find the money to travel to Provence, he was slowly establishing his contacts there. However fleeting, those friendships he valued most resulted in both painted and drawn portraits. Paul Eugène Milliet was a second lieutenant in a French Zouave regiment to whom he gave drawing lessons based on Cassagne's *Guide de l'alphabet du dessin*, and it was he who most probably introduced the artist to another member of the regiment. This resulted in two drawings ultimately related to paintings. The sitter was described by Van Gogh as having 'eyes like a cat's, watchful . . . a small head on a neck like a bull's' (653). In *Seated Zouave*, the figure is posed in front of a roughly indicated window or niche (Fig. 128). The style is distinctly caricatural, even allowing for the eccentricities of the uniform, which was based on the tribal costume of the Zwawa in Algeria to whom the Zouave regiments owed their origins. The long pipe and splayed legs on which the sitter's gnarled hands are positioned are surely humorous in intent or the result of spontaneous observation. The modelling of the face, cap and jacket provide some solidity to a rather unsatisfactory composition and execution, in which the figure seated on a low chair seems somewhat squashed within the rectangular format of the paper.

The Zouave, on the other hand, is more accomplished and livelier, partly owing to the combination of wax crayon and watercolour (Fig. 129). This is essentially a colour study for the

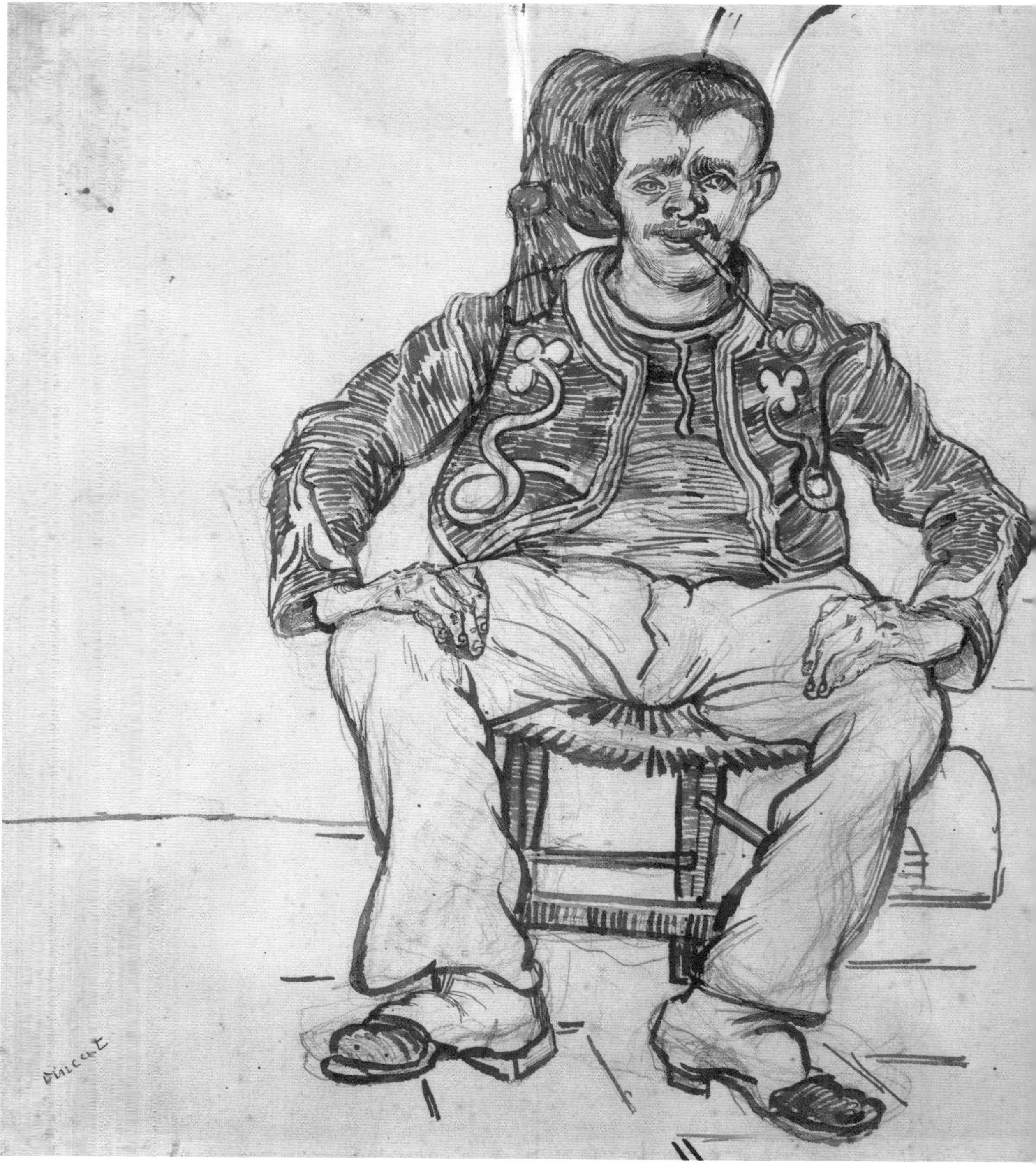
Vincent

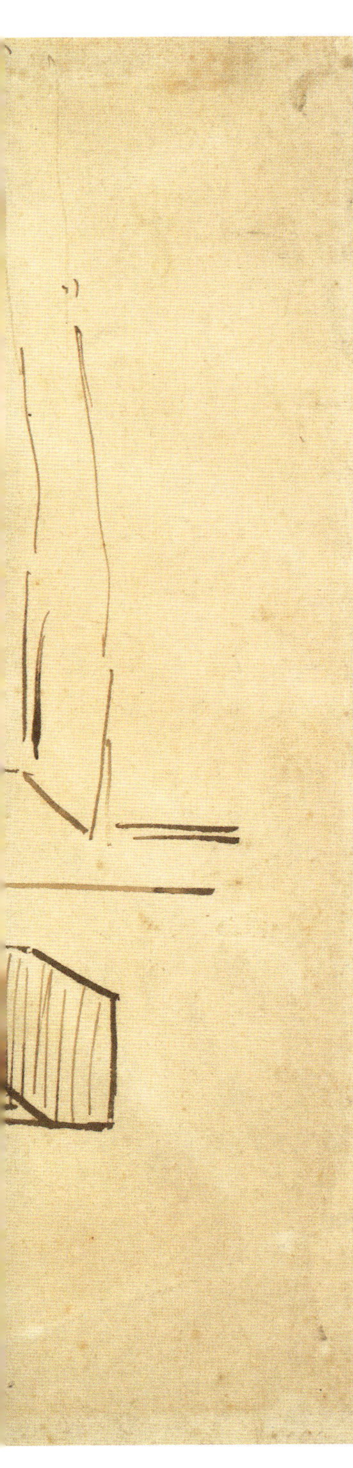

128 *Seated Zouave*, June 1888.
Pencil, reed pen and ink, watercolour, on paper, 49.3 × 61.2 cm (19½ × 24⅛ in.).
VAN GOGH MUSEUM, AMSTERDAM

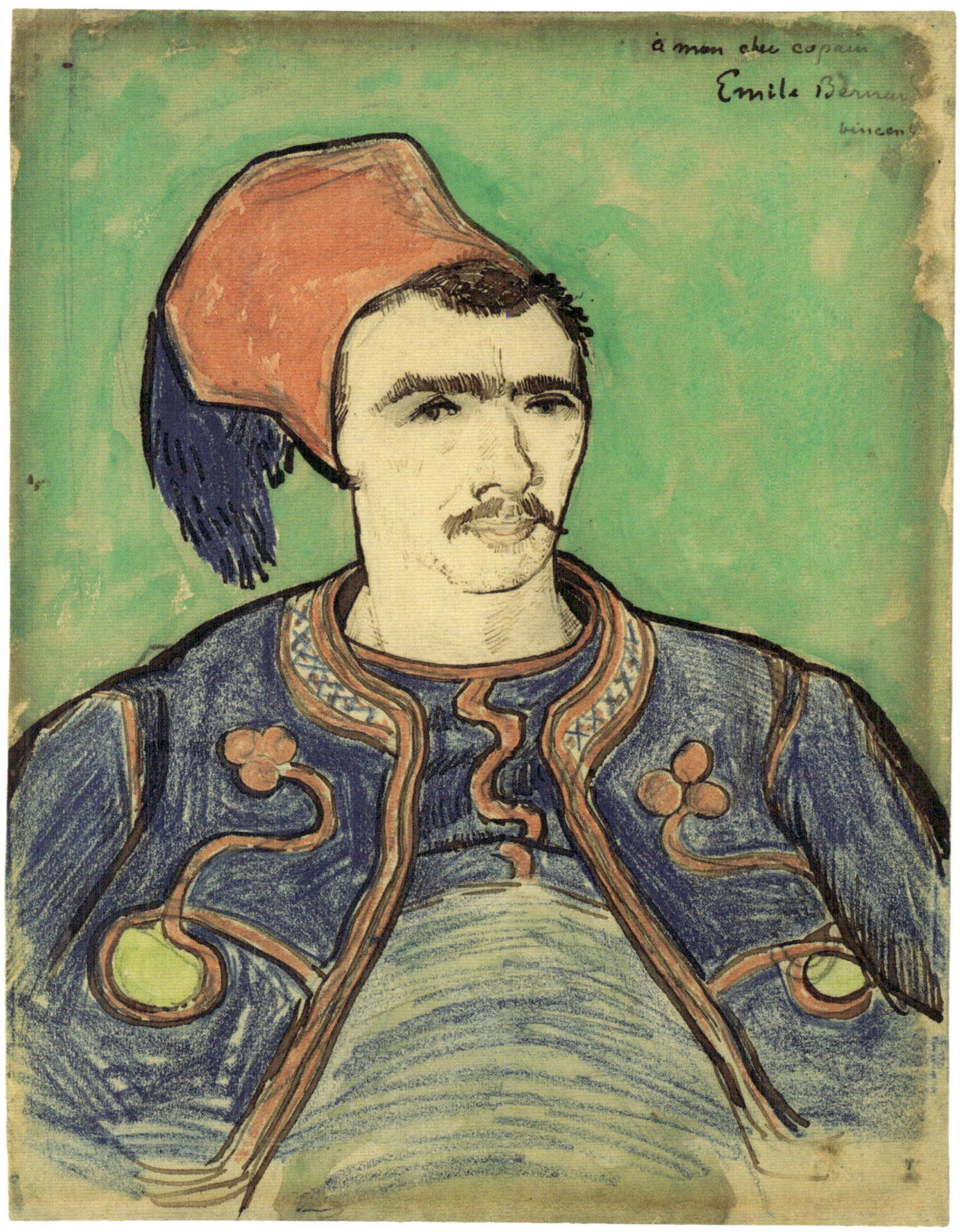

129 *The Zouave*, June 1888. Watercolour, reed pen and ink, wax crayon over pencil, on paper, 31.5 × 23.6 cm (12½ × 9⅜ in.). THE METROPOLITAN MUSEUM OF ART, NEW YORK

painting (Van Gogh Museum, Amsterdam), in which the face is more fully modelled and enhanced by warmer tones. In the drawing, Van Gogh revels in the sinuous decorative motifs of the uniform, the embroidered collar of which indicates that this particular soldier was a drummer in the regiment.

Other portraits drawn in the summer of 1888 were made in ink with a reed pen. Van Gogh's friendship with Joseph Roulin, who was technically an *entreposeur des postes*, employed to handle postage at the railway station in Arles, extended to his whole family: his wife, Augustine, who was the model for the composition entitled *La Berceuse*, known in no fewer than five versions, and their three children, Armand, Camille and the baby, Marcelle. Van Gogh was a neighbour of the Roulins, and they had similar political views. He compared Roulin's appearance with that of Socrates, adding that, 'The man is a fervent republican and socialist, reasons very well and knows many things' (653). He also liked drinking and, according to Van Gogh, 'lives a great deal in cafés. . . . But he's so much the opposite of *stupefied*, and his elation is so natural, so intelligent, and then he argues with such a broad sweep, à la Garibaldi' (702). Even after the artist left Arles, he received letters from Joseph Roulin, enquiring after his health and mental state. The drawing of Roulin is a resumé of a painting made at the same time, which is now in the Museum of Fine Arts in Boston (Figs 130 and 131). The pose and alert gaze echo that in the portrait of 1832 by Jean-Auguste-Dominique Ingres (1780–1867) of the director of the liberal *Journal des débats*, Louis-François Bertin (Musée du Louvre, Paris), which thereby gives a certain distinction to Van Gogh's friend. Masterly in every way is the handling of the reed pen in the cap, coat and the more lightly drawn facial features. The outlines of the chair and the creases in the trousers, which are otherwise left blank, are worthy of Manet. Here is Joseph Roulin in person, as alive to us as he was to Van Gogh.

Similarly, the drawings of the peasant Patience Escalier, who is depicted half-length in two contrasting characterizations, drawn at the beginning and the end of August 1888 respectively, reveal the supreme dexterity with which Van Gogh could handle the reed pen (Figs 132 and 133). Escalier was described by Van Gogh to Theo as 'an old Camargue oxherd, who's now a gardener at a farmstead in the Crau' (663). Confrontationally posed close to the picture plane, both the figures are placed against enlivened backgrounds. The skill lies in creating the contrast between the passages of close

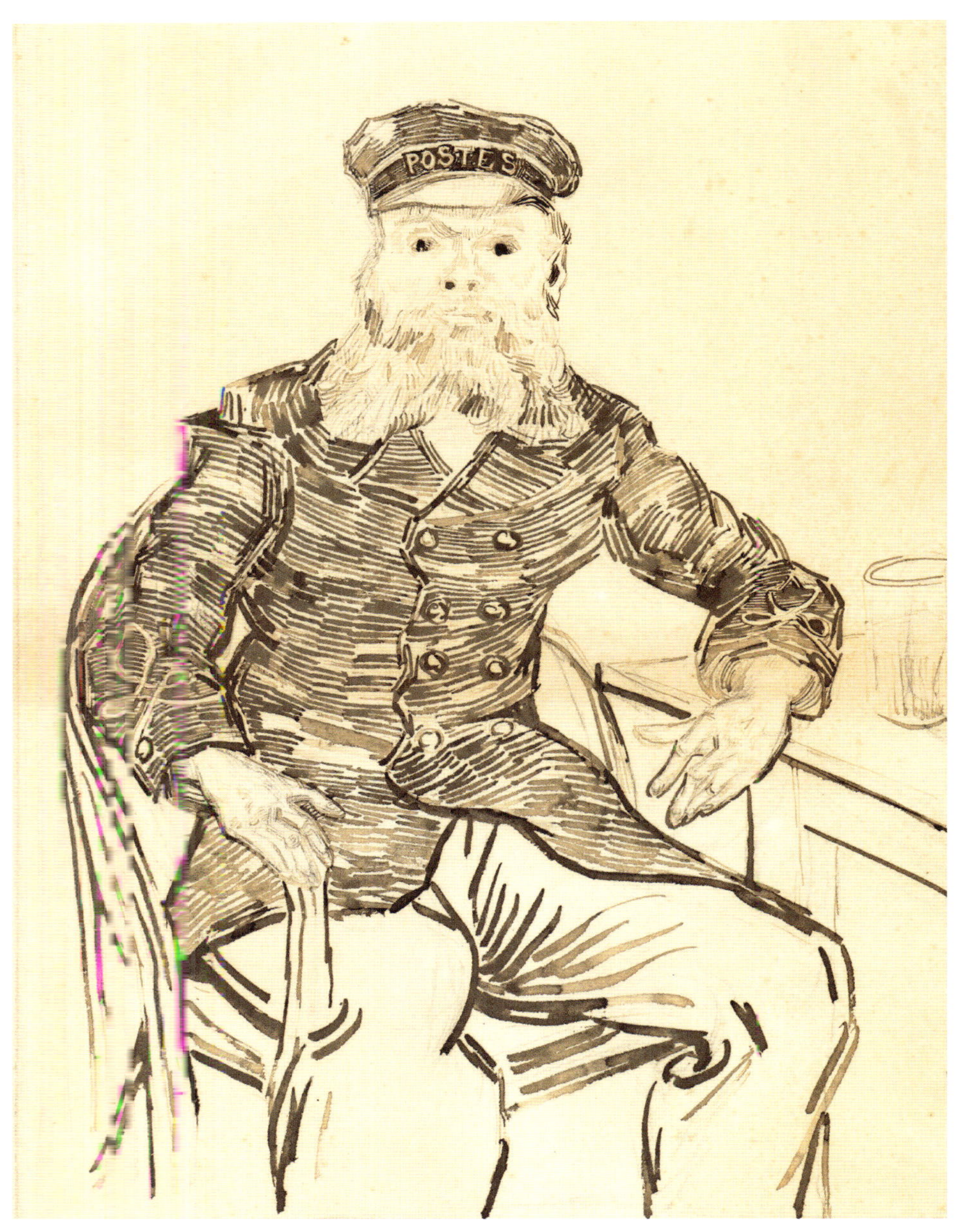

130 *The Postman Joseph Roulin*, early August 1888. Reed pen and ink over pencil, on paper, 51.4 × 42.2 cm (20¼ × 16⅝ in.). LOS ANGELES COUNTY MUSEUM OF ART

131 *Postman Joseph Roulin*, early August 1888. Oil on canvas, 81.3 × 65.4 cm (32 × 25¾ in.). MUSEUM OF FINE ARTS, BOSTON

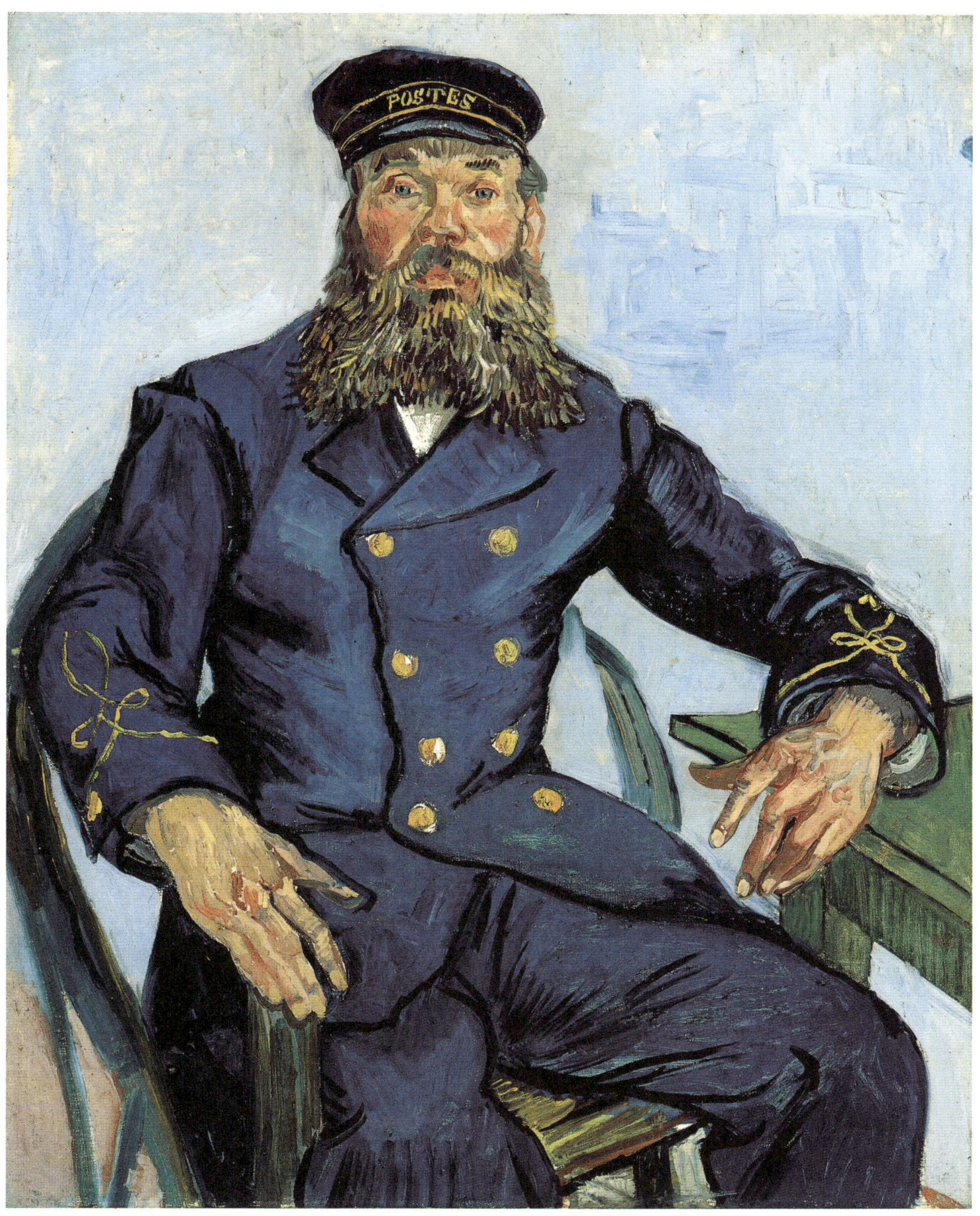
POSTES

modelling (facial features and neckerchief) and areas of blank paper (hat and coat). The peasant status of the sitter was one with which Van Gogh was in full sympathy, and it is interesting how the portraits are differentiated. The larger one in the Fogg Art Museum shows Escalier as though ennobled in the court of humanity, in so far as Van Gogh is reflecting on Millet's treatment of the peasant, as well as recalling Rembrandt's portrait etchings of the 1650s (Fig. 134). The other portrait is more animated, with the figure leaning slightly to one side, his hands crossed over the top of a stick. There is a sparkle and sense of energy, which suggests that a conversation is in progress between the artist and the sitter, perhaps discussing why the hat is so steeply turned up on one side. This is the world of Breugel the Elder and David Teniers the Younger (1610–1690).

132 *Portrait of Patience Escalier*, early August 1888. Reed pen and ink over pencil, on paper, 49.4 × 38 cm (19½ × 15 in.). FOGG MUSEUM, HARVARD ART MUSEUMS, CAMBRIDGE, MASS.

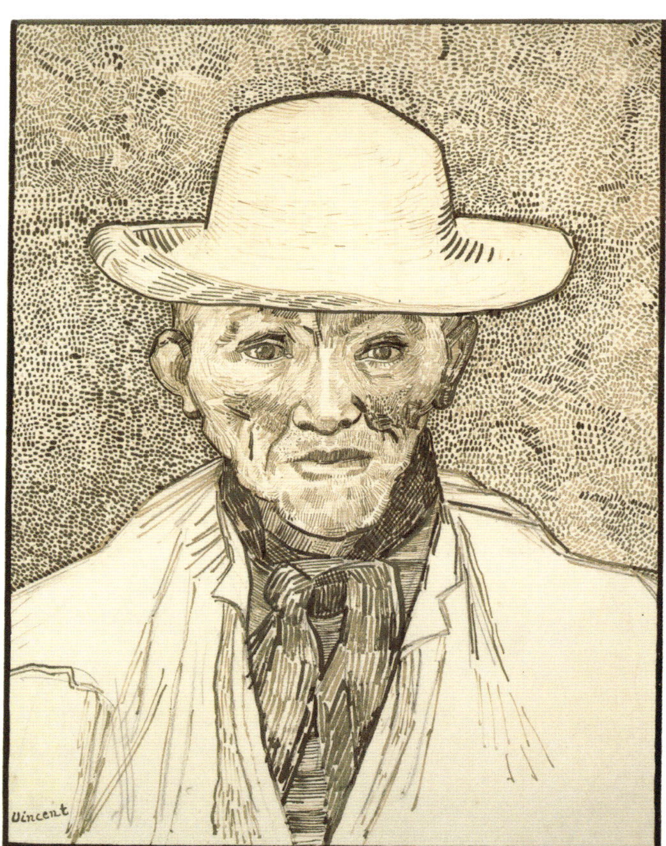

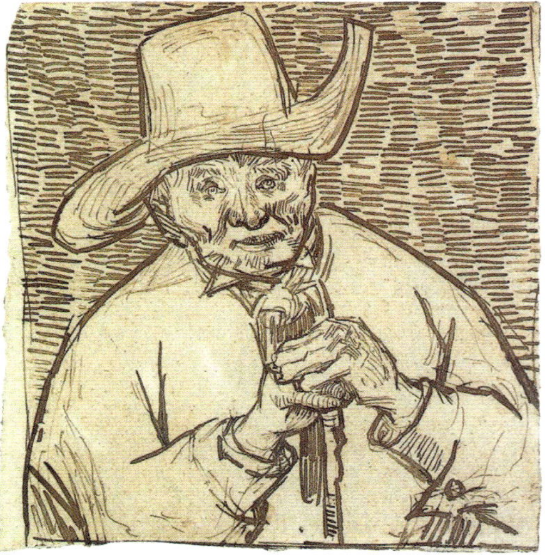

133 *Portrait of Patience Escalier*, late August 1888. Reed pen and ink, on paper, 13.5 × 13 cm (5³⁄₈ × 5¹⁄₈ in.). PRIVATE COLLECTION

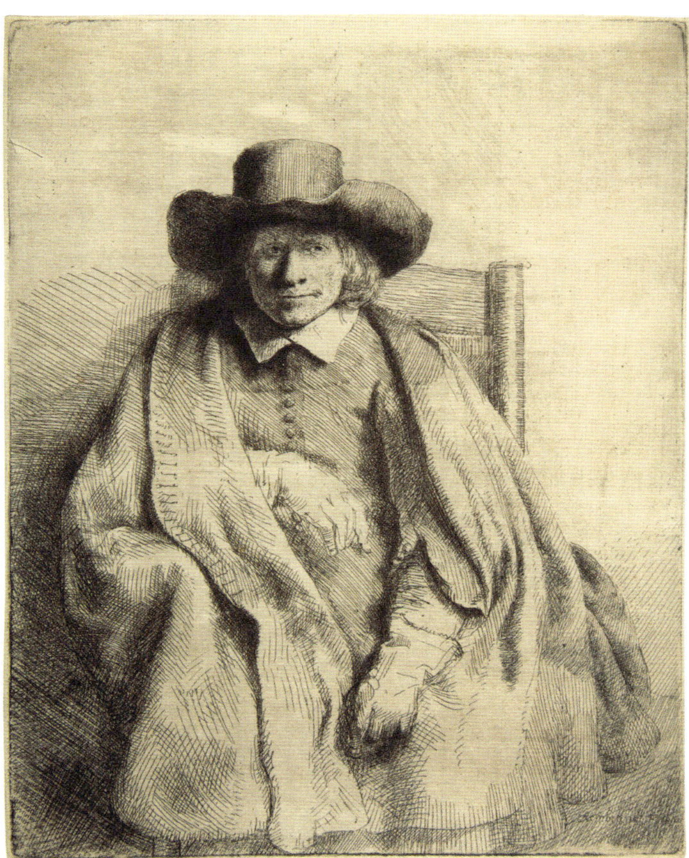

134 **Rembrandt van Rijn**
Portrait of Clement de Jonghe, 1651. Etching, drypoint and burin, 5th state, 20.6 × 16.1 cm (8⅛ × 6⅜ in.).
THE METROPOLITAN MUSEUM OF ART, NEW YORK

The virility exuded by the portraits of Roulin and Escalier is in direct contrast with the bewitchment of *La Mousmé*. Here the figure is inspired by a character Van Gogh was reading about in a novel by Pierre Loti set in Japan, *Madame Chrysanthème* of 1887. He first found a suitable model among the young Provençal girls to formulate his image of the idealized girl in the novel who was known as La Mousmé and who 'appeared . . . in full sunshine, and stood out in brilliant clearness like a fairy vision'. The painting is in the National Gallery of Art in Washington (Fig. 135), and the drawing made after it is in essence an undeniably brilliant extrapolation (Fig. 136). In contrast with the painting, the figure in the drawing is reduced to head and shoulders and moved closer to the picture plane. Van Gogh displays his knowledge of Japanese art in his

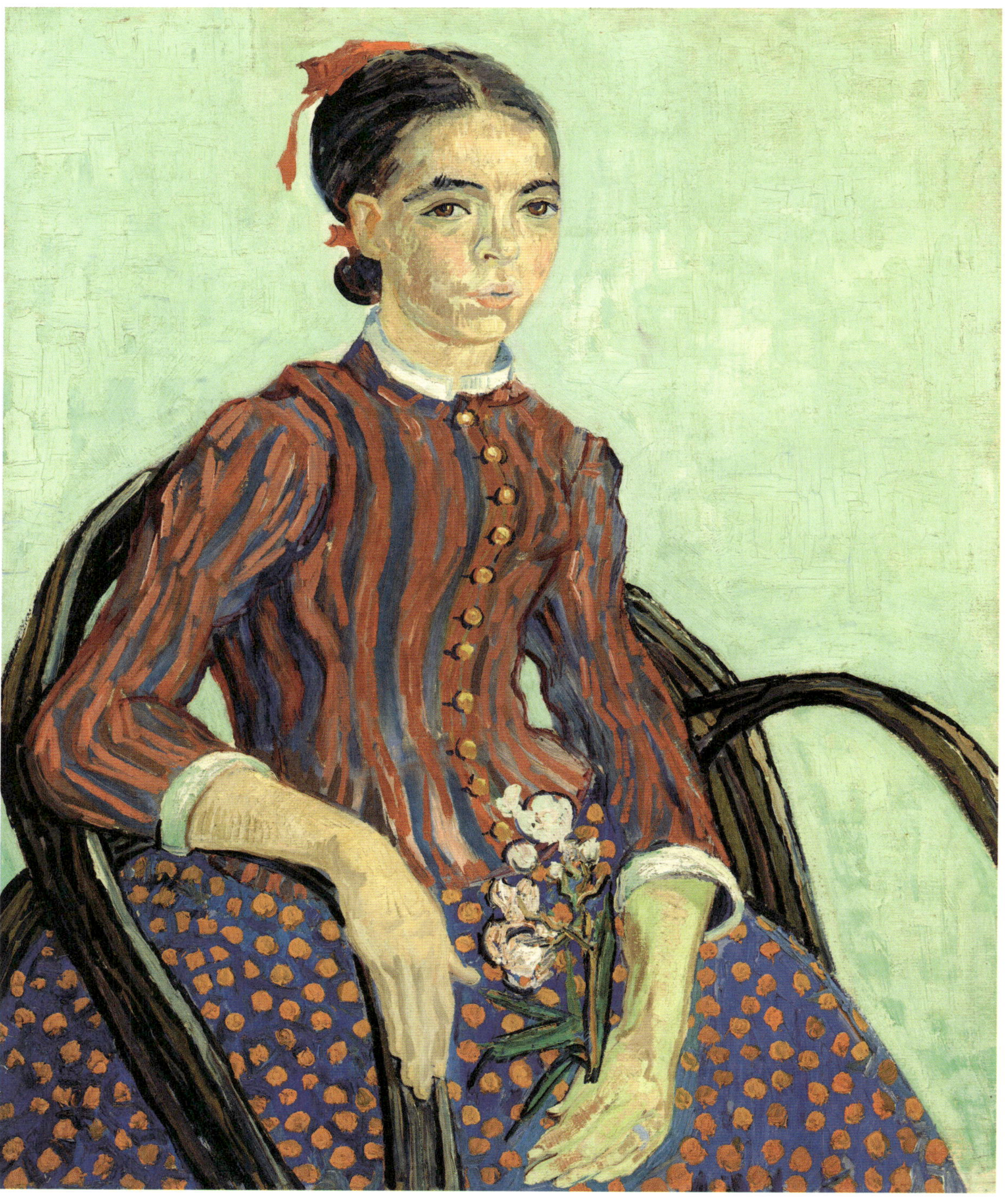

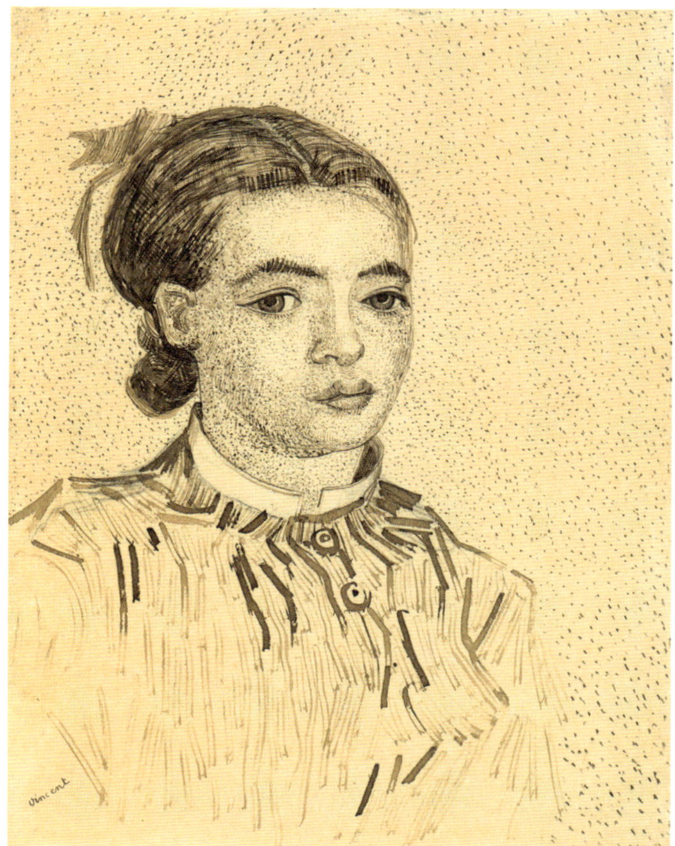

135 *La Mousmé*, July 1888. Oil on canvas, 73.3 × 60.3 cm (28⅞ × 23¾ in.). NATIONAL GALLERY OF ART, WASHINGTON, DC

136 *La Mousmé*, *c.* 31 July–3 August 1888. Reed and quill pen and ink over pencil, on paper, 31.5 × 24 cm (12⅜ × 9½ in.). PRIVATE COLLECTION

treatment of the face, particularly in the eyes. The technique throughout is of the greatest eloquence. Two types of pen have been used: the finer quill pen for the hair and the facial features, with the reed pen mainly reserved for the stripes in the dress. Clever use has been made in this last area of the broad cut of the reed pen as, under increasing pressure, it runs out of ink. The gently stippled background creates a radiant luminosity like the sun playing on water and an atmosphere that blends perfectly with the gentle contours of the face. Such an image positions Van Gogh among the greatest portraitists on paper, combining the equipoise and demureness of Raphael (1483–1520) with the elegant refinement of Ingres.

Chapter 7

Repetitions

During a three-week period in the summer of 1888, Van Gogh made thirty-two drawings after some of his most recent paintings. They constitute one of the most astonishing feats of draughtsmanship in the history of European art. Taken as a whole, this sequence of drawings is in many ways the summa of Van Gogh's drawing practices. Between mid-July and early August, he made three varied groups of drawings with different recipients in mind: the artists Émile Bernard and John Russell and his own brother Theo. In each case, the drawings were made for a specific purpose, in which the choice of subjects was of particular relevance.

Van Gogh had often made sketches (or what he termed 'scratches') of his compositions or works in progress as an accompaniment to his letters to family and friends. As a result, his evolution as an artist can be closely plotted through his correspondence. By contrast, the drawings after paintings sent to Bernard, Russell and Theo in 1888 are generally referred to as repetitions (*répétitions*) and are on independent sheets of paper. Technically they are a form of hybrid. They cannot be defined in Renaissance terms as presentation drawings, since they are not highly finished in style. Neither are they *ricordi*, since they are not conscious copies of the paintings they are reproducing, as are, for example, the *Liber Veritatis* of Claude Lorrain (1600–1682), now in the British Museum in London (Fig. 137), and the *Liber Studiorum* of J. M. W. Turner, made between 1807 and 1819 and comprising prints after paintings and watercolours. Rather, they are improvisations or, occasionally, variations of compositions already committed to canvas and still redolent in the artist's mind and eye. Stylistically, the result is in essence a translation of the brushstrokes on the canvas into marks made with a reed pen on paper. The repetitions, therefore, amount to an exercise in the reinterpretation of the technique of Van Gogh's paintings in terms of the grammar of drawing. This meant that, by some means, he had to suggest on paper the raised impasto left by a heavily loaded

Boats at Sea: Saintes-Maries-de-la-Mer, *c.* 6–8 August 1888 (detail of Fig. 143A).

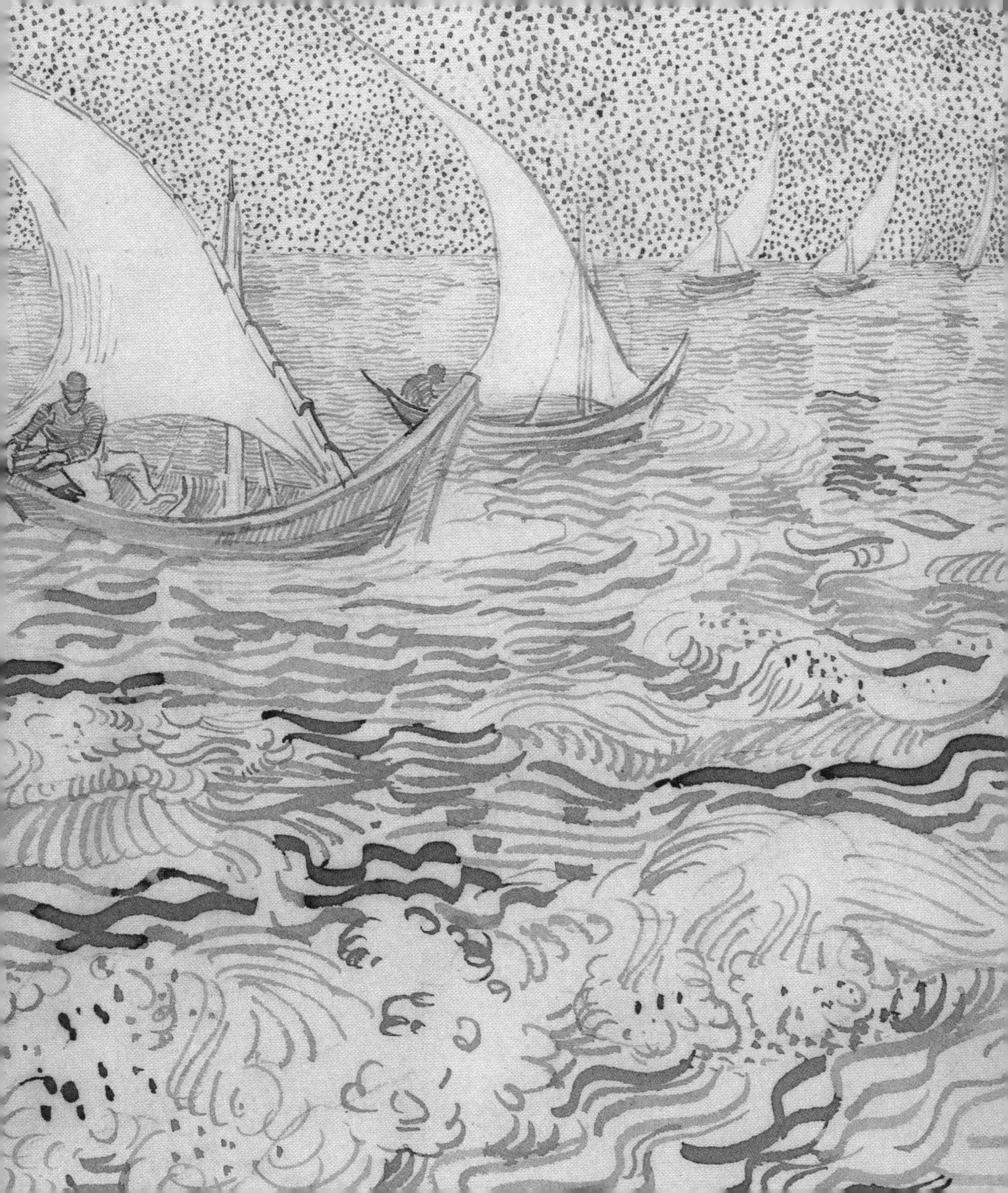

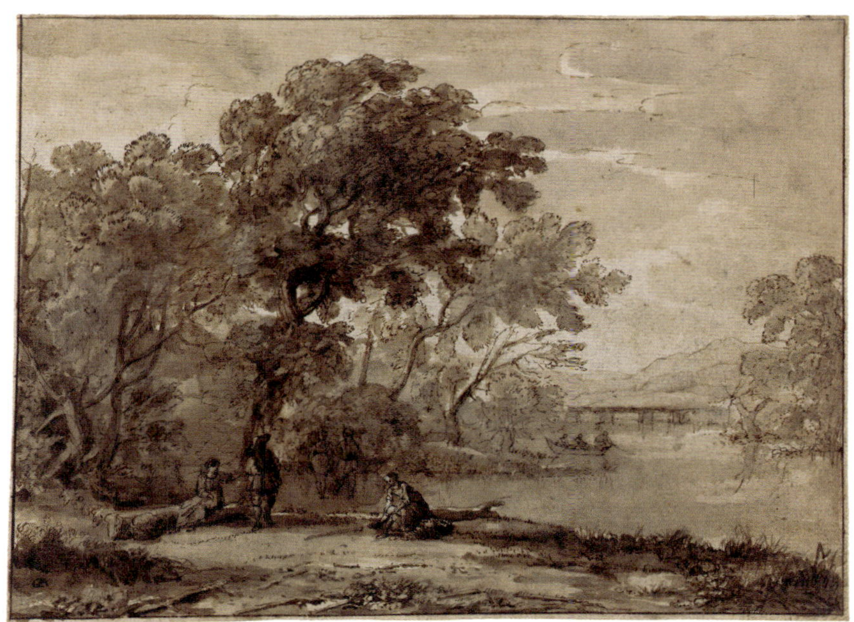

137 Claude Lorrain
Landscape with Peasants Crossing a Ford, from the *Liber Veritatis*, 1636. Pen and brown ink and brown wash, with grey-brown wash, on paper, 19 × 25 cm ($7\frac{1}{2}$ × $9\frac{7}{8}$ in.).
BRITISH MUSEUM, LONDON

brush on the canvas and the intensity of vibrant colour impinging on the viewer's eye. This was not actually a new challenge, since printmakers had often striven to simulate such pictorial effects in their work, either by the manipulation of pure line, as in the case of portraits by Claude Mellan and Robert Nanteuil in seventeenth-century France, or by creating the rich tonal qualities of the mezzotints produced in England during the late eighteenth and early nineteenth centuries. By contrast, Van Gogh's main instrument was simply the reed pen, which he occasionally used in conjunction with other types of nib.

The representations were distributed unevenly among the recipients: Bernard was sent fifteen drawings in two batches on 15 and 17 July. Twelve drawings were dispatched to Russell between 31 July and around 3 August. Originally, Van Gogh intended also to send his brother twelve examples, but only five were posted in the end, sometime in early August. Subsequently, none of the groups remained intact and were dispersed through dealers and the saleroom. The contents of each group have, therefore, been reconstituted by scholars using the correspondence and the provenances as their main sources of evidence.

Van Gogh overlapped with the much younger Bernard for a short time at Cormon's studio in Paris in 1886. Their independent approach to art cemented their friendship, which was developed through shared painting sessions in the suburb of Asnières, where Bernard's parents lived, and an appreciation of Japanese art. Van Gogh genuinely admired Bernard's early works, such as the painting *Breton Women at a Pardon* (1888; private collection), of which he made a fine copy in watercolour (Fig. 138), and he also admired the younger man's championship of Cézanne. Both artists had changeable, often volatile, temperaments, and, in reality, their friendship was relatively short-lived. It was not helped by Van Gogh's departure for Provence in February 1888 or by Bernard's return to Brittany, which he had been visiting since 1886. Their epistolary contact continued until the autumn of 1889, but, as a consequence of Bernard's having established

138 *Breton Women (after Émile Bernard)*, 1888. Watercolour on paper, 47.5 × 62 cm (18¾ × 24½ in.). GALLERIA D'ARTE MODERNA, MILAN

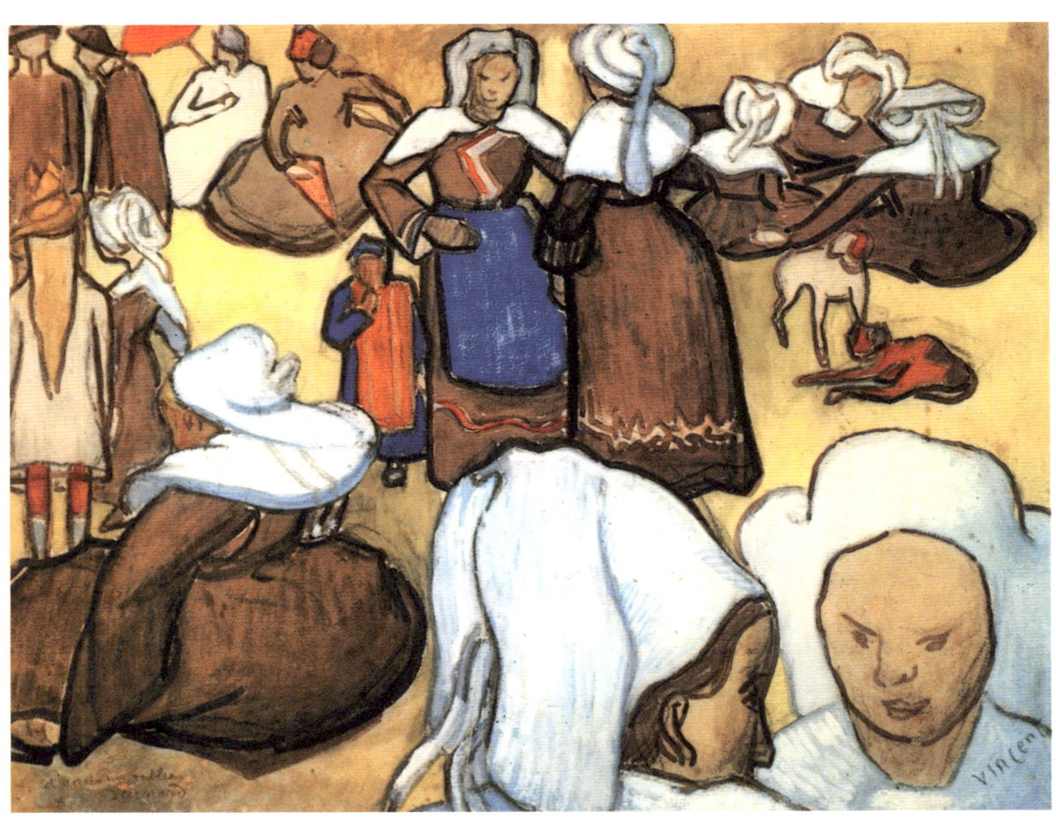

a close working relationship with Gauguin, his art began to change, and he went through a series of stylistic transformations away from Impressionism through Neo-Impressionism, Cloisonnism and finally Symbolism – the last of which Van Gogh disapproved of, particularly when it became imbued with religious connotations.

Van Gogh's motive in sending his fifteen repetitions to Bernard was in response to an initiative made by the younger artist to begin a series of exchanges. This was begun in the late spring or early summer of 1888 and was followed by several other such exchanges. As promised, Van Gogh passed on Bernard's numerous drawings to Theo in the hope that his brother would use them to promote Bernard's work and possibly that he would buy one of the paintings for their own collection.

Van Gogh chose the subjects of his repetitions with the intention of introducing Bernard – and ultimately Gauguin – to the array of suitable subjects for painting presented by Provence (Figs 139A–O). Seven of the drawings are connected with the harvest; two are of Saintes-Maries-de-la-Mer (one of them a seascape); four are of Arles, including scenes of the river, the canal and the public garden; one is a view of the landscape of La Crau; and, finally, there is the watercolour and wax crayon portrait of the Zouave soldier

Drawings sent to Émile Bernard

139A *A Corner of a Garden in the place Lamartine*, mid-July 1888. Reed pen and ink over pencil, on paper, 24.2 × 31.6 cm (9½ × 12½ in.). PRIVATE COLLECTION

139B *The Langlois Bridge, Arles*, mid-July 1888. Reed pen and ink over pencil, on paper, 24.5 × 31.9 cm (9¾ × 12⅝ in.). LOS ANGELES COUNTY MUSEUM OF ART

139C *Boats at Sea: Saintes-Maries-de-la-Mer*, mid-July 1888. Reed pen and ink over pencil, on paper, 24 × 32 cm (9½ × 12⅝ in.). KUPFERSTICHKABINETT, STAATLICHE MUSEEN, BERLIN

139D *Street in Saintes-Maries-de-la-Mer*, mid-July 1888. Reed pen and ink over pencil, on paper, 24.3 × 31.7 cm (9⅝ × 12½ in.). THE METROPOLITAN MUSEUM OF ART, NEW YORK

139E *Laundry on 'La Roubine du Roi' Canal*, mid-July 1888. Reed pen and ink over pencil, on paper, 31.5 × 24 cm (12⅜ × 9½ in.) KRÖLLER-MÜLLER MUSEUM, OTTERLO

139F *The Trinquetaille Bridge*, mid-July 1888. Reed pen and ink over pencil, on paper, 24.3 × 31.6 cm (9⅜ × 12½ in.). PRIVATE COLLECTION

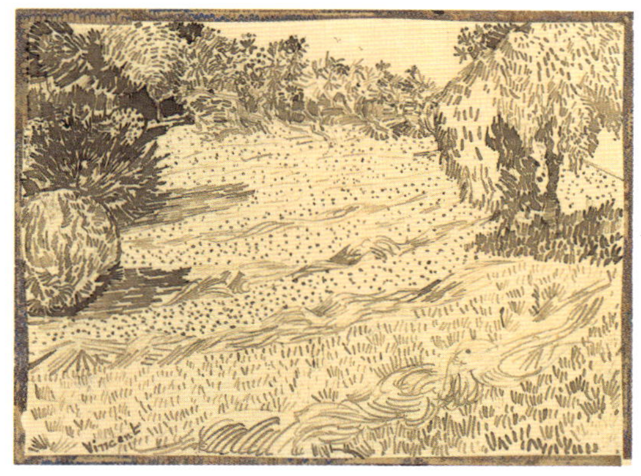
Vincent

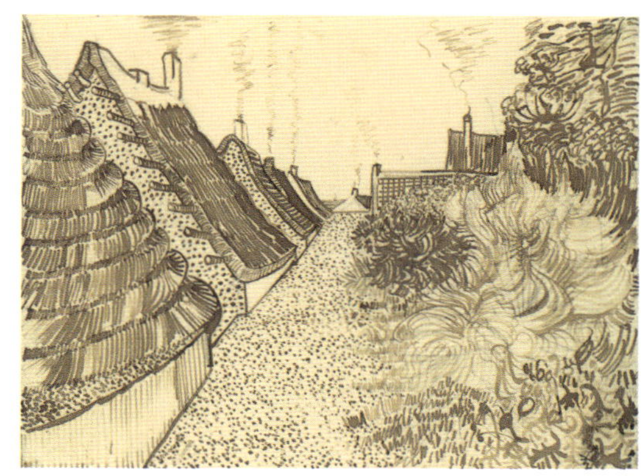

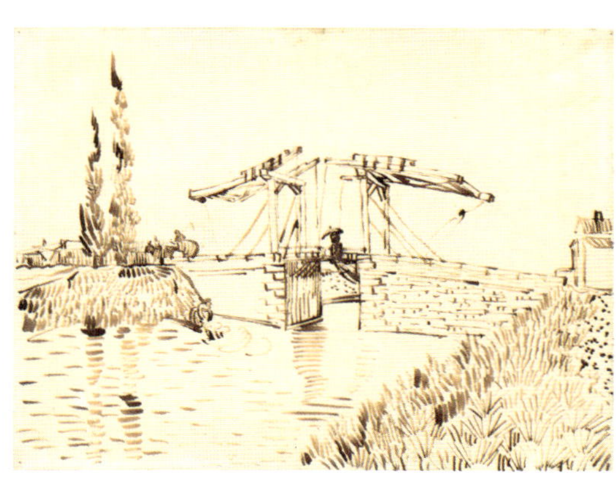

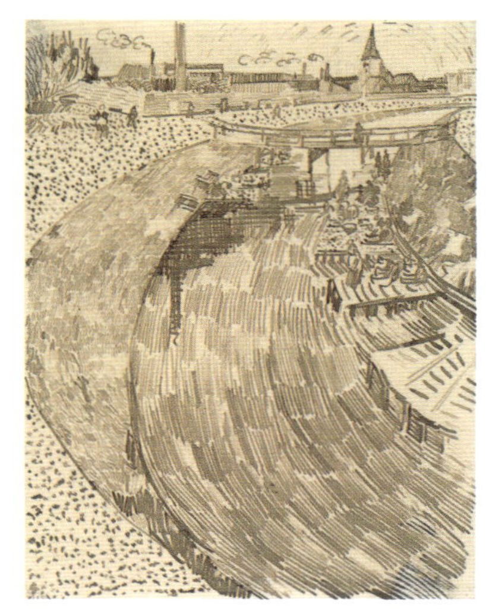

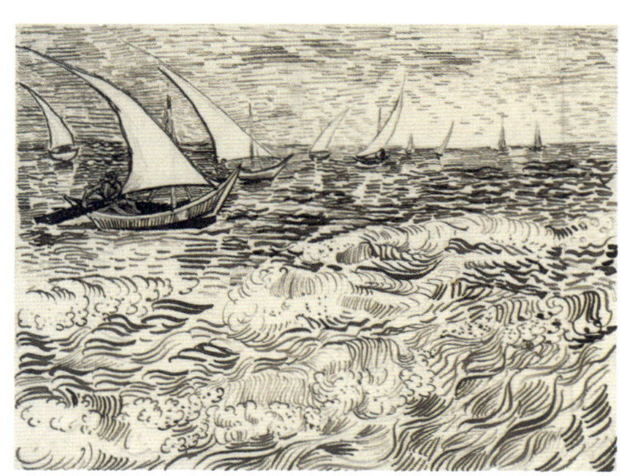

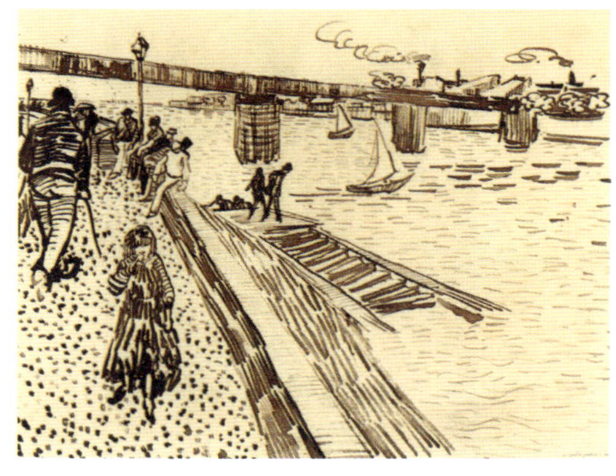

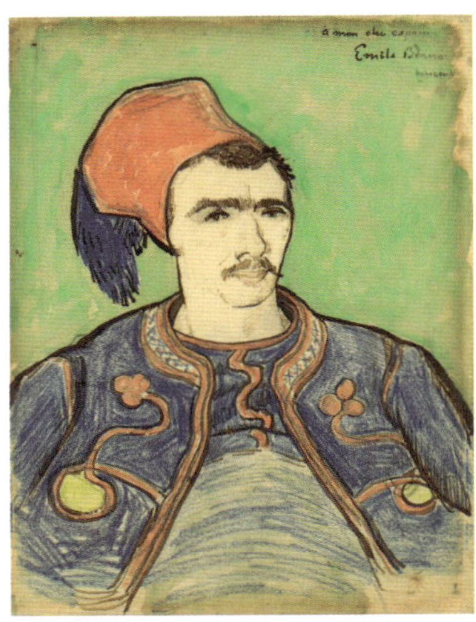

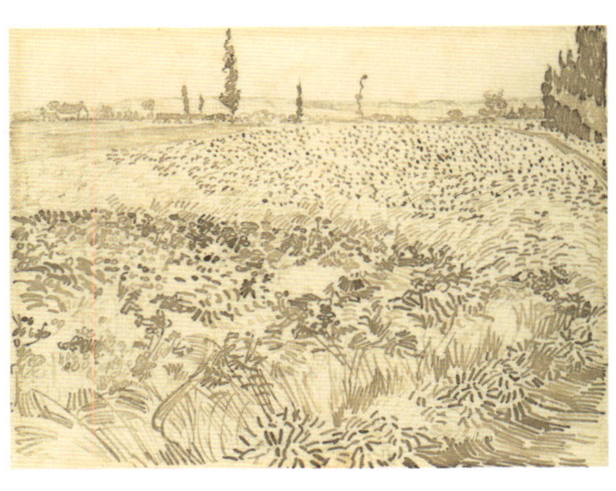

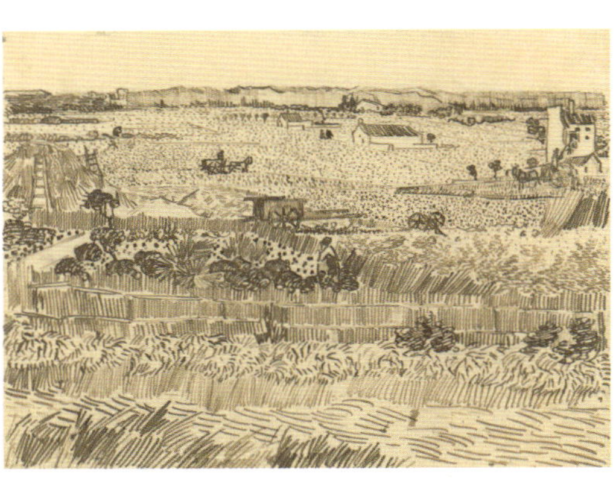

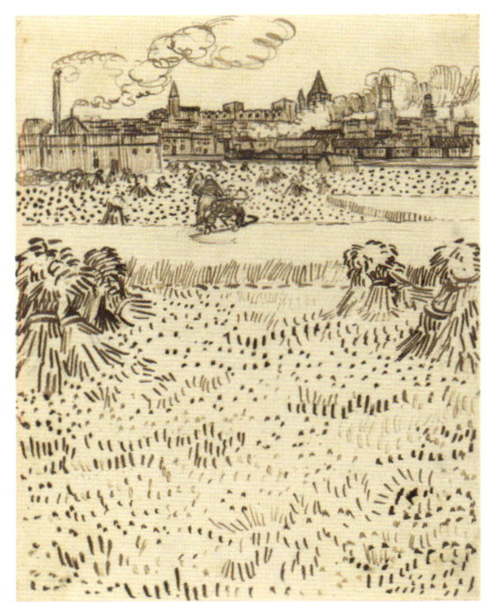

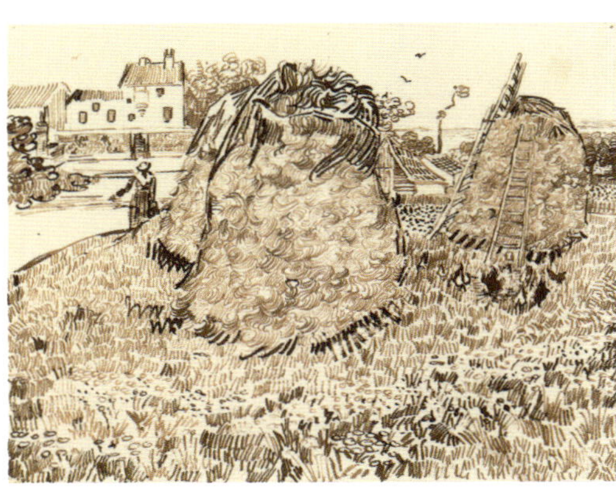

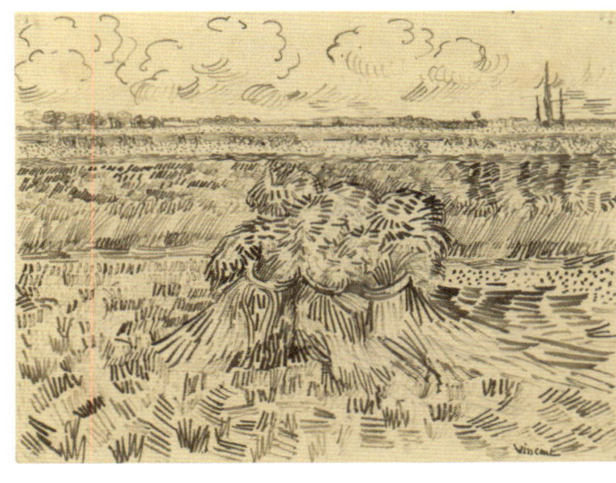
Vincent

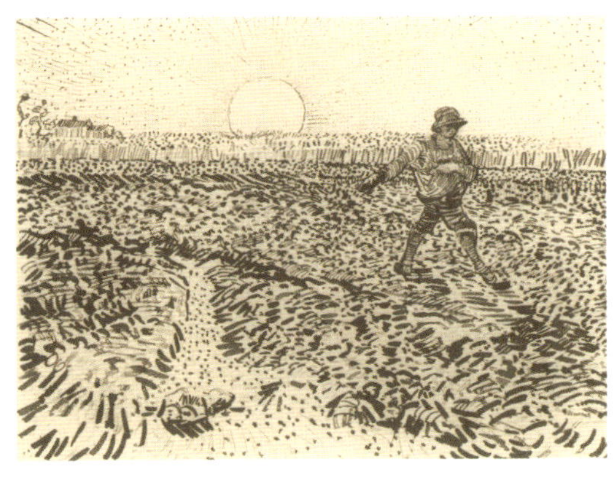

139G *The Zouave*, *c.* 20 June 1888. Watercolour, reed pen and ink, wax crayon over pencil, on paper, 31.5 × 23.6 cm ($12\frac{1}{2} \times 9\frac{3}{8}$ in.). THE METROPOLITAN MUSEUM OF ART, NEW YORK

139J *Wheatfield*, mid-July 1888. Reed pen and ink over pencil, on paper, 24.1 × 31.8 cm ($9\frac{7}{8} \times 12\frac{1}{2}$ in.). THE METROPOLITAN MUSEUM OF ART, NEW YORK

139M *The Sower*, mid-July 1888. Reed pen and ink over pencil, on paper, 24.5 × 31.7 cm ($9\frac{5}{8} \times 12\frac{1}{2}$ in.). PRIVATE COLLECTION

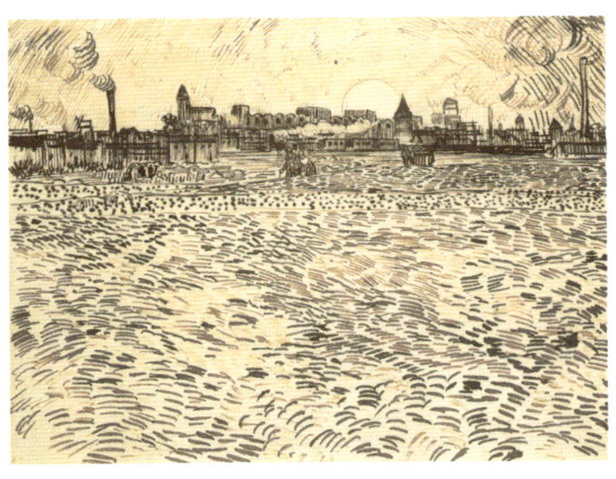

139H *Harvest in Provence*, mid-July 1888. Reed and quill pen and ink over pencil, on paper, 24 × 31.9 cm ($9\frac{1}{2} \times 12\frac{5}{8}$ in.). KUPFERSTICHKABINETT, STAATLICHE MUSEEN, BERLIN

139K *The Harvest*, mid-July 1888. Reed pen and brown ink over pencil, on paper, 31.7 × 24.2 cm ($12\frac{1}{2} \times 9\frac{1}{2}$ in.). NATIONAL GALLERY OF ART, WASHINGTON, DC

139N *A Summer Evening*, mid-July 1888. Reed pen and ink over pencil, on paper, 24 × 31.5 cm ($9\frac{1}{2} \times 12\frac{1}{8}$ in.). KUNST MUSEUM WINTERTHUR

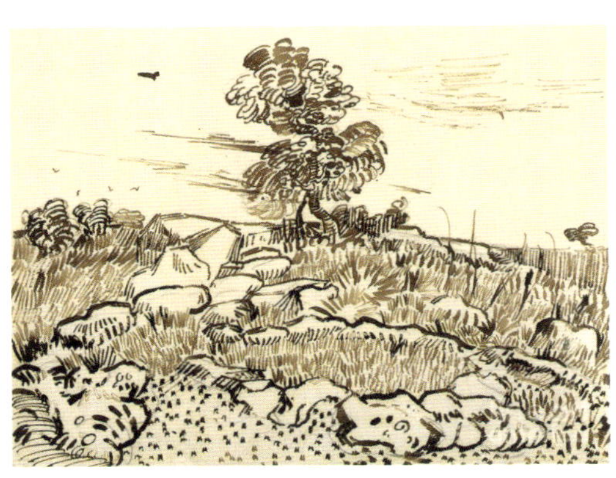

139I *Haystacks*, mid-July 1888. Reed pen and ink, on paper, 24 × 31.5 cm ($9\frac{1}{2} \times 12\frac{3}{8}$ in.). MUSEUM OF FINE ARTS, BUDAPEST

139L *Wheatfield with Bundles of Grain*, mid-July 1888. Reed pen and ink over pencil, on paper, 24.4 × 31.9 cm ($9\frac{5}{8} \times 12\frac{5}{8}$ in.). KUPFERSTICHKABINETT, STAATLICHE MUSEEN, BERLIN

139O *Rocks with Tree*, mid-July 1888. Reed pen and ink over pencil, on paper, 24 × 31 cm ($9\frac{1}{2} \times 12\frac{1}{4}$ in.). PRIVATE COLLECTION

(Fig. 129). Bernard's reaction was to mount the drawings in an album, which he did eventually show to Gauguin and other artists in his circle in Pont-Aven. He later promoted these drawings in various articles he wrote about Van Gogh and interviews he gave.

The most striking stylistic feature in the sequence for Bernard is the freedom of the penwork within each drawing – a veritable vortex of frequently repeated hatched lines, varying according to the pressure applied to the pen, over brief indications in pencil. The penwork then spirals out into a wide range of short horizontal and vertical strokes, dashes, whorls and flicks. On the other hand, there is only a limited number of Pointillist dots, since by this date Bernard had reacted strongly against Neo-Impressionism. Amazingly, although Van Gogh was drawing with such abandon, he manages throughout to retain control over the key compositional elements.

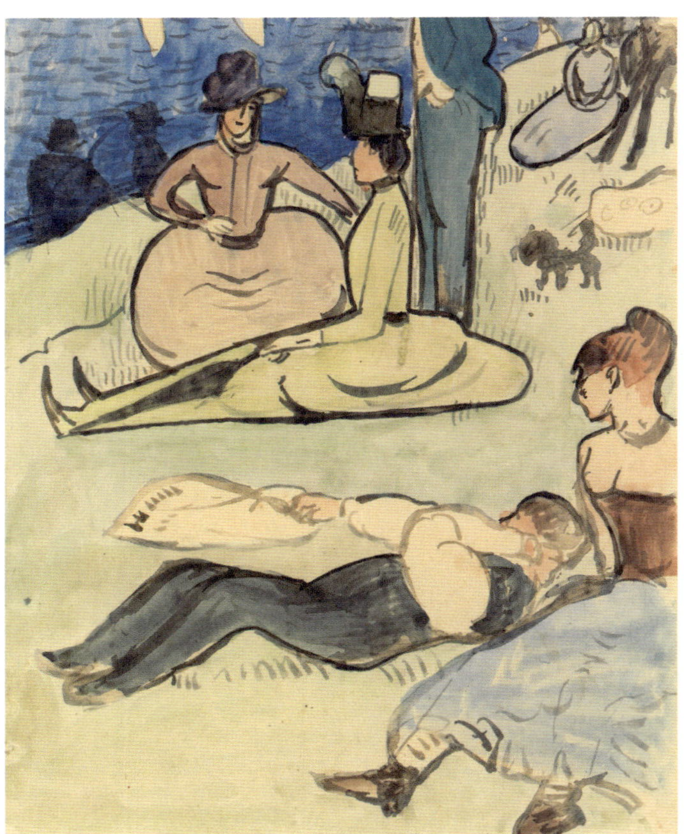

140 Émile Bernard
Figures by the Riverside, September 1888. Reed pen and brush and ink and watercolour, on paper, 32 × 26 cm (12⅝ × 10¼ in.).
VAN GOGH MUSEUM, AMSTERDAM

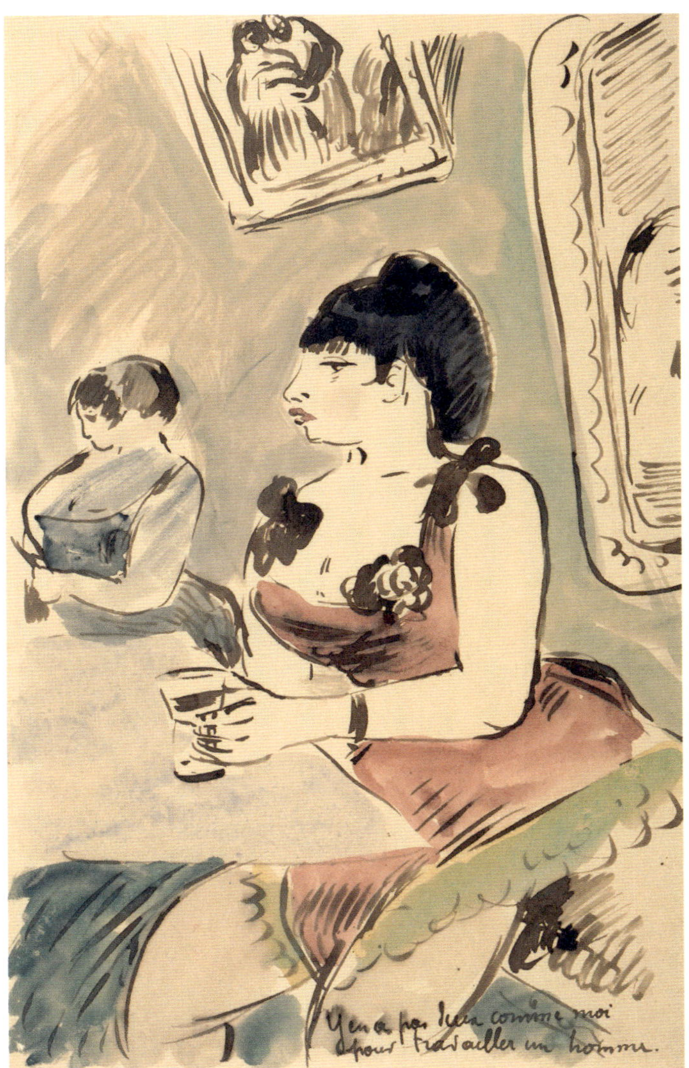

141 Émile Bernard
No One Can Pull a Man's Strings as Well as Me, 1888. Brush and ink and watercolour, on paper, 40.5 × 26.9 cm (16 × 10⅝ in.).
VAN GOGH MUSEUM, AMSTERDAM

The watercolours with pen and ink that Bernard sent in batches to Van Gogh in return are of a different order. They are varied in subject but united by his fascination with brothel scenes (Figs 140 and 141). These may not have been what Van Gogh was expecting, and he may even have been disappointed by them, though he loyally passed them on to Theo. Certainly, both artists shared an interest in brothels, and such subject matter reflects the more ribald passages in their correspondence, such as Van Gogh's remarks about the sexual incontinence of Rubens and Courbet compared with Degas's inadequacies in this department (655).

Van Gogh's motive in sending twelve of his repetitions to John Russell was largely altruistic. The idea was to encourage Russell to purchase a painting by Gauguin, and this would help to offset the expenses incurred when Gauguin made the trip to Arles to join Van Gogh and set up the 'Studio of the South'. Russell was born in Australia into a wealthy family. His father was an iron-founder, who, when he died in 1879, left his son a considerable fortune.

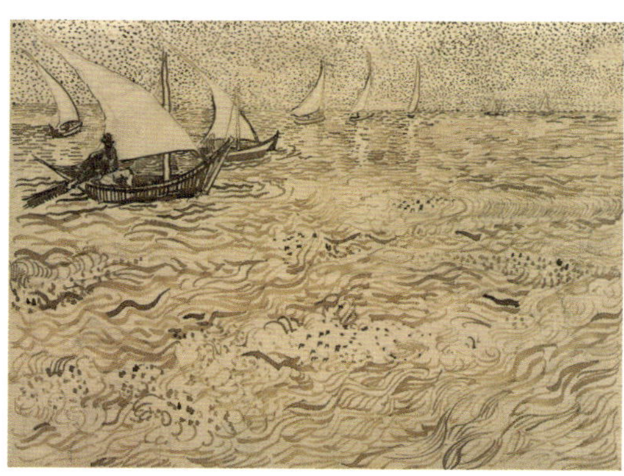

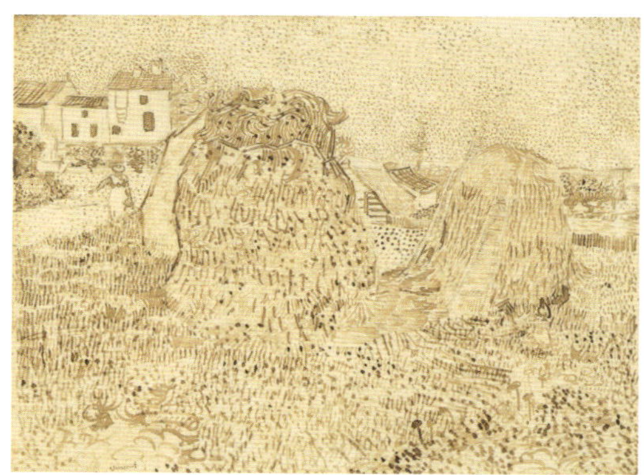

Drawings sent to John Russell

142A *Boats at Sea: Saintes-Maries-de-la-Mer*, *c.* 31 July–3 August 1888. Reed pen and ink over pencil, on paper, 24.3 × 31.9 cm (9⅝ × 12⅝ in.). SOLOMON R. GUGGENHEIM MUSEUM, NEW YORK

142B *Haystacks*, *c.* 31 July–3 August 1888. Reed and quill pens and brown ink over pencil, on paper, 24.1 × 31.8 cm (9½ × 12½ in.). PHILADELPHIA MUSEUM OF ART

142C *A Corner of a Garden in the place Lamartine*, *c.* 31 July–3 August 1888. Reed pen and ink over pencil, on paper, 31.5 × 24.5 cm (12½ × 9¾ in.). PRIVATE COLLECTION

142D *Boats at Sea: Saintes-Maries-de-la-Mer*, *c.* 31 July–3 August 1888. Reed pen and ink over pencil, on paper, 24.4 × 31.9 cm (9⅝ × 12½ in.). SAINT LOUIS ART MUSEUM

142E *Garden with Flowers*, *c.* 31 July–3 August 1888. Reed pen and ink, on paper, 24 × 31.5 cm (9½ × 12⅜ in.). PRIVATE COLLECTION

142F *Harvest: The Plain of La Crau*, *c.* 31 July–3 August 1888. Reed pen and brown ink over pencil, on paper, 24.2 × 31.9 cm (9½ × 12⅝ in.). NATIONAL GALLERY OF ART, WASHINGTON, DC

After travelling in England and Spain, Russell attended Cormon's studio in Paris in 1886 where he became friends with Van Gogh. In 1887, he left Paris and built a house on Belle-Île, off the south coast of Brittany, where he continued to paint until returning to Australia in 1919. Russell patronized several avant-garde artists and formed an important collection of their work. Monet visited him on Belle-Île in 1886, as did Matisse in 1896 and 1897, and Auguste Rodin (1840–1917) was among his friends.

The selection of drawings made by Van Gogh for Russell was deliberately enticing (Figs 142A–L), not only illustrating the wide

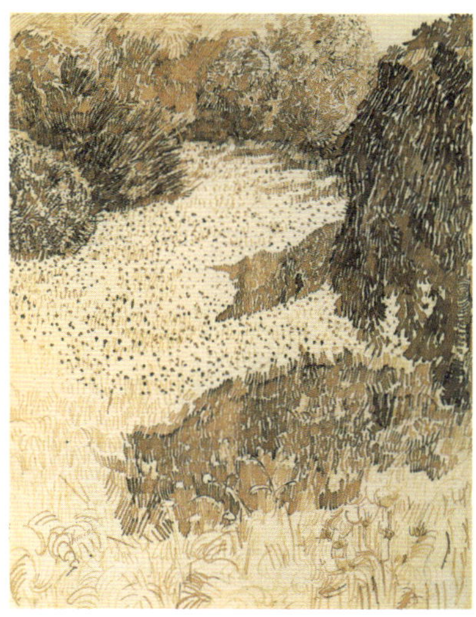

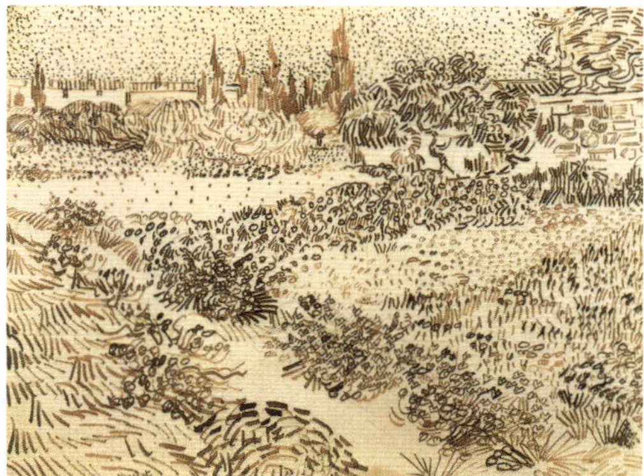

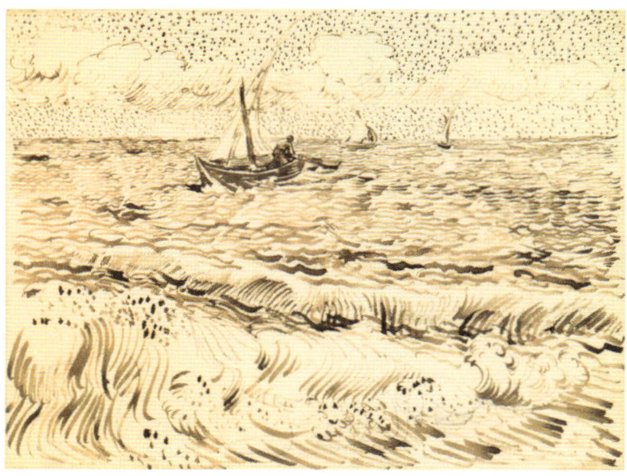

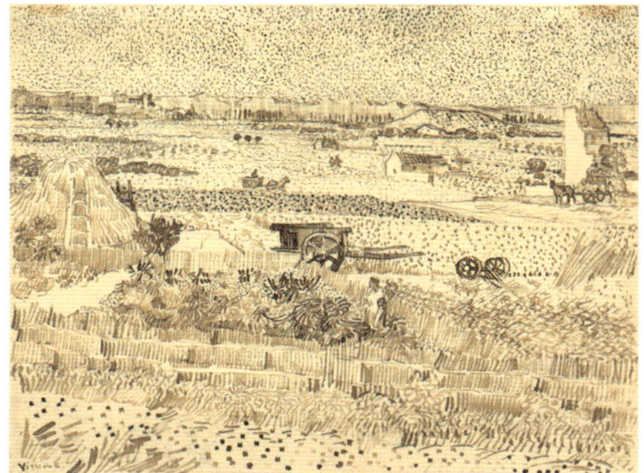

range of the artist's work being done in Provence, but also subtly reflecting Russell's own proclivities as a painter. There are four harvesting scenes, two seascapes of Saintes-Maries-de-le-Mer, two garden scenes, one view of the road leading from Arles to Tarascon and, perhaps most importantly, three portraits – the Zouave, La Mousmé and Joseph Roulin. Five of the subjects were repeats from the selection sent to Bernard, albeit with slight compositional changes and one in a different format. Unfortunately, Russell declined to purchase any paintings by Gauguin on this occasion,

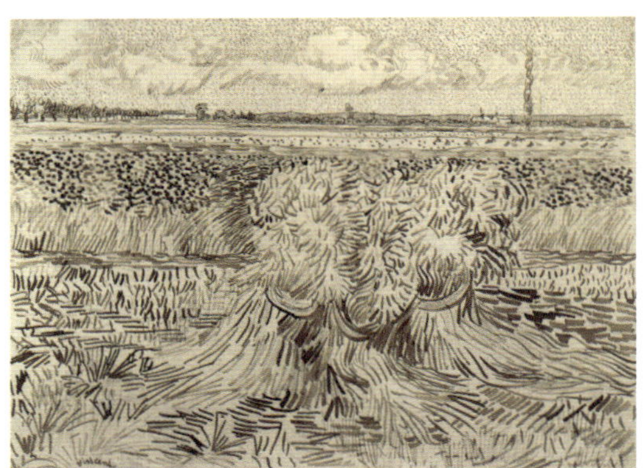

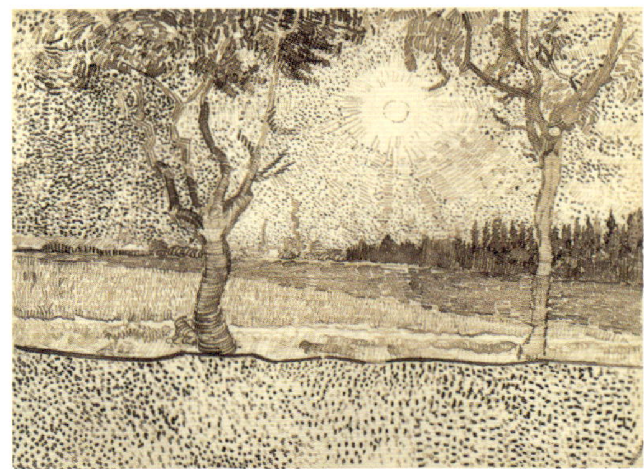

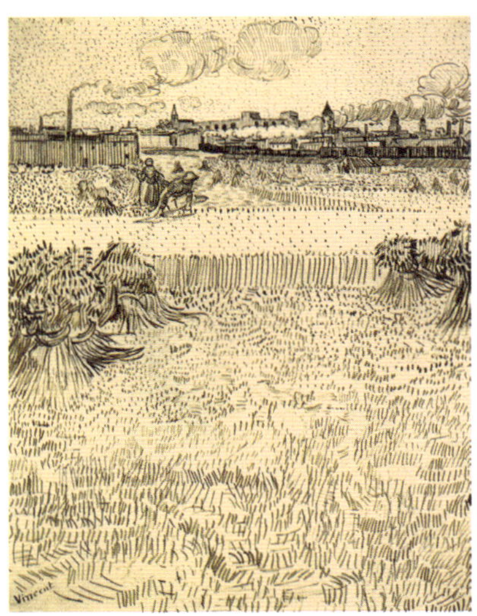

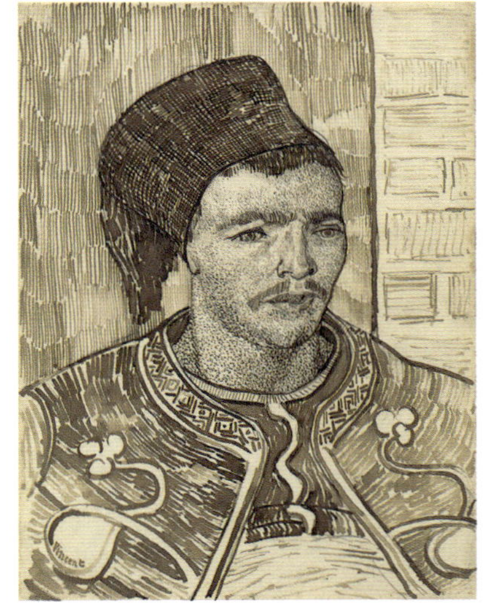

and so Van Gogh's ultimate purpose was a failure. Russell began to dispose of the drawings discreetly in 1920, having given one (*Haystacks*, now in the Philadelphia Museum of Art; Fig. 142B) to Matisse, and eventually left the three remaining to his daughter in 1930.

The quality of these repetitions suggests that Van Gogh was doing his utmost to support Gauguin's cause, but that he was also keen to demonstrate to Russell the quantity and high quality of his own recent output. The sense of achievement in this sequence of

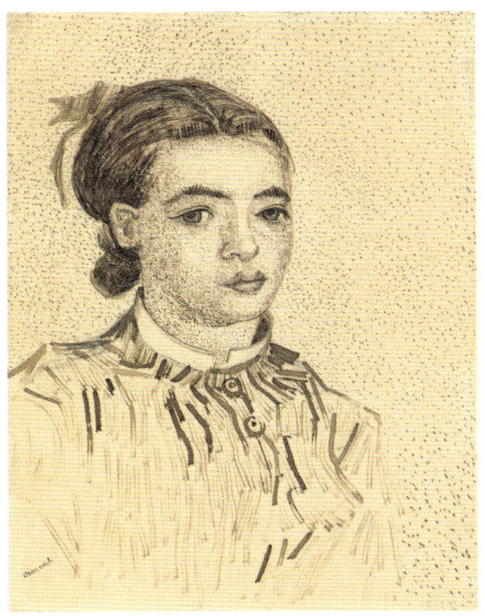

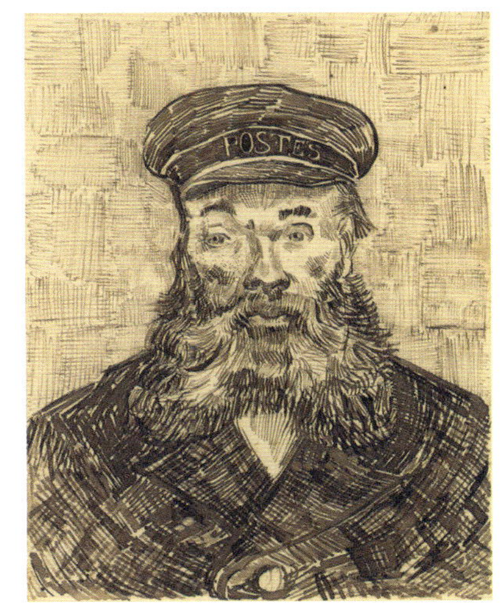

142G *Wheat Field with Sheaves*, *c.* 31 July–3 August 1888. Reed and quill pen and ink over pencil, on paper, 24.2 × 31.7 cm (9½ × 12½ in.). PRIVATE COLLECTION

142H *Arles: View from the Wheatfields*, *c.* 31 July–3 August 1888. Reed and quill pen and ink over pencil, on paper, 31.5 × 23.5 cm (12½ × 9¼ in.). PRIVATE COLLECTION

142I *The Road to Tarascon*, *c.* 31 July–3 August 1888. Reed pen and ink over pencil, on paper, 24.3 × 31.9 cm (9⅝ × 12⅝ in.). SOLOMON R. GUGGENHEIM MUSEUM, NEW YORK

142J *The Zouave*, *c.* 31 July–3 August 1888. Reed pen and pen and brown ink over pencil, on paper, 31.9 × 24.3 cm (12⅝ × 9⅝ in.). SOLOMON R. GUGGENHEIM MUSEUM, NEW YORK

142K *La Mousmé*, *c.* 31 July–3 August 1888. Reed and quill pen and ink over pencil, on paper, 31.5 × 24 cm (12⅜ × 9½ in.). PRIVATE COLLECTION

142L *Portrait of Joseph Roulin*, *c.* 31 July–3 August 1888. Reed and quill pen and brown ink over black chalk, on paper, 32.1 × 24.4 cm (12⅝ × 9⅝ in.). J. PAUL GETTY MUSEUM, LOS ANGELES

drawings is impressive. It is as though Van Gogh were determined to show how he could spread his technical skills evenly across each separate category of painting – landscape, marine, portraiture. This gives the drawings a sense of unity, which is enhanced to a certain extent by a greater uniformity of pen stroke, notably in the horizontal and vertical lines, as well as in the use of the Pointillist dot, which occurs in every one of the drawings. This stylistic coherence lends the sequence a finished and deliberate appearance.

Theo van Gogh was sent fewer repetitions than Bernard or Russell, although in the first instance he was told he would receive twelve (Figs 143A–E). Van Gogh, in fact, gave up after preparing five, although he did provide three supplementary garden scenes on a grander scale in an attempt to make up the shortfall. However, it may have been that the artist was by now moving away from

Drawings sent to Theo van Gogh

143A *Boats at Sea: Saintes-Maries-de-la-Mer*, *c.* 6–8 August 1888. Reed pen and grey-brown ink over pencil, on paper, 24.2 × 31.9 cm (9½ × 12½ in.). MUSÉES ROYAUX DES BEAUX-ARTS DE BELGIQUE, BRUSSELS

143B *Boats at Sea: Saintes-Maries-de-la-Mer*, *c.* 6–8 August 1888. Reed pen and ink over pencil, on paper. 24 × 32 cm (9½ × 12¾ in.). SAINT LOUIS ART MUSEUM

143C *The Sower*, *c.* 6–8 August 1888. Pencil, pen and reed pen and ink, on paper, 24.4 × 32 cm (9⅝ × 12⅝ in.). VAN GOGH MUSEUM, AMSTERDAM

143D *Arles: View from the Wheatfields*, *c.* 6–8 August 1888. Reed and quill pen and brown ink, on paper, 31.2 × 24.1 cm (12⅜ × 9½ in.). J. PAUL GETTY MUSEUM, LOS ANGELES

143E *A Corner of a Garden in the place Lamartine*, *c.* 6–8 August 1888. Reed and quill pen and ink over pencil, on paper, 24.4 × 32.1 cm (9⅝ × 12⅝ in.). THE MENIL COLLECTION, HOUSTON

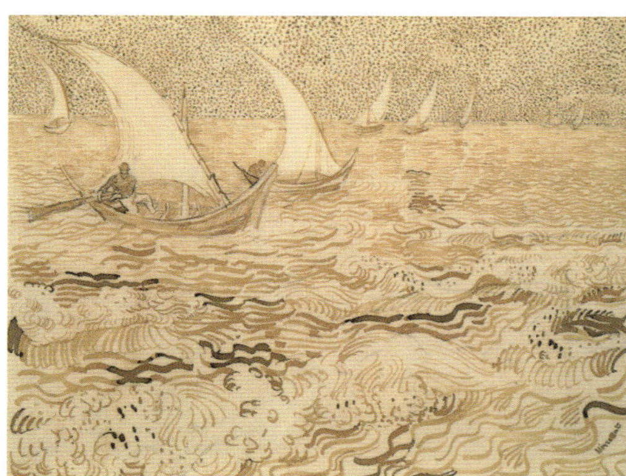

further exploration of his concept of producing official repetitions after his paintings. Furthermore, in the case of the group for Theo, Van Gogh may simply have been compiling a progress report for his brother. There are two marine subjects made at Saintes-Maries-de-la-Mer, two harvesting scenes, including *The Sower*, and one view of the public garden in Arles. The style of these drawings – possibly because Van Gogh was now much more practised in the art of drawing his repetitions – is a further development of those done for Russell. Comparison between those drawings with motifs that are common to all three sequences – *The Harvest* and *Arles: View*

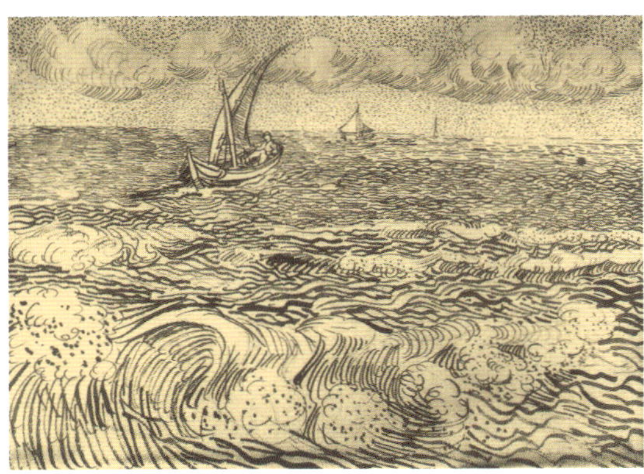

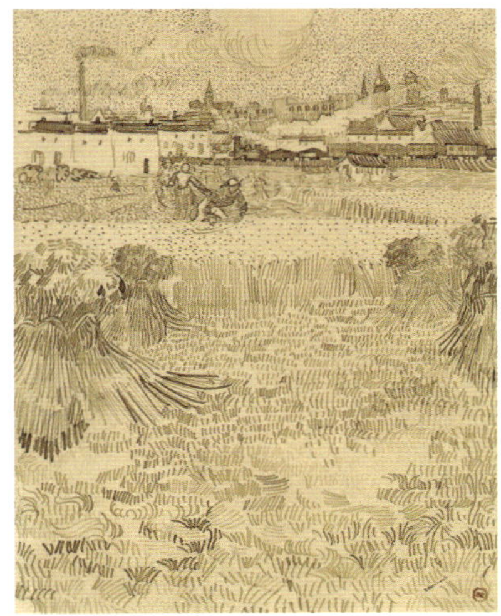

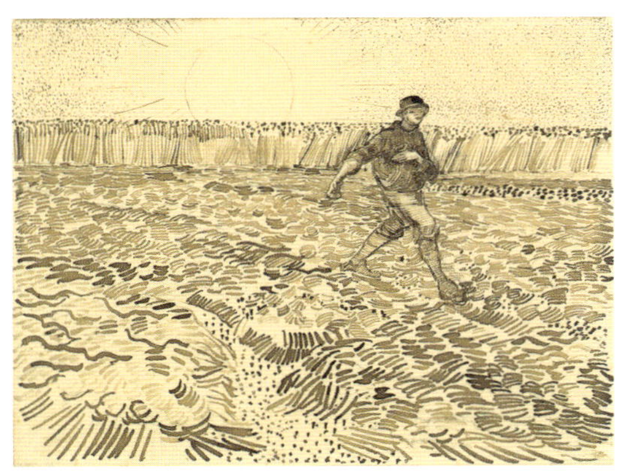

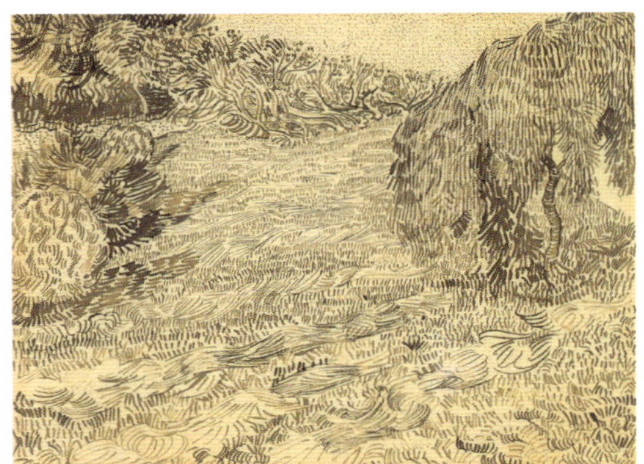

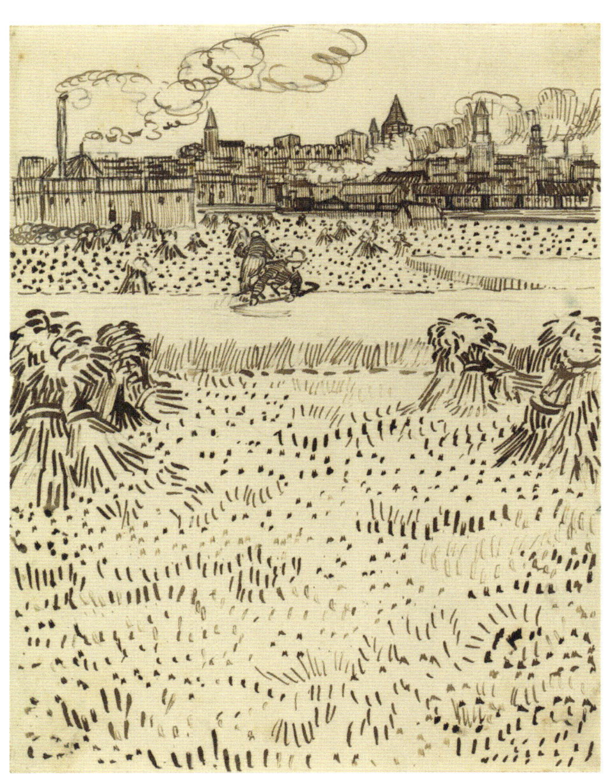

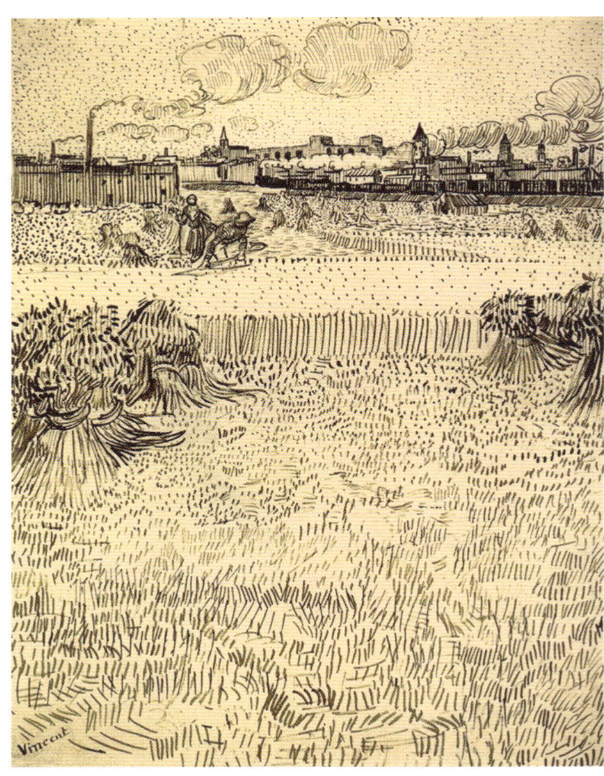
Vincent

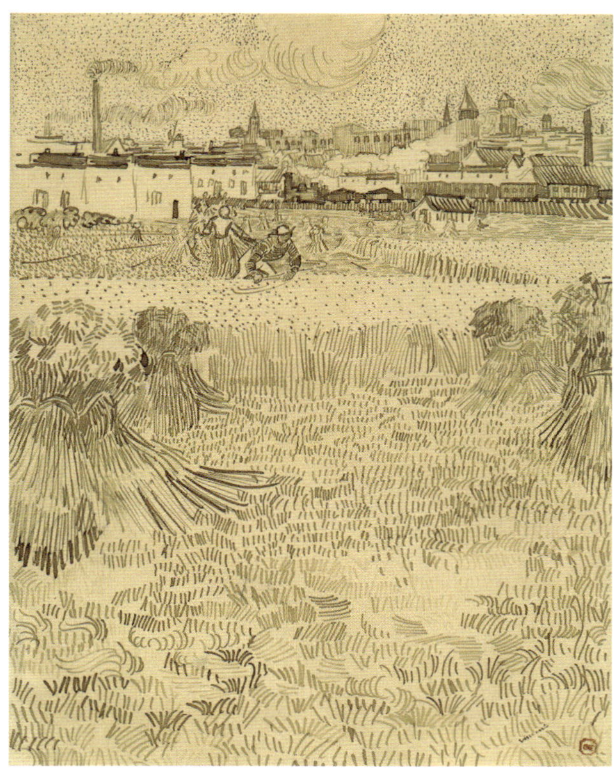

144 *The Harvest*, mid-July 1888. Reed pen and brown ink over pencil, on paper, 31.7 × 24.2 cm (12½ × 9½ in.).
NATIONAL GALLERY OF ART, WASHINGTON, DC

145 *Arles: View from the Wheatfields*, *c.* 31 July–3 August 1888. Reed and quill pen and ink over pencil, on paper, 31.5 × 23.5 cm (12½ × 9¼ in.).
PRIVATE COLLECTION

146 *Arles: View from the Wheatfields*, *c.* 6–8 August 1888. Reed and quill pen and brown ink, on paper, 31.2 × 24.1 cm (12¼ × 9½ in.).
J. PAUL GETTY MUSEUM, LOS ANGELES

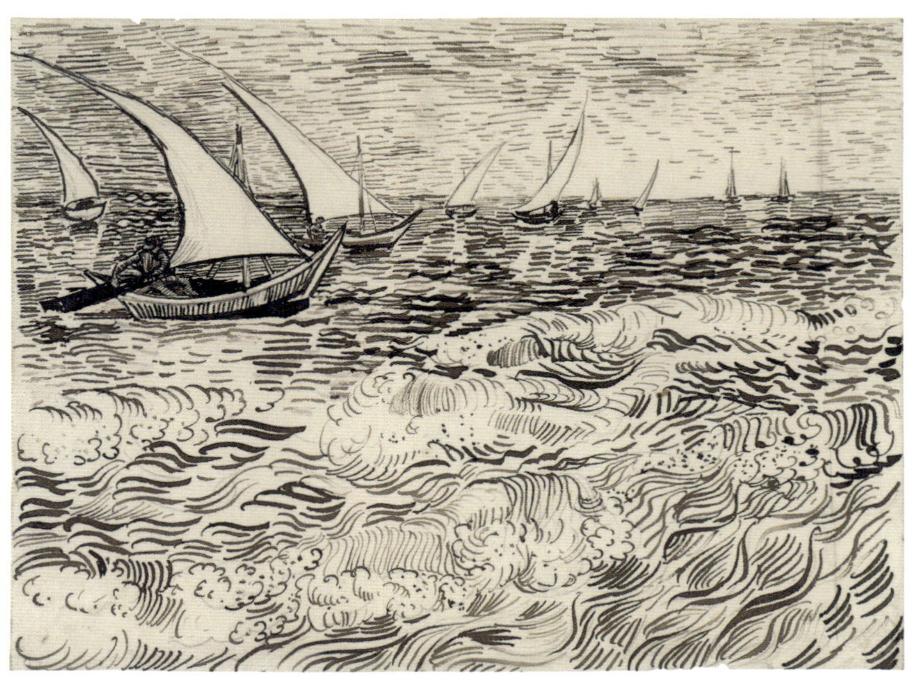

147 *Boats at Sea: Saintes-Maries-de-la-Mer*, mid-July 1888. Reed pen and ink over pencil, on paper, 24 × 32 cm (9½ × 12⅝ in.). KUPFERSTICHKABINETT, STAATLICHE MUSEEN, BERLIN

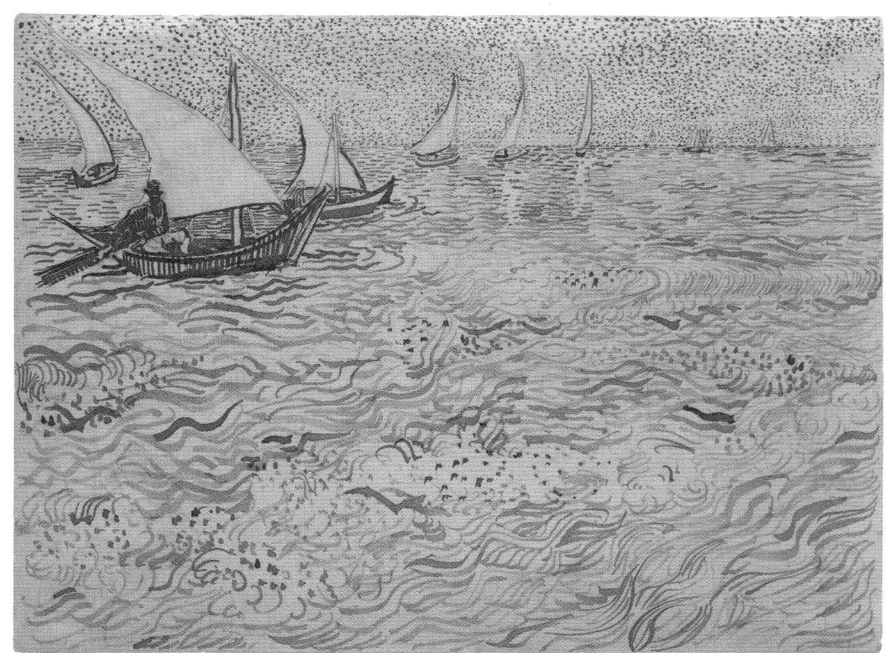

148 *Boats at Sea: Saintes-Maries-de-la-Mer*, *c.* 31 July–3 August 1888. Reed pen and ink over pencil, on paper, 24.3 × 31.9 cm ($9\frac{5}{8} \times 12\frac{5}{8}$ in.). SOLOMON R. GUGGENHEIM MUSEUM, NEW YORK

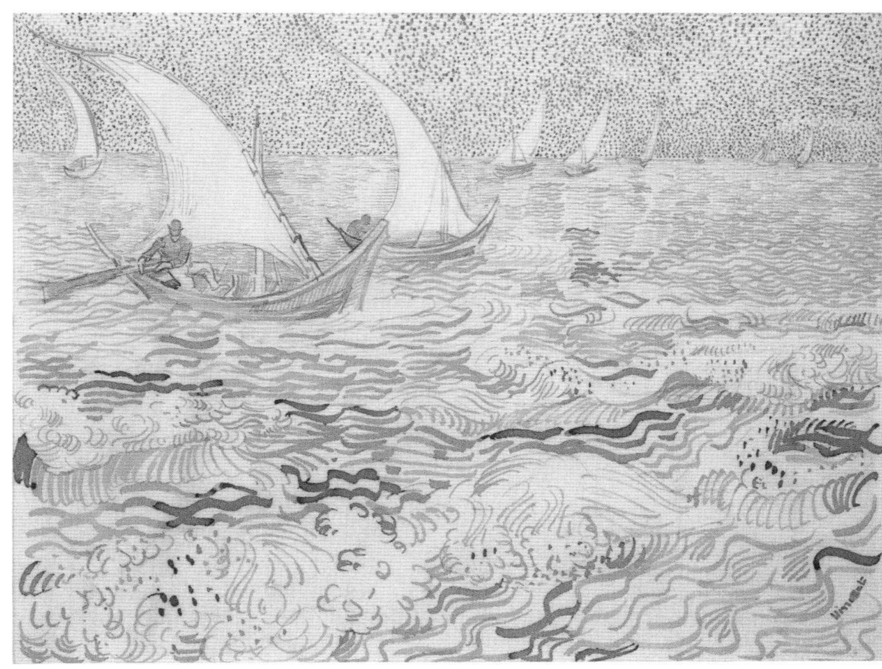

149 *Boats at Sea: Saintes-Maries-de-la-Mer*, *c.* 6–8 August 1888. Reed pen and grey-brown ink over pencil, on paper, 24.2 × 31.9 cm ($9\frac{1}{2} \times 12\frac{1}{2}$ in.). MUSÉES ROYAUX DES BEAUX-ARTS DE BELGIQUE, BRUSSELS

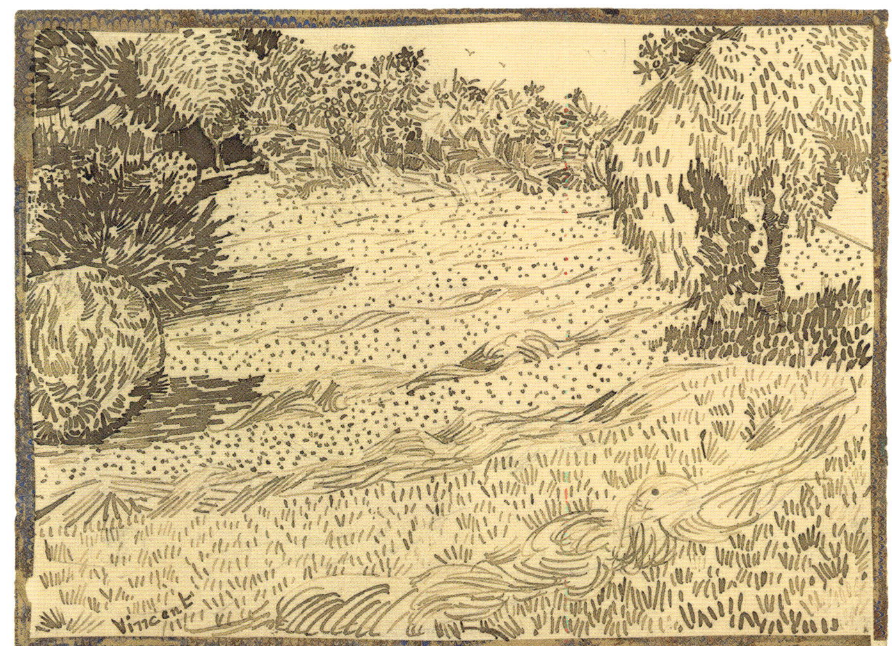

150 *A Corner of a Garden in the place Lamartine*, mid-July 1888. Reed pen and ink over pencil, on paper, 24.2 × 31.6 cm (9⅝ × 12½ in.).
PRIVATE COLLECTION

151 *A Corner of a Garden in the place Lamartine*, c. 6–8 August 1888. Reed and quill pen and ink over pencil, on paper, 24.4 × 32.1 cm (9⅝ × 12⅝ in.).
THE MENIL COLLECTION, HOUSTON

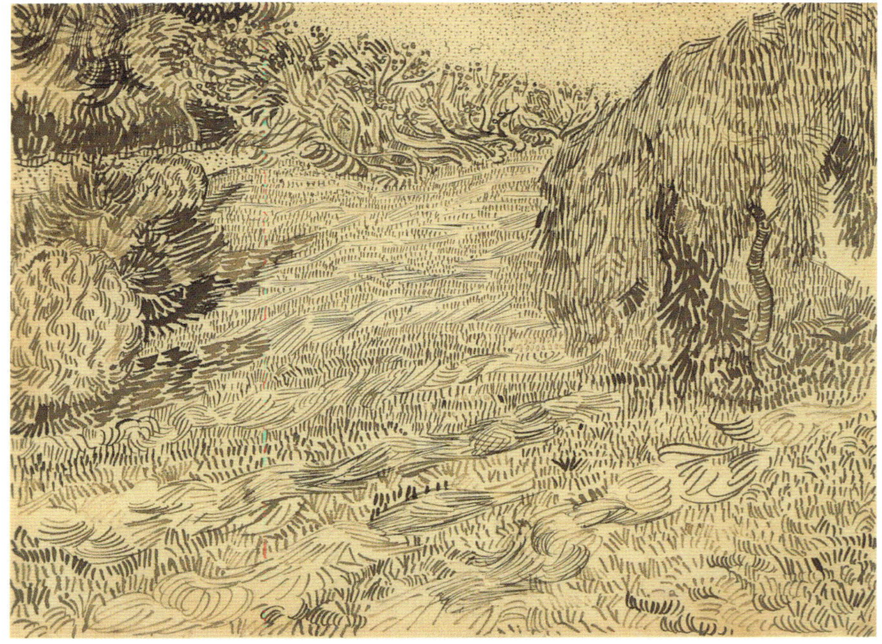

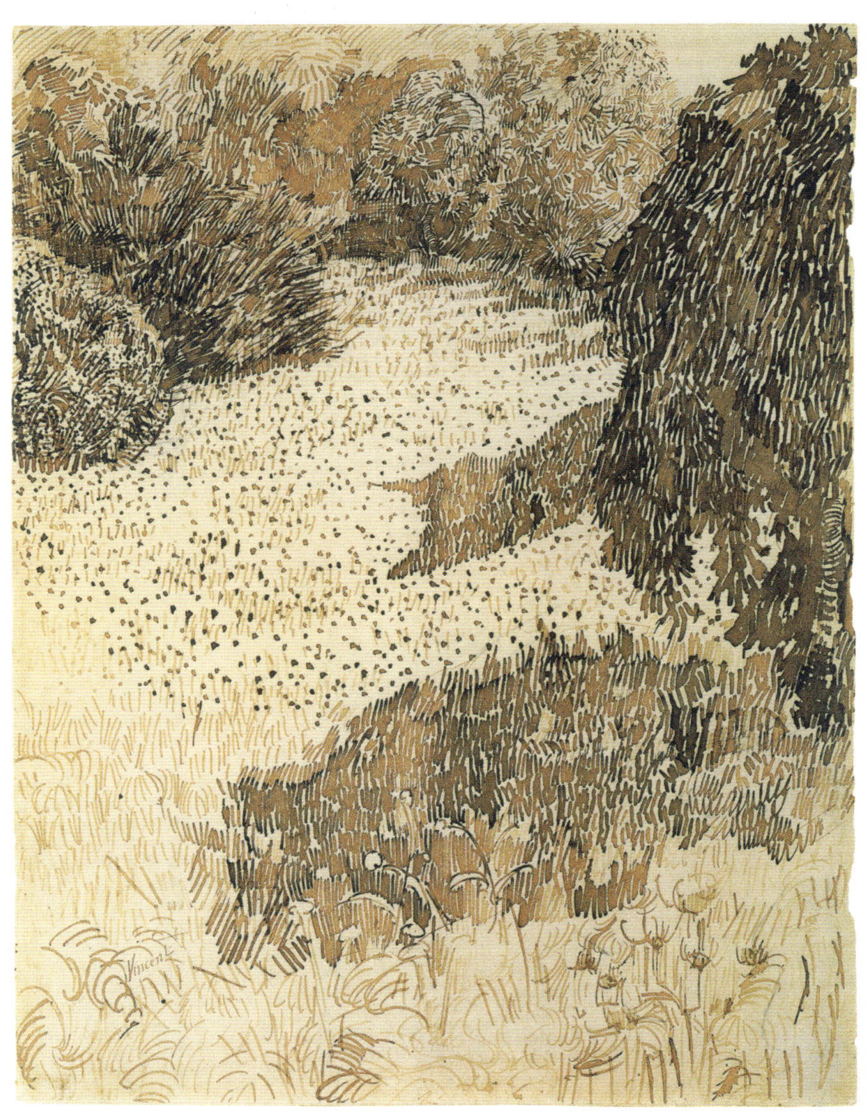

152 *A Corner of a Garden in the place Lamartine*, *c.* 31 July–3 August 1888. Reed pen and ink over pencil, on paper, 31.5 × 24.5 cm (12½ × 9¾ in.). PRIVATE COLLECTION

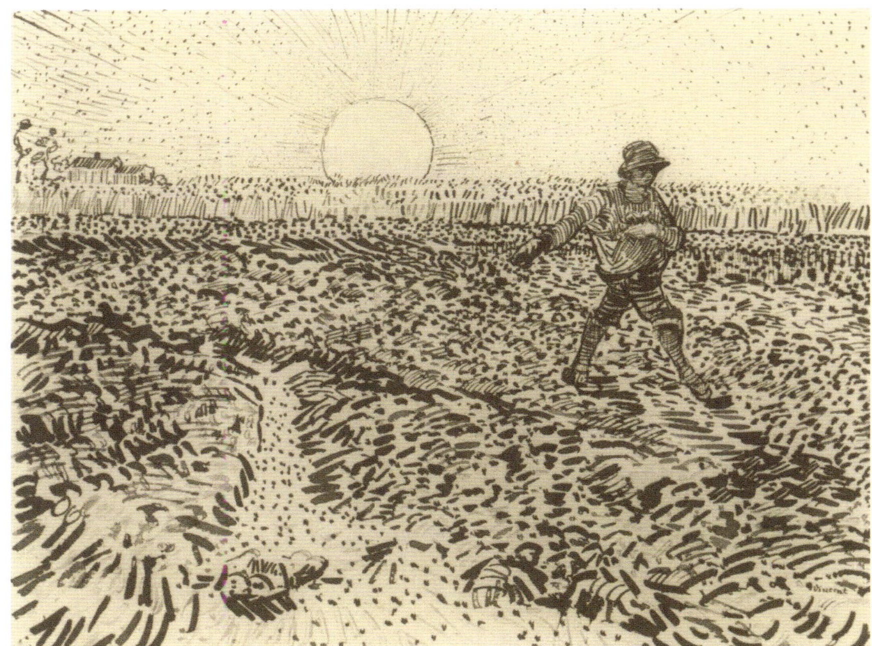

153 *The Sower*, mid-July 1888. Reed pen and ink over pencil, on paper, 24.5 × 31.7 cm (9¾ × 12½ in.).
PRIVATE COLLECTION

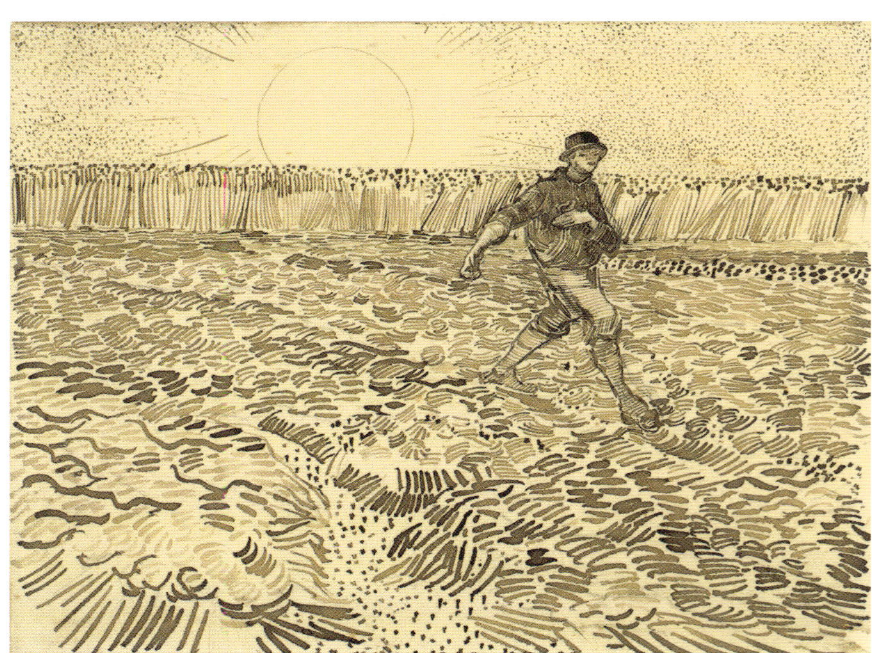

154 *The Sower*, *c.* 6–8 August 1888. Pencil, pen and reed pen and ink, on paper, 24.4 × 32 cm (9⅝ × 12⅝ in.).
VAN GOGH MUSEUM, AMSTERDAM

from the Wheatfields (Figs 144–46); *Boats at Sea: Saintes-Maries-de-la-Mer* (Figs 147–49); *A Corner of a Garden in the place Lamartine* (Figs 150–52) – reveals that, in the progression, small adjustments and refinements have been made in placement and proportions, as well as, on one occasion, in format. This is also true in the case of that archetypal image in Van Gogh's work, *The Sower*, repetitions of which were sent to Bernard and Theo (Figs 153 and 154). The lines in all these sequences become progressively more schematized, even inclining towards the abstract, as though familiarity has taken precedence over the specific, or the essential has overwhelmed the particular. These traits show Van Gogh finding new possibilities in the purity of line.

The repetitions made by the artist in 1888 may at first seem to be something of a detour in a general account of his drawings. In fact, the opposite is the case. They are a memorable climax, in that they incorporate so many aspects of his draughtsmanship and, in its move towards abstraction, indicate its significance for the development of modern art. These sequences present in microcosm the very essence of Van Gogh's drawing skills: selection, judgment and execution combined with vision and commitment. Acuity of eye acting in accordance with dexterity of hand are united to create a totally convincing and compelling expression of the artist's personal reflections on the external world. These special drawings, although not the last he did, are one of the peaks in Van Gogh's short but intense journey from his uncertain beginnings.

Epilogue

'Art demands persistent work, work in spite of everything, and unceasing observation' (249). So Van Gogh stated in a letter written to his brother Theo from The Hague in July 1882. Whatever self-doubts he may have harboured, there can be no question in the modern mind of Van Gogh's commitment to hard work or, indeed, of his powers of observation. His prodigious output and wide range of subject matter are testimony to his determination to succeed in his chosen profession. Yet, although Van Gogh's art is immensely popular in almost every country of the world, its essence lies, perhaps, not so much in those works for which he is justly famed as in those that, in his case, could be so easily overlooked. The private nature of drawings presents many occasions when an artist often reveals in his works on paper more than was intended. In this respect, the incidental is as important as the grand statement and is sometimes a more accurate measure of an artist's ambition. There are many examples among some of Van Gogh's most distinguished predecessors of which this may be said: Leonardo's awareness of the forces of nature; Dürer's excitement at his crossing the Alps in 1494–95 and 1520–21; Rembrandt's fascination for exotic beasts and ghoulish scenes; Rubens's love of his children and of his country estate at Het Steen – such moments fill the interstices of an artist's life and are where their real feelings and beliefs are, albeit briefly, exposed.

It is easy to overlook the fact that, by birth, Van Gogh was a Dutch artist. His initial instinct was for landscape (including, in a minor way, marine subjects), but at the cost, perhaps, of still-life painting, which was, of course, the other great strength of Dutch art. His interest in still life only really started in Paris, when he began to broaden his horizons in the light of the recent advances made by the avant-garde. Paradoxically, it was Paris that made Van Gogh into more than just a complete Dutch painter, in the sense that he now became a practitioner of two altogether different genres of painting, which most other artists kept separate. It was in 1886–88 that he

Tassel Hyacinth, May 1889 (detail of Fig. 162).

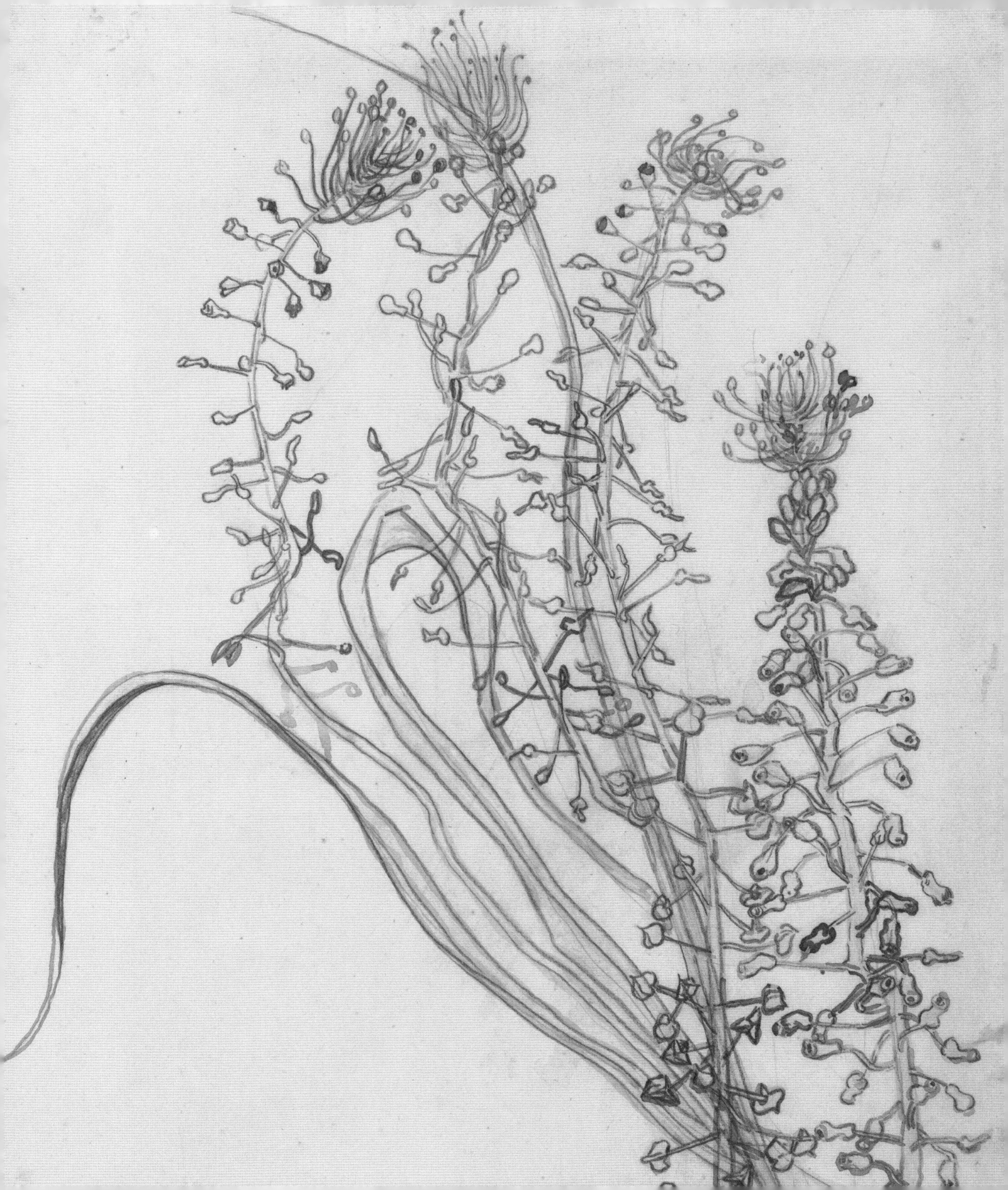

began to paint compositions of flowers, various types of vegetation, fruit and objects as diverse as his books and his boots. He continued to do this in Provence and again after his return to the north, but these were essentially subjects that he executed on canvas rather than on paper.

On first arriving in Arles in February 1888, however, he began by looking at the fields and orchards, not as a northern painter but like an Impressionist dedicated to creating an effusive blur of decorative colour, which can also be detected in his drawings (Fig. 155). Gradually, he turned back to his former, more personal identification with nature, choosing sunflowers, irises and blossom for closer scrutiny. This development intensified while he was in the asylum at Saint-Rémy, restricted to working in the overgrown garden and among the olive trees in the surrounding fields. His detailed attention to individual trees and plants growing in the garden equates with the northern Romantic tradition of scrutinizing and depicting nature, while, at the same time, the combination of landscape and still life situates Van Gogh within the context of the Dutch school of art (Fig. 156).

155 *Provençal Orchard*, March–April 1888. Pencil, pen, reed pen and ink, watercolour, on paper, 39.5 × 53.6 cm (15⅝ × 21⅛ in.). VAN GOGH MUSEUM, AMSTERDAM

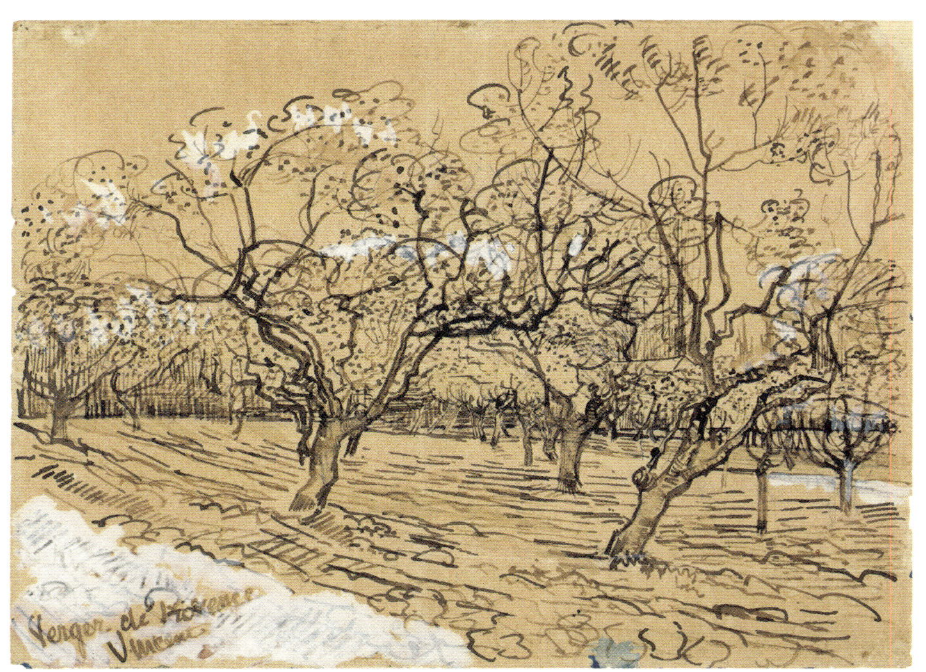

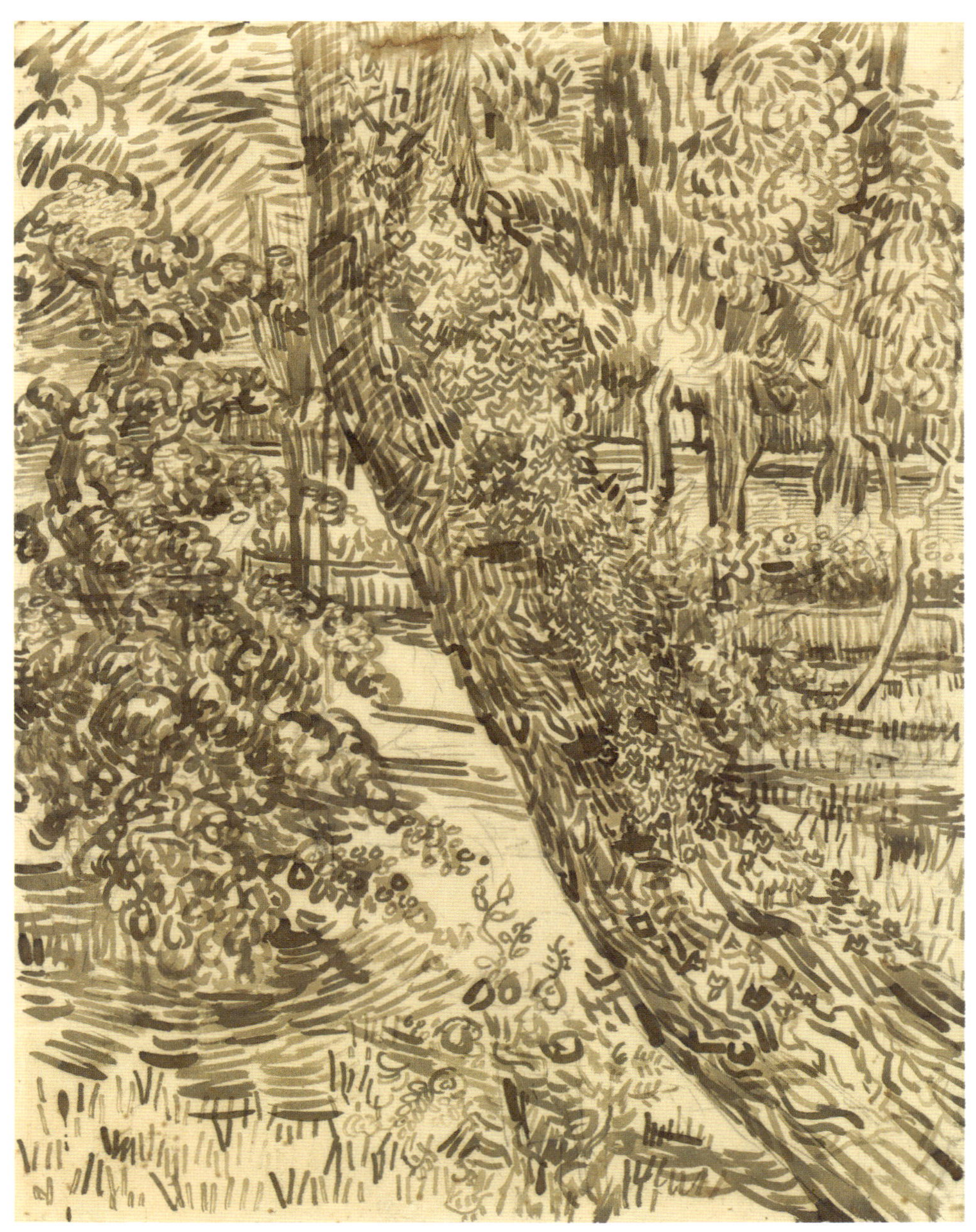

156 *Tree with Ivy in the Garden of the Asylum*, May–June 1889. Pencil, reed pen, brush and ink, on paper, 61.8 × 47.1 cm (24⅜ × 18⅝ in.).
VAN GOGH MUSEUM, AMSTERDAM

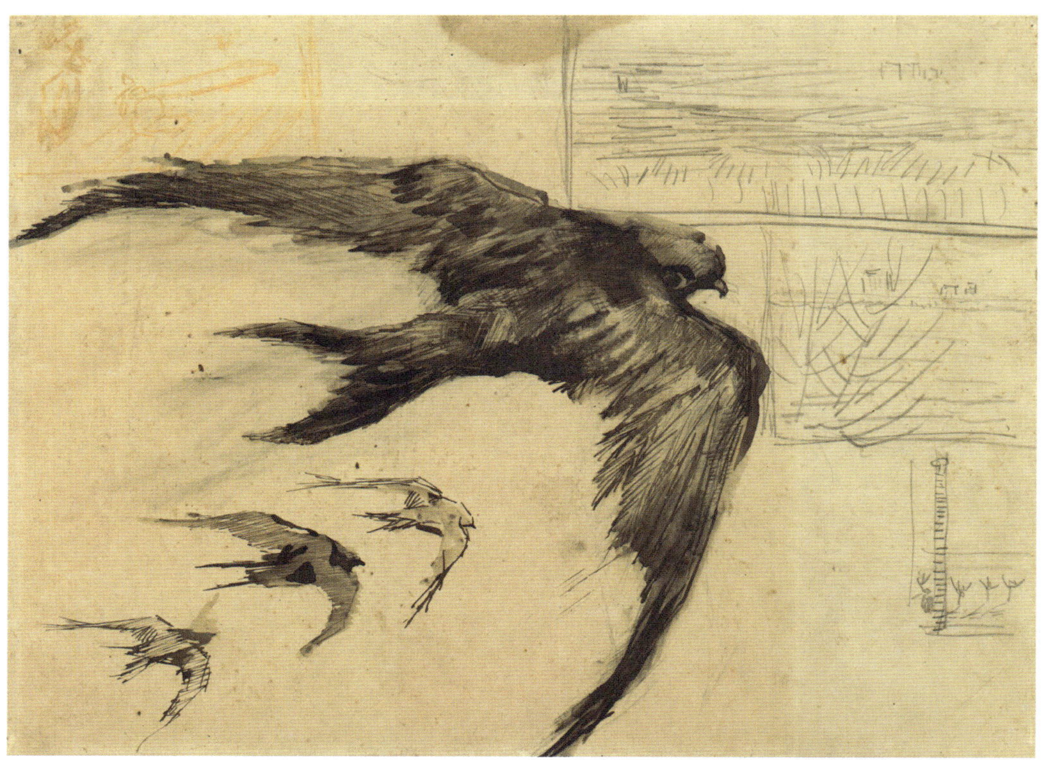

157 *Four Swifts with Landscape Sketches*, April–September 1887. Pencil, pen and ink, chalk, on paper, 26.9 × 35.2 cm (10⅝ × 13⅞ in.).
VAN GOGH MUSEUM, AMSTERDAM

A few drawings – unfortunately, very few – made at intervals combine Van Gogh's deeply felt love of nature and his great skill in recording it. They may not perhaps be counted among his most famous drawings, but, nonetheless, they demonstrate powers of observation and concentration not shared by many other artists. Birds occur frequently in Van Gogh's landscapes, but specific studies of them by the artist are unusual. *Four Swifts with Landscape Sketches* seems to have been drawn in Paris (Fig. 157). Often such drawings were done from preserved specimens, which Van Gogh himself collected or had access to, but he might in this case have used a dead bird that he had found. The drawing, however, expertly shows the bird on the wing, flying diagonally across the sheet of paper.

In Provence, Van Gogh was struck by the noise of the cicadas, which 'sing at least as loudly as a frog' (638). While at Saint-Rémy, he made a drawing of them annexed to a letter written to Theo, in which he says that 'Their song in times of great heat holds the same charm for me as the cricket in the peasant's hearth at home' (790) (Fig. 158). A comparable drawing of a giant peacock moth, which occurs in a painting of 1889, also done at Saint-Rémy, raised a different issue: 'Yesterday I drew a very large, rather rare night moth there [in the garden] which is called a death's head, its coloration astonishingly distinguished: black, grey, white, shaded, and with glints of carmine or vaguely tending towards olive green; it's very big. To paint it I would have to kill it, and that would have been a shame since the animal was so beautiful' (776) (Fig. 159). In the same letter, he refers to drawings of plants identifiable as *Periwinkle* and *Tassel Hyacinth*, which demonstrates the wide span of visual references that can be applied to Van Gogh's art: in the former, the response to plants by masters of the early Italian Renaissance and in the latter, Japanese art (Figs 160–63).

158 Sketch of three cicadas, from a letter to Theo van Gogh (Letter 790), 14–15 July 1889. Pen and ink, on paper, 20.1 × 17.8 cm (8 × 7⅛ in.)
VAN GOGH MUSEUM, AMSTERDAM

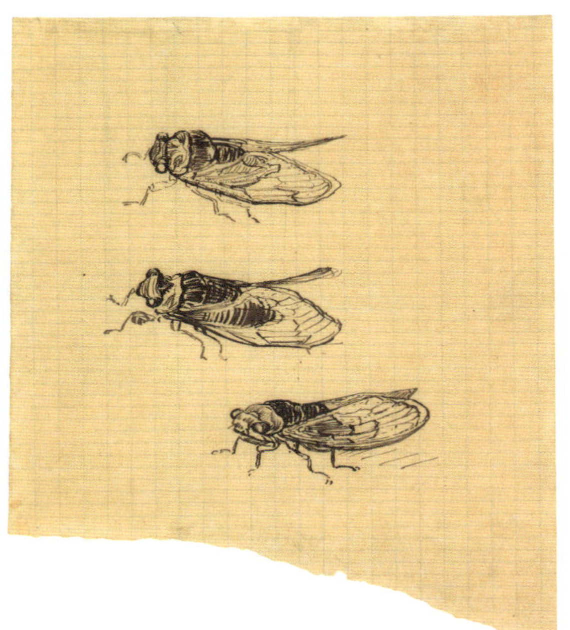

159 *Giant Peacock Moth*, May 1889. Chalk, pen and brush and ink, on paper, 16.3 × 24.2 cm (6½ × 9⅝ in.).
VAN GOGH MUSEUM, AMSTERDAM

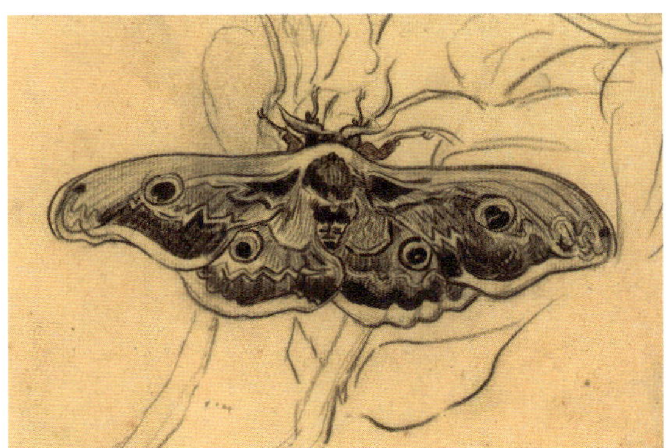

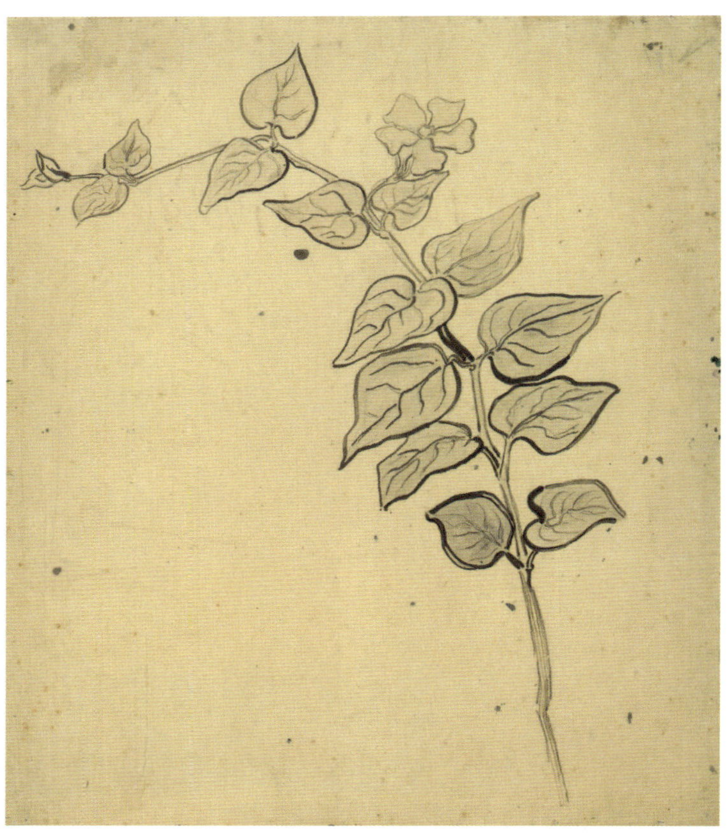

160 *Periwinkle*, May 1889. Pencil, chalk, brush and ink, on paper, 47.6 × 40 cm (18¾ × 15¾ in.).
VAN GOGH MUSEUM, AMSTERDAM

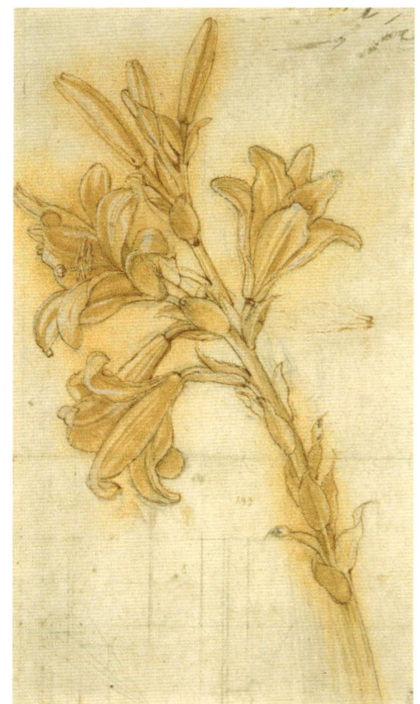

161 Andrea del Verrocchio (formerly attributed to Leonardo da Vinci) *A Lily*, *c.* 1475. Stylus, pinpointing, leadpoint, pen and ink, brown wash, ochre wash and rubbing, white heightening (partly discoloured), pricked through, on paper, 31.4 × 17.7 cm (12⅜ × 7 in.).
ROYAL COLLECTION TRUST, LONDON

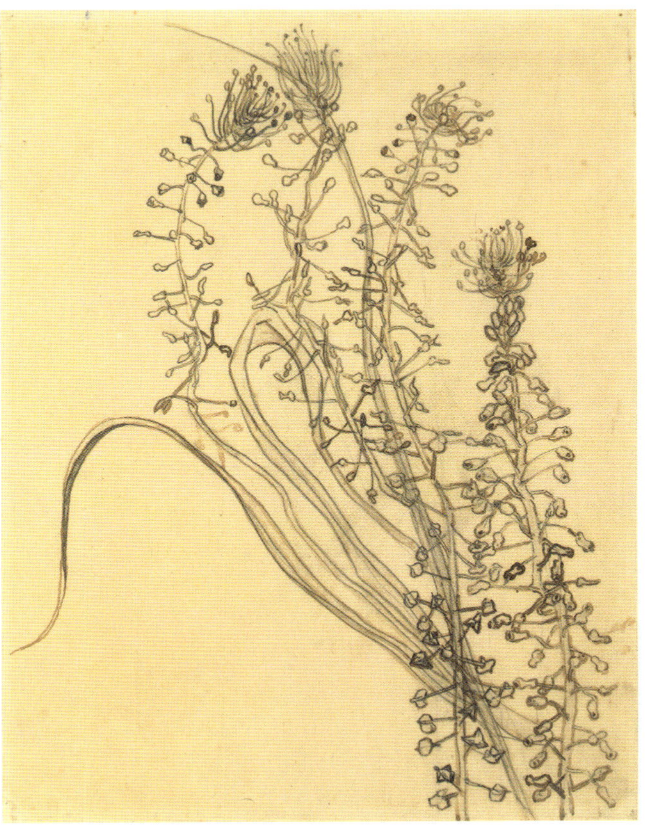

162 *Tassel Hyacinth*, May 1889.
Pencil, brush and ink, on paper,
41.2 × 30.9 cm (16¼ × 12¼ in.).
VAN GOGH MUSEUM, AMSTERDAM

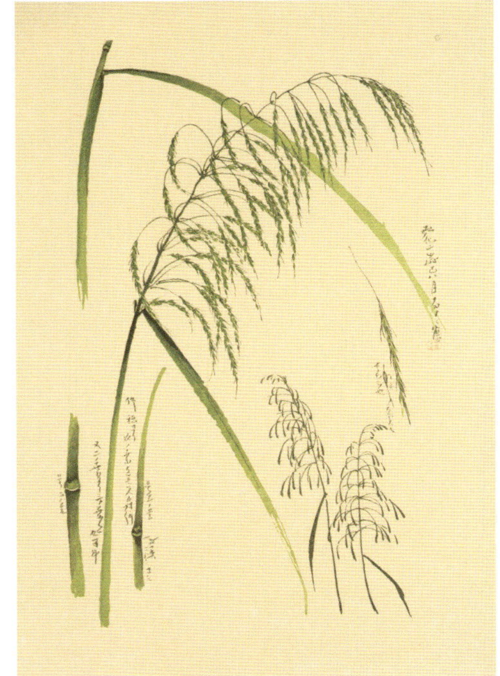

163 Anonymous Japanese artist
Study of Grass, 1845 (from *Le Japon artistique*, May 1888).
Media and dimensions unknown.
VAN GOGH MUSEUM, AMSTERDAM

In the context of Van Gogh's Dutch origins, these detailed drawings of the natural world can be seen to have been made in the spirit of scientific enquiry as conducted during the late Renaissance by such artists as Joris Hoefnagel (1542–1601) in Prague or Jacques de Gheyn the Younger (1565–1629) in the United Provinces, whose patrons supported the study of natural phenomena (Figs 164 and 165). The desire to investigate the natural world and to examine it at such close quarters was a particular trait of north European artists and increased during the seventeenth century. The art of Van Gogh ultimately belongs within this tradition.

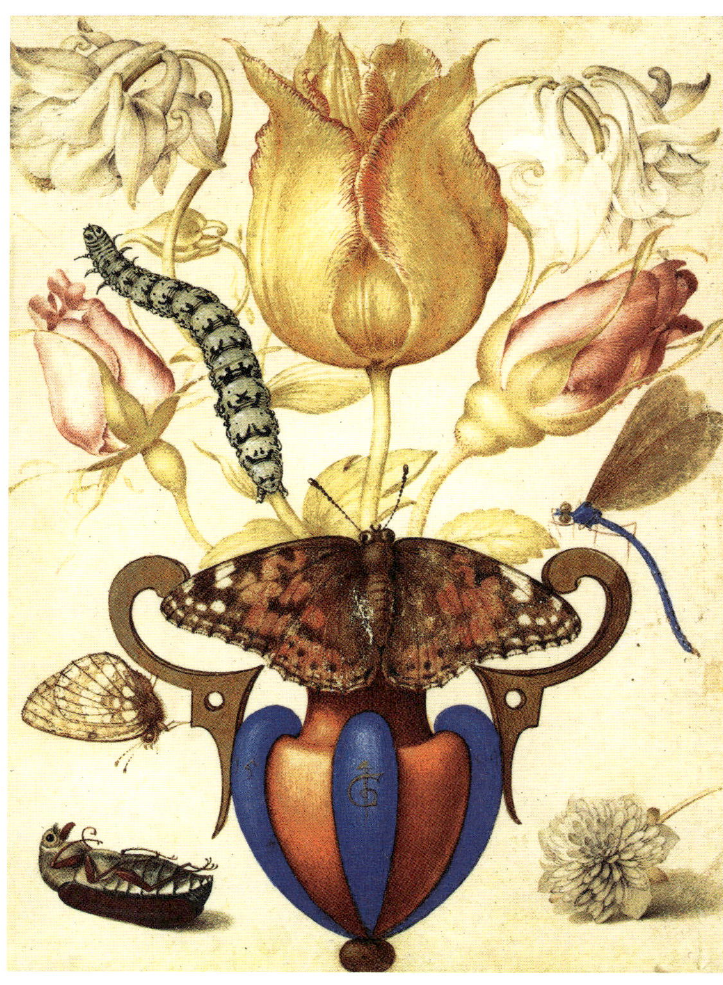

164 Joris Hoefnagel
Arrangement of Flowers in a Vase with Insects, 1594. Gouache and watercolour with gold leaf, on vellum, 16.1 × 12 cm (6⅜ × 4¾ in.).
ASHMOLEAN MUSEUM, OXFORD

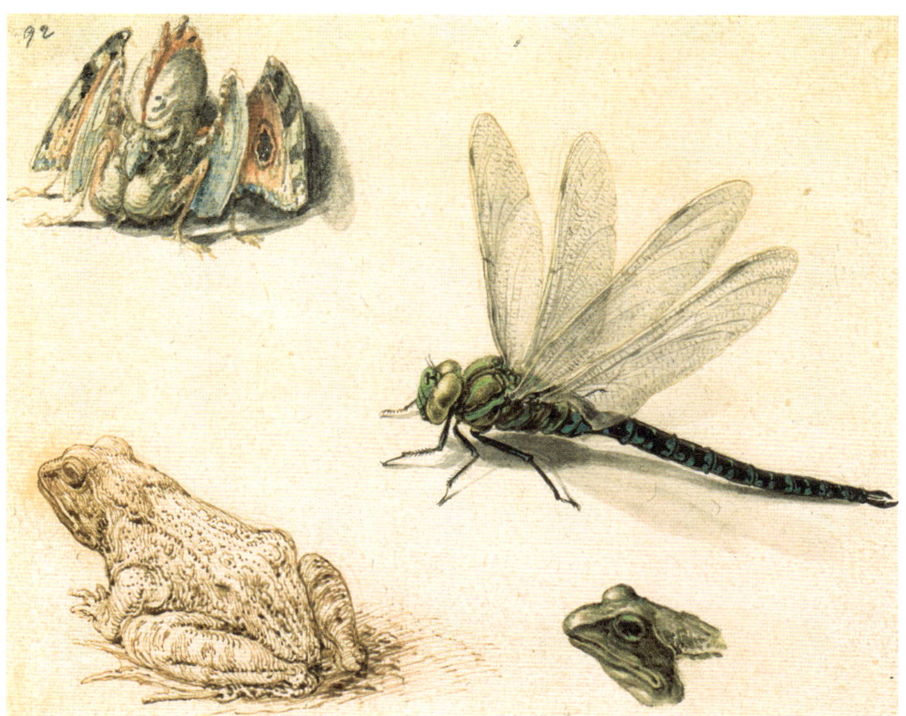

165 Jacques de Gheyn the Younger *Animal Studies*, *c.* 1596–1600. Pen and brown ink, watercolour and opaque watercolour, over traces of metalpoint, on paper prepared with white ground, 11.5 × 14 cm (4½ × 5½ in.). THE MORGAN LIBRARY & MUSEUM, NEW YORK

Many artists from Dürer (Fig. 166) to Henry Moore (1898–1986) have drawn their own hands for a variety of reasons. Van Gogh became interested in hands at Nuenen, when making his studies of those peasants that culminated in *The Potato Eaters* (Figs 48 and 50). The idea of repeating the composition of this painting was expressed while he was at Saint-Rémy and resulted in the artist's returning to the subject, for which he made yet more studies of hands. The layout of one of these shows Van Gogh's own hand (or hands) in eight positions (Fig. 167). Five are views of his left hand and three, seemingly, of the right hand, although these may have been made from the left hand using a mirror. Artists observed hands in connection with the gestures and signs that are essential components of their figurative compositions, but depictions of their own hands suggest a different dimension to the exercise, since their artistic competence rested as much in their manual dexterity as in their imagination. Such a drawing, therefore, may be seen as being indicative of the way artists express wonderment at the gifts

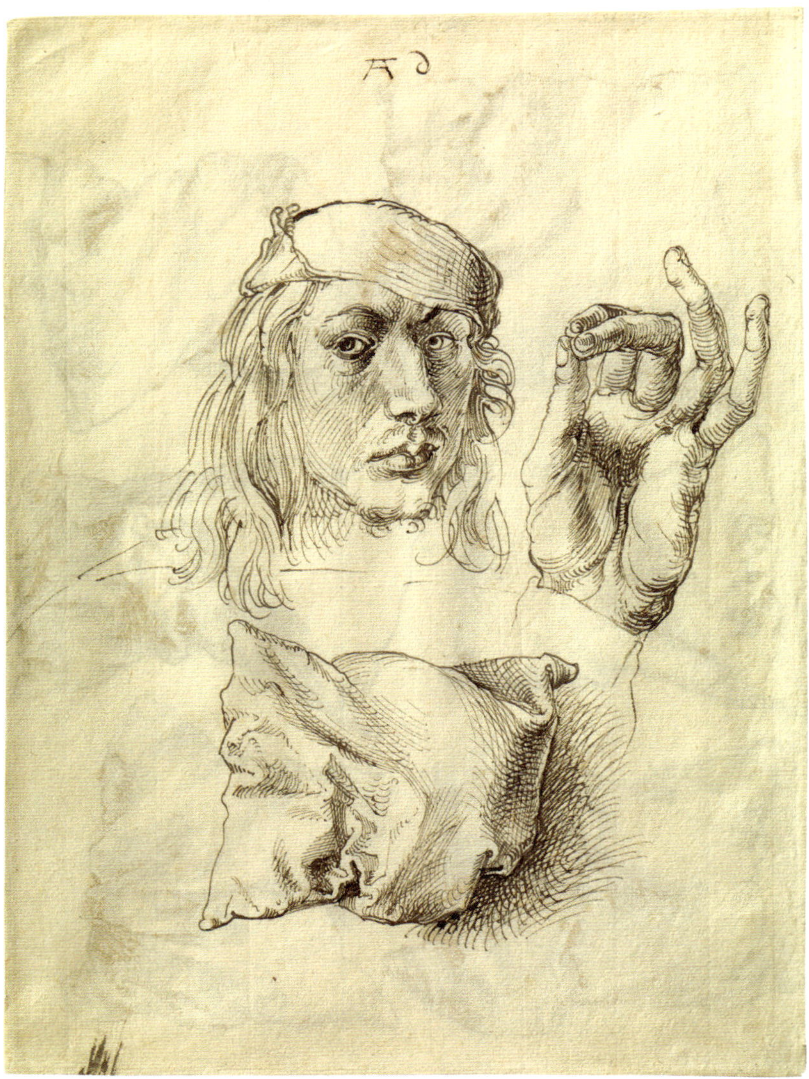

166 Albrecht Dürer
Self-portrait with Studies of the Artist's Left Hand and a Cushion, *c.* 1493.
Pen and brown ink, on paper,
27.6 × 20.2 cm (10⅞ × 8 in.).
THE METROPOLITAN MUSEUM OF ART, NEW YORK

they have been given or even of the search for the source of their manifold skills, evidence for which can be found, for example, as early as in prehistoric cave art. Investigative, questioning drawings of this type lie at the heart of Van Gogh's art, which was dominated at every stage by uncertainty. Early in 1882, having finally decided to become an artist, Van Gogh wrote to his brother with some prescience:

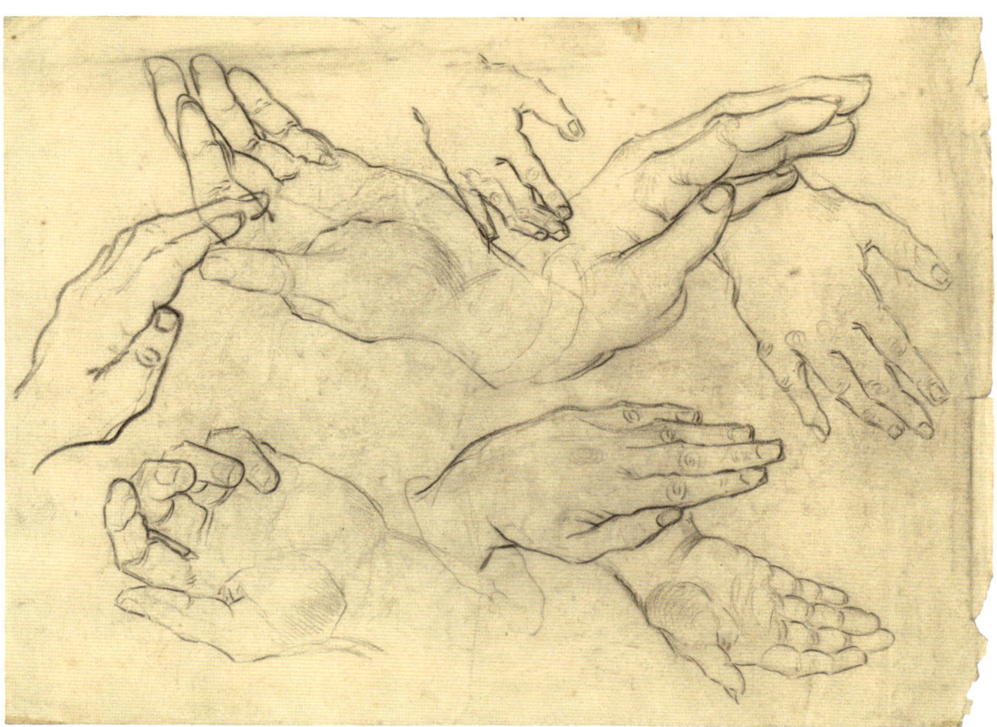

167 *Studies of a Hand*, March–April 1890. Chalk on paper, 23.8 × 31.6 cm (9⅜ × 12½ in.). VAN GOGH MUSEUM, AMSTERDAM

> What am I in the eyes of most people? A nonentity or an oddity or a disagreeable person – someone who has and will have no position in society, in short a little lower than the lowest.
>
> Very well – assuming that everything is indeed like that, then through my work I'd like to show what there is in the heart of such an oddity, such a nobody.
>
> This is my ambition, which is based less on resentment than on love in spite of everything, based more on a feeling of serenity than on passion (249).

Assuredly, Van Gogh's ambition was fulfilled in his drawings as much as in his paintings.

Bibliography

The following publications have been consulted in the preparation for this book and are listed within four sections in chronological order of publication.

Sources and Works of Standard Reference

La Faille, Jacob-Baart de, *L'Oeuvre de Vincent van Gogh: Catalogue raisonné*, 4 vols, Paris and Brussels, 1928; rev. edn, *The Works of Vincent van Gogh: His Paintings and Drawings*, Amsterdam, 1970

Gulik, Willem van, and Fred Orton, *Japanese Prints Collected by Vincent van Gogh*, Amsterdam, 1978

Hulsker, Jan, *The Complete Van Gogh: Paintings, Drawings, Sketches*, New York, 1980.

The Van Gogh Museum Journal (1995–2003)

Hulsker, Jan, *The New Complete Van Gogh: Paintings, Drawings, Sketches*, rev. and enlarged edn, Amsterdam and Meulenhoff, 1996

Vincent van Gogh Drawings, vol. 1: *1880–1883*, by Sjraar van Heugten, Amsterdam and London, 1996; vol. 2: *Nuenen 1883–1885*, by Sjraar van Heugten, Amsterdam and London, 1997; vol. 3: *Antwerp and Paris 1885–1888*, by Marije Vellekoop and Sjraar van Heugten, Amsterdam and London, 2001; vol. 4: *Arles, Saint-Rémy and Auvers-sur-Oise 1888–1890*, by Marije Vellekoop and Roelie Zwikker, Amsterdam and London, 2007

Jansen, Leo, and Jan Robert (eds), *Brief Happiness: The Correspondence of Theo van Gogh and Jo Bunger*, Amsterdam, 1999

Jansen, Leo, Hans Luijten and Nienke Bakker, *Vincent van Gogh: Painted with Words. The Letters to Émile Bernard*, New York and Amsterdam, 2007

Meedendorp, Teio, *Drawings and Prints by Vincent van Gogh in the Collection of the Kröller-Müller Museum*, Otterlo, 2007

Van Gogh Studies (2007–12), nos. 1–4

Jansen, Leo, Hans Luijten and Nienke Bakker (eds), *Vincent van Gogh: The Letters. The Complete Illustrated and Annotated Edition*, vol. 1: *The Hague–Etten 1872–1881*; vol. 2: *The Hague 1881–1883*; vol. 3: *Drenthe–Paris 1883–1887*; vol. 4: *Arles 1888–1889*; vol. 5: *Saint-Rémy-de-Provence–Auvers-sur-Oise 1889–1890*, vol. 6: *Commentary and Indexes*, New York and London, 2009

Leo Jansen, Hans Luijten and Nienke Bakker (eds), *Van Gogh: The Letters*, www.vangoghletters.org

Books

Meier-Graefe, Julius, *Vincent van Gogh*, 2 vols, London and Boston, 1922

Brouwer, Jaap W., Jan Laurens Siesling and Jacques Vis, *Anthon van Rappard, Companion & Correspondent of Vincent van Gogh: His Life & All His Works*, Amsterdam, 1974

Wolk, Johannes van der, *The Seven Sketchbooks of Vincent Van Gogh*, New York, 1987

Pabst, Fieke (ed.), *Vincent van Gogh's Poetry Albums*, Cahier Vincent 1, Amsterdam, 1988

Bailey, Martin, *Young Vincent: The Story of Van Gogh's Years in England*, London, 1990

Pollock, Griselda, 'On Not Seeing Provence: Van Gogh and the Landscape of Consolation, 1888–89', in *Framing France: The Representation of Landscape in France, 1870–1914*, ed. Richard Thomson, Manchester, 1998

Botton, Alain de, 'On Eye-opening Art', in *The Art of Travel*, London, 2002

Heugten, Sjraar van, with Marije Vellekoop and Roelie Zwikker, *Van Gogh Master Draughtsman*, London, 2005

Veen, Wouter van der, *Vincent Van Gogh à Auvers*, Paris, 2009

Fowle, Frances, *The Scottish Art Dealer Alexander Reid 1854–1928: Van Gogh's Twin*, Edinburgh, 2010

Naifeh, Steven, and Gregory White Smith, *Van Gogh: The Life*, London, 2011

Vincent Van Gogh: The Sketchbooks, facsimile edition. Commentary by Marije Vellekoop and Renske Suijver. London and Amsterdam, 2013

Jansen, Leo, et al., *Van Gogh's Studio Practice*, New Haven and London, 2013

Kendall, Richard, *'Studying Nature as a Hunter, a Savage': Vincent van Gogh and Karl Bodmer*, Edinburgh, 2014

Guzzoni, Mariella, *Vincent's Books: Van Gogh and the Writers Who Inspired Him*, London, 2021

Luijten, Hans, *Jo van Gogh-Bonger: The Woman who Made Vincent Famous*, London, 2022

Exhibition Catalogues

Pickvance, Ronald, *English Influences on Vincent van Gogh*, Arts Council of Great Britain exhibition held in Nottingham (University Art Gallery), Newcastle upon Tyne (Laing Art Gallery), London (Victoria and Albert Museum), Leigh (Turnpike Gallery), Sheffield (Graves Art Gallery), Bradford (Cartwright Hall), Brighton (Gardner Centre Gallery), Reading (Museum and Art Gallery), 1974[–75]

Welsh-Ovcharov, Bogomila, *Vincent van Gogh and the Birth of Cloisonism*, Art Gallery of Ontario, Toronto, and Van Gogh Museum, Amsterdam, 1981

Leeuw, Ronald de, John Sillevis and Charles Dumas, *The Hague School: Dutch Masters of the 19th Century*, Grand Palais, Paris, Royal Academy of Arts, London, Gemeentemuseum, The Hague, 1983

Pickvance, Ronald, *Van Gogh in Arles*, Metropolitan Museum of Art, New York, 1984
Vincent van Gogh Exhibition, National Museum of Western Art, Tokyo, and Nagoya-City Museum, 1985[–86]
Pickvance, Ronald, *Van Gogh in Saint-Rémy and Auvers*, Metropolitan Museum of Art, New York, 1986[–87]
Cachin, Françoise, and Bogomila Welsh-Ovcharov, *Van Gogh à Paris*, Musée d'Orsay, Paris, 1988
Wolk, Johannes van der, Ronald Pickvance and E. B .F. Pey, *Vincent van Gogh: Drawings* , Kröller-Müller Museum, Otterlo, 1990
Bionda, Richard, and Carel Blotkamp, *The Age of Van Gogh: Dutch Painting 1880–1895*, Burrell Collection, Glasgow, and Van Gogh Museum, Amsterdam, 1990[–91]
Bailey, Martin, *Van Gogh in England: Portrait of the Artist as a Young Man*, Barbican Art Gallery, London, 1992
Kendall, Richard, *Van Gogh's Van Goghs: Masterpieces from the Van Gogh Museum, Amsterdam*, National Gallery of Art, Washington, DC, and Los Angeles County Museum of Art, 1998[–99]
Stolwijk, Chris, and Richard Thomson, *Theo van Gogh 1857–1891: Art Dealer, Collector and Brother of Vincent*, Van Gogh Museum, Amsterdam, and Musée d'Orsay, Paris, 1999[–2000]
Dorn, Roland, et al., *Van Gogh Face to Face*, Detroit Institute of Arts, Philadelphia Museum of Art, and Museum of Fine Arts, Boston, 2000
Homburg, Cornelia (ed.), *Vincent van Gogh and the Painters of the Petit Boulevard*, Saint Louis Art Museum and Städelsches Kunstinstitut und Städtische Galerie, Frankfurt, 2001
Druick, Douglas K., and Peter Kort Zegers, *Van Gogh and Gauguin: The Studio of the South*, Art Institute of Chicago and Van Gogh Museum, Amsterdam, 2001[–02]
Kosinski, Dorothy, with contributions by Bradley Fratello and Laura Bruck, *Van Gogh's Sheaves of Wheat*, Dallas Museum of Art, 2006–7
Heugten, Sjraar van, Joachim Pissarro and Chris Stolwijk, with contributions by Geeta Bruin, Maita van Dijk and Jennifer Field, *Van Gogh and the Colours of the Night*, Museum of Modern Art, New York, and Van Gogh Museum, Amsterdam, 2008–9
Blotkamp, Carel, et al., *Vincent Van Gogh: Between Earth and Heaven. The Landscapes*, Kunstmuseum, Basel, 2009
Stolwijk, Chris, et al., *Vincent's Choice: The Musée imaginaire of Van Gogh,* Van Gogh Museum, Amsterdam, 2003
Ives, Colta, et al., *Van Gogh Draftsman: The Masterpieces*, Van Gogh Museum, Amsterdam, 2005, and *Vincent van Gogh: The Drawings*, The Metropolitan Museum of Art, New York, 2005
Bailey, Martin, with an essay by Frances Fowle, *Van Gogh and Britain: Pioneer Collectors*, Compton Verney, Warwickshire, and the Dean Gallery, Edinburgh, 2006
Dumas, Ann, et al., *The Real Van Gogh: The Artist and his Letters*, Royal Academy of Arts, London, 2010
Homburg, Cornelia, et al., *Van Gogh Up Close*, National Gallery of Canada, Ottawa, and Philadelphia Museum of Art, 2012
Standring, Timothy, and Louis van Tilborgh, *Becoming Van Gogh*, Denver Museum of Art, 2012–13
Vellekoop, Marije, et al., *Van Gogh at Work*, Van Gogh Museum, Amsterdam, 2013–14
Jacobi, Carol (ed.), *The EY Exhibition: Van Gogh and Britain*, Tate Britain, London, 2019
Gerritse, Bregie, *The Potato Eaters: Van Gogh's First Masterpiece*, Van Gogh Museum, Amsterdam. 2021[–22]
Serres, Karen (ed.), *Van Gogh: Self-portraits*, Courtauld Gallery, London, 2022

Articles

Murray, Ann, '"Strange and Subtle Perspective . . . ": Van Gogh, The Hague School and the Dutch Landscape Tradition', *Art History*, 3 (1980), pp. 410–24
Pollock, Griselda, 'Stark Encounters: Modern Life and Urban Work in Van Gogh's Drawings of The Hague 1881–3', *Art History*, 6 (1983), pp. 330–58
Zemel, Carol, 'The "Spook" in the Machine: Van Gogh's Pictures of Weavers in Brabant', *Art Bulletin,* 67 (1985), pp. 123–37
Zemel, Carol, 'Sorrowing Women, Rescuing Men: Van Gogh's Images of Women and Family', *Art History*, 10 (1987), pp. 351–68
Pollock, Griselda, 'Van Gogh and the Poor Slaves: Images of Rural Activities as Modern Art', *Art History*, 11 (1988), pp. 408–32
Bailey, Martin, 'Memories of Van Gogh and Gauguin: Hartrick's reminiscences', *Van Gogh Museum Journal,* 2001, pp. 96–105

Sources of Illustrations

Sources of illustrations by page number

Frontispiece Museum of Fine Arts, Budapest; **5** Van Gogh Museum, Amsterdam (Vincent van Gogh Foundation); **6–7** Solomon R. Guggenheim Museum, New York. Thannhauser Collection, Gift, Justin K. Thannhauser, 1978; **9** Photo President and Fellows of Harvard College; **13** Van Gogh Museum, Amsterdam (Vincent van Gogh Foundation); **41** Kröller-Müller Museum, Otterlo; **67** The Baltimore Museum of Art. The Cone Collection, formed by Dr. Claribel Cone and Miss Etta Cone of Baltimore, Maryland; **95** Van Gogh Museum, Amsterdam (Vincent van Gogh Foundation); **123** Rijksmuseum, Amsterdam. Purchased with the support of the Vereniging Rembrandt and the Prins Bernhard Fonds; **153** Los Angeles County Museum of Art. George Gard De Sylva Collection; **179** Musée Royaux des Beaux Arts, Brussels; **203, 222-3** Van Gogh Museum, Amsterdam (Vincent van Gogh Foundation)

Sources of illustrations by Fig. number

1, 2, 3, 4, 5 Van Gogh Museum, Amsterdam (Vincent van Gogh Foundation); **6, 7** Van Gogh Museum, Amsterdam; **8** Kröller-Müller Museum, Otterlo; **9** Van Gogh Museum, Amsterdam (Vincent van Gogh Foundation); **10** Van Gogh Museum, Amsterdam (Vincent van Gogh Foundation). Purchased with support from the VriendenLoterij; **11** Van Gogh Museum, Amsterdam (Vincent van Gogh Foundation); **12** Photo CSG CIC Glasgow Museums Collection/Gifted by Sir William and Lady Burrell to the City of Glasgow, 1944/Bridgeman Images; **13** Van Gogh Museum, Amsterdam (Vincent van Gogh Foundation); **14** Musée d'Orsay, Paris; **15** Museum of Dordrecht, The Netherlands; **16** Kröller-Müller Museum, Otterlo; **17** Centraal Museum, Utrecht; **18** Kröller-Müller Museum, Otterlo; **19, 20, 21, 22** Van Gogh Museum, Amsterdam (Vincent van Gogh Foundation); **23** Tate, London; **24, 25** Kröller-Müller Museum, Otterlo; **26** P. and N. de Boer Foundation, Amsterdam; **27, 28** Van Gogh Museum, Amsterdam (Vincent van Gogh Foundation); **29** Witt Library, Courtauld Institute of Art, London; **30, 31, 32** Van Gogh Museum, Amsterdam (Vincent van Gogh Foundation); **33, 34, 35, 36** Kröller-Müller Museum, Otterlo; **37, 38, 39** Van Gogh Museum, Amsterdam (Vincent van Gogh Foundation); **40** The Art Institute, Chicago. Bequest of Kate L. Brewster; **41, 42** Kröller-Müller Museum, Otterlo; **43** Kupferstichkabinett Berlin State Museums; **44, 45** Van Gogh Museum, Amsterdam (Vincent van Gogh Foundation); **46** The Baltimore Museum of Art, Baltimore. The Cone Collection, formed by Dr. Claribel Cone and Miss Etta Cone of Baltimore, Maryland; **47, 48, 49, 50, 51** Van Gogh Museum, Amsterdam (Vincent van Gogh Foundation); **52** The Royal Collection Trust, London; **53, 54, 55, 56, 57** Van Gogh Museum, Amsterdam (Vincent van Gogh Foundation); **58** Rijksmuseum, Amsterdam. Purchased with the support of the Vereniging Rembrandt, the Prins Bernhard Fonds and the Rijksmuseum-Stichting; **59** RISD Museum, Providence; **60** Private Collection, on deposit at The Morgan Library & Museum, New York; **61** Dallas Museum of Art, The Wendy and Emery Reves Collection; **62, 63** Van Gogh Museum, Amsterdam (Vincent van Gogh Foundation); **64** Kröller-Müller Museum, Otterlo; **65, 66** Van Gogh Museum, Amsterdam (Vincent van Gogh Foundation); **67, 68** Kröller-Müller Museum, Otterlo; **69** akg-images/CDA/Guillemot; **70, 71, 72** Van Gogh Museum, Amsterdam (Vincent van Gogh Foundation); **73** The Clark Art Institute, Williamstown, Massachusetts. Acquired by the Clark, 1996; **74** Stedelijk Museum, Amsterdam. Donation VVHK, 1949; **75** Whitworth Art Gallery/Bridgeman Images; **76** Van Gogh Museum, Amsterdam (Vincent van Gogh Foundation); **77** National Gallery, Oslo; **78** Oskar Reinhart collection Am Römerholz, Winterthur; **79** Boijmans van Beuningen Museum, Rotterdam; **80, 81, 82, 83** Van Gogh Museum, Amsterdam (Vincent van Gogh Foundation); **84** The Metropolitan Museum of Art, New York. Bequest of Abby Aldrich Rockefeller, 1948; **85** Van Gogh Museum, Amsterdam (Vincent van Gogh Foundation); **86** Tate, London; **87** National Gallery of Canada, Ottawa; **88** The Whitworth Art Gallery, University of Manchester, Manchester; **89** Kröller-Müller Museum, Otterlo; **90** The J. Paul Getty Museum, Los Angeles; **91** Van Gogh Museum, Amsterdam; **92** Groninger Museum, The Netherlands; **93, 94** Van Gogh Museum, Amsterdam (Vincent van Gogh Foundation); **95** The Metropolitan Museum of Art, New York. Robert Lehman Collection, 1975; **96** Kröller-Müller Museum, Otterlo; **97** The New Art Gallery Walsall, United Kingdom; **98** Museum of Fine Arts, Budapest; **99** Promised bequest to the British Museum. Photo The Trustees of the British Museum; **100** Grafische Sammlung, Kunsthaus Zürich; **101** Van Gogh Museum, Amsterdam (Vincent van Gogh Foundation); **102** Museum Folkwang, Essen, Germany; **103** Van Gogh Museum, Amsterdam (Vincent van Gogh Foundation); **104** Musée Des Beaux-Arts, Tournai; **105** Rijksmuseum, Amsterdam, Purchased with the support of the Vereniging Rembrandt and the Prins Bernhard Fonds, 1962; **106** Teylers Museum, Haarlem, The Netherlands; **107** Van Gogh Museum, Amsterdam (Vincent van Gogh Foundation); **108** The British Museum, London; **109** Private Collection; **110** The Art Institute of Chicago; **111** Kröller-Müller Museum, Otterlo; **112** Staatliche Graphische Sammlung, Munich; **113** Brooklyn Museum, New York. Frank L. Babbott Fund and A. Augustus Healy Fund; **114** Norton Simon Museum, Pasadena, California; **115** The Hermitage, St Petersburg; **116** Private Collection; **117, 118, 119, 120, 121, 122** Van Gogh Museum, Amsterdam

(Vincent van Gogh Foundation); **123** Kröller-Müller Museum, Otterlo; **124** Museum of Fine Arts Boston. William Francis Warden Fund; **125** The British Museum, London; **126** Van Gogh Museum, Amsterdam (Vincent van Gogh Foundation); **127** Museum of Fine Art, Budapest; **128** Van Gogh Museum, Amsterdam (Vincent van Gogh Foundation); **129** The Metropolitan Museum of Art, New York. Gift of Emanie Philips, 1962; **130** Los Angeles County Museum of Art. George Gard De Sylva Collection; **131** Boston Museum of Fine Arts, USA; **132** Photo © President and Fellows of Harvard College; **133** Private Collection; **134** The Metropolitan Museum of Art, New York. H. O. Havemeyer Collection, Bequest of Mrs. H. O. Havemeyer, 1929; **135** National Gallery of Art, Washington, DC. Chester Dale Collection; **136** Private Collection; **137** Photo The Trustees of the British Museum; **138** Civica Galleria d'Arte Moderna, Milan; **139A** Private Collection; **139B** Los Angeles County Museum of Art. George Gard De Sylva Collection; **139C** Kupferstichkabinett, Berlin State Museums; **139D** The Metropolitan Museum of Art, New York. Bequest of Abby Aldrich Rockefeller, 1948; **139E** Kröller-Müller Museum, Otterlo; **139F** Private Collection; **139G** The Metropolitan Museum of Art, New York. Gift of Emanie Philips, 1962; **139H** Kupferstichkabinett, Berlin State Museums; **139I** Museum of Fine Arts Budapest; **139J** The Metropolitan Museum of Art, New York. Gift of Mrs. Max J.H. Rossbach, 1964; **139K** The National Gallery of Art, Washington DC. Collection of Mr. and Mrs. Paul Mellon; **139L** Kupferstichkabinett, Berlin State Museums; **139M** Private Collection; **139N** Kunst Museum, Winterthur; **139O** Private Collection; **140, 141** Van Gogh Museum, Amsterdam (Vincent van Gogh Foundation); **142A** Solomon R. Guggenheim Museum, New York. Thannhauser Collection, Gift, Justin K. Thannhauser, 1978; **142B** Philadelphia Museum of Art. The Samuel S. White 3rd and Vera White Collection, 1962; **142C** Private Collection; **142D** The Saint Louis Art Museum, Missouri. Gift of Mr. and Mrs. Joseph Pulitzer Jr.; **142E** Private Collection; **142F** National Gallery of Art, Washington DC. Collection of Mr. and Mrs. Paul Mellon, in Honor of the 50th Anniversary of the National Gallery of Art; **142G, 142H** Private Collection; **142I, 142J** Solomon R. Guggenheim Museum, New York. Thannhauser Collection, Gift, Justin K. Thannhauser, 1978; **142K** Private Collection; **142L** The J. Paul Getty Museum, Los Angeles; **143A** Musée Royaux des Beaux Arts de Belgique, Brussels; **143B** The Saint Louis Art Museum, Missouri. Gift of Mr. and Mrs. Joseph Pulitzer Jr.; **143C** Van Gogh Museum, Amsterdam (Vincent van Gogh Foundation); **143D** The J.Paul Getty Museum, Los Angeles; **143E** The Menil Collection, Houston; **144** National Gallery of Art, Washington. Collection of Mr. and Mrs. Paul Mellon; **145** Private Collection; **146** The J.Paul Getty Museum, Los Angeles; **147** Kupferstichkabinett, Berlin State Museums; **148** Solomon R. Guggenheim Museum, New York. Thannhauser Collection, Gift, Justin K. Thannhauser, 1978; **149** Musée Royaux des Beaux Arts de Belgique, Brussels; **150** Private Collection; **151** The Menil Collection, Houston; **152, 153** Private Collection; **154, 155, 156, 157, 158, 159, 160** Van Gogh Museum, Amsterdam (Vincent van Gogh Foundation); **161** The Royal Collection Trust, London; **162** Van Gogh Museum, Amsterdam (Vincent van Gogh Foundation); **163** Van Gogh Museum Library, Amsterdam. Heritage Image Partnership Ltd/ Alamy Stock Photo; **164** Heritage Image Partnership Ltd/ Alamy Stock Photo; **165** The Morgan Library & Museum, Thaw Collection, New York; **166** The Metropolitan Museum of Art, New York. Robert Lehman Collection, 1975; **167** Van Gogh Museum, Amsterdam (Vincent van Gogh Foundation)

Index

Index

Acknowledgments

As on two previous occasions, when writing on Picasso (2018) and Matisse (2022), I have been greatly assisted by the loan of a quantity of books from the superb library belonging to my near neighbour in Suffolk, Tim Hilton. His generosity was doubly welcome in this respect, since I embarked on writing the present book during the onset of the Coronavirus pandemic with its accompanying restrictions. I also benefited greatly at a later stage from being allowed to roam freely along the shelves of the extensive and highly specialized library of Richard and Belinda Thomson. Carol Richardson, Alesa Boyle and Ann Dumas helped in similar ways regarding access to sources. Jane McAusland kindly fielded a question on the papers used by Van Gogh.

My wife, Frances, was once again on hand with her technical skills to prepare the manuscript for publication. She also read the text closely at a preliminary stage and commented on it, for which I am most grateful.

At Thames & Hudson, I am greatly indebted to Roger Thorp, Mohara Gill, Gillian Malpass, Aman Phull, Anabel Navarro, Sam Wythe, Sadie Butler and Elisa Merino, who, at different stages and in diverse ways, all contributed constructively and sympathetically to the completion of this book.

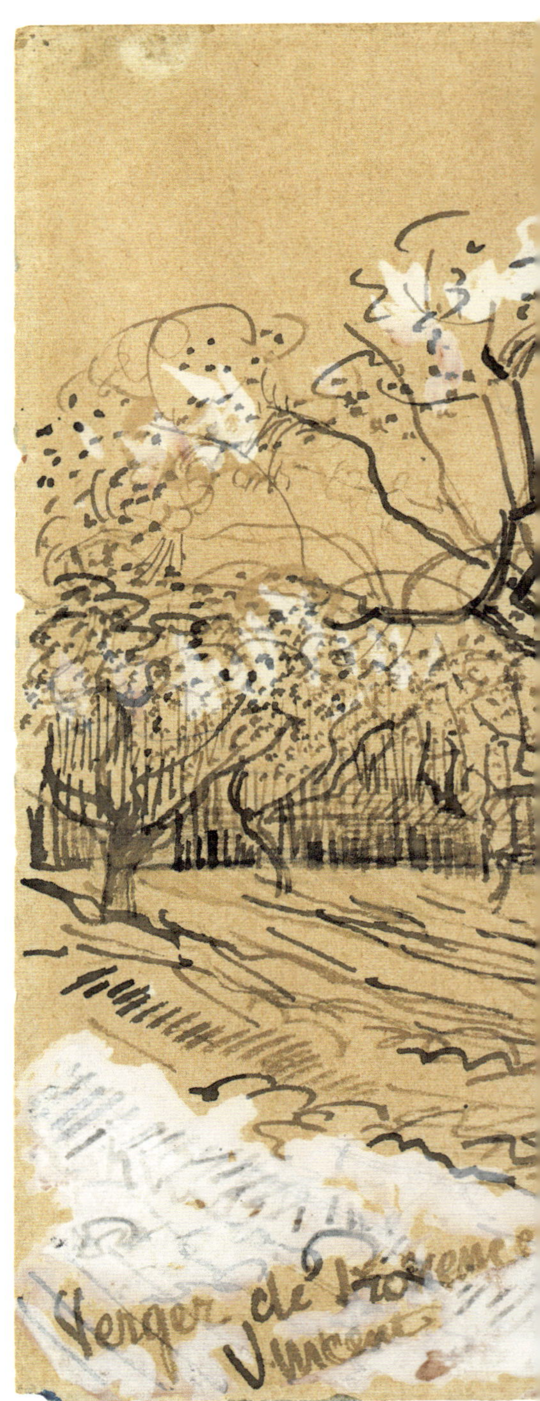

Provençal Orchard, March–April 1888.
Pencil, pen, reed pen and ink, watercolour, on paper,
39.5 × 53.6 cm ($15\frac{5}{8}$ × $21\frac{1}{8}$ in.).
VAN GOGH MUSEUM, AMSTERDAM

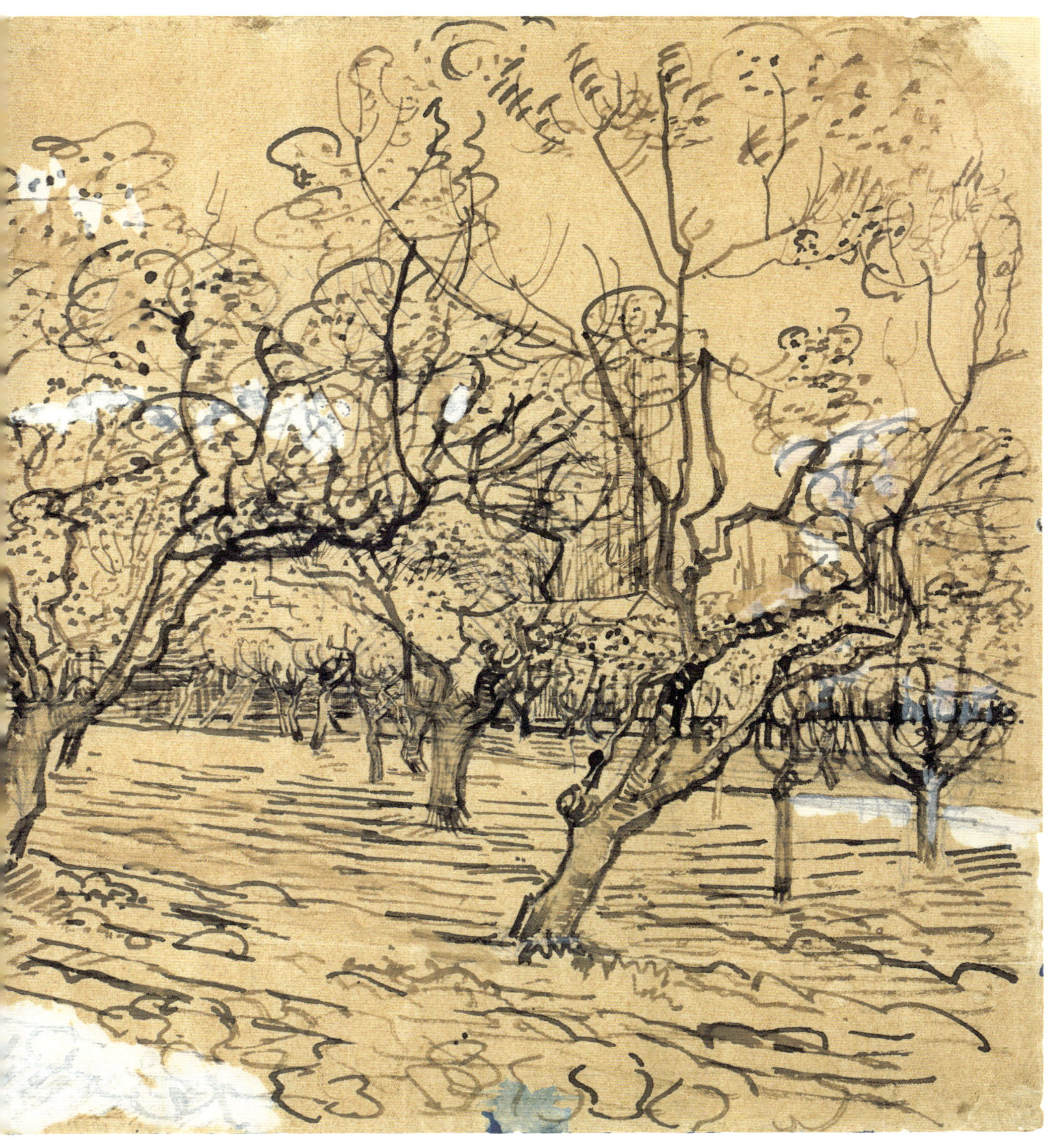

In memory of Richard Brettell
(1949–2020)

Christopher Lloyd is a British art historian. He was Surveyor of The Queen's Pictures from 1988 to 2005. His publications include monographs on painters, particularly Camille Pissarro, official catalogues of museum collections, and general surveys of the British Royal Collection. In addition, he has organized and curated numerous exhibitions and in 1992 made a six-part television series on the paintings in the Royal Collection.

ON THE JACKET, FRONT: *The Oise at Auvers*, late May–early June 1890. TATE, LONDON

FRONTISPIECE: *Haystacks*, mid-July 1888 (detail of Fig. 1391).
PAGE 5: *Old Vineyard with Peasant Woman*, 20–23 May 1890 (detail of Fig. 39).
PAGES 6–7: *Boats at Sea: Saintes-Maries-de-la-Mer*, *c.* 31 July–3 August 1888 (detail of Fig. 142A).

First published in the United Kingdom in 2023 by
Thames & Hudson Ltd, 6–24 Britannia Street, London WC1X 9JD

First published in the United States of America in 2023 by
Thames & Hudson Inc., 500 Fifth Avenue, New York, New York 10110

This compact edition published in 2026

EU Authorized Representative: Interart S.A.R.L.
19 rue Charles Auray, 93500 Pantin, Paris, France
productsafety@thameshudson.co.uk
interart.fr

A CIP catalogue record for this book is available from the British Library

Library of Congress Control Number 2023934836

ISBN 978-0-500-03139-1
01

Printed and bound in China by C&C Offset Printing Co. Ltd

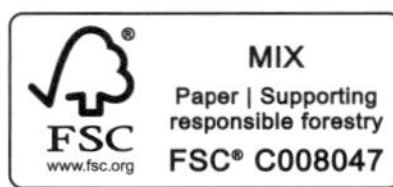